Fodor's 98

Santa Fe, Taos, Albuquerque

The complete guide, thoroughly up-to-date

Packed with details that will make your trip

The must-see sights, off and on the beaten path

What to see, what to skip

Vacation itineraries, walking tours, day trips

Smart lodging and dining options

Essential local do's and taboos

Transportation tips

Key contacts, savvy travel advice

When to go, what to pack

Clear, accurate, easy-to-use maps

Books to read, videos to watch, background essays

Fodor's Travel Publications, Inc.
New York • Toronto • London • Sydney • Auckland
www.fodors.com/

Fodor's Santa Fe, Taos, Albuquerque

EDITOR: Alison B. Stern

Editorial Contributors: David Brown, Marilyn Haddrill, Christina Knight, Rebecca Miller, M. T. Schwartzman (Gold Guide editor), Heidi Sarna, Craig Seligman, Dinah A. Spritzer, Lois Taylor, Nancy Zimmerman

Editorial Production: Tracy Patruno

Maps: David Lindroth, *cartographer*; Steven K. Amsterdam, *map editor*

Design: Fabrizio La Rocca, *creative director*; Guido Caroti, *associate art director*; Jolie Novak, *photo editor*

Production/Manufacturing: Mike Costa

Cover Photograph: Thomas Hoepker/Magnum Photos, Inc.

Copyright

Special Sales

CONTENTS

Maps

ON THE ROAD WITH FODOR'S

WE'RE ALWAYS THRILLED to get letters from readers, especially one like this:

It took us an hour to decide what book to buy and we now know we picked the best one. Your book was wonderful, easy to follow, very accurate, and good on pointing out eating places, informal as well as formal. When we saw other people using your book, we would look at each other and smile.

Our editors and writers are deeply committed to making every Fodor's guide "the best one"—not only accurate but always charming, brimming with sound recommendations and solid ideas, right on the mark in describing restaurants and hotels, and full of fascinating facts that make you view what you've traveled to see in a rich new light.

About Our Writers

Our success in achieving our goals—and in helping to make your trip the best of all possible vacations—is a credit to the hard work of our extraordinary and editors.

Ron Butler, who wrote earlier editions of this guidebook, has traveled extensively around the Southwest. His books include *Esquire's Guide to Modern Etiquette* and *The Best of the Old West,* and his articles have appeared in *Travel & Leisure, Travel Holiday,* and *Ladies' Home Journal.*

As a New Mexico native, **Marilyn Haddrill** has explored many overlooked crannies of the rugged southern New Mexico region, which she shares with you in the Carlsbad and Southern New Mexico chapter. She is also an invaluable source for practical information, which makes her the perfect updater for Destination: Santa Fe, Taos, Albuquerque and for our Gold Guide. Marilyn has coauthored two suspense novels and writes for various publications including *Space News* and the *Chicago Tribune.* Her hardest assignment ever? Trying to get past a herd of hungry, bleating sheep.

Lois Taylor lives in New Mexico, where she works for *Town and Country* as a researcher and also for the Speaker of the House for New Mexico, when it's in session.

Nancy Zimmerman, updater of the Santa Fe and Vicinity and Taos chapters, is a freelance writer, editor, and translator based in Tesuque, a village just outside of Santa Fe.

New This Year

This year we've added terrific **Great Itineraries** that will lead you through the best of the city, taking into consideration how long you have to spend.

And this year, Fodor's joins Rand McNally, the world's largest commercial mapmaker, to bring you a **detailed color map** of Santa Fe, Taos, and Albuquerque. Just detach it along the perforation and drop it in your tote bag.

We're also proud to announce that the American Society of Travel Agents has endorsed Fodor's as its guidebook of choice. ASTA is the world's largest and most influential travel trade association, operating in more than 170 countries, with 27,000 members pledged to adhere to a strict code of ethics reflecting the Society's motto, "Integrity in Travel." ASTA shares Fodor's devotion to providing smart, honest travel information and advice to travelers, and we've long recommended that our readers consult ASTA member agents for the experience and professionalism they bring to the table.

On the Web, check out **Fodor's site** (www.fodors.com/) for information on major destinations around the world and travel-savvy interactive features. The Web site also lists the 85-plus radio stations nationwide that carry the **Fodor's Travel Show,** a live call-in program that airs every weekend. Tune in to hear guests discuss their wonderful adventures—or call in to get answers for your most pressing travel questions.

How to Use This Book

Organization

Up front is the **Gold Guide,** an easy-to-use section divided alphabetically by topic. Under each listing you'll find tips and information that will help you accomplish what you need to in Santa Fe, Albuquerque, and Taos. You'll also find addresses and telephone numbers of organizations and companies that offer destination-related services and detailed information and publications.

The first chapter in the guide, **Destination: Santa Fe, Taos, Albuquerque,** helps get you in the mood for your trip. New and Noteworthy cues you in on trends and happenings; What's Where gets you oriented; Pleasures and Pastimes describes the activities and sights that really make Santa Fe, Taos, and Albuquerque unique; Great Itineraries helps you decide what to visit in the time you have; Fodor's Choice showcases our top picks; and Festivals and Seasonal Events alerts you to special events you'll want to seek out.

Chapters in *Santa Fe, Taos, Albuquerque* are arranged by city and by region. Each city chapter begins with an Exploring section, which is subdivided by neighborhood; each subsection recommends a walking or driving tour and lists sights in alphabetical order. The Carlsbad and Southern New Mexico chapter is divided by geographical area; a suggested itinerary is given for the region as a whole, and within each area, towns are covered in logical geographical order. Throughout, "Off the Beaten Path" sights appear alphabetically, under Sights to See. And within town sections, all restaurants and lodgings are grouped together. The A to Z section that ends all chapters covers getting there, getting around, and helpful contacts and resources.

At the end of the book you'll find **Portraits**—a wonderful essay about New Mexico by D. H. Lawrence, followed by suggestions for pretrip reading, both fiction and nonfiction, and movies on tape with New Mexico as a backdrop. Finally, there's a glossary of frequently used terms.

Icons and Symbols

★   Our special recommendations
✕   Restaurant
🏠   Lodging establishment
✕🏠   Lodging establishment whose restaurant warrants a special trip
⚠   Campgrounds
🐥   Good for kids (rubber duckie)
☞   Sends you to another section of the guide for more information
✉   Address
☎   Telephone number

🕐   Opening and closing times
☎   Admission prices (those we give apply to adults; substantially reduced fees are almost always available for children, students, and senior citizens)

Numbers in white and black circles that appear on the maps, in the margins, and within the tours correspond to one another.

Dining and Lodging

The restaurants and lodgings we list are the cream of the crop in each price range. Price charts appear in the dining and lodging sections of each chapter and in the Pleasures and Pastimes section that follows the introduction in the Carlsbad and Southern New Mexico chapter.

Hotel Facilities

We always list the facilities that are available—but we don't specify whether they cost extra: When pricing accommodations, always ask what's included. In addition, assume that all rooms have private baths unless otherwise noted.

Restaurant Reservations and Dress Codes

Reservations are always a good idea; we note only when they're essential or when they are not accepted. Book as far ahead as you can, and reconfirm when you get to town. Unless otherwise noted, the restaurants listed are open daily for lunch and dinner. We mention dress only when men are required to wear a jacket or a jacket and tie. Look for an overview of local habits under Dining in the Gold Guide.

Credit Cards

The following abbreviations are used: **AE,** American Express; **D,** Discover; **DC,** Diners Club; **MC,** MasterCard; and **V,** Visa.

Don't Forget to Write

You can use this book in the confidence that all prices and opening times are based on information supplied to us at press time; Fodor's cannot accept responsibility for any errors. Time inevitably brings changes, so always confirm information when it matters—especially if you're making a detour to visit a specific place. In addition, when making reservations be sure to mention if you have a disability or are traveling with children, if you prefer a private bath or a certain type of bed, or if you have specific dietary needs or other concerns.

Were the restaurants we recommended as described? Did our hotel picks exceed your expectations? Did you find a museum we recommended a waste of time? If you have complaints, we'll look into them and revise our entries when the facts warrant it. If you've discovered a special place that we haven't included, we'll pass the information along to our correspondents and have them check it out. So send us your feedback, positive *and* negative: email us at editors@fodors.com (specifying the name of the book on the subject line) or write the Santa Fe/Taos/Albuquerque editor at Fodor's, 201 East 50th Street, New York, New York 10022. Have a wonderful trip!

Karen Cure
Editorial Director

The United States

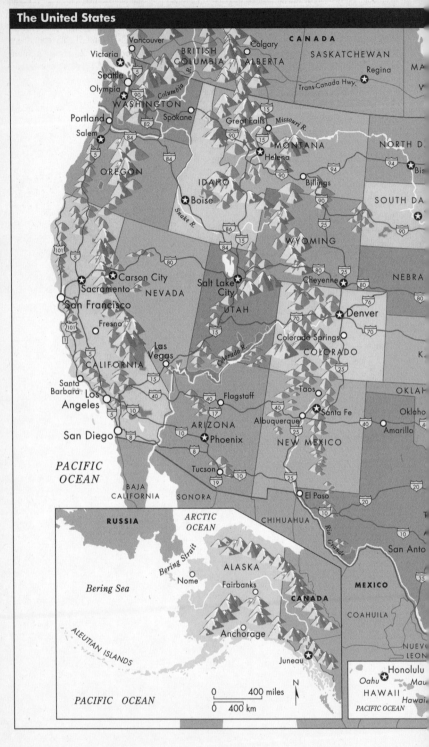

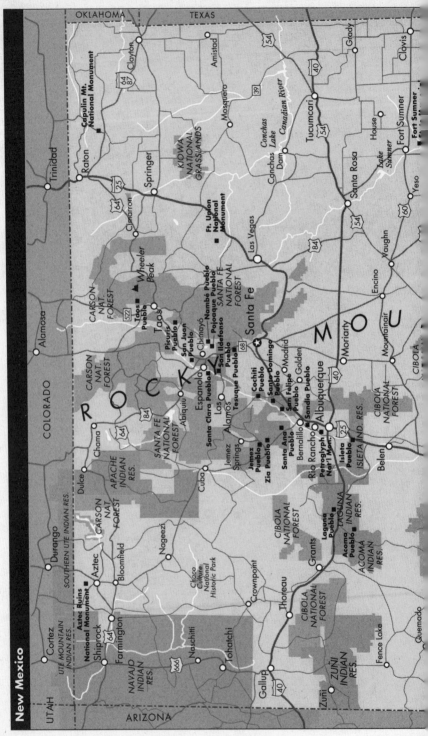

New Mexico

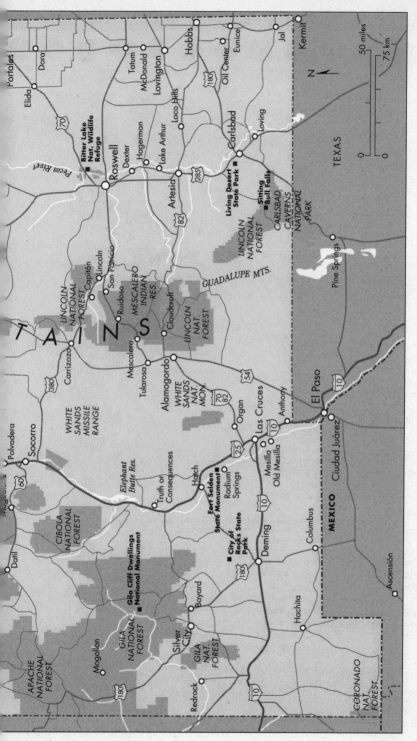

World Time Zones

Numbers below vertical bands relate each zone to Greenwich Mean Time (0 hrs.).
Local times frequently differ from these general indications,
as indicated by light-face numbers on map.

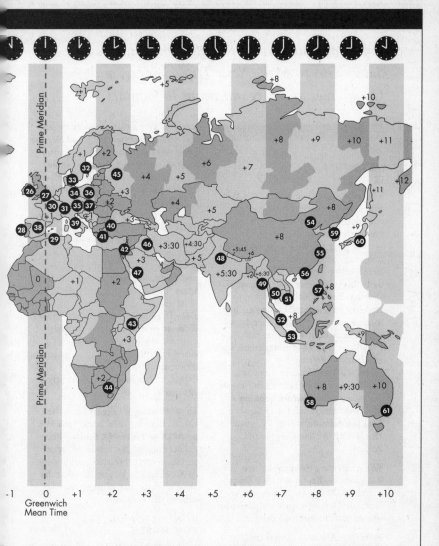

SMART TRAVEL TIPS A TO Z

Basic Information on Traveling in New Mexico, Savvy Tips to Make Your Trip a Breeze, and Companies and Organizations to Contact

A

AIR TRAVEL

MAJOR AIRLINE OR LOW-COST CARRIER?

Most people choose a flight based on price. Yet there are other issues to consider. Major airlines offer the greatest number of departures; smaller airlines—including regional, low-cost and no-frill airlines—usually have a more limited number of flights daily. Major airlines have frequent-flyer partners, which allow you to credit mileage earned on one airline to your account with another. Low-cost airlines offer a definite price advantage and fewer restrictions, such as advance-purchase requirements. Safety-wise, low-cost carriers as a group have a good history, but **check the safety record before booking** any low-cost carrier; call the Federal Aviation Administration's Consumer Hotline (☞ Airline Complaints, *below*).

When traveling from the United Kingdom, flights on British Airways travel via Dallas; Delta flies via Atlanta and Albuquerque; and United is routed via Chicago and Denver.

➤ MAJOR AIRLINES: **American** (☎ 800/433–7300). **Continental** (☎ 800/525–0280). **Delta** (☎ 800/221–1212). **Northwest** (800/692–7000). **TWA** (☎ 800/221–2000). **United** (☎ 800/241–6522). **US Airways** (☎ 800/428–4322).

➤ SMALLER AIRLINES: **America West** (☎ 800/235–9292). **Frontier** (☎ 800/432–1359). **Mesa Air** (☎ 800/637–2247). **Reno Air** (☎ 800/736–6247). **Southwest** (☎ 800/531–5601).

➤ FROM THE U.K.: **British Airways** (☎ 0345/222111). **Delta** (☎ 0800/414767). **United Airlines** (☎ 0800/888555).

GET THE LOWEST FARE

The least-expensive airfares to New Mexico are priced for round-trip travel. Major airlines usually require that you **book in advance and buy the ticket within 24 hours,** and you may have to **stay over a Saturday night.** It's smart to **call a number of airlines, and when you are quoted a good price, book it on the spot**—the same fare may not be available on the same flight the next day. Airlines generally allow you to change your return date for a fee $25–$50. If you don't use your ticket you can apply the cost toward the purchase of a new ticket, again for a small charge. However, most low-fare tickets are nonrefundable. To get the lowest airfare, **check different routings.** If your destination or home city has more than one gateway, compare prices to and from different airports. Also price off-peak flights, which may be significantly less expensive.

To save money on flights from the United Kingdom and back, **look into an APEX or Super-PEX ticket.** APEX tickets must be booked in advance and have certain restrictions. Super-PEX tickets can be purchased at the airport on the day of departure—subject to availability.

DON'T STOP UNLESS YOU MUST

When you book, **look for nonstop flights** and **remember that "direct" flights stop at least once.** Try to **avoid connecting flights,** which require a change of plane. Two airlines may jointly operate a connecting flight, so ask if your airline operates every segment—you may find that your preferred carrier flies you only part of the way.

USE AN AGENT

Travel agents, especially those who specialize in finding the lowest fares (☞ Discounts & Deals, *below*), can be especially helpful when booking a plane ticket. When you're quoted a price, **ask your agent if the price is likely to get any lower.** Good agents know the seasonal fluctuations of airfares and can usually anticipate a sale or fare war. However, waiting can be risky: The fare could go *up* as seats become scarce, and you may wait so long that your preferred flight sells out. A wait-and-see strategy works best if your plans are flexible, but if you must arrive and depart on certain dates, don't delay.

AVOID GETTING BUMPED

Airlines routinely overbook planes, knowing that not everyone with a ticket will show up, but sometimes everyone does. When that happens, airlines ask for volunteers to give up their seats. In return these volunteers usually get a certificate for a free flight and are rebooked on the next flight out. If there are not enough volunteers the airline must choose who will be denied boarding. The first to get bumped are passengers who checked in late and those flying on discounted tickets, so **get to the gate and check in as early as possible,** especially during peak periods.

ENJOY THE FLIGHT

For better service, **fly smaller or regional carriers,** which often have higher passenger-satisfaction ratings. Sometimes you'll find leather seats, more legroom, and better food.

For more legroom, **request an emergency-aisle seat**; don't, however, sit in the row in front of the emergency aisle or in front of a bulkhead, where seats may not recline.

If you don't like airline food, **ask for special meals when booking.** These can be vegetarian, low-cholesterol, or kosher, for example.

COMPLAIN IF NECESSARY

If your baggage goes astray or your flight goes awry, complain right away. Most carriers require that you file a claim immediately.

➤ AIRLINE COMPLAINTS: U.S. Department of Transportation **Aviation Consumer Protection Division** (✉ C-75, Room 4107, Washington, DC 20590, ☎ 202/366–2220). **Federal Aviation Administration (FAA) Consumer Hotline** (☎ 800/322–7873).

AIRPORTS & TRANSFERS

The major gateway to Santa Fe is Albuquerque International Airport, 65 mi southwest of Santa Fe and 130 mi south of Taos. There is no regular air service between Albuquerque and Santa Fe, but air shuttle service is offered from Albuquerque to Carlsbad and Las Cruces on Mesa Air (☞ Smaller Airlines, *above*).

Always **bring a photo ID to the airport.** You may be asked to show it before you are allowed to check in.

➤ AIRPORT INFORMATION: **Albuquerque International Airport** (☎ 505/842–4366). **Santa Fe Municipal Airport** (☎ 505/473–7243).

TRANSFERS

Shuttle buses operate between the Albuquerque Airport and Santa Fe and take about 1 hour and 20 minutes. The cost is about $20 each way. There's also a shuttle between Albuquerque Airport and Taos, which takes about 2¾ hours and costs $35 each way. In southern New Mexico there are daily trips between El Paso International Airport in Texas and Las Cruces. The trip is about 50 minutes and costs about $23. Reservations are advised on all shuttles.

➤ BETWEEN ALBUQUERQUE AIRPORT AND SANTA FE: **Shuttlejack** (☎ 505/982–4311).

➤ BETWEEN ALBUQUERQUE AIRPORT AND TAOS: **Faust Transportation** (☎ 505/758–7359).

➤ BETWEEN EL PASO AND LAS CRUCES: **Las Cruces Shuttle** (☎ 505/525–1784).

B

BUS TRAVEL

Bus service is available between major cities and towns in New Mexico. A one-way ticket from Albuquerque to Santa Fe costs about $12; to Taos about $22. Silver Stage offers personalized service, dropping passengers off at preferred destinations between cities including El Paso, Carlsbad, Las Cruces and Silver City.

➤ WITHIN NEW MEXICO: **Greyhound Albuquerque** (✉ 300 2nd St. SW, ☎ 505/243–4435 or 800/231–2222). **Faust Transportation** (☞ Transfers, *above*). **Shuttlejack** (☞ Transfers, *above*). **Silver Stage** (☎ 800/522–0162).

THE GOLD GUIDE / SMART TRAVEL TIPS

BUSINESS HOURS

Banks are open in Santa Fe weekdays 9–3 and Saturday 9–noon. In Taos they are open weekdays 9–5 and in Albuquerque weekdays 9–4, and, in some cases, Saturday 10–2.

In Santa Fe, Taos, and Albuquerque museums are generally open daily from 9 or 10 AM to 5 or 6 PM, although hours may vary from season to season.

In Santa Fe and Albuquerque the post office is open weekdays 8–5 and in Taos, weekdays 9–5.

General business hours in Santa Fe, Taos, and Albuquerque are 9–5; most shops and galleries are open 10–5 or 6, with limited hours on weekends. Store and commercial hours may vary from place to place and season to season (remaining open longer in summer than in winter) in Santa Fe and Taos.

C

CAMERAS, CAMCORDERS, & COMPUTERS

Always **keep your film, tape, or computer disks out of the sun.** Carry an extra supply of batteries, and **be prepared to turn on your camera, camcorder, or laptop** to prove to security personnel that the device is real. Always **ask for hand inspection of film,** which becomes clouded after successive exposure to airport X-ray machines, and **keep videotapes and computer disks away from metal detectors.**

➤ PHOTO HELP: Kodak Information Center (☎ 800/242–2424). *Kodak Guide to Shooting Great Travel Pictures,* available in bookstores or from Fodor's Travel Publications (☎ 800/533–6478); $16.50 plus $4 shipping.

CAR RENTAL

Rates in Santa Fe begin at about $30 a day and $160 a week for an economy car with air conditioning, an automatic transmission, and unlimited mileage. This does not include tax on car rentals, which is 10.75%, and a $2 per day surcharge. If you rent at the airport, there is an additional 2% tax.

➤ MAJOR AGENCIES: **Avis** (☎ 800/331–1212, 800/879–2847 in Canada). **Budget** (☎ 800/527–0700, 0800/181181 in the U.K.). **Hertz** (☎ 800/654–3131, 800/263–0600 in Canada, 0345/555888 in the U.K.).

➤ SMALLER AGENCIES: **Sears** (☎ 800/527–0770). **Enterprise** (☎ 800/322–8007). **PayLess** (☎ 800/541–1566). **Rent Rite** (☎ 800/554–7483). **Rich Ford** (☎ 800/331–3271). **Thrifty** (☎ 800/367–2277).

CUT COSTS

To get the best deal, **book through a travel agent who is willing to shop around.** When pricing cars, **ask about the location of the rental lot.** Some off-airport locations offer lower rates, and their lots are only minutes from the terminal via complimentary shuttle. You also may want to **price local car-rental companies,** whose rates may be lower still, although their service and maintenance may not be as good as those of a name-brand agency. Remember to ask about required deposits, cancellation penalties, and drop-off charges if you're planning to pick up the car in one city and leave it in another.

Also **ask your travel agent about a company's customer-service record.** How has it responded to late plane arrivals and vehicle mishaps? Are there often lines at the rental counter, and, if you're traveling during a holiday period, does a confirmed reservation guarantee you a car?

Be sure to **look into wholesalers,** companies that do not own fleets but rent in bulk from those that do and often offer better rates than traditional car-rental operations. Prices are best during off-peak periods.

➤ RENTAL WHOLESALERS: **Kemwel Group** (☎ 914/835–5555 or 800/678–0678, FAX 914/835–5126).

NEED INSURANCE?

When driving a rented car you are generally responsible for any damage to or loss of the vehicle. You also are liable for any property damage or personal injury that you may cause while driving. Before you rent, **see what coverage you already have** under the terms of your personal auto-insurance policy and credit cards.

For about $14 a day, rental companies sell protection, known as a collision- or loss-damage waiver (CDW or LDW) that eliminates your liability for damage to the car; it's always optional and should never be automatically added to your bill.

In most states you don't need CDW if you have personal auto insurance or other liability insurance. However, **make sure you have enough coverage to pay for the car.** If you do not have auto insurance or an umbrella policy that covers damage to third parties, purchasing CDW or LDW is highly recommended.

BEWARE SURCHARGES

Before you pick up a car in one city and leave it in another, **ask about drop-off charges or one-way service fees,** which can be substantial. Note, too, that some rental agencies charge extra if you return the car before the time specified on your contract. To avoid a hefty refueling fee, **fill the tank just before you turn in the car,** but be aware that gas stations near the rental outlet may overcharge.

MEET THE REQUIREMENTS

In the United States you must be 21 to rent a car, and rates may be higher if you're under 25. You'll pay extra for child seats (about $3 per day), which are compulsory for children under five, and for additional drivers (about $2 per day). Residents of the U.K. will need a reservation voucher, a passport, a U.K. driver's license, and a travel policy that covers each driver, in order to pick up a car.

CHILDREN & TRAVEL

Be sure to plan ahead and **involve your youngsters** as you outline your trip. When packing, include things to keep them busy en route. On sightseeing days try to schedule activities of special interest to your children. If you are renting a car don't forget to **arrange for a car seat** when you reserve.

LODGING

Many hotels in Santa Fe and Taos accommodate kids in all different ways. Some provide activities, while others actually allow kids to stay free. Holiday Inns permit children under 19 to stay with adults at no extra cost; at the Best Western the cutoff is 12 years old. Some hotels, however, charge them as extra adults; be sure to **ask about the cutoff age for children's discounts.** Another lodging option when traveling with kids is to consider resort accommodations. In many cases, especially for larger families, these work out to be much cheaper than hotels. For families that are looking for a little more activity, adventure holidays for children and families abound in the Southwest. Operators will organize wagon rides, safaris, and numerous other activities for children and adults.

➤ ADVENTURE HOLIDAYS: **Santa Fe Detours** (✉ 54½ E. San Francisco St., Santa Fe 87501, ☎ 505/983–6565 or 800/338–6877).

➤ CONDOMINIUMS AND RESORTS: **Ft. Marcy Hotel Suites** (✉ 320 Artist Rd., Santa Fe 87501, ☎ 505/982–6636).

➤ KID-FRIENDLY HOTELS: **Best Western Hotels** (☎ 800/528–1234). **Bishop's Lodge** (☎ 505/983–6377). **Holiday Inns** (☎ 800/465–4329).

FLYING

As a general rule, infants under two not occupying a seat fly free. If your children are two or older **ask about children's airfares.**

In general the adult baggage allowance applies to children paying half or more of the adult fare.

According to the FAA it's a good idea to use safety seats aloft for children weighing less than 40 pounds. Airlines, however, can set their own policies: U.S. carriers allow FAA-approved models but usually require that you buy a ticket, even if your child would otherwise ride free, since the seats must be strapped into regular seats. Airline rules vary regarding their use, so it's important to **check your airline's policy about using safety seats during takeoff and landing.** Safety seats cannot obstruct any of the other passengers in the row, so get an appropriate seat assignment as early as possible.

When making your reservation, **request children's meals or a free-standing bassinet** if you need them; the latter are available only to those seated at the bulkhead, where there's enough legroom. Remember, however, that bulkhead seats may not have their own overhead bins, and there's no storage space in front of you—a major inconvenience.

GROUP TRAVEL

If you're planning to take your kids on a tour, look for companies that specialize in family travel.

➤ FAMILY-FRIENDLY TOUR OPERATORS: **Grandtravel** (✉ 6900 Wisconsin Ave., Suite 706, Chevy Chase, MD 20815, ☎ 301/986–0790 or 800/247–7651) for people traveling with grandchildren ages 7–17. **Families Welcome!** (✉ 92 N. Main St., Ashland, OR 97520, ☎ 541/482–6121 or 800/326–0724, FAX 541/482–0660).

CONSUMER PROTECTION

Whenever possible, **pay with a major credit card** so you can cancel payment if there's a problem, provided that you can provide documentation. This is a good practice whether you're buying travel arrangements before your trip or shopping at your destination.

If you're doing business with a particular company for the first time, **contact your local Better Business Bureau and the attorney general's offices** in your state and the company's home state, as well. Have any complaints been filed?

Finally, if you're buying a package or tour, always **consider travel insurance** that includes default coverage (☞ Insurance, *below*).

➤ LOCAL BBBs: **Council of Better Business Bureaus** (✉ 4200 Wilson Blvd., Suite 800, Arlington, VA 22203, ☎ 703/276–0100, FAX 703/525–8277).

CUSTOMS & DUTIES

ENTERING THE U.S.

Visitors age 21 and over may import the following into the United States: 200 cigarettes or 50 cigars or 2 kilograms of tobacco, 1 liter of alcohol, and gifts worth $100. Prohibited items include meat products, seeds, plants, and fruits.

ENTERING CANADA

If you've been out of Canada for at least seven days you may bring in C$500 worth of goods duty-free. If you've been away for fewer than

seven days but more than 48 hours, the duty-free allowance drops to C$200; if your trip lasts 24–48 hours, the allowance is C$50. You may not pool allowances with family members. Goods claimed under the C$500 exemption may follow you by mail; those claimed under the lesser exemptions must accompany you.

Alcohol and tobacco products may be included in the seven-day and 48-hour exemptions but not in the 24-hour exemption. If you meet the age requirements of the province or territory through which you reenter Canada you may bring in, duty-free, 1.14 liters (40 imperial ounces) of wine or liquor *or* 24 12-ounce cans or bottles of beer or ale. If you are 16 or older you may bring in, duty-free, 200 cigarettes and 50 cigars; these items must accompany you.

You may send an unlimited number of gifts worth up to C$60 each duty-free to Canada. Label the package UNSOLICITED GIFT—VALUE UNDER $60. Alcohol and tobacco are excluded.

➤ INFORMATION: **Revenue Canada** (✉ 2265 St. Laurent Blvd. S, Ottawa, Ontario K1G 4K3, ☎ 613/993–0534, 800/461–9999 in Canada).

ENTERING THE U.K.

From countries outside the EU, including the United States, you may import, duty-free, 200 cigarettes or 50 cigars; 1 liter of spirits or 2 liters of fortified or sparkling wine or liqueurs; 2 liters of still table wine; 60 milliliters of perfume; 250 milliliters of toilet water; plus £136 worth of other goods, including gifts and souvenirs.

➤ INFORMATION: **HM Customs and Excise** (✉ Dorset House, Stamford St., London SE1 9NG, ☎ 0171/202–4227).

D

DISABILITIES & ACCESSIBILITY

ACCESS IN SANTA FE

Most of the region's national parks and recreational areas have accessible visitor centers, rest rooms, campsites, and trails, and more are being added every year.

➤ LOCAL RESOURCES: **National Park Service, Southwest Support Office** (✉ Box 728, Santa Fe 87504, ☎ 505/ 988–6011).

TIPS & HINTS

When discussing accessibility with an operator or reservationist, **ask hard questions.** Are there any stairs, inside *or* out? Are there grab bars next to the toilet *and* in the shower/tub? How wide is the doorway to the room? To the bathroom? For the most extensive facilities meeting the latest legal specifications, **opt for newer accommodations,** which are more likely to have been designed with access in mind. Older buildings or ships may offer more limited facilities. Be sure to **discuss your needs before booking.**

➤ COMPLAINTS: **Disability Rights Section** (✉ U.S. Department of Justice, Box 66738, Washington, DC 20035–6738, ☎ 202/514–0301 or 800/514–0301, FAX 202/307–1198, TTY 202/514–0383 or 800/514–0383). **Aviation Consumer Protection Division** (☞ Air Travel, *above*). **Civil Rights Office** (✉ U.S. Department of Transportation, Departmental Office of Civil Rights, S-30, 400 7th St. SW, Room 10215, Washington, DC, 20590, ☎ 202/366–4648).

TRAVEL AGENCIES & TOUR OPERATORS

The Americans with Disabilities Act requires that travel firms serve the needs of all travelers. That said, you should note that some agencies and operators specialize in making travel arrangements for individuals and groups with disabilities.

➤ TRAVELERS WITH MOBILITY PROBLEMS: **Access Adventures** (✉ 206 Chestnut Ridge Rd., Rochester, NY 14624, ☎ 716/889–9096).**Accessible Journeys** (✉ 35 W. Sellers Ave., Ridley Park, PA 19078, ☎ 610/521–0339 or 800/846–4537, FAX 610/521–6959), for escorted tours exclusively for travelers with mobility impairments. **Hinsdale Travel Service** (✉ 201 E. Ogden Ave., Suite 100, Hinsdale, IL 60521, ☎ 630/325–1335), a travel agency that benefits from the advice of wheelchair traveler Janice Perkins. **Wheelchair Journeys** (✉ 16979 Redmond Way, Redmond, WA 98052, ☎ 206/885–2210 or 800/313–4751), for general travel arrangements.

Be a smart shopper and **compare all your options before making a choice.** A plane ticket bought with a promotional coupon may not be cheaper than the least expensive fare from a discount ticket agency. For high-price travel purchases, such as packages or tours, keep in mind that what you get is just as important as what you save. Just because something is cheap doesn't mean it's a bargain.

LOOK IN YOUR WALLET

When you use your credit card to make travel purchases you may get free travel-accident insurance, collision-damage insurance, and medical or legal assistance, depending on the card and the bank that issued it. American Express, MasterCard, and Visa provide one or more of these services, so **get a copy of your credit card's travel-benefits policy.** If you are a member of the American Automobile Association (AAA) or an oil-company-sponsored road-assistance plan, always **ask hotel or car-rental reservationists about auto-club discounts.** Some clubs offer additional discounts on tours, cruises, or admission to attractions. And don't forget that auto-club membership entitles you to free maps and trip-planning services.

DIAL FOR DOLLARS

To save money, **look into "1-800" discount reservations services,** which use their buying power to get a better price on hotels, airline tickets, even car rentals. When booking a room, always **call the hotel's local toll-free number** (if one is available) rather than the central reservations number—you'll often get a better price. Always ask about special packages or corporate rates.

➤ AIRLINE TICKETS: ☎ 800/FLY–4–LESS. ☎ 800/FLY–ASAP.

➤ HOTEL ROOMS: **RMC Travel** (☎ 800/245–5738).

SAVE ON COMBOS

Packages and guided tours can both save you money, but don't confuse the two. When you buy a package your travel remains independent, just as though you had planned and booked the trip yourself. Fly/drive packages, which combine airfare and car rental, are often a good deal. In cities, ask the local visitors bureau about hotel packages.

JOIN A CLUB?

Many companies sell discounts in the form of travel clubs and coupon books, but these cost money. You must use participating advertisers to get a deal, and only after you recoup the initial membership cost or book price do you begin to save. If you plan to use the club or coupons frequently you may save considerably. Before signing up, find out what discounts you get for free.

➤ DISCOUNT CLUBS: **Entertainment Travel Editions** (⊠ 2125 Butterfield Rd., Troy, MI 48084, ☎ 800/445–4137); $23–$48, depending on destination. **Great American Traveler** (⊠ Box 27965, Salt Lake City, UT 84127, ☎ 800/548–2812); $49.95 per year. **Moment's Notice Discount Travel Club** (⊠ 7301 New Utrecht Ave., Brooklyn, NY 11204, ☎ 718/234–6295); $25 per year, single or family. **Privilege Card International** (⊠ 237 E. Front St., Youngstown, OH 44503, ☎ 330/746–5211 or 800/236–9732); $74.95 per year. **Sears's Mature Outlook** (⊠ Box 9390, Des Moines, IA 50306, ☎ 800/336–6330); $14.95 per year. **Travelers Advantage** (⊠ CUC Travel Service, 3033 S. Parker Rd., Suite 1000, Aurora, CO 80014, ☎ 800/548–1116 or 800/648–4037); $49 per year, single or family. **Worldwide Discount Travel Club** (⊠ 1674 Meridian Ave., Miami Beach, FL 33139, ☎ 305/534–2082; $50 per year family, $40 single).

DRIVING

I–40 runs east–west across the middle of the state; I–10 cuts across the southern part of the state from the Texas border at El Paso to the Arizona line, through Las Cruces, Deming, and Lordsburg; I–25 runs north from the state line at El Paso through Albuquerque and Santa Fe, then angles northeast to the Colorado line near Raton.

U.S. highways connect all major cities and towns with a good network of paved roads. State roads go to the smaller towns; most of them are paved, two-lane thoroughfares. Roads

on Native American lands are designated by wooden, arrow-shape signs; these, like roads in national forests, are usually not paved.

Technically, there may not be a lot of true desert in New Mexico, but there is a lot of high, dry, lonesome country. For a safe trip, **keep your gas tank full and abide by the signs**—you shouldn't have any trouble.

Arroyos, dry washes or gullies, are bridged on major roads, but lesser roads often dip down through them. These can be a hazard during the rainy season of July, August, and September. Even if it looks shallow, **don't try to cross an arroyo filled with water**—it may have an axle-breaking hole in the middle. Just wait a little while, and it will drain off almost as quickly as it filled. If you stall in a running arroyo, get out of the car and onto high ground if possible. If you are in backcountry, never drive (or walk) in a dry arroyo bed if the sky is dark anywhere upstream. A sudden thunderstorm 15 miles away could send a raging flash flood down a wash that was perfectly dry a few minutes earlier.

Unless they are well graded and graveled, **avoid unpaved roads in New Mexico when they are wet.** The soil has a lot of caliche, or clay, in it that gets very slick when mixed with water. During winter storms, roads may be shut down entirely; call the State Highway Department to find out road conditions.

➤ AUTO CLUBS: In the U.S., **American Automobile Association** (☎ 800/564–6222). In the U.K., **Automobile Association** (AA; ☎ 0990/500–600), **Royal Automobile Club** (RAC; ☎ 0990/722–722 for membership, 0345/121–345 for insurance).

➤ ROAD CONDITIONS: **State Highway Department** (☎ 800/432–4269).

G

GAY & LESBIAN TRAVEL

➤ GAY- AND LESBIAN-FRIENDLY TRAVEL AGENCIES: **Advance Damron** (⊠ 1 Greenway Plaza, Suite 800, Houston, TX 77046, ☎ 713/850–1140 or 800/695–0880, FAX 713/888–1010). **Club Travel** (⊠ 8739 Santa Monica Blvd., West Hollywood, CA 90069, ☎ 310/

358–2200 or 800/429–8747, FAX 310/358–2222). **Islanders/Kennedy Travel** (✉ 183 W. 10th St., New York, NY 10014, ☎ 212/242–3222 or 800/988–1181, FAX 212/929–8530). **Now Voyager** (✉ 4406 18th St., San Francisco, CA 94114, ☎ 415/626–1169 or 800/255–6951, FAX 415/626–8626). **Yellowbrick Road** (✉ 1500 W. Balmoral Ave., Chicago, IL 60640, ☎ 773/561–1800 or 800/642–2488, FAX 773/561–4497). **Skylink Women's Travel** (✉ 3577 Moorland Ave., Santa Rosa, CA 95407, ☎ 707/585–8355 or 800/225–5759, FAX 707/584–5637), serving lesbian travelers.

I

INSURANCE

Travel insurance is the best way to **protect yourself against financial loss.** The most useful policies are trip-cancellation-and-interruption, default, medical, and comprehensive insurance.

Without insurance you will lose all or most of your money if you cancel your trip, regardless of the reason. It's essential that you **buy trip-cancellation-and-interruption insurance,** particularly if your airline ticket, cruise, or package tour is nonrefundable and cannot be changed. When considering how much coverage you need, look for a policy that will cover the cost of your trip plus the nondiscounted price of a one-way airline ticket, should you need to return home early. Also **consider default or bankruptcy insurance,** which protects you against a supplier's failure to deliver.

Citizens of the United Kingdom can buy an annual travel-insurance policy valid for most vacations during the year in which it's purchased. If you are pregnant or have a preexisting medical condition, make sure you're covered. According to the Association of British Insurers, a trade association representing 450 insurance companies, it's wise to buy extra medical coverage when you visit the United States.

If you have purchased an expensive vacation, comprehensive insurance is a must. It's best to **look for comprehensive policies that include trip-delay insurance,** which will protect you in the event that weather problems cause

you to miss your flight, tour, or cruise. A few insurers sell waivers for preexisting medical conditions. Companies that offer both features include Access America, Carefree Travel, Travel Insured International, and Travel Guard (☞ *below*).

Always **buy travel insurance directly from the insurance company;** if you buy it from a travel agency or tour operator that goes out of business you probably will not be covered for the agency or operator's default, a major risk. Before you make any purchase, **review your existing health and home-owner's policies** to find out whether they cover expenses incurred while traveling.

➤ U.S. TRAVEL INSURERS: **Access America** (✉ 6600 W. Broad St., Richmond, VA 23230, ☎ 804/285–3300 or 800/284–8300). **Carefree Travel Insurance** (✉ Box 9366, 100 Garden City Plaza, Garden City, NY 11530, ☎ 516/294–0220 or 800/323–3149). **Near Travel Services** (✉ Box 1339, Calumet City, IL 60409, ☎ 708/868–6700 or 800/654–6700). **Travel Guard International** (✉ 1145 Clark St., Stevens Point, WI 54481, ☎ 715/345–0505 or 800/826–1300). **Travel Insured International** (✉ Box 280568, East Hartford, CT 06128–0568, ☎ 860/528–7663 or 800/243–3174). **Travelex Insurance Services** (✉ 11717 Burt St., Suite 202, Omaha, NE 68154-1500, ☎ 402/445–8637 or 800/228–9792, FAX 800/867–9531). **Wallach & Company** (✉ 107 W. Federal St., Box 480, Middleburg, VA 20118, ☎ 540/687–3166 or 800/237–6615).

➤ IN CANADA: **Mutual of Omaha** (✉ Travel Division, 500 University Ave., Toronto, Ontario M5G 1V8, ☎ 416/598–4083, 800/268–8825 in Canada).

➤ IN THE U.K.: **Association of British Insurers** (✉ 51 Gresham St., London EC2V 7HQ, ☎ 0171/600–3333).

L

LODGING

In addition to hotels, New Mexico offers a broad range of alternative accommodations, from charming bed-and-breakfasts in quaint residential areas to small alpine lodges near the

primary ski resorts. Of course, you'll
also find major-chain hotels. Low-
season rates, which fluctuate, tend to
be 20% lower than during the peak
tourist months of July and August.
Reservations are also easier to obtain
during low season (☞ When to Go,
below).

APARTMENT & VILLA RENTALS

If you want a home base that's roomy
enough for a family and comes with
cooking facilities, **consider a furnished
rental.** These can save you money,
however some rentals are luxury
properties, economical only when
your party is large. Home-exchange
directories list rentals (often second
homes owned by prospective house
swappers), and some services search
for a house or apartment for you
(even a castle if that's your fancy) and
handle the paperwork. Some send an
illustrated catalog; others send photographs only of specific properties,
sometimes at a charge. Up-front
registration fees may apply.

➤ RENTAL AGENTS: **Europa-Let/
Tropical Inn-Let** (✉ 92 N. Main
St., Ashland, OR 97520, ☎ 541/
482–5806 or 800/462–4486, FAX
541/482–0660). **Property Rentals
International** (✉ 1008 Mansfield
Crossing Rd., Richmond, VA 23236,
☎ 804/378–6054 or 800/220–3332,
FAX 804/379–2073). **Rent-a-Home
International** (✉ 7200 34th Ave. NW,
Seattle, WA 98117, ☎ 206/789–9377
or 800/488–7368, FAX 206/789–
9379). **Hideaways International** (✉
767 Islington St., Portsmouth, NH
03801, ☎ 603/430–4433 or 800/
843–4433, FAX 603/430–4444) is a
travel club whose members arrange
rentals among themselves; yearly
membership is $99.

BED-AND-BREAKFASTS

➤ RESERVATIONS: **Taos Bed-and-
Breakfast Directory** (✉ Box 2772,
Taos, NM 87571, ☎ 505/758–4747
or 800/876–7857).

HOME EXCHANGES

If you would like to exchange your
home for someone else's, **join a home-
exchange organization,** which will
send you its updated listings of available exchanges for a year and will
include your own listing in at least
one of them. Making the arrangements is up to you.

➤ EXCHANGE CLUBS: **HomeLink
International** (✉ Box 650, Key West,
FL 33041, ☎ 305/294–7766 or 800/
638–3841, FAX 305/294–1148)
charges $83 per year.

M

MONEY

ATMS

Before leaving home, **make sure that
your credit cards have been pro-
grammed for ATM use.**

➤ ATM LOCATIONS: **Cirrus** (☎ 800/
424–7787). **Plus** (☎ 800/843–7587).

P

PACKING FOR NEW MEXICO

Typical of the Southwest, temperatures can vary considerably from
sunup to sundown. You should **pack
for warm days and chilly nights.**

The areas of higher elevation are, of
course, considerably cooler than are
Carlsbad and other low-lying southern portions of the state. That means
winter visitors should pack warm
clothes—coats, parkas, and whatever
else your body's thermostat and your
ultimate destination dictate. Sweaters
and jackets will also be needed for
summer visitors, because while days
are warm, nights at the higher alti-
tudes can be extremely chilly. And
bring comfortable shoes; you're likely
to be doing a lot of walking.

New Mexico is one of the most
informal and laid-back areas of the
country, which for many is much a
part of its appeal. Probably no more
than three or four restaurants in the
entire state enforce a dress code, even
for dinner meals, though men are
likely to feel more comfortable wearing a jacket in the major hotel dining
rooms, and anyone wearing tennis
shoes may receive a look of stern
disapproval from the maître d'.

The Western look, popular throughout the country a few years back has,
of course, never lost its hold on the
West. But Western dress has become
less corny and more subtle and refined. Western-style clothes are no
longer a costume; they're being mixed
with tweed jackets, for example, for a
more conservative, sophisticated
image. Which is to say, you can dress
Western with your boots and big belt

buckles in even the best places in Santa Fe, Taos, Albuquerque, or Carlsbad, but if you come strolling through the lobby of the Eldorado Hotel looking like Hopalong Cassidy, you'll get some funny looks.

Depending on where you're headed in New Mexico, you may find the sun strong, the air dry, and the wind hot and relentless. Don't neglect to **bring skin moisturizers** if dry skin's a problem, and **bring sunglasses** to protect your eyes from the glare of lakes or ski slopes. High altitude can be a problem (it may cause headaches and dizziness), so check with your doctor about medication to alleviate symptoms.

Bring an extra pair of eyeglasses or contact lenses in your carry-on luggage, and if you have a health problem, **pack enough medication** to last the entire trip. It's important that you **don't put prescription drugs or valuables in luggage to be checked**: it might go astray.

LUGGAGE

In general you are entitled to check two bags on flights within the United States. A third piece may be brought on board, but it must fit easily under the seat in front of you or in the overhead compartment.

Airline liability for baggage is limited to $1,250 per person on flights within the United States. On international flights it amounts to $9.07 per pound or $20 per kilogram for checked baggage (roughly $640 per 70-pound bag) and $400 per passenger for unchecked baggage. Insurance for losses exceeding these amounts can be bought from the airline at check-in for about $10 per $1,000 of coverage; note that this coverage excludes a rather extensive list of items, which is shown on your airline ticket.

Before departure, **itemize your bags' contents** and their worth, and label the bags with your name, address, and phone number. (If you use your home address, cover it so that potential thieves can't see it readily.) Inside each bag, **pack a copy of your itinerary.** At check-in, **make sure that each bag is correctly tagged** with the destination airport's three-letter code. If your bags arrive damaged or fail to arrive at all, file a written report with the airline before leaving the airport.

PARKS, FORESTS, & MONUMENTS

There are 12 national monuments in New Mexico, and a few state monuments and parks. Several of the monuments give insight into the 19th-century territorial period of New Mexico, including exploits of the infamous Billy the Kid. New Mexico also has Carlsbad National Park, in the southeastern part of the state (27 mi southwest of Carlsbad on U.S. 62/180), with one of the largest and most spectacular cave systems in the world.

For information on New Mexico's five national forests and the Kiowa National Grasslands (part of the Cibola National Forest), contact the USDA Forest Service (☞ Visitor Information, *below*).

See also Pleasures and Pastimes *in* Chapter 1, *and* individual park and monument listings *in* Chapters 2, 3, 4, and 5.

➤ GENERAL INFORMATION: **Monument Division, Museum of New Mexico** (⊠ Box 2087, Santa Fe 87504, ☎ 505/827–6334). **State Parks and Recreational Division** (⊠ Energy, Minerals, and Natural Resources Dept., 408 Galisteo St., Box 1147, Santa Fe 87504, ☎ 505/827–7465 or 800/451–2451), for maps and brochures. **National Parks Service** (⊠ Box 728, Santa Fe 87504–0728, ☎ 505/988–6011).

➤ NATIONAL MONUMENTS AND PARKS: **Aztec Ruins National Monument** (⊠ Box 640, Aztec 87410, ☎ 505/334–6174). **Bandelier National Monument** (⊠ HCR 1, Box 1, Suite 15, Los Alamos 87544, ☎ 505/672–0343). **Capulin Volcano National Monument** (⊠ Box 94, Capulin 88414, ☎ 505/278–2201). **Chaco Culture National Historic Park** (⊠ Star Rte. 4, Box 6500, Bloomfield 87413, ☎ 505/786–7014). **El Malpais National Monument and Conservation Area** (⊠ Box 939, Grants 87020, ☎ 505/285–4641). **El Morro National Monument** (⊠ NM 2, Box 43, Ramah 87321-9603, ☎ 505/783–4226). **Fort Union National Monument** (⊠ Box 127, Watrous 87753, ☎ 505/425–8025). **Gila Cliff Dwellings National Monument** (⊠ NM 11, Box 100, Silver City 88061, ☎ 505/536–9461 or 505/757–

6032). **Pecos National Historical Park** (⊠ Drawer 418, Pecos 87552, ☎ 505/757–6414). **Petroglyph National Monument** (⊠ 6900 Unser Blvd. NW, Albuquerque 87120, ☎ 505/897–8814). **Salinas Pueblo Missions National Monument** (⊠ Box 517, Mountainair 87036, ☎ 505/847–2585). **White Sands National Monument** (⊠ Box 1086, Holloman AFB, NM 88330-1086, ☎ 505/479–6124). **Carlsbad Caverns National Park** (⊠ 3225 National Parks Hwy., Carlsbad 88220, ☎ 505/785–2251).

➤ NATIONAL FORESTS: **Carson National Forest** (⊠ Forest Service Bldg., 208 Cruz Alta Rd., Box 558, Taos 87571, ☎ 505/758–6200). **Cibola National Forest** (⊠ 2113 Osuna Rd. NE, Suite A, Albuquerque 87113, ☎ 505/761–4650). **Gila National Forest** (⊠ 3005 E. Camino del Bosque, Silver City 88061, ☎ 505/388–8201). **Lincoln National Forest** (⊠ Federal Bldg., 1101 New York Ave., Alamogordo 88310, ☎ 505/434–7200). **Santa Fe National Forest** (⊠ 1220 St. Francis Dr., Box 1689, Santa Fe 87504, ☎ 505/988–6940).

➤ STATE MONUMENTS: **Coronado State Monument** (⊠ NM 44, off I–25, Box 95, Bernalillo 87004, ☎ 505/867–5351). **Jemez State Monument** (⊠ NM 4, 1 mi north of Jemez Springs, Box 143, Jemez Springs 87025, ☎ 505/829–3530). **Lincoln State Monument** (⊠ U.S. 380, 12 mi east of Capitan, Courthouse Museum, Lincoln 88338, ☎ 505/653–4372), **Fort Selden** (⊠ Radium Springs exit off I–25, 13 mi north of Las Cruces, Box 58, Radium Springs 88054, ☎ 505/ 526–8911). **Fort Sumner** (⊠ 2 mi east of the town Fort Sumner, on Billy the Kid Rd., NM 1, Box 356, Fort Sumner 88119, ☎ 505/355–2573).

PASSES

You may be able to **save money on park entrance fees** by getting a discount pass. The Golden Eagle Pass ($50) gets you and your companions free admission to all parks for one year. (Camping and parking are extra). Both the Golden Age Passport, for U.S. citizens or permanent residents age 62 and older, and the Golden Access Passport, for travelers with disabilities, entitle holders to free entry to all national parks plus 50%

off fees for the use of many park facilities and services. Both passports are free; you must show proof of age and U.S. citizenship or permanent residency (such as a U.S. passport, driver's license, or birth certificate) or proof of disability. All three passes are available at all national park entrances. Golden Eagle and Golden Access passes are also available by mail.

➤ PASSES BY MAIL: **National Park Service** (⊠ Department of the Interior, Washington, DC 20240).

PASSPORTS & VISAS

CANADIANS

A passport is not required to enter the United States.

U.K. CITIZENS

British citizens need a valid passport to enter the United States. If you are staying for fewer than 90 days on vacation, with a return or onward ticket, you probably will not need a visa. However, you will need to fill out the Visa Waiver Form, 1-94W, supplied by the airline.

➤ INFORMATION: **London Passport Office** (☎ 0990/21010) for fees and documentation requirements and to request an emergency passport. **U.S. Embassy Visa Information Line** (☎ 01891/200–290) for U.S. visa information; calls cost 49p per minute or 39p per minute cheap rate. **U.S. Embassy Visa Branch** (⊠ 5 Upper Grosvenor St., London W1A 2JB) for U.S. visa information; send a self-addressed, stamped envelope. Write the **U.S. Consulate General** (⊠ Queen's House, Queen St., Belfast BTI 6EO) if you live in Northern Ireland.

S

SENIOR-CITIZEN TRAVEL

To qualify for age-related discounts, **mention your senior-citizen status up front** when booking hotel reservations (not when checking out) and before you're seated in restaurants (not when paying the bill). Note that discounts may be limited to certain menus, days, or hours. When renting a car, **ask about promotional car-rental discounts**, which can be cheaper than senior-citizen rates.

➤ EDUCATIONAL TRAVEL PROGRAMS:
Elderhostel (✉ 75 Federal St., 3rd
floor, Boston, MA 02110, ☎ 617/
426–8056).

BICYCLING

➤ CYLCING EVENTS: **New Mexico
Touring Society** (☎ 505/298–0085).

BIRD-WATCHING

New Mexico is fortunate to be home
to tens of thousands of migrating
birds, and the refuges offer viewing
platforms for observing the flocks of
snow geese, sandhill cranes, and other
migratory birds using this popular
stopover.

➤ REFUGES: **Bitter Lake National
Wildlife Refuge** (✉ Box 7, Roswell
88202, ☎ 505/622–6755). **Bosque
del Apache National Wildlife Refuge**
(✉ Box 1246, Socorro 87801, ☎
505/835–1828).

CAMPING

For information on camping in New
Mexico's National Forest, *see* Parks,
Forests, & Monuments, *above*.

CANOEING, KAYAKING, & RIVER RAFTING

Most of the hard-core river rafting is
done in the Taos area; for statewide
information concerning river recreational activities, contact the New
Mexico Department of Tourism (☞
Visitor Information, *below*).

➤ OUTFITTERS: **Santa Fe Detours** (✉
54½ E. San Francisco St., Santa Fe
87501, ☎ 505/983–6565 or 800/
338–6877). **Taos County Chamber of
Commerce** (✉ 1139 Paseo del Pueblo
Sur, Drawer I, Taos 87571, ☎ 505/
758–3873 or 800/732–8267) for list
of local outfitters.

FISHING

Anyone over 12 who wishes to fish
must **buy a New Mexico fishing
license.** Including a trout-validation
stamp, the license costs out-of-state
visitors $8 per day or $16 for five
days. Habitat stamps also must be
purchased for an extra $5 for fishing
on U.S. Forest Service or Bureau of
Land Management lands. About 225
stores, in addition to game-and-fish
offices, sell fishing and hunting licenses.

Fishing on Native American reservations is not subject to state regulations but will require tribal permits;
the Indian Pueblo Cultural Center (☞
Visitor Information, *below*) can
provide further information.

➤ INFORMATION: **New Mexico Game
and Fish Department** (✉ Villagra
Bldg., 408 Galisteo St., Box 25112,
Santa Fe 87503, ☎ 505/827–7911)
for state fishing regulations and maps.
Sport Fishing Promotions Council
toll-free hot line (☎ 800/275–3474)
for 24-hour up-to-date information
on fishing conditions, regulations,
and boat-launch sites.

GOLF

➤ INFORMATION: **Sun Country Ama-
teur Golf Association** (✉ 10035
Country Club La. NW, No. 5, Albuquerque 87114, ☎ 505/897–0864)
for a list of courses and greens fees
and hours for each club.

HIKING

➤ INFORMATION AND MAPS: **State
Parks and Recreation Division** (✉
Energy, Minerals, and Natural Resources Dept., 408 Galisteo St., Box
1147, Santa Fe 87504, ☎ 505/827–
7465 or 800/451–2541).

HORSE RACING

➤ TRACKS: **Downs at Santa Fe** (✉ 5
mi south of Santa Fe, ☎ 505/471–
3311).**Downs at Albuquerque** (✉
New Mexico State Fairgrounds, E.
Central Ave., ☎ 505/266–5555).
Ruidoso Downs Racetrack (☎ 505/
378–4431). **Sunland Park Racetrack**
(✉ 5 mi north of El Paso, Texas, ☎
505/589–1131).

SKIING

➤ INFORMATION: **Ski New Mexico** (☎
800/755–7669), for a free *Skier's
Guide*.

➤ DOWNHILL: **Angel Fire Resort** (✉
Drawer B, Angel Fire 87710, ☎ 800/
633–7463). **Enchanted Forest Cross
Country,** ✉ Box 521, Red River
87558, ☎ 505/754–2374). **Pajarito
Mountain Ski Area** (✉ Box 155, Los
Alamos 87544, ☎ 505/ 662–7669 or
505/662–5725). **Red River Ski Area**
(✉ Box 900, Red River 87558, ☎
505/ 754–2223). **Sandia Peak Ski
Area** (✉ 10 Tramway Loop NE,
Albuquerque 87122, ☎ 505/242–
9133). **Santa Fe Ski Area** (✉ 1210
Louisa St., Suite 5, Santa Fe 87505–

THE GOLD GUIDE / SMART TRAVEL TIPS

4126, ☎ 505/982–4429). **Sipapu Lodge and Ski Area** (✉ Box 29, Vadito 87579, ☎ 505/587–2240). **Ski Apache** (✉ Box 220, Ruidoso 88345, ☎ 505/336–4356). **Snow Canyon** (✉ Box 498, Cloudcroft 88317, ☎ 800/ 333–7542). **Taos Ski Valley** (✉ Box 90, Taos Ski Valley 87525, ☎ 505/776–2291).

STUDENTS

➤ STUDENT IDs AND SERVICES: **Council on International Educational Exchange** (CIEE; ✉ 205 E. 42nd St., 14th floor, New York, NY 10017, ☎ 212/822–2600 or 888/268–6245, FAX 212/822–2699), for mail orders only, in the United States. **Travel Cuts** (✉ 187 College St., Toronto, Ontario M5T 1P7, ☎ 416/979–2406 or 800/ 667–2887) in Canada.

➤ HOSTELING: **Hostelling International—American Youth Hostels** (✉ 733 15th St. NW, Suite 840, Washington, DC 20005, ☎ 202/783–6161, FAX 202/783–6171). **Hostelling International—Canada** (✉ 400-205 Catherine St., Ottawa, Ontario K2P 1C3, ☎ 613/237–7884, FAX 613/237–7868). **Youth Hostel Association of England and Wales** (✉ Trevelyan House, 8 St. Stephen's Hill, St. Albans, Hertfordshire AL1 2DY, ☎ 01727/855215 or 01727/845047, FAX 01727/844126); membership U.S.$25, C$26.75, or £9.30.

➤ STUDENT TOURS: **Contiki Holidays** (✉ 300 Plaza Alicante, Suite 900, Garden Grove, CA 92840, ☎ 714/740–0808 or 800/266–8454, FAX 714/740–2034).

T

TELEPHONES

CALLING HOME

AT&T, MCI, and Sprint long-distance services make calling home relatively convenient and let you avoid hotel surcharges. Typically you dial an 800 number in the United States.

➤ TO OBTAIN ACCESS CODES: **AT&T USADirect** (☎ 800/874–4000). **MCI Call USA** (☎ 800/444–4444). **Sprint Express** (☎ 800/793–1153).

TOUR OPERATORS

Buying a prepackaged tour or independent vacation can make your trip to Santa Fe less expensive and more

hassle-free. Because everything is prearranged you'll spend less time planning.

Operators that handle several hundred thousand travelers per year can use their purchasing power to give you a good price. Their high volume may also indicate financial stability. But some small companies provide more personalized service; because they tend to specialize, they may also be more knowledgeable about a given area.

A GOOD DEAL?

The more your package or tour includes, the better you can predict the ultimate cost of your vacation. Make sure you know exactly what is covered, and **beware of hidden costs.** Are taxes, tips, and service charges included? Transfers and baggage handling? Entertainment and excursions? These can add up.

If the package or tour you are considering is priced lower than in your wildest dreams, **be skeptical.** Also, **make sure your travel agent knows the accommodations** and other services. Ask about the hotel's location, room size, beds, and whether it has a pool, room service, or programs for children, if you care about these. Has your agent been there in person or sent others you can contact?

BUYER BEWARE

Each year consumers are stranded or lose their money when tour operators—even very large ones with excellent reputations—go out of business. So **check out the operator.** Find out how long the company has been in business, and ask several agents about its reputation. **Don't book unless the firm has a consumer-protection program.**

Members of the National Tour Association and United States Tour Operators Association are required to set aside funds to cover your payments and travel arrangements in case the company defaults. Nonmembers may carry insurance instead. Look for the details, and for the name of an underwriter with a solid reputation, in the operator's brochure. Note: When it comes to tour operators, **don't trust escrow accounts.** Although the Department of Transportation watches over charter-flight operators, no regulatory body prevents tour operators from raiding the till. You may want to protect yourself by buying travel insurance that includes a tour-operator default provision. For more information, *see* Consumer Protection, *above.*

It's also a good idea to choose a company that participates in the American Society of Travel Agents' Tour Operator Program (TOP). This gives you a forum if there are any disputes between you and your tour operator; ASTA will act as mediator.

➤ TOUR-OPERATOR RECOMMENDATIONS: **American Society of Travel Agents** (☞ Travel Agencies, *below*). **National Tour Association** (NTA; ✉ 546 E. Main St., Lexington, KY 40508, ☎ 606/226–4444 or 800/755–8687). **United States Tour Operators Association** (USTOA; ✉ 342 Madison Ave., Suite 1522, New York, NY 10173, ☎ 212/599–6599, FAX 212/599–6744).

USING AN AGENT

Travel agents are excellent resources. In fact, large operators accept bookings made only through travel agents. But it's a good idea to **collect brochures from several agencies,** because some agents' suggestions may be influenced by relationships with tour and package firms that reward them for volume sales. If you have a special interest, **find an agent with expertise in that area;** ASTA (☞ Travel Agencies, *below*) has a database of specialists worldwide. Do some homework on your own, too: Local tourism boards can provide information about lesser-known and small-niche operators, some of which may sell only direct.

SINGLE TRAVELERS

Prices for packages and tours are usually quoted per person, based on two sharing a room. If traveling solo, you may be required to pay the full double-occupancy rate. Some operators eliminate this surcharge if you agree to be matched with a roommate of the same sex, even if one is not found by departure time.

GROUP TOURS

Among companies that sell tours to Santa Fe, the following are nationally known, have a proven reputation,

and offer plenty of options. The classifications used below represent different price categories, and you'll probably encounter these terms when talking to a travel agent or tour operator. The key difference is usually in accommodations, which run from budget to better, and better-yet to best.

➤ DELUXE: **Globus** (✉ 5301 S. Federal Circle, Littleton, CO 80123-2980, ☎ 303/797–2800 or 800/221–0090, FAX 303/347–2080). **Maupintour** (✉ 1515 St. Andrews Dr., Lawrence, KS 66047, ☎ 913/843–1211 or 800/255–4266, FAX 913/843–8351). **Tauck Tours** (✉ Box 5027, 276 Post Rd. W, Westport, CT 06881-5027, ☎ 203/226–6911 or 800/468–2825, FAX 203/221–6828).

PACKAGES

Like group tours, independent vacation packages are available from major tour operators and airlines. The companies listed below offer vacation packages in a broad price range.

➤ GENERAL ITINERARIES: **Amtrak's Great American Vacations** (☎ 800/321–8684).

➤ CUSTOM ITINERARIES: **Recursos de Santa Fe** (✉ 826 Camino de Monte Rey, Santa Fe, NM 87505, ☎ 505/982–9301, FAX 505/989–8608).

➤ FROM THE U.K.: **British Airways Holidays** (✉ Astral Towers, Betts Way, London Rd., Crawley, West Sussex RH10 2XA, ☎ 01293/723–121). **Trailfinders** (✉ 42–50 Earls Court Rd., London W8 6FT, ☎ 0171/937–5400; ✉ 58 Deansgate, Manchester M3 2FF, ☎ 0161/839–6969). **Jetsave** (✉ Sussex House, London Rd., East Grinstead, W. Sussex RH19 1LD, ☎ 01342/312–033).

THEME TRIPS

➤ ARCHAEOLOGY: **The Archaeological Conservancy** (✉ 5301 Central Ave. NE, #1218, Albuquerque 87108, ☎ 505/266–1540).

➤ ART/CULTURE: **Atwell Fine Art** (✉ 1430 Paseo Norteno St., Santa Fe 87505, ☎ 505/474–4263 or 800/235-8412, FAX 505/474–4602).

➤ BICYCLING: **Backroads** (✉ 801 Cedar St., Berkeley, CA 94710-1800,

Smart Travel Tips A to Z

THE GOLD GUIDE / SMART TRAVEL TIPS

☎ 510/527–1555 or 800/462–2848, FAX 510-527–1444).

➤ HIKING/WALKING: TrekAmerica (⊠ Box 189 Rockaway, NJ 07866, ☎ 201/983–1144 or 800/221–0596, FAX 201/983–8551). Native Sons Adventures (⊠ Box 6144, Taos, NM 87571, ☎ 505/758–9342 or 800/753–7559).

➤ LEARNING: National Audubon Society (⊠ 700 Broadway, New York, NY 10003, ☎ 212/979–3066, FAX 212/353–0190). Victor Emanual Nature Tours (⊠ Box 33008, Austin, TX 78764, ☎ 512/328–5221 or 800/328–8368, FAX 512/328–2919).

➤ RIVER RAFTING: Far Flung Adventures (⊠ Box 377, Terlingua, TX 79852, ☎ 915/371–2489 or 800/359–4138, FAX 915/371–2325). New Wave Rafting Company (⊠ Rte. 5, Box 302A, Santa Fe 87501, ☎ 505/984–1444 or 800/984–1444, FAX 505/984–1197).

A good travel agent puts your needs first. Look for an agency that has been in business at least five years, emphasizes customer service, and has someone on staff who specializes in your destination. In addition, **make sure the agency belongs to the American Society of Travel Agents** (ASTA). If your travel agency is also acting as your tour operator, *see* Tour Operators, *above.*

➤ LOCAL AGENT REFERRALS: American Society of Travel Agents (ASTA, ☎ 800/965–2782 for 24-hr hot line, FAX 703/684–8319). Alliance of Canadian Travel Associations (⊠ Suite 201, 1729 Bank St., Ottawa, Ontario K1V 7Z5, ☎ 613/521–0474, FAX 613/521–0805). Association of British Travel Agents (⊠ 55–57 Newman St., London W1P 4AH, ☎ 0171/637–2444, FAX 0171/637–0713).

Travel catalogs specialize in useful items, such as compact alarm clocks and travel irons, that can **save space when packing.**

➤ MAIL-ORDER CATALOGS: Magellan's (☎ 800/962–4943, FAX 805/568–5406). Orvis Travel (☎ 800/541–3541, FAX 540/343–7053).

TravelSmith (☎ 800/950–1600, FAX 800/950–1656).

The U.S. government can be an excellent source of inexpensive travel information. When planning your trip, **find out what government materials are available.**

➤ ADVISORIES: U.S. Department of State (⊠ Overseas Citizens Services Office, Room 4811 N.S., Washington, DC 20520); enclose a self-addressed, stamped envelope. Interactive hot line (☎ 202/647–5225, FAX 202/647–3000). Computer bulletin board (☎ 301/946–4400).

➤ PAMPHLETS: Consumer Information Center (⊠ Consumer Information Catalogue, Pueblo, CO 81009, ☎ 719/948–3334) for a free catalog that includes travel titles.

For general information before you go, contact the city and state tourism bureaus. If you're interested in learning more about the area's national forests, contact the USDA. And, for information about Native American attractions, call or visit the Indian Pueblo Cultural Center.

➤ CITY INFORMATION: Albuquerque Convention & Visitors Bureau (⊠ 20 First Plaza NW, Suite 20, Albuquerque, 87102, ☎ 505/768–4575 or 800/733–9918). Santa Fe Convention & Visitors Bureau (⊠ Box 909, Santa Fe, 87504, ☎ 505/984–6760 or 800/777–2489, FAX 505/984–6679). Taos County Chamber of Commerce (⊠ Drawer I, Taos, 87571, ☎ 505/758–3873 or 800/732–8267, FAX 505/758–3872).

➤ STATEWIDE INFORMATION: New Mexico Department of Tourism (⊠ 491 Old Santa Fe Trail, Santa Fe, 87503, ☎ 505/827–7400 or 800/733–6396, FAX 505/827–7402).

➤ NATIONAL FORESTS: USDA Forest Service, Southwestern Region (⊠ Public Affairs Office, 517 Gold Ave. SW, Albuquerque, 87102, ☎ 505/842–3292, FAX 505/842–3800).

➤ NATIVE ATTRACTIONS: **Indian Pueblo Cultural Center** (✉ 2401 12th St. NW, Albuquerque, 87102, ☎ 505/843–7270 or 800/766–4405 outside NM, ℻ 505/842–6959.

➤ FROM THE U.K.: **New Mexico Tourism Bureau** (✉ 302 Garden Studios, 11–15 Betterton St., Covent Garden, London WC2H 9BP, ☎ 0171/470–8803, ℻ 0171/470–8810).

W
WHEN TO GO

When to visit New Mexico is a matter of personal preference. If you're interested in a particular sport, activity, or special event, go when that's available and don't worry too much about the weather. Most ceremonial dances at the Native American pueblos occur in the summer, early fall, and at Christmas and Easter. The majority of other major events—including the Santa Fe Opera, Chamber Music Festival, and Indian and Spanish markets—are geared to the traditionally heavy tourist season of July and August. The Santa Fe Fiesta and New Mexico State Fair in Albuquerque are held in September, and the Albuquerque International Balloon Fiesta is in October.

The relatively cool climates of Santa Fe and Taos are a lure in summer, as is the skiing in Taos and Santa Fe in winter. Christmas is a wonderful time to be in New Mexico because of Native American ceremonials as well as the Hispanic religious folk plays, special foods, and musical events. Hotel rates are generally highest during the peak summer season but fluctuate less than those in most major resort areas. If you plan to come in summer, be sure to **make reservations in advance for July and August.** You can avoid most of the tourist crowds by coming during spring or fall. Spring weather is unpredictable; sudden storms may erupt. October is one of the best months to visit: The air is crisp, colors are brilliant, and whole mountainsides become fluttering cascades of red and gold.

➤ FORECASTS: **Weather Channel Connection** (☎ 900/932–8437), 95¢ per minute from a Touch-Tone phone.

Climate in New Mexico

What follows are average daily maximum and minimum temperatures for Santa Fe and Albuquerque.

SANTA FE

Jan.	39F	4C	May	68F	20C	Sept.	73F	23C
	19	– 7		42	6		48	9
Feb.	42F	6C	June	78F	26C	Oct.	62F	17C
	23	– 5		51	11		37	3
Mar.	51F	11C	July	80F	27C	Nov.	50F	10C
	28	– 2		57	14		28	– 2
Apr.	59F	15C	Aug.	78F	26C	Dec.	39F	4C
	35	2		55	13		19	– 7

ALBUQUERQUE

Jan.	46F	8C	May	78F	26C	Sept.	84F	29C
	24	– 4		51	11		57	14
Feb.	53F	12C	June	89F	32C	Oct.	71F	22C
	28	– 2		60	16		44	7
Mar.	60F	16C	July	91F	33C	Nov.	57F	14C
	33	1		64	18		32	0
Apr.	69F	21C	Aug.	89F	32C	Dec.	48F	9C
	42	6		64	18		26	– 3

1 Destination: Santa Fe, Taos, Albuquerque

A LAND APART

ALMOST EVERY New Mexican has a tale or two to tell about being perceived as a "foreigner" by the rest of the country. There is the well-documented plight of the Santa Fe man who tried to purchase tickets to the 1996 Olympic Games in Atlanta, only to be shuffled over to the department handling international ticket requests. (It wasn't until nationwide publicity embarrassed the Olympics committee that the error was corrected.) Even the U.S. Postal Service, which should know better, occasionally returns New Mexico–bound mail to its senders for lack of sufficient "international" postage.

While annoying to residents, such cases of mistaken identity are oddly apt. New Mexico is, in many ways, a foreign country; it has its own language, cuisine, architecture, fashion, and culture, all of these an amalgam of the designs and accidents of a long and intriguing history. In prehistoric times, Native Americans hunted game in New Mexico's mountains and farmed along its riverbanks. Two thousand years ago, Pueblo Indians began expressing their reverence for the land through flat-roofed earthen architecture, drawings carved onto rocks, and rhythmic chants and dances. The late 16th and early 17th centuries brought the Spanish explorers who, along with the Franciscan monks, founded Santa Fe as a northern capital of the empire of New Spain, a settlement that was contemporaneous with the Jamestown colony of Virginia.

Although the clash of the Native American and Spanish cultures was often violent, over the course of several hundred years, tolerance has grown and traditions have commingled. Pueblo Indians passed on their innovative uses for chile, beans, and corn, while the Spanish shared their skill at metalwork, influencing the Native American jewelry that has become symbolic of the region. They also shared their architecture, which itself had been influenced by 700 years of Arab domination of Spain, as was the acequia system, the irrigation method still in use today in the villages of northern New Mexico.

The last of the three main cultures to arrive was that of the Anglo (any non-Native American, non-Hispanic person in New Mexico is considered an Anglo—even groups who don't normally identify with the Anglo-Saxon tradition). Arriving throughout the 19th century, they mined the mountains for gold, other precious metals, and gemstones, and uncovered vast deposits of coal, oil, and natural gas. Their contributions to New Mexican life include the railroad, the highway system, and—for better or worse—the atomic bomb.

The resulting melange of cultures has produced a character that is uniquely New Mexican: Spanish words are sprinkled liberally throughout everyday English parlance; Spanish itself, still widely spoken in the smaller villages, contains a number of words from the Pueblo Indian dialects. Architectural references and culinary terms in particular tend to hew to the original Spanish: You'll admire the vigas and *bancos* that adorn the restaurant where you'll partake of *posole* or *chiles rellenos*.

But beyond the linguistic quirks, gastronomic surprises, and cultural anomalies that give New Mexico its sense of uniqueness, there remains the most distinctive feature of all: the landscape. At once subtle and dramatic, the mountains and mesas seem almost surreal as they glow gold, terracotta, and pink in the clear, still air of the high desert. The shifting clouds overhead cast rippling shadows across the land, illuminating the delicate palette of greens, grays, and browns that contrast with a sky that can go purple or dead black or eye-searingly blue in a matter of seconds. It's a landscape that has inspired writers (such as D. H. Lawrence and Willa Cather), painters (Georgia O'Keeffe), and countless poets, dreamers, and assorted iconoclasts for centuries.

Indeed, watching the ever-changing sky is something of a spectator sport here, especially during the usual "monsoons" of mid- to late summer. So regular that you could almost set your watch by them, the thunderheads start to gather in late afternoon, giving enough visual warning to let viewers run for cover before the inevitable shower. In the meantime, the sky dazzles with its interplay of creamy white clouds edged by charcoal, sizzling flashes of lightning, and dramatic shafts of light shooting earthward from some ethereal perch between the sun and the clouds.

The mountains absorb and radiate this special light, transforming themselves daily according to the whims of light and shadow. The very names of the major ranges attest to the profound effect their light show had on the original Spanish settlers: The Franciscan monks named the mountains to the east of Santa Fe *Sangre de Cristo,* or "blood of Christ," because of their tendency to glow deep red at sunset. To the south, just east of Albuquerque, the Sandia Mountains ("watermelon" in Spanish) also live up to their colorful name when the sun sets.

It's spectacles like these that render New Mexico's tag lines more than just marketing clichés. The state is truly a "Land of Enchantment," and Santa Fe is indisputably "the City Different." Surrounded by mind-expanding mountain views and filled with sinuous streets that discourage car traffic but invite leisurely exploration, Santa Fe welcomes with characteristic warmth, if not some trepidation. Rapid growth and development have taken their toll, prompting many local residents to worry about becoming too much like "everywhere else," and you'll hear various complaints about encroaching commercialism and its attendant T-shirt shops and fast-food restaurants that interfere with the rhythms of life here.

But despite (or perhaps, occasionally, because of) a surfeit of trendy restaurants, galleries, and boutiques touting regional fare and wares, both authentic and artificial, Santa Fe remains a special place to visit. Commercialism notwithstanding, its deeply spiritual aura affects even non-religious types in surprising ways, inspiring a reverence probably not unlike that which inspired the Spanish monks to name it the "City of Holy Faith." (Its full name is La Villa Real de la Santa Fe de San Francisco de Asìs, or the Royal City of the Holy Faith of St. Francis of Assisi.) A kind of mystical Catholicism blended with ancient Native American lore and beliefs flourishes throughout northern New Mexico in the tiny mountain villages that have seen little change over the centuries. Tales of miracles, spontaneous healings, and spiritual visitations thrive in the old adobe churches that line the High Road that leads north of Santa Fe up to Taos.

IF SANTA FE IS SPIRITUAL, sophisticated, and occasionally superficial, Taos, some 60 mi away, is very much an outpost despite its relative proximity to the capital. Compared with Santa Fe, Taos is smaller, feistier, quirkier, tougher, and very independent. Taoseños are a study in contradictions: Wary of strangers and suspicious of outsiders, they nevertheless accept visitors with genuine warmth and pride; rustic and delightfully unpretentious, the town still lays claim to a handful of upscale restaurants with cuisines and wine lists as innovative as what you might find in New York. It's a haven for aging hippies, creative geniuses, cranky misanthropes, and anyone else who wants a good quality of life in a place that accepts people without a lot of questions—as long as they don't offend longtime residents with their city attitudes.

Sixty miles south of Santa Fe, Albuquerque adds another distinctive perspective to the mix. New Mexico's only big city by most standards, it shares many traits with cities its size elsewhere: traffic, noise, crime, and congestion. But what sets it apart is its dogged determination to remain a friendly small town, a place where pedestrians still greet one another as they pass, and where downtown's main street is lined with angle parking (a modern-day version of the hitching post). Old Town, an oddly congenial site of authentic historical appeal tempered by the unabashed pursuit of the tourist buck, is a typical example of how traditional small-town New Mexico flourishes amid a larger, more demanding economy, without sacrificing the heart and soul of the lifestyle. The historic San Felipe de Neri Catholic church is still attended by local worshipers, and civic celebrations of history and culture, while welcoming to visitors, are designed to enliven the existence of local residents, not tourists.

The unifying factor among these different towns and the terrain around them is the appeal of the land and the people. From the stunning natural formations of Carlsbad Caverns to the oceanic sweep of the "badlands" north of Santa Fe, it's the character of the residents and their attitude toward the land that imbues New Mexico with its enchanted spirit. Newcomers learn to find pleasure in the simple, albeit unexpected, pleasures of a place where time is measured not by linear calculations of hours, days, weeks, and years but in a circular sweep of crop cycles, gestation periods, the rotation of generations, and the changing of seasons.

Summer is traditionally the high season, when the arts scene explodes with gallery openings, opera performances at Santa Fe's distinctive open-air opera house, and a variety of festivals and celebrations. In autumn, when the towering cottonwoods that hug the riverbanks turn gold, residents enjoy warm, sunny days and crisp nights. Those popular kiva fireplaces get a workout in winter, a time when the rhythm of life slows down to accommodate occasional snowstorms, and the scent of aromatic firewood like piñon and cedar fill the air like an earthy incense.

Whatever the season, New Mexico will sneak into your consciousness in unexpected ways. As much a state of mind as it is a geographic entity, it's a place where nature can be glimpsed simultaneously at its most fragile, and most powerful—truly a land of enchantment.

—Nancy Zimmerman

WHAT'S WHERE

Santa Fe and Vicinity

Perched on a 7,000-ft-high plateau at the base of the Sangre de Cristo Mountains in north-central New Mexico, Santa Fe is one of the most popular cities in the United States, with an abundance of museums, one-of-a-kind cultural events, art galleries, first-rate restaurants, and shops selling Southwestern furnishings and cowboy gear. Among the smallest state capitals in the country, the city is characterized by its many fine examples of traditional Pueblo Revival–style homes and buildings made of adobe. Remnants of a 2,000-year-old Pueblo civilization surround the city, and this also echoes its nearly 250 years of Spanish and Mexican rule. Other area highlights are the Pecos National Historic Park, with

ruins of Spanish missions and an ancient Native American pueblo; Las Vegas, a town that time seems to have bypassed; Los Alamos, the birthplace of the atomic bomb; and Chimayo, a small Hispanic village famous for weaving, regional food, and the Santuario, which attracts thousands of worshipers each year.

Taos

Some 65 mi north of Santa Fe, on a rolling mesa at the base of the Sangre de Cristo Mountains, Taos is a world-famous artistic and literary center that attracts artists and collectors to its museums and galleries. This enchanted town has romantic courtyards, stately elms and cottonwood trees, narrow streets, and a profusion of adobe buildings. Three miles northwest of the commercial center lies Taos Pueblo, while 4 mi south of town is Ranchos de Taos, a farming and ranching community first settled centuries ago by the Spanish. Taos is also renowned for its fabulous ski slopes.

Albuquerque and Vicinity

With the state's only international airport, Albuquerque is the gateway to New Mexico and the state's business, finance, education, and industry capital. Like many other areas of the state, this large, sprawling city is filled with artists, writers, poets, filmmakers, and musicians. Its population, as well as its architecture, foods, art, and ambience, reflects the state's three primary cultures: the original Native Americans and its subsequent Hispanic and Anglo settlers.

Carlsbad and Southern New Mexico

In southeastern New Mexico along the Pecos River, Carlsbad is a popular tourist destination with historic museums, 30 parks, 27 mi of beaches, and the nearby Living Desert State Park and Carlsbad Caverns National Park, the latter enclosing one of the largest and most spectacular cave systems in the world. Northwest of Carlsbad are the historic towns of Lincoln County (Ruidoso, San Patricio, and Lincoln, where Billy the Kid was jailed) and White Sands National Monument, an eerie wonderland of shifting sand dunes 60 ft high. Southwestern New Mexico has its own mystique, including the authentic Mexican-style town of Old Mesilla near Las Cruces with its appealing shops and galleries. Silver City, too, is establishing a growing reputation as an artists' haven in the lofty grandeur of the Gila Forest.

NEW AND NOTEWORTHY

The glitter and bright lights of **casinos** no longer are confined to the gambling mecca of Las Vegas. Gaming is a growing industry in New Mexico, especially with the 1997 state Legislature's endorsement of new laws allowing the spread of casinos outside reservations owned by Native American tribes. Horse racing tracks along with fraternal and veterans' organizations won the right to add slot machines at their facilities, although there were a few legal snafus to be worked out. Barring unforeseen obstacles, new gaming establishments are expected to be seen springing up throughout the state in 1998.

The newly opened $33 million **Albuquerque Biological Park,** celebrated with a ribbon-cutting in December 1996, charmed crowds throughout 1997 and expects to do the same in 1998. The park combines the new Albuquerque Aquarium and Rio Grande Botanic Garden with existing facilities at the Rio Grande Zoo. New attractions include a 285,000-gallon shark tank and a tubular eel cave, where slitherings can be watched up close. The botanic gardens are ultramodern, with computer-controlled climates that can produce fog or mist.

The historic **La Posada de Albuquerque** hotel is expected in 1998 to unveil a new $4.5 million addition—a six-floor, 90-room tower just south of the existing structure. Architects have pledged to preserve the classic look of the original property, first built by Conrad Hilton in 1939. Ground breaking for the project is scheduled to happen by 1998.

The summer of 1997 saw the opening of the **Georgia O'Keeffe Museum** in Santa Fe, where more than 80 works of the famed artist are displayed in the new 13,000-square-ft museum downtown. The comprehensive collection includes drawings, paintings, pastels, watercolors, and sculptures created from 1914 through 1982.

Another unique attraction scheduled to open in the spring of 1998 is the **New Mexico Farm and Ranch Heritage Museum,** occupying 46 acres of land near Las Cruces. Under construction during 1997, the $8 million museum includes a dairy barn, greenhouse, outdoor pastures, and artifacts from the state's early agricultural heritage.

Meanwhile, near Farmington, an **unusual bed-and-breakfast** opened in 1997: a home carved from rock above the La Plata River valley. Parking is offered atop a 300-ft-high cliff, after which you will descend 70 ft into the rock walls of the 1,650-square-ft cave home owned by Bruce Black. Black said his inspiration came from nearby ruins of the ancient Anasazi cave dwellers.

At Ruidoso, renowned architect Antoine Predock of Albuquerque designed the wedge-shaped, imposing structure housing the new $20 million **Spencer Theater for the Performing Arts,** occupying a mesa east of this mountain resort community. The theater, scheduled to open in October 1997, contains only 523 seats to offer an intimate atmosphere for guests and performing artists. The theater's primary donors are Jackie Spencer of nearby Alto and her husband, Dr. A.N. Spencer, who grew up in nearby Carrizozo.

After wrecking New Mexico's ski industry with drought and accompanying fires during the winter of 1995–96, Mother Nature relented and graced the state with generous snows that sparkled in mountain resorts both early and late in the 1996–97 winter season. New Mexico's 1996 **tourist visitation** numbers were down 7% from the previous year, but 1997 figures were expected to show a rally since ski resorts were packed. Bucking trends, Albuquerque persevered as a popular destination with lodgers' tax revenues continuing to increase in the state's largest city, which also has become a popular convention site.

PLEASURES AND PASTIMES

Dining

New Mexico's cuisine is a delicious and extraordinary mixture of Pueblo, Spanish Colonial, and Mexican and American frontier cooking. Recipes that came from Spain via Mexico were adapted for local ingredients—chiles, corn, pork, wild game, pinto beans, honey, apples, and piñon nuts—and have remained much the same ever since.

In northern New Mexico, babies cut their teeth on fresh flour tortillas and quickly develop a taste for sopaipillas, deep-fried, puff-pastry pillows, drizzled with honey. But it is the chile pepper, whether red or green, that is the heart and soul of northern New Mexican cuisine. You might be a bit surprised to learn that *ristras,* those strings of bright red chiles that seem to hang everywhere, are sold more for eating here than for decoration. More varieties of chiles—upward of 90—are grown in New Mexico than anywhere else in the world. Mighty wars have been waged over the spelling of chile and chili, but in New Mexico they have finally reached a consensus: Chile refers to the actual chile peppers, whereas chili defines the spicy dish with red chile, beans, and meat. *See* the Menu Guide *in* the glossary at the back of this book for names and terms of traditional New Mexican dishes.

New Mexican restaurants are especially popular and are almost universally inexpensive. Some offer buffalo meat (stews, steaks, and burgers), particularly in southern New Mexico—"cowboy country." Of course, there are a fair share of trendy and contemporary restaurants, particularly in the Santa Fe and Taos areas, as well as a respectable offering of gourmet grill rooms, and French, Italian, Japanese, Greek, and other ethnic establishments.

In most restaurants you can dress as casually as you like. Those in the major business hotels tend to be a bit more formal, but as the evening wears down, so do the restrictions.

Outdoor Activities and Sports

BICYCLING➤ **Albuquerque** is a biker's paradise, with miles and miles of bike lanes and trails crisscrossing and skirting the city. Not only is Albuquerque's Parks and Recreation Department aware of bikers' needs, but bike riding is heavily promoted as a means of cutting down on traffic congestion and pollution. Santa Fe and Taos, because of hilly terrain and narrow, frequently congested downtown streets, are less hospitable to cyclists. However, mountain biking along back roads and trails is popular. Cycling events in New Mexico include the **Santa Fe Century** (50- or 100-mi recreational rides), the **Sanbusco Hill Climb** (an annual race to the Santa Fe Ski Area), and the **Tour de Los Alamos** (road race and criterium).

BIRD-WATCHING➤ Bird-watchers have wonderful opportunities to spot birds migrating along the **Rio Grande flyway** from the jungles of South America to the tundra of the Arctic Circle. The **Bosque del Apache National Wildlife Refuge,** 90 mi south of Albuquerque, is the winter home of tens of thousands of migrating birds, including one of only two wild flocks of the rare whooping crane. The **Bitter Lake National Wildlife Refuge,** north of Roswell, also serves as a stopover for migrating flocks of snow geese, sandhill cranes, and other exotic birds.

CANOEING AND RIVER RAFTING➤ New Mexico's rivers offer a choice: Lazy glides along a serpentine waterway, past colorful mesas and soaring cliffs, or heart-thumping rides through white-water rapids. The **Taos Box,** a 17-mi run through the churning rapids of the Rio Grande, is one of America's most exciting rafting experiences. Most of the hard-core river rafting is done in the Taos area. More leisurely trips can be had aboard the sightseeing craft that ply the Rio Chama and other meandering rivers. Depending on the amount of spring runoff from snow melts, river rafting also is popular in the **Silver City** area of the **Gila Forest.**

FISHING➤ Fishing spots include the **Rio Grande,** which traverses New Mexico north to south; **Abiquiu Lake,** 40 mi northwest of Santa Fe; **Heron Lake,** 20 mi southwest of Chama via U.S. 64 and N.M. 96; and **Blue Water Lake,** 28 mi west of Grants via N.M. 371. The San Juan's high-quality-water regulations make for some of the best trout fishing in the country. Six-thousand-acre Heron Lake offers rainbow trout, lake trout, and kokanee salmon. Trout fishermen will also find nirvana in the sparkling streams of the **Sangre de Cristo range,** north of Santa Fe. The **Pecos River** and its tributaries offer excellent backcountry fishing. Anglers also can try their luck in the rivers, lakes, and streams of the **Gila Forest** and **Lincoln Forest** of southern New Mexico. Fishing on Native American reservations is not subject to state regulations but requires tribal permits.

GOLF➤ The state has a respectable share of turf, with more than 60 courses offering recreation throughout the year. The dry climate here makes playing very comfortable. There are excellent public courses in **Albuquerque, Angel Fire, Las Vegas, Los Alamos, Ruidoso, Santa Fe,** and **Taos.**

HIKING➤ Bring your walking shoes: Few states in the nation are as blessed with such a diverse network of trails. New Mexico's air is clean and crisp, and its ever-changing terrain is aesthetically rewarding as well. **Carlsbad Caverns National Park** in the southeast has more than 50 mi of scenic hiking trails.

HORSE RACING➤ Horse racing with pari-mutuel betting is very popular in New Mexico. Two of the more favored of the state's tracks are **Downs at Santa Fe,** 5 mi south of Santa Fe, and **Downs at Albuquerque,** a glass-enclosed facility in the center of the city at the New Mexico State Fairgrounds. Quarter-horse racing's Triple Crown events—Kansas Futurity, Rainbow Futurity, and All-American Futurity—take place in mid-June, mid-July, and Labor Day, respectively, at the **Ruidoso Downs** tracks in Lincoln County. The **Sunland Park Racetrack** is located 5 mi north of El Paso, Texas, and 40 mi south of Las Cruces.

HOT-AIR BALLOONING➤ The **Albuquerque International Balloon Fiesta** in early October draws the largest number of spectators (an estimated 1.5 million people) of any sporting event in the state (☞ Festivals and Seasonal Events, *below*).

RODEOS➤ Rodeos are a big draw from early spring through autumn. Besides big events in **Santa Fe, Albuquerque,** and **Gallup,** every county in the state has a rodeo competition during its county fair. Major Native American rodeos take place at Stone Lake on the **Jicarilla Reservation,** on the **Mescalero Apache Reservation,** at the **Inter-Tribal Ceremonial** in Gallup, and at the **National Indian Rodeo Finals** in Albuquerque.

SKIING➤ New Mexico offers many world-class downhill ski areas. Snowmaking equipment is used in most areas to ensure a long season, usually from Thanksgiving through Easter. The **Santa Fe Ski Area** averages 250 inches of dry-powder snow a year; it accommodates all levels of skiers on more than 40 trails. Within a 90-mi radius, Taos offers four ski resorts with excellent slopes for all levels of skiers, as well as snowmobile and cross-country ski trails. **Taos Ski Valley** resort is renowned internationally for its challenging terrain and European ambience.

For cross-country skiing, **Enchanted Forest** near Red River offers miles of groomed trails in the state's major Nordic ski area. Head to the **Sangre de Cristos, the Jemez, the Sandias,** or the **Manzano Mountains** for other cross-country skiing terrain. There are also exciting cross-country trails north of Chama along the New Mexico–Colorado border, and in the south in the **Gila Wilderness,** and the **Sacramento Mountains** adjacent to White Sands National Monument.

Parks and Monuments

New Mexico has a plethora of outstanding parks and monuments, which offer outdoor recreational facilities, camping, and historic exhibits. Established in the 1930s, New Mexico's state park system is composed of 45 parks, ranging from high-mountain lakes and pine forests in the north to the Chihuahuan Desert lowlands of the south. There are also five national forests—Carson, Cibola, Gila, Lincoln, and Santa Fe—and the Kiowa National Grasslands (part of the Cibola National Forest), as well as a number of state monuments and historic parks with ruins of prehistoric Native American pueblos and 17th-century mission churches, and exhibits on the infamous Billy the Kid.

Parks and monuments close to Santa Fe include Pecos National Historic Park, Chaco Culture National Historic Park, and Jemez State Monument. Carson National Forest is near Taos. Around Albuquerque you'll find Coronado State Monument, Petroglyph National Monument, Salinas Pueblo Missions National Monument, and Rio Grande Nature Center State Park. Carlsbad Caverns National Park, White Sands National Monument, Bottomless Lake State Park, Brantley Lake State Park, Living Desert State Park, and Smokey Bear Historical State Park are all in southern New Mexico.

Reservations and Pueblos

The Native American reservations of New Mexico are among the few places left in the United States where traditional Native

American culture and skills are retained in largely undiluted form. There are two general classifications of Native Americans in New Mexico: Pueblo, who established an agricultural civilization here more than seven centuries ago, and the descendants of the nomadic tribes who later came into the area—the Navajos, Mescalero Apaches, and Jicarilla Apaches.

The **Jicarilla Apaches** live on a reservation of ¾ million acres in north-central New Mexico, the capital of which is Dulce. The terrain varies from mountains, mesas, and lakes to high grazing land, suited to cattle and horse ranching. The tribe has a well-defined tourist program promoting fishing and camping on a 20,000-acre game preserve. Nearly all the tribe members gather at Stone Lake on September 14 and 15 for the fall festival—two days of dancing, races, and a rodeo. For more information, contact the Tourism Department, Jicarilla Apache Tribe (✉ Box 507, Dulce 87528, ☎ 505/759–3242, FAX 505/759–3005).

A reservation of a half million acres of timbered mountains and green valleys is home to the **Mescalero Apaches** in southeastern New Mexico. The tribe owns and operates the famous resort, Inn of the Mountain Gods, as well as Ski Apache, 16 mi from Ruidoso. For detailed information, *see* Roswell and Lincoln County *in* Chapter 5.

The **Navajo Reservation,** home to the largest Native American group in the United States, covers 17.6 million acres in New Mexico, Arizona, and Utah. Many Navajos are still seminomadic, herding flocks of sheep from place to place and living in hogans (mud-and-pole houses). There are a few towns on the reservation, but for the most part it is a vast area of stark pinnacles, colorful rock formations, high desert, and mountains. The land encompasses several national and tribal parks, some of which include campgrounds. Navajos are master silversmiths and rug weavers, and their work is available at trading posts scattered throughout the reservation. The tribe encourages tourism; for more information, contact the Navajo Nation Tourism Office (✉ Box 663, Window Rock, AZ 86515, ☎ 520/871–6436 or 520/871–7371, FAX 520/871–7381).

New Mexico's 19 remaining Pueblo cultures, each with its own reservation, and distinct but overlapping history, culture, art, and customs, are descendants of the highly civilized Anasazi culture that built Chaco Canyon. Pueblos dating back centuries are located near Santa Fe, Taos, and Albuquerque; the best time to visit them is during one of their many year-round public dance ceremonies. Admission is free to pueblos unless otherwise indicated. Donations, however, are always welcome.

Before venturing off to visit any one of the pueblos, you might want to visit the striking **Indian Pueblo Cultural Center** (☞ Old Town *in* Chapter 4) in Albuquerque, which exhibits and sells the best of arts and crafts from all the New Mexico pueblos, or the **Museum of Indian Arts and Culture** (☞ Upper Old Santa Fe Trail *in* Chapter 2) in Santa Fe. Going to these will help you decide which of the pueblos to visit, and you may also have the opportunity to photograph one of the frequent ceremonial dances held at these locales; photographing Native American rituals is generally not allowed at any of the individual pueblos.

Fall, when the pueblos celebrate the harvest with special ceremonies, dances, and sacred rituals, is the best time to visit. The air is fragrant with curling piñon smoke. Clusters of ristras decorate many homes, with the chiles destined to add their distinct flavor to stews and sauces throughout the year. Drums throb with insistent cadence. Dancers adorn themselves with some of the most beautiful turquoise jewelry seen anywhere. The atmosphere is lighthearted, evocative of a country fair.

The pueblos around Santa Fe—San Ildefonso, Nambe, Pojoaque, and Santa Clara—are more infused with Spanish culture than are the pueblos in other areas. Pueblo dwellers here also have the keenest business sense when dealing with the sale of handicrafts and art and with matters touristic. The famous Taos Pueblo, unchanged over the centuries, is the personification of classic Pueblo Native American culture. It and the Picuris Pueblo near Taos offer first-rate recreational facilities as well as a glimpse into the past. Sports enthusiasts from Albuquerque regularly escape the confines of urban life to fish in the well-stocked lakes and reservoirs of the nearby pueblos—Acoma ("Sky

City"), Isleta, Jemez, Laguna, and Santo Domingo. The legendary Acoma Pueblo, probably the most spectacular of the pueblo communities, is only a short drive from the city. For detailed information about the individual pueblos, *see* listings *in* Chapters 2, 3, and 4.

When visiting pueblos and reservations, you're expected to follow a certain etiquette. Each pueblo has its own regulations for the use of still and video cameras and video and tape recorders, as well as for sketching and painting. Some pueblos, such as Santo Domingo, prohibit photography altogether. Others, such as Santa Clara, prohibit photography at certain times, such as during ritual dances. Still others allow photography but require a permit, which usually costs about $5 for a still camera and up to $35 for the privilege of setting up an easel and painting all day. Be sure to ask permission before photographing anyone in the pueblos; it's also customary to give the subject a dollar or two for agreeing to be photographed. Native American law prevails on the pueblos, and violations of photography regulations could result in confiscation of cameras.

Specific restrictions for the various pueblos are noted in the individual descriptions. Other rules are described below.

- Possessing or using drugs and/or alcohol on Native American land is forbidden.

- Ritual dances often have serious religious significance and should be respected as such. Silence is mandatory. That means no questions about ceremonies or dances while they're being performed. Don't walk across the dance plaza during a performance, and don't applaud afterward.

- Kiva and ceremonial rooms are restricted to pueblo members only.

- Cemeteries are sacred. They're off-limits to all visitors and should never be photographed.

- Unless pueblo dwellings are clearly marked as shops, don't wander or peek inside. Remember, these are private homes.

- Many of the pueblo buildings are hundreds of years old. Don't try to scale adobe walls or climb on top of buildings, or you may come tumbling down.

- Don't litter. Nature is sacred on the pueblos, and defacing of land can be a serious offense.

Shopping

Santa Fe, Old Mesilla near Las Cruces, Taos, and Old Town in Albuquerque, are all filled with one-of-a-kind, locally owned specialty shops; national boutique chain stores have only recently arrived. From leather goods and handwoven shawls to Mexican imports, crafts, household items, local foods, and wonderful bookstores, New Mexico will satisfy.

ANTIQUES➤ As New Mexico is the oldest inhabited region of the United States, it can be great fun to browse through the antiques shops and roadside museums that dot the landscape. You'll find everything in these shops, from early Mexican typewriters to period saddles, ceramic pots, farm tools, pioneer aviation equipment, and yellowed newspaper clippings about Kit Carson and D. H. Lawrence.

ART➤ Santa Fe, with more than 150 galleries, is the arts capital of the Southwest and a leading arts center nationally. Albuquerque and Taos are not far behind. Native American art, Western art, Hispanic art, contemporary art, sculpture, photography, prints, ceramics, jewelry, folk art, junk art—it's all for sale in New Mexico, produced by artists of both international and local renown.

CRAFTS➤ Hispanic handcrafted furniture and santos command high prices from collectors; santos are religious carvings and paintings in the form of *bultos* (three-dimensional carvings in the round) and *retablos* (holy images painted on wood or tin). Colorful handwoven Hispanic textiles, tinwork, ironwork, and straw appliqué are also in demand. Native American textiles, rugs, kachina dolls, baskets, silver jewelry, turquoise, pottery, beadwork, ornamental shields, drums, and ceramics can be found almost everywhere in New Mexico, from Santa Fe Plaza to the Native American pueblos throughout the state. Prices range from thousands of dollars for a rare 1930s kachina doll to just a few cents for handwrapped bundles of sage, juniper, sweet grass, and lavender that are used by Native Americans in healing ceremonies, gatherings, and daily cleansing of the home. Ignited like incense, this herbal combination gives off a sacred smoke; passing it once around the room is enough to change and charge the air.

SPICES➤ You'll find stands beside the road selling chile ristras, strings of crimson chiles to hang in the kitchen or beside the front door, or to use for cooking, and you'll find shops everywhere selling chile powder and other spices. You'll catch the smell from the road; walk in the store and your eyes will water and your mouth will salivate. For many, especially natives of the Southwest, *picante* is the purest, finest word in the Spanish language. It means hot—spicy hot. All around you, in boxes, bags, packets, jars, and cans, there's everything picante—salsas, chile pastes, powders, herbs, spices, peppers, barbecue sauce, and fiery potions in bottles.

GREAT ITINERARIES

Probably more than any other state, New Mexico is blessed with varied destinations appealing to almost any taste—from urban sophistication to pristine outdoor pleasure. It's difficult to single out only a few of the several hundred worthwhile attractions for travelers with limited time. But there are some must-see sites.

If You Have 1 Day

You must visit Santa Fe, the nation's oldest settlement, and explore on foot the adobe charms of the downtown central **Plaza.** Stop first at the **Palace of the Governors** on the plaza's north side, then investigate the crafts and wares of Native American outdoor vendors. Be sure and visit the **Museum of Fine Arts** to view exhibits of Southwestern artists. The **Saint Francis Cathedral,** built in Romanesque style, also is worth a look just east of the plaza. For lunch consider stopping by the **Plaza Cafe** on Lincoln Avenue for a sandwich or a bowl of chili, topped off with ice cream from the soda fountain.

Spend the afternoon exploring the area's cultural roots, with its 19 pueblos inhabited by Native Americans who continue to embrace their heritage. Orient yourself with a visit to the **Museum of Indian Arts and Culture** at 710 Camino Lejo. Then start your tour of a sampling of pueblos at **Pojoaque Pueblo** 12 mi north of Santa Fe off U.S. 84/285. The visitor's center here will explain the origins of this particular population. If you have time, proceed north 7 mi more on the highway to **San Ildefonso Pueblo.** The **Santa Clara Pueblo** is 27 mi northwest of Santa Fe. From San Ildefonso Pueblo, take NM 502 to NM 30 and turn north.

If You Have 3 Days

After spending the first day in **Santa Fe** exploring the downtown **Plaza** and area pueblos, travel to **Albuquerque** and spend the night in a historic bed-and-breakfast or in the Southwest decor of the 10-story **La Posada de Albuquerque** originally built in 1939 by Conrad Hilton.

Begin your second day with a morning tour of **Old Town Plaza,** with its restaurants, galleries, and shaded nooks. You can spend several hours perusing other sites near this area, including the **New Mexico Museum of Natural History and Science.** Devote the afternoon to a visit to the new **Albuquerque Biological Park,** which includes the **Albuquerque Aquarium** and **Rio Grande Botanic Garden** combined with existing facilities at the **Rio Grande Zoo.** In the early evening, take a ride on the **Sandia Aerial Tramway** for a breathtaking view, and hike along the rim of the Sandia Mountains.

On the third day head for the old frontier town of **Taos,** noted for its galleries and collection of independent artists. Visit the **Fechin Institute,** a Southwestern adobe house that hosts art exhibits and workshops. The Taos Society of Artists has established its headquarters at the **Blumenschein Home,** filled with paintings and antiques near the southeast corner of the plaza. Reserve some time for a visit to the **Taos Pueblo,** which still retains the mud-and-straw adobe walls of its original construction almost 1,000 years ago. Check schedules for ceremonial dances, many of them open to the public throughout the year.

If You Have 5 Days

It's a long drive to **Carlsbad Caverns,** but after you've spent the first three days visiting **Santa Fe, Albuquerque,** and **Taos,** you should make southern New Mexico your next destination. Set aside the morning of the fourth day to drive the 300 mi from Albuquerque to Carlsbad. Use up the rest of the day visiting **Living Desert Zoo And Garden State Park** and strolling scenic pathways along the Pecos River banks at **Lake Carlsbad Recreation Area.**

On the fifth day take the walking tour into the enormous caves of **Carlsbad Caverns National Park.** You can spend at least a half day there. If you need to head back to the northern part of the state, consider driving northwest through the mountain area of **Cloudcroft** and drop down into **Alamogordo,** where—depending on your time—you can visit both the **Space Center** and **White Sands National Monument.** If you have only a few hours of daylight left, make **White Sands** your priority. It's a dazzling vista of glistening white dunes.

FODOR'S CHOICE

Historic Buildings

★ **KiMo Theater, Albuquerque.** At this 1927 movie palace on Central Avenue, restored to its original design—Pueblo Deco–style architecture painted in bright colors—a varied program is offered, including everything from traveling road shows to local song-and-dance acts.

★ **Palace of the Governors, Santa Fe.** The oldest public building in the United States, this Pueblo-style structure has served as the residence for 100 Spanish, Native American, Mexican, and American governors; it is now the state history museum.

★ **San Francisco de Asìs Church, Ranchos de Taos.** First built in the 18th century as a spiritual and physical refuge from raiding Apaches, Utes, and Comanches, and reconstructed in 1979, this church is a spectacular example of adobe Mission architecture that has inspired generations of painters and photographers, including Georgia O'Keeffe, Paul Strand, and Ansel Adams.

★ **San Miguel Mission, Santa Fe.** The oldest church still in use in the continental United States, this simple, earth-hued adobe structure built in about 1625 has priceless statues and paintings on display,

as well as the San José Bell, said to have been cast in Spain in 1356.

★ **Santuario de Chimayo, Chimayo.** Tens of thousands flock each year to this small, frontier adobe church built on the site where, believers say, a mysterious light came from the ground on Good Friday night in 1810; today the chapel sits above a sacred *pozito* (a small well), the dirt from which is believed to have miraculous healing properties.

★ **Taos Pueblo, Taos.** For nearly 1,000 years, the Taos Pueblos have lived at or near this site, the largest existing multistory pueblo structure in the United States; within its mud-and-straw adobe walls—frequently several feet thick—it preserves a way of life barely changed by time's passage.

Lodging

★ **Inn of the Anasazi, Santa Fe.** In the heart of the historic Plaza district, this decidedly upscale hotel has individually designed rooms, each with a beamed ceiling, kiva fireplace, four-poster bed, and handcrafted desk, dresser, and tables. *$$$$*

★ **Hyatt Regency Albuquerque, Albuquerque.** In the heart of downtown, this gorgeous hotel's soaring desert-colored tower climbs high above the city skyline. It is totally modern and luxurious, from the on-site spa to the well-regarded restaurant and shopping promenade. *$$$*

★ **Inn of the Mountain Gods, Mescalero.** The Mescalero Apaches own and operate this spectacular year-round resort on the banks of Mescalero Lake, about 3 mi southwest of Ruidoso. *$$$*

★ **Casas de Sueños, Albuquerque.** Long a historic gathering spot for artists, the two-acre grounds of Casas de Suenos—Houses of Dreams—provide a magical setting of attractively decorated casitas amid lush English gardens and quiet patios; it's adjacent to Old Town on Rio Grande Boulevard SW. *$$–$$$*

★ **La Posada de Albuquerque, Albuquerque.** This historic, highly lauded hotel in downtown Albuquerque overflows with Southwestern charm, from its tiled lobby fountain, massive vigas, encircling balcony, and fixtures of etched glass and tin, to the Native American war-dance murals behind the reception desk. *$$–$$$*

★ **Touchstone Inn, Taos.** This peaceful, elegant bed-and-breakfast overlooking the Taos Pueblo is filled with a tasteful mix of antiques and modern artwork by the talented owner, artist Ben Price. *$$–$$$*

★ **Hacienda del Sol, Taos.** Once a house for guests of art patron Mabel Dodge Luhan, this bed-and-breakfast features kiva-style fireplaces, Spanish antiques, Southwestern-style handcrafted furniture, and original artwork. *$$*

★ **Best Western Motel Stevens, Carlsbad.** Tasteful surroundings at bargain prices can be found at this locally owned establishment. There's also an excellent steak restaurant and a popular bar. *$*

Restaurants

★ **Anasazi, Santa Fe.** A half block from the Plaza, the restaurant combines New Mexican and Native American flavors in exotic offerings served in the large dining room filled with beautiful, solid-wood tables and adobe banquettes upholstered with handwoven textiles from Chimayo. *$$$*

★ **Geronimo, Santa Fe.** The menu changes daily at this popular restaurant in the historic Borrego House. Enjoy such dishes as mesquite-grilled Black Angus rib eye with a spicy smoked corn and tomato salsa or the superb Sunday brunch. *$$$*

★ **Trading Post Cafe, Taos.** Imagination, talent, and simplicity make this newcomer a favorite in Taos. Look forward to delicately prepared Continental cuisine with a twist. *$$–$$$*

★ **Artichoke Cafe, Albuquerque.** In a turn-of-the-century brick building just east of downtown on Central Avenue, diners appreciate the excellent service and variety of cuisines—new American, Italian, French—at this outstanding café with dishes prepared using organically grown ingredients. *$$*

★ **Rancho de Chimayo, Chimayo.** This favorite for northern New Mexico cuisine, more notable for its ambience than its food, has cozy dining rooms within a century-old adobe hacienda tucked into the mountains. *$$*

★ **Andre's, Albuquerque.** Chef-owner Andre Diddy's popular restaurant offers delicious, imaginative food at amazingly reasonable prices. *$–$$*

★ **La Posta, Old Mesilla.** Dine on authentic Mexican dishes and fine Southwestern favorites at this old adobe structure that was once a way station for the Butterfield Overland Mail and Wells Fargo stages. *$–$$*

★ **Casa Fresen Bakery, Taos.** Perfectly packed picnic baskets are a specialty at this espresso bar, bakery, and Italian deli; its gorgeous breads, meats, and cheeses would even make a New Yorker smile. *$*

★ **Plaza Café, Santa Fe.** A fixture on the Santa Fe Plaza since 1918, this large, busy restaurant serves excellent American fare, along with New Mexican and Greek specialties. *$*

Romantic Sites

★ **Any spot beside the road under a cottonwood tree during chile-harvesting season.** In August through September, enterprising farmers set up tumble dryer–like roasting machines under cottonwood trees to roast freshly picked chiles for sale to passing motorists.

★ **Millicent Rogers Museum, Taos.** At this Native American and Hispanic art museum, the courtyard with its Native American maiden statue by R. C. Gorman provides an enchanted atmosphere.

★ **Outdoor hot tubs at Ten Thousand Waves, Santa Fe.** Come to this Japanese-style health spa to unwind after a day's cavorting on the slopes or in the dusty desert.

★ **Santa Fe at Christmastime.** New Mexico's capital is at its most festive at the end of December, with incense and piñon smoke sweetening the air and the winter darkness illuminated by thousands of *farolitos* (tiny candle lanterns in paper sacks).

★ **Santa Fe Opera.** It's hard to surpass the excitement of the curtain rising and the music swelling at a SFO world opera premier as lightning crackles over the distant Jemez Mountains.

Scenic Drives

★ **Enchanted Circle.** This 100-mi loop from Taos winds through canyon and alpine country, with a few colorful mining towns along the way.

★ **High Road to Taos.** On the old road linking Santa Fe and Taos, the stunning drive—with a rugged alpine mountain backdrop—encompasses rolling hillsides studded with orchards and tiny picturesque villages noted for weavers and wood-carvers.

★ **Lake Valley National Back Country Byway.** View some of southwestern New Mexico's historic mining towns, while traveling this winding, two-lane paved highway through 48 mi of scenic forest, desert, and distant mountain ranges. The route is accessible 18 mi south of Truth or Consequences. Take the Hillsboro exit off I–25.

★ **Mountains to Desert.** For a dramatic ride that runs from high, cool, green mountains to hot, dry desert near White Sands National Monument, drive the stretch of U.S. 82 that drops some 6,000 ft in altitude between Alamogordo and Cloudcroft in south-central New Mexico.

★ **Turquoise Trail.** This old route full of ghost towns between Albuquerque and Santa Fe ventures into backcountry, where the pace is slow, talk is all about weather and crops, and horses have the right of way.

FESTIVALS AND SEASONAL EVENTS

WINTER

➤ DEC.: **Christmas Native American Dances** (☎ 505/758–1028) take place at most pueblos. The Spanish-inspired dance/drama *Los Matachines* is performed at Picuris Pueblo. There are also pine-torch processions and Kachina dances at Taos Pueblo, and Basket, Buffalo, Deer, Harvest, Rainbow, and Turtle dances at Acoma, Cochiti, San Ildefonso, Santa Clara, and Taos pueblos.

During the **Christmas season,** Santa Fe is at its most festive, with incense and piñon smoke sweetening the air and the darkness of winter illuminated by thousands of farolitos. A custom believed to have derived from the Chinese lanterns, the glowing farolitos are everywhere, lining walkways, doorways, rooftops, walls, windowsills, and sometimes even grave sites with soft puddles of light. The songs of Christmas are sung around corner bonfires (luminarias, as the holiday bonfires are called in Santa Fe), and mugs of hot cider and melt-in-your-mouth Christmas cookies, *bizcochitos,* are offered to all who pass by. With glowing lights reflected on the snow, Santa Fe is never lovelier.

Numerous religious pageants and processions take place. Early in the month are 10 days of **Las Posadas** at San Miguel Mission (✉ 401 Old Santa Fe Trail, ☎ 505/983-3974), during which the story of Mary and Joseph's journey to Bethlehem is reenacted. The **Feast Day of Our Lady of Guadalupe,** December 12, is grandly celebrated at Santuario de Guadalupe, and **Christmas at the Palace** resounds with hours of festive music emanating from the Palace of the Governors.

Christmas on the Pecos (☎ 505/887–6516) at Carlsbad offers evening boat rides and views of glittering backyard displays. Tickets usually sell out early and are available beginning in August.

➤ JAN.: During **Native American New Year's Celebrations** (☎ 505/758–1028) at many pueblos, Comanche, Deer, Turtle, and other traditional dances are performed.

➤ FEB.: **Santa Fe's Winterfestival** (☎ 505/982–4429) takes place in late February, both in town and on the slopes of the Santa Fe Ski Area. Events include snow-sculpture competitions, downhill racing, hot-air ballooning, music, and drama.

SPRING

➤ MAR.: The annual one-weekend **Fiery Foods Show** (☎ 505/298–3835) in Albuquerque specializes in everything you ever wanted to know about New Mexico's favorite spicy food. Chile is featured here in all its incarnations, from sizzling salsas and dips to unusual beer and chocolate concoctions. Product demonstrations, panel discussions, and book signings all highlight the culinary qualities of this versatile state vegetable, making this free public event one of the hottest tickets in town.

The annual **Border Book Festival** (☎ 505/524–8521) in Las Cruces attracts renowned writers and authors from both sides of the United States–Mexico border and continues to grow in prestige. Lectures, workshops, and publishers' booths are offered among several days of events.

➤ MAR.–APR.: The **Chimayo Pilgrimage** (☎ 505/753–2831) takes place on Good Friday; thousands of New Mexicans and out-of-state pilgrims trek on foot to the Santuario de Chimayo, a small church north of Santa Fe, which is believed to induce miracles. People line U.S. 285 for miles en route to this sacred spot.

➤ APR.: **Albuquerque Founder's Day** (☎ 800/284–2282) commemorates the April 23, 1706, founding of Albuquerque by Governor Francisco Cuervo y Valdés, whose costumed persona presides over the event. The celebration takes place at the Old Town Plaza.

Gathering of Nations Powwow (☎ 505/758–1028), in Albuquerque, is the largest powwow in the nation. This popular annual event attracts Native American dancers from across North America, who are dressed in incredible costumes and compete for large prizes. Arts and crafts exhibitions, traditional foods, and a beauty contest are other highlights.

➤ MAY: The **Taos Spring Arts Celebration** (☎ 800/ 732–TAOS), an annual, two-week festival, features contemporary visual arts, music, poetry readings, dance, and many other special events.

The week-long **Mescal Roast & Mountain Spirit Dances** (☎ 505/887– 5516), at Carlsbad's Living Desert Zoo and Garden State Park, celebrates the mystic connection Mescalero Apaches have long had with the sacred Guadalupe Mountains of this area, where mescal plants traditionally were gathered for food.

SUMMER

➤ JUNE: On the last weekend of the month, Albuquerque's New Mexico State Fairgrounds hosts the **New Mexico Arts and Crafts Fair** (☎ 505/884–9043), where more than 200 artists and craftspeople come together to display their talents. Spanish, Native American, and other North American cultures are represented, and there's plenty of food and entertainment.

➤ LATE JUNE OR EARLY JULY–AUG.: In 1998, the world-famous indoor/outdoor **Santa Fe Opera** (☎ 505/986–5900) will mark its 42nd season, staged in a beautiful facility tucked into a hillside. Annual world premieres and classics offer opera fans a wide range of options. Opening night is one of *the* social events of the year in New Mexico.

➤ JULY: Out-of-this-world **Encounter** festivities celebrate Roswell's notoriety as the home of the legendary 1947 crash of a supposed UFO, purportedly covered up by the U.S. government. Guest lecturers and events such as alien costume competitions are part of the fun.

➤ MID-JULY: **Rodeo de Santa Fe** (☎ 505/471– 4300) brings a taste of the Old West, with calf roping, bull riding, and a traditional rodeo parade. World-champion rodeo competitors come from all parts of the United States and Canada to this event, held since 1959.

The festive **Spanish Market** (✉ Box 1611, Santa Fe 87501, ☎ 505/983– 4038), held on the Santa Fe Plaza, features Hispanic arts, crafts, and good food—you can smell the burritos, tamales, and chile from blocks around. Many exhibitors are from remote villages, where outstanding handicrafts are produced. Contact the Spanish Colonial Arts Society.

➤ JULY–AUG.: **Shakespeare in Santa Fe** (☎ 505/982–2910) means theater fans reserve Friday, Saturday, and Sunday for free performances of great Shakespearean plays. An outdoor theater in the hills east of Santa Fe provides a beautiful backdrop for the immortal words of the Bard.

➤ AUG.: Carlsbad's **Bat Flight Breakfast** (☎ 505/ 785–2232), on the second Thursday of the month, is when early risers gather at the entrance to Carlsbad Caverns to eat breakfast and watch tens of thousands of bats, who have been out for the night feeding on insects, fly back into the cave.

Launched in 1922, Gallup's **Intertribal Indian Ceremonial** (☎ 800/233– 4528) is one of the oldest Native American gatherings in the nation; the Ceremonial is an informal and festive reunion of old friends and visitors. Native American dances, a huge arts and crafts fair, several parades, and an all Native American rodeo are just some of the attractions of this event, held just outside town in spectacular Red Rocks State Park.

Santa Fe's **Indian Market** is the world's most prestigious gathering of Native American potters, jewelers, weavers, painters, basket makers, kachina carvers, and other artists and craftspeople—and their avid collectors. Held annually on the Plaza on the third weekend in August, many of the town's 150 art galleries feature special shows of leading Native American artists. At least 800 artists and craftspeople show their work at this event. Contact the Southwestern Association of Indian Affairs (SWAIA; ✉ 142 Palace Ave., Suite 104, Santa Fe 87501, ☎ 505/ 983–5220).

During **Old Lincoln Days** (☎ 505/653–4025), this Old West town's early prominence in the violent Lincoln County Wars is displayed in numerous events lasting several days, including performances of the "Last Escape of Billy the Kid" Pageant.

AUTUMN

➤ SEPT.: **Las Fiestas de Santa Fe** (✉ Box 4516, Santa Fe 87505, ☎ 505/988–7575), the city's biggest celebration, begins the first Friday after Labor Day and commemorates the reconquest of Santa Fe from the Pueblos by Don Diego de Vargas in 1692. A pet parade, dancing, religious observances, ethnic foods, fireworks, and the burning of *Zozobra* (Old Man Gloom) are all part of the fun.

The **New Mexico State Fair** (☎ 505/265–1791), one of the nation's liveliest, takes place at the New Mexico State Fairgrounds in Albuquerque, with a large midway, arts, crafts, livestock shows, entertainment, a rodeo, and living early Spanish and Native American villages.

➤ OCT.: Albuquerque's **Kodak International Balloon Fiesta** (☎ 505/821–1000) is the single most popular event in the state, with as many as 1.5 million spectators coming to see the mass ascensions of more than 700 hot-air and gas balloons at sunrise. This major event in the world of ballooning—you'll never see anything like it—takes place at Balloon Fiesta Park the first two weekends in October.

The Whole Enchilada Fiesta (☎ 505/527–3939), in Las Cruces, lasts several days and attracts thousands with food, arts and crafts, and the concoction of the world's largest enchilada—which is shared with the crowd.

At the **Lincoln County Cowboy Symposium** (☎ 505/378–4142), cowboy poets, musicians, chuck-wagon cooks, and artisans congregate in Ruidoso's rugged mountain settings for festivities lasting several days.

➤ NOV.: The Las Cruces **Renaissance Craftfaire** (☎ 505/523–6403) has costumed characters representing the Middle Ages' song and culture and selling their wares in a local park that's magically converted into scenes from centuries ago.

2 Santa Fe

Take a high desert plateau with crystalline air at the foot of the snow-capped peaks, layer in almost 400 years of Spanish, Mexican, and Native American influences, and sprinkle on an odd assortment of artists, writers, health nuts, and modern urban refugees, and you get Santa Fe, America's most un-American city.

ITH ITS CRISP, CLEAR AIR and bright, sunny weather, Santa Fe couldn't be more welcoming. Perched on a plateau at the base of the Sangre de Cristo Mountains—at an elevation of 7,000 ft—the city is surrounded by remnants of a 2,000-year-old Pueblo civilization and filled with reminders of almost four centuries of Spanish and Mexican rule. Add rows of chic art galleries, superb restaurants, and shops selling Southwestern furnishings and cowboy gear, and you have this uniquely appealing destination.

Updated by
Nancy
Zimmerman

La Villa Real de la Santa Fe de San Francisco de Asís (the Royal City of the Holy Faith of St. Francis of Assisi) was founded as early as 1607 by Don Pedro de Peralta, who planted his banner in the name of Spain. The Santa Fe Plaza has been the site of bullfights, public floggings, gunfights, battles, political rallies, promenades, and public markets.

In 1680 most of the region's Pueblo people rose in revolt against the Spanish, burning homes and churches and killing hundreds of Spaniards. After an extended siege in Santa Fe, the Pueblo people successfully drove the Spanish colonists out of New Mexico. But the tide turned again 12 years later, in 1692, when General Don Diego de Vargas returned with a new army from El Paso and recaptured Santa Fe. To commemorate de Vargas's victory, Las Fiestas de Santa Fe *have* been held every year since 1712. The country's oldest community celebration takes place the weekend after Labor Day, with parades, mariachis, pageants, and nonstop parties. Though the best-known festival in Santa Fe, "Fiesta" (as it's referred to locally) is but one of numerous opportunities for revelry throughout the year—from the arrival of the annual rodeo and the opening week of the Santa Fe Opera to traditional Pueblo dances at Christmastime.

Following de Vargas's defeat of the Pueblos, the once-grand Camino Real (Royal Highway), originally stretching from Mexico City to Santa Fe, brought an army of conquistadors, clergymen, and settlers to the northernmost reaches of Spain's New World conquests. In 1820 the first flood of covered wagons rolled into the Plaza from Missouri along the Santa Fe Trail—a prime artery of U.S. expansion to the West—and a booming trade with the United States was born. Mexico's independence from Spain in 1821, and its subsequent rule of New Mexico, further increased this exchange.

But the Santa Fe Trail's heyday ended with the arrival of the Atchison, Topeka, and Santa Fe railroad in 1880. The trains, and then the nation's first roads, brought a new type of settler to Santa Fe—artists who fell in love with its cultural diversity, its history, and its magical color and light. Their presence soon attracted tourists who quickly became a primary source of income for the largely poor populace.

Today, Santa Fe is renowned for its arts, tri-cultural heritage (Native American, Hispanic, and Anglo), and adobe architecture. The Pueblo people were already using adobe—though in a slightly different form—to build their multistory "condos" when the Spanish arrived. In a relatively dry climate and a treeless region, adobe was a naturally suitable building material. Melding into the landscape with their earthen colors and rounded, flowing lines, the pueblos and villages were hard to see from afar and thus protected, to some degree, from the ravages of raiding nomadic tribes. The distinctive Pueblo-style architecture no longer repels visitors, it attracts them—but the predominance of adobe, pure or ersatz, flat-roof Colonial style or climbing Pueblo fashion, can be a bit overwhelming.

Among the smallest state capitals in the country, Santa Fe is without a major airport (Albuquerque's is the nearest). The city's population, an estimated 62,000, swells to nearly double that figure in summer and, to a lesser degree, again in winter, when skiers arrive, lured by the challenging slopes of the Santa Fe Ski Area and nearby Taos Ski Valley. Geared for tourists, Santa Fe can put a serious dent in your travel budget. Prices are highest in June, July, and August; lower from September through November and April; and lowest (except for the major holidays) from December through March.

EXPLORING SANTA FE

Humorist Will Rogers said on his first visit to Santa Fe, "Whoever designed this town did so while riding on a jackass, backwards, and drunk." Although the maze of narrow streets and alleyways may confound motorists, it's a delight for shoppers and pedestrians, who will find attractive shops and restaurants, a flowered courtyard, or an eye-catching gallery at just about every turn.

Santa Fe Plaza

Getting acquainted with Santa Fe begins, logically enough, with its central Plaza. Much of the history of Santa Fe, New Mexico, the Southwest, and even the West has roots in this small town square, the heart of the city. Originally laid out around 1607 by New Mexico governor Don Pedro de Peralta, the Plaza witnessed the revolt of the Pueblos in 1680 and the Spanish recapture of Santa Fe in 1692. It was the site of a bullring and of fiestas and fandangos. Freight wagons unloaded here—at the end of the Santa Fe Trail—after completing their arduous journeys. The American flag was raised over it in 1846 in the first military action of the Mexican War. For a time it was a tree-shaded park with a white picket fence, then later, in the 1890s, an expanse of lawn, where uniformed bands played in an ornate gazebo at its center. Today it is filled with shops, art galleries, restaurants, and Native American vendors.

Numbers in the text correspond to numbers in the margin and on the Santa Fe map.

A Good Walk

You can get an overview of the history of the city and the state at the **Palace of the Governors** ①, bordering the northern side of the Plaza on Palace Avenue. Outside, under the Palace portals, dozens of Native American craftspeople sell their wares. From the Palace, cross Lincoln Street to the **Museum of Fine Arts** ②, where the works of regional masters are on display. There's more art by New Mexico's best-known painter, Georgia O'Keeffe, at the new **Georgia O'Keeffe Museum** ③ on nearby Johnson Street.

After you've visited the Georgia O'Keeffe museum, return to the Plaza and stroll over to its southeast corner on Old Santa Fe Trail, where you can find the town's oldest hotel, **La Fonda** ④. Go inside to soak up a little of Santa Fe gone by. When you leave La Fonda, you can't miss the imposing facade of **St. Francis Cathedral** ⑤ looming above East San Francisco Street. Inside is an old adobe church reminiscent of those scattered across northern New Mexico.

Cross Cathedral Place, away from the church, to get to the **Museum of the Institute of American Indian Arts** ⑥, where the world's largest collection of contemporary Native American art is housed. A stone's throw away from the museum is cool, quiet **Sena Plaza** ⑦, where you can sit and bask in the feeling of another place and time.

TIMING

It's possible to zoom through this compact area in about five hours—two hours exploring the Plaza and the Palace of the Governors, two hours seeing the Museum of Fine Arts and the Museum of the Institute of American Indian Arts, and an hour visiting the other sites. But you might also want to take your time in the Plaza, which is a great place to sit on a bench in the sun and soak up the ambience of the city's soul. Particularly festive times on the Plaza are the weekend after Labor day, during Las Fiestas de Santa Fe, and at Christmas, when all the trees are filled with lights and lanterns line the rooftops. It can, however, get a bit crowded during major Plaza events.

Sights to See

❸ **Georgia O'Keeffe Museum.** O'Keeffe was one of many East Coast artists who came to New Mexico in the 1920s–'40s, fell in love with the region, and returned to live here. Unlike those artists who are still generally unknown, O'Keeffe emerged as a kind of demigoddess of New Mexico and of the art world as a whole. This new, private museum dedicated to her work opened in July 1997. The museum's founders plan to eventually house the world's largest collection of works by O'Keeffe. ⊠ *217 Johnson St.,* ☎ *505/995–0785.* ⌨ *$5, 4-day pass $8 (good at all 4 state museums in Santa Fe), free Fri.* ☉ *Tues.–Thurs. and weekends 10–5, Fri. 10–8.*

❹ **La Fonda.** This landmark hotel (☞ Lodging, *below*) facing the southeast corner of the Plaza, where Old Santa Fe Trail and East San Francisco Street meet, is Santa Fe's oldest lodging place. A *fonda* (inn) has stood on the spot for centuries, though the current hotel was built only in 1922. It is still known fondly as "The Inn at the End of the Trail" because of its proximity to the Plaza and its history as a gathering place for cowboys, trappers, traders, soldiers, and frontier politicians. Many of Santa Fe's major social events still take place here. ⊠ *E. San Francisco St.,* ☎ *505/982–5511.*

★ ❷ **Museum of Fine Arts.** This understated building is home to one of America's finest regional art museums and was Santa Fe's first Pueblo Revival–style structure. Completed in 1917, it inspired the region's distinctive architectural look. The ceilings are made of split cedar *latillas* (branches set in a crosshatch pattern) and hand-hewn vigas; many excellent examples of Spanish Colonial–style furniture are on display. The 8,000-piece permanent collection emphasizes the work of regional artists, including Georgia O'Keeffe; the "Cinco Pintores" (five painters) of Santa Fe (including Fremont Elis and Will Shuster); the Taos Masters (Ernest Blumenschein, Bert Geer Philips, Joseph Henry Sharp, and Eanger Irving Couse, among others); as well as works by Mexican (such as Diego Rivera), Southwestern, and Native American artists. A beautiful interior *placita* (small plaza) with fountains, murals, and sculpture, and the breathtaking St. Francis Auditorium are other highlights. Concerts and lectures are often held in the auditorium: Call for information. ⊠ *W. Palace Ave.,* ☎ *505/827–4455.* ⌨ *$5, 4-day pass $8 (good at the Georgia O'Keeffe Museum and all 4 state museums in Santa Fe), free Fri.* ☉ *Tues.–Thurs. and weekends 10–5, Fri. 10–8.*

❻ **Museum of the Institute of American Indian Arts.** This handsomely renovated former Federal Post Office houses the largest collection of contemporary Native American art in the United States. The paintings, photography, sculpture, prints, and traditional crafts showcase the works of students and teachers, past and present, of the seminal

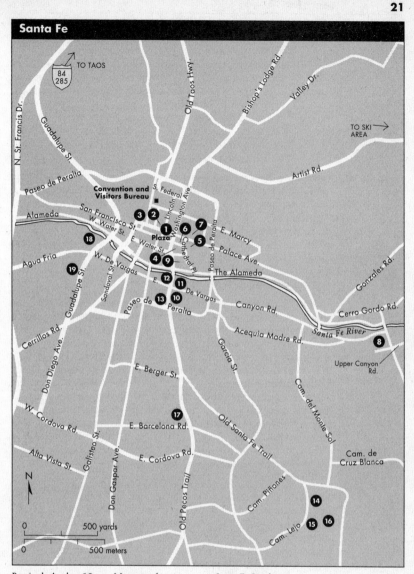

Santa Fe

Barrio de Analco, **12**

Cristo Rey Church, **8**

Georgia O'Keeffe Museum, **3**

La Fonda, **4**

Loretto Chapel, **9**

Museum of Fine Arts, **2**

Museum of Indian Arts and Culture, **14**

Museum of the Institute of American Indian Arts, **6**

Museum of International Folk Art, **15**

The Oldest House, **11**

Palace of the Governors, **1**

St. Francis Cathedral, **5**

San Miguel Mission, **10**

Santa Fe Children's Museum, **17**

Santa Fe Southern Railway, **19**

Santuario de Guadalupe, **18**

Sena Plaza, **7**

State Capitol Building, **13**

Wheelright Museum of the American Indian, **16**

Institute of American Indian Arts. The Institute, across town on Cerrillos Road, was founded as a one-room studio classroom in the early 1930s by Dorothy Dunn, a beloved art teacher who played a critical role in launching the careers of many well-known Native American artists. In the 1960s and '70s, it blossomed into the major center for Native American arts in the country, sparking the international appeal it has now. Famed artist Fritz Scholder taught here for years, as did renowned sculptor Allan Houser. Among their best-known disciples was T. C. Cannon, who died in a car accident in 1978. ⊠ *108 Cathedral Pl.,* ☎ *505/988–6211 for events and parking information.* ⊒ *$4.* ⊗ *Mon.–Sat. 10–5, Sun. noon–5.*

★ ♺ ❶ **Palace of the Governors.** This humble-looking one-story adobe on the north side of the Plaza is the oldest public building in the United States. Built at the same time as the Plaza, circa 1607, it has been the key seat of government under four separate flags—Spain, Mexico, the Confederacy, and the U.S. territory that preceded New Mexico's statehood in 1912. It served as the residence for 100 Spanish, Mexican, and American governors, including Governor Lew Wallace, who wrote his epic *Ben Hur* in its then drafty rooms, while complaining of the dust and mud that fell from its earthen ceiling.

Since 1913, the Palace has been the central headquarters of the Museum of New Mexico; it houses the primary unit of the **State History Museum.** Permanent exhibits chronicle 450 years of New Mexico history using maps, furniture, clothing, housewares, weaponry, and village models. It is also home to the **Museum of New Mexico Press,** which prints books, cards, and booklets on antique presses and offers bookbinding demonstrations, lectures, and slide shows. With advance permission, students and researchers have access to the museum's extensive historical-research library and its collection of rare maps, manuscripts, and photographs (more than 120,000 prints and negatives). There is also an outstanding gift shop and bookstore. ⊠ *Palace Ave. (north side of the Plaza),* ☎ *505/827–6483.* ⊒ *$5, 4-day pass $8 (good at all 4 state museums in Santa Fe, as well as the Georgia O'Keeffe Museum), free Fri.* ⊗ *Tues.–Sun. 10–5.*

Dozens of **Native American vendors** gather daily under the portal of the Palace of the Governors to display and sell pottery, jewelry, bread, and other goods. With few exceptions, the more than 500 artists and craftspeople registered to sell under the portals are all members of New Mexico Pueblos or tribes. All merchandise on sale is required to meet Museum of New Mexico standards: Items are all handmade or handstrung in Native American households; silver jewelry is either sterling (92.5% pure) or coin silver (90% pure); all metal jewelry bears the maker's mark, which is registered with the museum. Prices tend to reflect the high quality of the merchandise. Photographs should not be taken without permission.

★ ❺ **Saint Francis Cathedral.** A block east of the Plaza is this magnificent Romanesque-style cathedral, one of the rare departures from the city's steadfast pueblo architecture. Construction was begun in 1869 by Jean Baptiste Lamy, Santa Fe's first archbishop, working with French architects and Italian stonemasons. The inspiration for Willa Cather's novel *Death Comes for the Archbishop,* Lamy, the controversial circuit-riding archbishop, is buried in the crypt beneath the church's high altar.

A small adobe chapel on the northeast side of the cathedral, the remnant of an earlier church built on the site, reveals the Hispanic architectural influence so noticeably missing from the cathedral itself. Inside this older chapel is *Nuestra Señora de la Paz* (Our Lady of Peace)—the oldest Madonna statue in the United States. It accompanied Don Diego de Vargas on his reconquest of Santa Fe in 1692, a feat attributed to the statue's spiritual intervention. Every Friday the faithful adorn the statue, now the patron saint of New Mexico, with a new dress. ⊠ *231 Cathedral Pl.,* ☎ *505/982–5619.* ☉ *Daily; Mass celebrated daily at 7 and 8:15 AM, 12:10 and 5:15 PM; Sun. at 6, 8, and 10 AM, noon, and 7 PM.*

❼ Sena Plaza. This courtyard, surrounded on all sides by two-story buildings, can be entered only through two small doorways on Palace Avenue. Flowering fruit trees, a fountain, and inviting benches provide a nice place to rest weary feet. Originally built in the 1700s as a single-family residence—with quarters for blacksmiths, bakers, farmers, and all manner of help—it harkens back to a much quieter and simpler time in Santa Fe. ⊠ *125 E. Palace Ave.*

Canyon Road

Canyon Road, nicknamed "the Art and Soul of Santa Fe" because of its many art galleries, shops, and restaurants, stretches for 2 mi from the Plaza. It was once a Native American trail, and, during the early part of this century, a route for woodcutters coming into town with their loaded burros. If you're walking, be aware that Canyon Road is a long stretch, all slightly uphill. If you're driving, note that street parking is at a premium, but there is a lot in the shopping complex at the lower end of the street (⊠ 225 Canyon Rd.) and another city-owned lot at the corner of Camino del Monte Sol.

A Good Walk

Begin your walk along Canyon Road at its intersection with Paseo de Peralta, and follow it for 2 mi, along the Santa River, back into the hills above the city. Take your time exploring the street's numerous galleries and shops and take a break at one of its many fine restaurants. At the intersection of Upper Canyon and Cristo Rey, you'll find the massive **Cristo Rey Church** ⑧.

TIMING

A thorough exploration of Canyon Road could take a day, especially if you like to shop and see galleries. With a car, and limited stops, you could cut your visit down to about three hours. Even on a cold day, the walk can be lovely, with massive, glistening icicles hanging off roofs and a silence shrouding the tiny streets like a comfortable old shawl. There are few places as festive as Canyon Road on Christmas Eve, when thousands of votive candles shimmer inside brown paper bags on walkways, walls, roofs, and even in trees.

Sights to See

❽ Cristo Rey Church. Built in 1940 to commemorate the 400th anniversary of Coronado's exploration of the Southwest, this church is the largest adobe structure in the United States and is considered by many to be the finest example of Pueblo-style architecture anywhere. It was constructed the old-fashioned way by parishioners, who mixed the more than 200,000 mud-and-straw adobe bricks themselves and hauled them into place. The church's magnificent 225-ton stone reredos (altar screen) is equally impressive. ⊠ *1120 Canyon Rd.,* ☎ *505/983–8528.* ☉ *Daily 8–7.*

NEED A
BREAK?

When you need a respite, drop into the **Backroom Coffeebar** (✉ 616
Canyon Rd., ☎ 505/988–5323) for a light snack and something to
drink.

Lower Old Santa Fe Trail

It was along the Old Santa Fe Trail that wagon trains from Missouri
rolled into town in the 1800s, forever changing Santa Fe's destiny. This
area, just off the Plaza, is one of Santa Fe's most historic.

A Good Walk

The delicate **Loretto Chapel** ⑨, facing the Old Santa Fe Trail, behind
La Fonda hotel (☞ Santa Fe Plaza, *above*), is the best place to start
your walk on this street that resounds with history. Turning away from
La Fonda, head southeast on Old Santa Fe Trail to the **San Miguel Mission** ⑩, which contains a priceless collection of Spanish Colonial religious art.

Across from the Mission, on De Vargas Street, is **The Oldest House** ⑪,
a title of questionable, but interesting merit. Up and down narrow De
Vargas stretches the **Barrio de Analco** ⑫, one of America's oldest neighborhoods; plaques on the houses attest to more than 350 years of occupation. After you've explored this street, return to Old Santa Fe Trail
and walk farther away from downtown until you come to the round
State Capitol Building ⑬, probably one of the most unusually shaped
government buildings in the United States.

TIMING

Plan on spending a half hour in each church, an hour exploring the
Barrio de Analco, and an hour in the State Capitol. Overall, this walk
should take about 3½ hours, depending on how long you spend at each
place.

Sights to See

⑫ **Barrio de Analco.** Along the south bank of the Santa Fe River is one
of America's oldest neighborhoods, settled in the early 1600s by the
Tlaxcalans, Mexican–Native American mercenaries who were forbidden
to live on the north side of the river around the Spanish Plaza. Plaques
on houses on East De Vargas Street highlight some of the most historic
houses, including the Crespin, Alarid, Bandelier, and Boyle homes.

⑨ **Loretto Chapel.** Started in 1873, this delicate Romanesque church,
modeled after the famous Sainte-Chapelle chapel in Paris, was built at
the same time as St. Francis Cathedral by the same French architects
and Italian stonemasons. The chapel is known for the "Miraculous Staircase" that leads to the choir loft. Legend has it that the chapel was almost finished when it became obvious that there wasn't room enough
to complete a staircase to the choir loft. In answer to the prayers of
the cathedral's sisters, an old, bearded man arrived on a donkey, built
a 20-ft staircase—using only a square, a saw, and a tub of water to
season the wood—and then disappeared as quickly as he came. Many
of the faithful believe it was St. Joseph himself. The staircase contains
two complete 360-degree turns with no central support; no nails were
used in its construction. The chapel is maintained by the Inn at Loretto
(☞ Lodging, *below*), which adjoins it. ✉ *211 Old Santa Fe Trail,* ☎
505/984–7971. 🎫 *$1.* ☉ *Mid-Oct.–mid-May, Mon.–Sat. 9–5, Sun.
10:30–5; mid-May–mid-Oct., Mon.–Sat. 8–6, Sun. 10:30–5.*

⑪ **The Oldest House.** First built by the Pueblo people more than 800 years
ago out of "puddled" adobe (liquid mud poured between upright
wooden frames), which predates the adobe brick introduced by the Span-

ish, this house is said to be the most ancient dwelling in the United States. The building is now a gift shop. ⊠ *215 E. De Vargas St.* ☉ *Mon.–Sat. 10–5.*

★ ❿ **San Miguel Mission.** The oldest church still in use in the continental United States, this simple, earth-hued adobe structure was built in about 1625 by the Tlaxcalan Indians of Mexico, who originally came to New Mexico as servants of the Spanish. Badly damaged in the 1680 Pueblo Revolt, the church was rebuilt in 1710. On display in the chapel are priceless statues and paintings and the San José Bell, weighing nearly 800 pounds, believed to have been cast in Spain in 1356 and brought to Santa Fe several centuries later. Mass is held Sunday at 5 PM. ⊠ *401 Old Santa Fe Trail,* ☎ *505/983–3974.* ⊠ *Donations suggested.* ☉ *May–Sept., daily 9–4:30; Oct.–Apr., daily 10–4.*

NEED A BREAK? Have a slice of pizza on the patio of **Upper Crust Pizza** (⊠ 329 Old Santa Fe Trail, ☎ 505/982-0000), next to the San Miguel Mission.

★ ⓭ **State Capitol.** Built in 1966, the state capitol—known as "the Roundhouse"—was modeled after the Zia Pueblo symbol, which represents the Circle of Life. Doorways at opposing sides of the building symbolize the four winds, four directions, and the four seasons. The **State Legislature** and the **Office of the Governor** are here. You can view works of art from the outstanding Capitol Art Foundation's collection, historical and cultural displays, and handcrafted local furniture throughout public areas of the building. There are also temporary art exhibitions in the **Governor's Gallery.** Six acres of imaginatively landscaped gardens shelter many outstanding sculptures. ⊠ *Old Santa Fe Trail at Paseo de Peralta,* ☎ *505/986–4589.* ⊠ *Free.* ☉ *Sept.–May, weekdays 8–5; June–Aug., Mon.–Sat. 8–5; guided tours at 10 AM and 2 PM.*

Upper Old Santa Fe Trail

This outing to Santa Fe's finest museums is easiest to do with a car, but if you have two hours, and you're in good shape, you could walk it. Three of the museums are grouped together just off Old Santa Fe Trail, and another is on Old Pecos Trail, just south of its intersection with Old Santa Fe Trail.

A Good Drive

Begin at the **Museum of Indian Arts and Culture** ⑭, a state institution that honors the significant cultural achievements of New Mexico's Native American people. To get there from the Plaza, drive uphill on Old Santa Fe Trail to Camino Lejo, a mile from where Old Santa Fe Trail intersects with Old Pecos Trail. From the Indian Arts and Culture Museum, cross the parking lot to the **Museum of International Folk Art** ⑮, a truly one-of-a-kind marvel dedicated to the human creative spirit. Next, walk to the **Wheelwright Museum of the American Indian** ⑯, a few minutes away. When you've finished there—and if you have kids with you—drive back downhill to the **Santa Fe Children's Museum** ⑰.

TIMING

Set aside 4–6 hours to see all the museums on the Upper Santa Fe Trail. An hour and a half at each museum will only begin to dent the collections—but it's better to see too little than to grow glassy-eyed. Kids usually have to be dragged from the Children's Museum after an hour or two. Check the papers for special exhibits and events.

Sights to See

★ ⑭ **Museum of Indian Arts and Culture.** Housed in this modern building is an extensive collection of New Mexico's oldest works of art—beautiful pottery vessels, fine stone and silver jewelry, extraordinary textiles, and other arts and crafts created by the state's Pueblo, Navajo, and Apache Native Americans. The museum also offers art demonstrations, interactive displays, and a film about the life and work of famed Pueblo potter Maria of San Ildefonso. In summer it hosts "Breakfast With Curators," a lecture series that includes breakfast and a private tour of the collection (cost $20). ⊠ 710 Camino Lejo, ☎ 505/827–6344. 🖾 $5, 4-day pass $8 (good at the Georgia O'Keeffe museum and all 4 state museums in Santa Fe). ☉ Tues.–Sun. 10–5.

★ ⑮ **Museum of International Folk Art.** This unique museum, considered the premier institution of its kind, is dedicated to the creations of folk artists from around the world. Everywhere you look there are amazingly inventive handmade objects—a tin Madonna, a devil made from bread dough, and all kinds of rag dolls. The original collection—of 4,000 works—was donated by Florence Dibell Bartlett, a collector who also donated money to found the museum in 1953. In 1978 designer and architect Alexander Girard gave the museum his lifelong collection of folk art—more than 106,000 items. The museum was again enriched in 1989 with the opening of a $1.1 million Hispanic Heritage Wing, designed to display Hispanic folk art from the Spanish Colonial period (in New Mexico, 1598–1821) to the present. The 5,000-piece exhibit includes religious folk art—particularly *bultos* (carved wooden statues of saints) and *retablos* (holy images painted on wood or tin). Along with the permanent collection, the museum presents temporary exhibits. The gift shop carries textiles, dolls, jewelry, ornaments, and other folk-art objects. ⊠ 706 Camino Lejo, ☎ 505/827–6350. 🖾 $5, 4-day pass $8 (good at the Georgia O'Keeffe Museum and all 4 state museums in Santa Fe). ☉ July–Dec., daily 10–5; Jan.–June, Tues.–Sun 10–5.

⑰ **Santa Fe Children's Museum.** Kids won't be bored at this museum. Stimulating hands-on exhibits, a solar greenhouse, oversize geometric forms, and a simulated 18-ft mountain-climbing wall all contribute to the museum's popularity. Special performances of puppet shows and storytellers are presented occasionally. ⊠ 1050 Old Pecos Trail, ☎ 505/989–8359. 🖾 $3. ☉ Sept.–May, Thurs.–Sat. 10–5, Sun. noon–5; June–Aug., Wed.–Sat. 10–5, Sun. noon–5.

⑯ **Wheelwright Museum of the American Indian.** This private institution, housed in a building shaped like a traditional Navajo hogan, first opened in 1937. Founded by Boston scholar Mary Cabot Wheelwright and Navajo medicine-man Hasteen Klah, the museum houses the works of many Native American cultures and mounts impressive special exhibitions year-round. The **Case Trading Post,** the museum shop on the lower level, is modeled after the trading posts that dotted the Southwestern frontier over a hundred years ago. ⊠ 704 Camino Lejo, ☎ 505/982–4636. 🖾 Donation suggested. ☉ Mon.–Sat. 10–5, Sun. 1–5.

Railroad District

Ten years ago this area at the western edge of downtown Santa Fe was crumbling; today it is filled with shops, restaurants, and galleries. But the highlight of the area is the restored scenic train line, which is once again putting the town's old depot to use.

A Good Walk
Start your walk of this area at the humble but historic **Santuario de Guadalupe** ⑱, 3½ blocks southwest of the Plaza, at the end of El Camino Real. From the Plaza, head west on San Francisco Street, then

take a left on Guadalupe Street. From here, head south along Guadalupe Street; take your time browsing through the shops and eating lunch in one of the restaurants along the way. At the corner of Montezuma Street, turn right and proceed a half block to the end of the railroad tracks on your left, where you'll find one of Santa Fe's two original train stations. If you have time, take the antique train run by the **Santa Fe Southern Railway** ⑲ to Lamy (20 mi away) and back for some scenic views of the distant Ortíz, Sandía, and Jemez Mountains.

TIMING

A visit to the Santuario de Guadalupe can take an hour or so—more if there is an art show is progress. If you like shopping, it's possible to spend hours browsing in the shops on and off Guadalupe Street. The trip to Lamy and back on the train takes five hours and is best on a warm, sunny day.

Sights to See

⑲ **Santa Fe Southern Railway.** Ride in the antique railroad cars or the caboose to Lamy, 20 mi away from Santa Fe. Trains depart from one of Santa Fe's two original train stations, which was once a stop on the "Chile Line." The tracks extend off the Santa Fe plateau and into the vast Galisteo Basin; views of over 120 mi are not uncommon. In the brick depot, great rail-history books, model trains, T-shirts, and other train-related objects are on sale. Eat lunch in Lamy or pack a picnic. In summer a special "Sunset Run" is offered, which leaves an hour before dusk and includes a light supper. ✉ *410 S. Guadalupe,* ☎ *505/989–8600.* ✑ *$21; sunset run $28.* ✆ *Departs May–Oct., Tues., Thurs., and weekends about 10:30 AM, returns 2:30–3:30 PM; sunset run departs anywhere 6 PM–7:15 PM. Call for winter schedule and sunset run times.*

⑱ **Santuario de Guadalupe.** This humble adobe structure is the oldest shrine in the United States to Our Lady of Guadalupe, patron saint of Mexico. It now houses a nonprofit cultural center, which sponsors art exhibits, concerts, and cultural events, although mass is still occasionally held here. Built by Franciscan missionaries between 1776 and 1795, it has adobe walls nearly 3 ft thick and contains several noteworthy paintings, including a priceless 16th-century work by Venetian painter Leonardo de Ponte Bassano depicting Jesus driving the money changers from the temple, and a portrait of Our Lady of Guadalupe by Mexico's renowned colonial painter José de Alzíbar. Other highlights are an authentic 19th-century sacristy; a pictorial-history archive; a library devoted to Archbishop Lamy, furnished with many of his personal possessions; and a garden containing plants from the Holy Land. ✉ *100 Guadalupe St.,* ☎ *505/988–2027.* ✑ *Donation suggested.* ✆ *May–Oct., Mon.–Sat. 9–4; Nov.–Apr., weekdays 9–4.*

DINING

Santa Fe cuisine is a delicious mixture of Pueblo, Spanish, Mexican, and Continental cuisine. From cheerful cafés serving superb Mexican dishes to elegant restaurants serving nouvelle New Mexican to hamburger joints, Santa Fe offers a range of dining options for every taste and budget.

CATEGORY	COST*
$$$	over $20
$$	$10–$20
$	under $10

*per person, excluding drinks, service, and sales tax (6.25%)

$$$ ✕ **Anasazi.** A soft light illuminates the stone and adobe interior of this
★   fine restaurant, which became a Santa Fe fixture the day it opened. Chef
      John Bobrick combines New Mexican and Native American flavors
      to produce such exotic offerings as Anasazi flat bread with fire-roasted
      sweet peppers, cinnamon-chile tenderloin of beef with *chipotle* (a hot,
      smoky chile) and white-cheddar mashed potatoes served with mango
      salsa. The large dining room has solid wood tables and *bancos* (adobe
      banquettes) upholstered with Chimayo handwoven textiles. Groups of
      up to 12 can dine in the private wine cellar, and groups of up to 40
      can be served in the library. ✉ *113 Washington Ave.,* ☎ *505/988–3030.
      AE, D, DC, MC, V.*

$$$ ✕ **Coyote Cafe.** The bright, cheerful modern room and the innovative
★   menu are the creations of well-known chef-owner Mark Miller. Try
      "The Cowboy," a 22-ounce rib eye served with barbecued black beans
      and red chile–dusted onion rings, the squash-blossom and corn-cake
      appetizers, or the ravioli filled with wild-boar-and-goat-cheese sausage.
      The wine list offers more than 500 selections. In summer the Rooftop
      Cantina serves equally exotic but less expensive dishes such as duck
      quesadillas. The **Coyote General Store,** under the café, sells a wide va-
      riety of Southwestern foodstuffs and Miller's best-selling cookbooks.
      ✉ *132 W. Water St.,* ☎ *505/983–1615. Reservations essential. AE,
      D, DC, MC, V.*

$$$ ✕ **Geronimo.** Chefs Steven and Kirstin Jarrett change the menu fre-
★   quently at this popular restaurant in the historic Borrego House (dat-
      ing from 1756). A typical meal might include mesquite-grilled elk
      tenderloin with jalapeño creamed corn or chile-rubbed grilled tuna with
      fettuccine and black beans in lime beurre blanc. Or make a meal out
      of the variety of generous appetizers. The Sunday brunch is also ex-
      cellent. The intimate, white dining rooms have beamed ceilings, wood
      floors, fireplaces, and cushioned bancos. In summer you can dine
      under the front portal; in winter the tiny bar and fireplace are invit-
      ing. ✉ *724 Canyon Rd.,* ☎ *505/982–1500. AE, MC, V. No lunch Mon.*

$$$ ✕ **La Casa Sena.** This elegant restaurant is in the lovely Sena Plaza.
      The menu includes a delicious mix of New Mexican and Continental
      fare. If you order the popular *trucha en terra-cotta* (fresh trout wrapped
      in corn husks and baked in clay), and be sure to ask them to save the
      clay head for you as a souvenir. Finish dinner with a strange but won-
      derful avocado cheesecake with a piñon nut crust. The incredible se-
      lection of more than 700 wines earned this restaurant the *Wine
      Spectator*'s award of excellence. For a musical meal (evenings only),
      sit in the restaurant's adjacent Cantina, where staff members serve up
      Broadway show tunes along with your food. ✉ *125 E. Palace Ave.,*
      ☎ *505/988–9232. AE, D, DC, MC, V.*

$$$ ✕ **Santacafé.** The thick adobe walls of this romantic restaurant—one
★   of Santa Fe's finest—2 blocks north of the Plaza in the historic Padre
      Gallegos House, are decorated with floral bouquets. The shrimp and
      spinach dumplings with tahini sauce and the Chimayó chile-spiced rack
      of lamb with green chile mashed potatoes are particularly good. Ser-
      vice is pleasant. In summer the delightful patio is a popular spot. ✉
      231 Washington Ave., ☎ *505/984–1788. AE, MC, V.*

$$–$$$ ✕ **Café Escalera.** Ride the only escalator in Santa Fe to the second floor
      for fine Mediterranean-influenced fare. The spacious restaurant and
      bar have a minimalist look, with billowy ceiling canopies and white
      tablecloths. The menu changes daily, but may include spaghettini with
      English peas, pancetta, and Romano cheese, or a fried oyster sandwich
      with smoked bacon and aïoli. ✉ *130 Lincoln Ave.,* ☎ *505/989–8188.
      AE, MC, V. Closed Sun.*

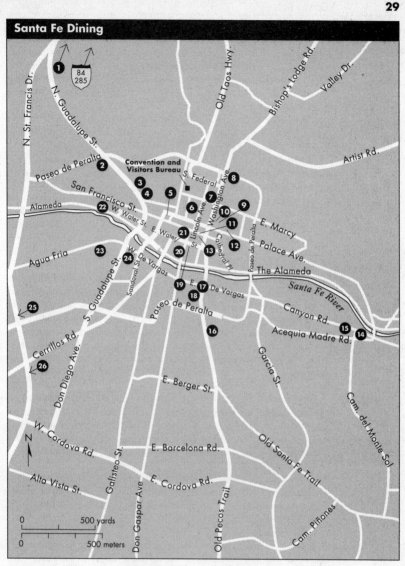

Santa Fe Dining

Anasazi, **10**
Bistro 315, **16**
Bert's Burger Bowl, **3**
Café Escalera, **6**
Cafe Pasqual's, **20**
Cowgirl Hall of
Fame, **24**
Coyote Cafe, **21**
Dave's Not Here, **25**
El Farol, **14**
El Nido, **1**

Geronimo, **15**
Guadalupe Cafe, **18**
Il Piatto, **7**
India Palace, **19**
La Casa Sena, **12**
La Tertulia, **23**
Old Mexico Grill, **26**
Ore House on the
Plaza, **11**
The Palace, **5**

Pink Adobe, **17**
Plaza Café, **13**
Santacafé, **8**
The Shed, **9**
Shohko, **4**
Vanessie, **22**
Whistling Moon
Cafe, **2**

$$–$$$ ✕ **Cafe Pasqual's.** A block southwest of the Plaza, this tiny, cheerful restaurant offers regional specialties and possibly the best breakfast in town—served all day. Forget the pancakes and order a chorizo burrito (Mexican sausages, scrambled eggs, and home fries in a flour tortilla), or the succulent corned beef hash. For dinner, there's chile-rubbed pan-roasted salmon with a tomatillo-avocado salsa and chile-corn pudding. High ceilings and huge colorful murals lend a spacious feel, and piñatas, *ristras* (strings of red chile peppers), and ceramic pottery add a festive tone. Expect a line at breakfast and lunch. ⊠ *121 Don Gaspar Ave.,* ☎ *505/983–9340 or 800/722–7672. AE, MC, V.*

$$–$$$ ✕ **El Nido.** Since the 1920s, Santa Feans have made the 6-mi drive to the tiny village of Tesuque to eat at this former dance hall and trading post, now known for its cozy ambience and solid menu of choice aged beef, fresh seafood, and local specialties such as chunky green chile stew. Only a five-minute drive from the Santa Fe Opera, El Nido is a favorite of opera fans. Banquet facilities are also available. ⊠ *U.S. 285/84 (6 mi north of Santa Fe to first Tesuque exit, then about ¼ mi farther to restaurant),* ☎ *505/988–4340. AE, MC, V. Closed Mon.*

$$–$$$ ✕ **The Palace.** One of New Mexico's premier restaurants—and a pop-
   ★ ular spot for power lunches—the Palace has upholstered banquettes and a lively saloon with rich red wallpaper (a remnant from the days of Doña Tules, a famed madam and gambling tycoon who owned the building in the 1800s). The present owner, Lino Pertusini, is from Italy and he focuses on Italian and Continental cuisine. Try the sautéed sweetbreads, the linguine with shrimp, and the irresistible homemade pastries. The wine list and service are also notable. In summer there's patio dining. ⊠ *142 W. Palace Ave.,* ☎ *505/982–9891. AE, D, MC, V. No lunch Sun.*

$$–$$$ ✕ **Pink Adobe.** Rosalea Murphey has owned this restaurant—one of the best-known in town—for 50 years. The several cozy dining rooms have fireplaces and an array of artwork by well-known artists, including Rosalea herself. Continental, New Orleans Creole, and local New Mexican favorites are served: Steak Dunnigan smothered in green chile and mushrooms, and savory Shrimp Louisianne—fat and crispy deep-fried shrimp—are perennial specials, as is the apple pie drenched in rum sauce. A limited menu is served in the adjacent Dragon Room bar, a popular hangout. Smoking is not allowed in the dining areas. ⊠ *406 Old Santa Fe Trail,* ☎ *505/983–7712. AE, D, DC, MC, V. No lunch weekends.*

$$ ✕ **Bistro 315.** This place feels like something you might find on a trendy thoroughfare in Paris rather than on the Old Santa Fe Trail. Chef Matt Yohalem prepares classical bistro fare using organic vegetables, locally raised beef and lamb, free-range chicken, and fresh seafood. The ever-changing menu is highlighted by such seasonal specialties as potato-crusted salmon and mussels marinara with french fries. In good weather you can dine on the patio. ⊠ *315 Old Santa Fe Trail,* ☎ *505/ 986–9190. Reservations essential. AE, MC, V. Closed Sun.–Mon. in winter.*

$$ ✕ **El Farol.** Owner David Salazar sums up his food in one word: "Spanish." Feast on paella and tapas every night. There are 20 or so available—from tiny fried squid to wild mushrooms. It's a lively, relaxed place, with both indoor and outdoor dining. At 9:30 people push back the chairs and start dancing. ⊠ *808 Canyon Rd.,* ☎ *505/983–9912. D, DC, MC, V.*

$$ ✕ **Il Piatto.** This cozy Italian restaurant, opened in 1996 by the owners of Bistro 315, serves a variety of creative pasta dishes, such as risotto with duck, artichoke, and truffle oil; and seafood cannelloni with garlic toast. Entrées include pancetta-wrapped trout with rosemary and lemon, and roast chicken with Italian sausage, potatoes, peppers, and onions. ⊠ *95 W. Marcy,* ☎ *505/984–1091. AE, MC, V. Closed Sun. No lunch Sat.*

$$ ✕ **India Palace.** The idea of an East Indian restaurant in Santa Fe probably never occurred to most locals before the arrival of Indian Palace; now many locals wouldn't think of living without chef Bal Dev Singh's exotic and spicy dishes. The serene, deep pink interior sets the scene for such favorites as tender tandoori chicken and lamb and superb curried seafood and vegetables. Meals are cooked as hot or mild as you wish, and there's a wide selection of vegetarian dishes. ⊠ *227 Don Gaspar Ave. (at the rear of the El Centro shopping compound through the Water St. parking lot),* ☎ *505/986–5859. AE, D, MC, V.*

$$ ✕ **La Tertulia.** In a converted 19th-century convent, this popular restaurant serves good New Mexican cuisine and is home to a splendid Spanish Colonial art collection. Among the culinary highlights are tender *carne adovada* (red chile–marinated pork), *chalupas* (bowl-shape corn tortillas filled with beans, chicken, or beef), and flan for dessert. Be sure to have some of the extraordinary house sangria. ⊠ *416 Agua Fria St.,* ☎ *505/988–2769. AE, MC, V. Closed Mon.*

$$ ✕ **Old Mexico Grill.** For a taste of old Mexico in New Mexico, come
★ here to sample such dishes as *arracheras* (the traditional name for fajitas—grilled beef, chicken, or fish with peppers and onions and served with tortillas), and tacos *al carbón* (shredded pork cooked in a mole sauce and folded into corn tortillas). Start the meal with a fresh ceviche appetizer and a cool lime margarita. The restaurant's Cerrillos Road shopping center location makes parking a snap. ⊠ *2434 Cerrillos Rd., College Plaza S,* ☎ *505/473–0338. Reservations not accepted. D, MC, V. Closed weekend lunch.*

$$ ✕ **Ore House on the Plaza.** This restaurant is better known for its perfect location overlooking the Plaza than for its food. Salmon, swordfish, lobster, ceviche, and steaks are all solidly prepared, though rather ordinary. The specialty margaritas, however, are anything but ordinary: They come in more than 80 customized flavors, ranging from cool watermelon to zippy jalapeño. ⊠ *50 Lincoln Ave., upstairs on the southwest corner of the Plaza,* ☎ *505/983–8687. AE, MC, V.*

$$ ✕ **Shohko.** Tasty tempura—including, perhaps, the world's only greenchile tempura—and more than 35 kinds of sushi are on the menu at this small Japanese restaurant. If possible, sit at the 16-seat sushi bar and watch the masters at work. ⊠ *321 Johnson St.,* ☎ *505/983–7288. AE, D, MC, V.*

$$ ✕ **Vanessie.** Vanessie's is known for serving up huge portions of beef, chicken, fish, and rack of lamb, along with massive baked potatoes—even the salads are enormous and onion lovers will be awestruck by the size of the onion-loaf appetizer. High beamed ceilings and massive oak tables with high-back chairs create a cozy lodgelike ambience. After dinner, the popular piano bar is a perfect place to sit, listen to wistful tunes, and digest your food. ⊠ *434 W. San Francisco St.,* ☎ *505/982–9966. AE, DC, MC, V.*

$–$$ ✕ **Cowgirl Hall of Fame.** Part restaurant, part bar, part museum, and part theater—this fun place serves Texas-style brisket and barbecue (described by owner Barry Secular as "deep Southwest with a twist") and good New Mexican fare, including tasty *chiles rellenos* (peppers stuffed with cheese, dipped in batter, and fried), grilled-salmon soft tacos, and butternut-squash casserole. Frosty, long-neck Lone Stars reign in the beer lineup. In summer you can dine on the pleasant, tree-shaded patios, and kids can eat in "The Corral," a special area with its own kid's menu. After dinner there's live entertainment—from cowboy poetry readings to live music to skits. ⊠ *319 S. Guadalupe,* ☎ *505/982–2565. AE, D, MC, V.*

$ ✕ **Bert's Burger Bowl.** Since the 1950s, this tiny spot has been serving up yummy charbroiled burgers—the No. 6 (green chile with cheese) is a staple. You can also get excellent pressure-cooked chicken, tasty carne adovada, crispy fries, and old-fashioned shakes. There are tables outside and a few chairs indoors. ✉ *235 N. Guadalupe,* ☎ *505/ 982–0215. No credit cards.*

$ ✕ **Dave's Not Here.** In the running for title to Santa Fe's best burger, served with heaps of onions, mushrooms, avocado, or cheese, Dave's also has perhaps the town's best, made-from-scratch, chiles rellenos. For dessert, try the 1-pound slice of deep chocolate cake. There's a community table if you're eating solo. ✉ *1115 Hickox St.,* ☎ *505/983– 7060. Reservations not accepted. No credit cards.*

$ ✕ **Guadalupe Café.** This informal café, open from breakfast to dinner, serves quality American and New Mexican fare. Try any of a half-dozen enchiladas and tacos and a sizable sopaipilla served with honey or the restaurant's classic Adobe Pie—coffee ice cream on a chocolate cookie crust—for dessert. Breakfast is popular, undoubtedly due to the fresh raspberry pancakes (in season), and the imaginative breakfast burrito—sautéed spinach and mushrooms rolled in a flour tortilla and buried in red or green chile. If you don't show up early, be prepared to wait. Service is efficient. ✉ *422 Old Santa Fe Trail,* ☎ *505/982–9762. Reservations not accepted. D, MC, V. Closed Mon.*

$ ✕ **Plaza Café.** This large, busy restaurant has been a fixture on the Santa
★ Fe Plaza since 1918 and run with homespun care by the Razatos family since 1947. From all appearances, the decor hasn't changed much since then: red leather banquettes, black Formica tables, tile floors, vintage Santa Fe photos, a coffered tin ceiling, and a 1940s-style service counter. Standard American fare, such as hamburgers and tuna sandwiches, is served, along with New Mexican and Greek specialties including baklava. A bowl of green chile and beans will leave your tongue burning—that's the way the locals like it. You can cool it off, however, with an old-fashioned ice cream treat from the soda fountain or a towering slice of coconut cream pie. There's a good wine and beer selection. ✉ *54 Lincoln Ave.,* ☎ *505/982–1664. Reservations not accepted. D, MC, V.*

$ ✕ **The Shed.** The lunch lines attest to the fact that this charming downtown spot, serving classic New Mexican cuisine and fabulous homemade desserts, is a favorite of Santa Feans. Housed in a rambling adobe dating from 1692, the restaurant is decorated throughout with festive folk art. Specialties include red-chile enchiladas, green-chile stew (green chile with potatoes and pork), *posole* (lime hominy, pork, chile, and garlic soup), and charbroiled "Shedburgers." The neighborly service will make you feel as if you never left home. ✉ *113½ E. Palace Ave.,* ☎ *505/982–9030. Reservations not accepted. No credit cards. Closed Sun. No dinner Mon.–Wed.*

$ ✕ **Whistling Moon Cafe.** This place is a local favorite for quality innovative Middle Eastern and other Mediterranean fare. Simple, inexpensive, and scented with unusual spices, the menu includes pasta primavera, Greek salad, Moroccan lamb sausage, a Middle Eastern sampler, and Turkish coffee. The coriander-cumin fries are irresistible, as is the homemade Greek honey cheesecake. Although the small ocher dining room with red Moroccan weavings is a touch noisy, the food and prices more than make up for it. ✉ *402 N. Guadalupe,* ☎ *505/ 983–3093. Reservations essential for 6 or more. MC, V.*

LODGING

Santa Fe has a wide selection of lodgings, from no-frills motels on Cerrillos Road to historic hotels in the heart of town to luxurious resorts in the foothills to the north. There are also many cozy bed-and-breakfasts and a number of campsites. Since Santa Fe is a popular tourist destination, hotel prices can be high. You can, however, get lower rates off-season, from November through April (excluding Thanksgiving and Christmas).

CATEGORY	COST*
$$$$	over $150
$$$	$100–$150
$$	$65–$100
$	under $65

*All prices are for a standard double room, excluding tax (5.8%), in peak season.

Hotels and Resorts

$$$$ ⊞ **Eldorado Hotel.** This is the city's largest hotel—a bit too modern for some—in the heart of downtown, not far from the Plaza. Rooms are stylishly furnished with carved Southwestern-style desks and chairs, art prints, and large upholstered club chairs, all in warm desert colors. Many rooms have terraces or kiva-style fireplaces. Baths are spacious and completely tiled. Its **Old House Restaurant**, focusing on Continental cuisine, is highly rated. There's music nightly in the bar. ⊠ 309 W. San Francisco St., 87501, ☎ 505/988–4455 or 800/955–4455, FAX 505/995–4544. 201 rooms, 18 suites, and 19 casitas (including 8 condos). 2 restaurants, bar, pool, hot tub, sauna, health club, shops, concierge, convention center, meeting rooms, valet parking. AE, D, DC, MC, V.

$$$$ ⊞ **Inn of the Anasazi.** In the heart of the historic district, this hotel is
★ one of Santa Fe's finest. Each individually designed room has a beamed ceiling, kiva-style fireplace, and handcrafted furniture. Amenities include a personal attendant who acts as a concierge, twice-daily maid service, room delivery of exercise bikes upon request, and a library with books on New Mexico and the Southwest. The excellent **Anasazi Restaurant** serves a mix of Native American and North American cowboy cuisine. ⊠ 113 Washington Ave., 87501, ☎ 505/988–3030 or 800/688–8100, FAX 505/988–3277. 59 rooms and suites. Restaurant, in-room safes, minibars, in-room VCRs. AE, D, DC, MC, V.

$$$$ ⊞ **Inn on the Alameda.** Nestled between the Santa Fe Plaza and Canyon Road is one of the city's nicest small hotels. Alameda means "tree-lined lane," befitting its pleasant riverside location. The adobe architecture and enclosed courtyards combine a relaxed New Mexico country atmosphere with the luxury and amenities of a world-class hotel. Rooms have a Southwestern color scheme and handmade armoires, headboards, and ceramic lamps and tiles that exemplify local artistry. The gourmet breakfast included with your stay is a wonder. Service is friendly. ⊠ 303 E. Alameda, 87501, ☎ 505/984–2121 or 800/289–2122, FAX 505/986–8325. 66 rooms and suites. Bar, refrigerators, 2 hot tubs, spa, exercise room, library, laundry service. AE, D, DC, MC, V.

$$$–$$$$ ⊞ **Inn of the Governors.** This hotel, just two blocks from the Plaza, with its small, intimate lobby, makes the traveler feel quickly at home. Standard rooms have a Mexican theme, with bright colors, hand-painted folk art, Southwestern fabrics, and handmade furnishings; deluxe rooms have balconies and fireplaces. The dining room offers New Mexican dishes and lighter fare, such as wood-oven pizza. ⊠ 234 Don Gaspar Ave. (at W. Alameda), 87501, ☎ 505/982–4333 or 800/234–4534 outside NM, FAX 505/989–9149. 100 rooms. Piano bar, pool, free parking. AE, D, DC, MC, V.

Santa Fe Lodging

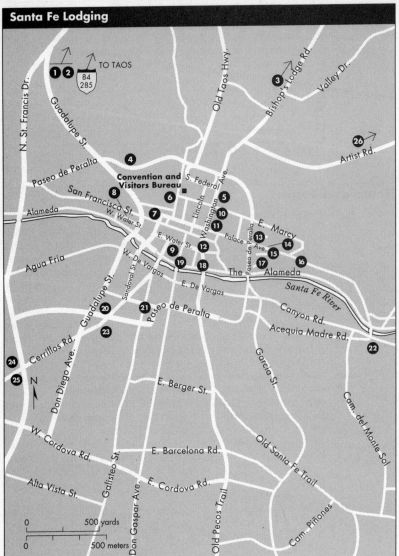

Alexander's Inn, **16**

Bishop's
Lodge, **3**

Dunshee's, **22**

Eldorado Hotel, **7**

El Rey Inn, **24**

Grant Corner
Inn, **6**

Hacienda del
Cerezo, **2**

Homewood Suites, **4**

Hotel Plaza Real, **10**

Hotel St. Francis, **9**

Hotel Santa Fe, **20**

Inn at Loretto, **18**

Inn of the
Anasazi, **11**

Inn of the Animal
Tracks, **13**

Inn of the
Governors, **19**

Inn on the
Alameda, **17**

La Fonda, **12**

La Posada de
Santa Fe, **14**

Motel 6, **25**

Preston House, **15**

Pueblo Bonito
B&B Inn, **21**

Rancho Encantado, **1**

Santa Fe Motel, **23**

Ten Thousand
Waves/Houses of
the Moon, **26**

Territorial Inn, **5**

Water Street Inn, **8**

$$–$$$$ ★ ⌂ **Bishop's Lodge.** This resort, established in 1918, offers a rare mix of relaxation and sophistication. Though only five minutes by car from the Plaza, in a lovely valley at the foot of the Sangre de Cristo Mountains, it feels much removed from the hustle and bustle of town. Behind the main building is a tiny, beautiful chapel, open for visitation, that was once the private retreat of Archbishop Lamy. The property offers a variety of outdoor activities, including horseback riding, organized trail rides (with meals) into the adjacent national forest, skeet-shooting, and trapshooting. It also runs daylong activity programs for children ages 4–12, so parents can have a vacation, too! Guest rooms and public spaces in the one- and three-story lodges have old Southwestern furnishings, such as shipping chests, tinwork from Mexico, and original Native American and Western art. The dining room offers a bountiful Sunday brunch, probably the best in Santa Fe. ⌧ *Bishop's Lodge Rd., 87504,* ☎ *505/983–6377 or 800/732–2240,* FAX *505/989–8739. 70 rooms, 18 suites. Bar, pool, hot tub, spa, 4 tennis courts, exercise room, hiking, horseback riding, fishing, airport shuttle, shuttle into town, free parking. AE, D, MC, V.*

$$–$$$$ ★ ⌂ **Rancho Encantado.** This world-class Santa Fe resort on 168 acres is an elegantly casual hideaway that has sheltered Robert Redford, Johnny Cash, Robert Plant, and the Dalai Lama. It has facilities for a range of outdoor activities. Rooms have Southwestern-style furniture, hand-made and hand-painted by local craftspeople, in addition to fine Spanish and Western antiques from the 1850s and earlier; some have fireplaces, private patios, and tiled floors; others have carpeting and refrigerators. The dining room, with a terrific view of the Jemez Mountains, serves up good Continental fare. ⌧ *NM 4; 8 mi north of Santa Fe off U.S. 84/285 near Tesuque, on NM 592 (Box 57C), 87501,* ☎ *505/982–3537 or 800/722–9339,* FAX *505/983–8269. 29 rooms, 29 villas. 2 pools, hot tub, 2 tennis courts, hiking. AE, D, DC, MC, V.*

$$$ ⌂ **Homewood Suites.** Situated five blocks north of the Plaza, this all-suite hotel offers one- and two-bedroom suites decorated in Southwest style—carved wooden furniture, desert colors, local artwork. Each suite has a separate living room, a fully equipped kitchen, two TVs, a VCR, and a sleeper sofa. A complimentary continental buffet breakfast is served daily, although there is no restaurant on the premises. The hotel provides a free grocery shopping service to guests, as well as a sundries shop with video rental. ⌧ *400 Griffin (at Paseo de Peralta), 87501,* ☎ *505/988–3000,* FAX *505/988–4700. 105 suites. Pool, 2 outdoor hot tubs, exercise room, free parking, AE, D, DC, MC, V.*

$$$ ⌂ **Hotel Plaza Real.** This handsome, brick-trimmed Territorial-style hotel, just a block from the Plaza, has large rooms decorated with Southwestern handcrafted furniture. Most have wood-burning fireplaces and patios or balconies; all are accessed from an interior brick courtyard. Continental breakfast and historic walking tours are complimentary. ⌧ *125 Washington Ave., 87501,* ☎ *505/988–4900 or 800/279–7325,* FAX *505/988–9322. 56 rooms and suites. Coffee shop, lounge, concierge, parking (fee). AE, D, DC, MC, V.*

$$$ ⌂ **Hotel Santa Fe.** Controlling interest in this Pueblo-style three-story hotel is owned by the Picurís Pueblo, smallest of the eight northern Pueblo tribes. Rooms and suites are decorated in traditional Southwestern style, with locally handmade furniture and Pueblo paintings (*Picurís* means "those who paint"), many by well-known artist Gerald Nailor. All suites have microwave ovens. A continental breakfast is served in the café. The hotel gift shop, the only tribal-owned store in Santa Fe, has lower prices than many nearby retail stores. ⌧ *1501 Paseo de Peralta, 87505,* ☎ *505/982–1200 or 800/825–9876 outside NM,* FAX *505/983–0785. 40 rooms, 91 suites. Café, pool, hot tub. AE, D, DC, MC, V.*

$$$ 🏨 **Hotel St. Francis.** Listed in the National Register of Historic Places,
★ this three-story building, constructed in 1920, has walkways lined
with turn-of-the-century lampposts. In addition to a prime location—
a block southwest of the Plaza—the hotel offers small, simple rooms
with high ceilings, casement windows, brass-and-iron beds, marble and
cherry antiques, and original artwork. A carved wooden angel floats
on the wall above each bed. Afternoon tea, with scones and finger sand-
wiches, is served daily in the huge lobby, which rises 50 ft from a floor
of blood-red tiles. The St. Francis Club restaurant offers an eclectic menu
in an English hunting room setting. The hotel bar is one of the only
places in town that serves food until midnight. ⊠ *210 Don Gaspar
Ave., 87501, ☎ 505/983–5700 or 800/529–5700 outside NM,* FAX *505/
989–7690. 82 rooms. Restaurant, bar, meeting rooms, free parking.
AE, D, DC, MC, V.*

$$$ 🏨 **Inn at Loretto.** Entirely refurbished in 1996 by the new owners, Nobel
House Hotels, this landmark establishment next to the Loretto Chapel
was modeled after a multistory Pueblo structure. Rooms are decorated
in Santa Fe–style decor, and there is a restaurant, Cafe Loretto, and a
lobby bar. ⊠ *211 Old Santa Fe Trail, 87501, ☎ 505/989–5531 or 800/
528–1234 outside NM,* FAX *505/989–7968. 143 rooms. Restaurant,
lounge, pool, beauty salon, shops. AE, D, DC, MC, V.*

$$$ 🏨 **La Fonda.** When Santa Fe was established in 1610, official records
★ show that the town already had an adobe fonda to accommodate trav-
elers. Two centuries later, the original hotel was still welcoming guests—
traders, trappers, mountain men, soldiers, and politicians. The present
structure, built in 1922 and enlarged many times since, is the only lodg-
ing directly on the Plaza and perhaps the only hotel in the world that
can boast having had both Kit Carson and John F. Kennedy as guests.
Its historic tiled lobby, with its welcoming leather chairs, is decorated
with antiques and classic Native American art. Each room is unique,
with hand-decorated wooden furniture, wrought-iron light fixtures,
beamed ceilings, and motifs painted by local artists; some of the suites
have fireplaces. On weekends there's live entertainment in the bar, a
favorite watering hole for centuries. ⊠ *100 E. San Francisco St.,
87501, ☎ 505/982–5511 or 800/523–5002 outside NM,* FAX *505/988–
2952. 132 rooms, 21 suites (14 new suites scheduled for 1998). Restau-
rant, bar, pool, 2 hot tubs, meeting rooms, parking (fee). AE, D, DC,
MC, V.*

$$$ 🏨 **La Posada de Santa Fe.** This relaxed, pleasant hotel only 2 blocks
from the Plaza is on 6 acres of beautifully landscaped gardens and lawns
shaded by giant elms, fruit trees, and cottonwoods. Some rooms have
fireplaces, beamed ceilings, and Native American rugs. The Staab
House Restaurant serves up a great Sunday brunch and has a cozy, romantic bar. ⊠ *330 E. Palace Ave., 87501, ☎ 505/986–0000 or 800/
727–5276 outside NM,* FAX *505/982–6850. 119 rooms and suites.
Restaurant, bar, pool, health club privileges available, free parking. AE,
D, DC, MC, V.*

$$$ 🏨 **Ten Thousand Waves/Houses of the Moon.** Santa Fe style gives way
★ to Japanese style in the moonlit mountains 4 mi above town at this
health spa and miniresort. You can choose from six small houses,
which are on a hillside and reached by a path through piñons. All have
brick floors, marble fireplaces, and adobe-color walls, plus Japanese
art, fine woodwork, and futon beds; two come with full kitchens. If
you are staying overnight, you get 10% off all services at the spa—the
perfect place to unwind after a day's cavorting. The facility offers pri-
vate and communal indoor and outdoor hot tubs, therapeutic massages,
facials, and herbal wraps. Towels, kimonos, soaps, shampoos, sandals,
and lockers are provided. Hot teas, juices, and pastries are available,
too. Tubs run from $13 per session to $25; massage and spa treatments

cost from $35 to $120, depending on the treatment. ⊠ *4 mi from the Plaza on road to Santa Fe Ski Basin (Box 10200), 87504, ☎ 505/982–9304, FAX 505/989–5077. 1 house sleeps 5, 4 houses sleep 4, 3 houses sleep 2. Outdoor hot tubs, spa. D, MC, V.*

$–$$$ ⊞ **El Rey Inn.** Founded in 1936, this is as nice a motel as you'll find anywhere. The well-maintained, whitewashed buildings with tile trim are surrounded by large trees, lawns, and an abundance of flowers from the motel's own greenhouses. Rooms are decorated in Southwest, Spanish Colonial, and Victorian style. Some have kitchenettes and fireplaces. The largest suite, with seven rooms, sleeps eight and has antique furniture, a full kitchen, a breakfast nook, and two patios. A Continental breakfast is included in the price of every room. ⊠ *1862 Cerrillos Rd., 87501, ☎ 505/982–1931 or 800/521–1349, FAX 505/989–9249. 79 rooms, 8 suites. Kitchenettes, pool, 2 hot tubs, sauna, playground, coin laundry. AE, DC, MC, V.*

$–$$ ⊞ **Santa Fe Motel.** Proximity is a prime asset of this property—an unusually nice upgrade of an older standard motel—which is walking distance from Santa Fe's Plaza. Rooms are decorated in contemporary Southwestern style. Casitas are also available. ⊠ *510 Cerrillos Rd., 87501, ☎ 505/982–1039 or 800/999–1039, FAX 505/986–1275. 13 rooms, 8 casitas, 2-story guest house sleeps 6. Kitchenettes. AE, MC, V.*

$ ⊞ **Motel 6.** This chain motel is the same from coast to coast—reliably clean, well maintained, and unexceptional. Santa Fe's offers an outdoor pool, free HBO and ESPN, and free local calls. Kids under 17 stay free with their parents. ⊠ *3007 Cerrillos Rd., 87505, ☎ 505/473–1380, FAX 505/473–7784. 104 rooms. Pool. AE, MC, V.*

Bed-and-Breakfasts

$$$$ ⊞ **Hacienda del Cerezo.** This beautiful, superbly detailed, very high-
★ end new inn rests on a splendidly isolated spot (the owners constructed the road) 25 minutes north of downtown Santa Fe. Each of the 10 rooms has its own theme (sun, corn, fans), subtly carried out in prints, ornaments, engravings on the beams of the vi̶.........chings in the glass shower doors. Each has a ki̶...........d, a g.....ous sitting area, a kiva fireplace, an enclosed p........a fine view of the mountains. The bathrooms are sumptuo.....ate includes three meals prepared by a master chef; dinner is a five-course candlelighted affair in the high-ceilinged great room or in the courtyard, looking out onto the vanishing-edge pool and the desert beyond. Staying here is like being the houseguest of a gracious family; the hacienda's remoteness makes it an ideal spot to get far, far away from it all, and the high tariff assures exclusivity. ⊠ *100 Camino del Cerezo, 87501, ☎ 505/982–8000 or 888/982–8001, FAX 505/983–7162. 10 rooms. In-room VCRs, pool, outdoor hot tub, tennis court, hiking, horseback riding.*

$$$ ⊞ **Water Street Inn.** The large rooms in this restored adobe five min-
★ utes from the Plaza are uniquely decorated with reed shutters, pine antique beds, hand-stenciled paintings, and a blend of cowboy, Hispanic, and Native American art and artifacts. Most have fireplaces, all have private baths, cable TV, phones, and voice mail. Breakfast—served in your room around a handsome dining table or out on a second-story patio overlooking downtown—consists of oven-fresh pastries, cereal, fruit, juice, and coffee. Afternoon wine and snacks are served in the living room. ⊠ *427 W. Water St., 87501, ☎ 505/984–1193 or 800/646–6752. 11 rooms. Free parking. AE, MC, V.*

$$–$$$ ⊞ **Territorial Inn.** Creature comforts are a high priority in this elegant 1890s brick structure, set back off a busy downtown street two blocks from the Plaza. The decor is Victorian throughout; among the well-maintained rooms, No. 9 has a canopied bed and a fireplace. A hot

tub is also available, with robes provided. In addition to Continental breakfast, the inn offers afternoon treats and brandy in the evening. ✉ *215 Washington Ave., 87501,* ☎ *505/989–7737,* 𝔽𝔸𝕏 *505/986–9212. 10 rooms, 8 with bath, 2 with shared bath. Free parking. AE, DC, MC, V.*

$$ ▣ **Alexander's Inn.** This 1903 two-story, Craftsman-style house in the
★ lovely Eastside residential area, only a few blocks from the Plaza and Canyon Road, exudes the charm of an old country inn. Rooms have American country–style wooden furnishings and flower arrangements. There are also two two-story cottages ideal for bigger groups and one adobe-style house, the Casa de Flores, which has a lovely Mexican-tiled kitchen. In summer a breakfast of homemade granola, bread, muffins, yogurt, fresh fruits, juice, and coffee is served on the deck and in winter in the dining room. ✉ *529 E. Palace Ave., 87501,* ☎ *505/ 986–1431. 5 rooms, 3 with bath; 4 cottages. Hot tub, health club privileges, mountain bikes. MC, V.*

$$ ▣ **Dunshee's.** This pretty B&B, in the quiet Eastside area just a mile from the Plaza, is so romantic that its patio has been used for weddings. You have two options: One is a spacious suite in the restored adobe home of artist Susan Dunshee, the proprietor; the other, more expensive choice, which is popular with families, is an adobe casita. The suite has a cozy living room, a bedroom with a queen bed, kiva-style fireplaces, and viga ceilings, and it is decorated with antiques and works by local artists. The casita has two bedrooms, a living room, a patio, a completely equipped and stocked kitchen, and a kiva-style fireplace, and it is adorned with decorative linens and folk art. All in all, this place is a good buy for Santa Fe. ✉ *986 Acequia Madre, 87501,* ☎ *505/982–0988. 1 suite, 1 small house. MC, V.*

$$ ▣ **Grant Corner Inn.** This long-standing B&B is downtown, but the small garden and portal around it make it feel private. Antique Spanish and American country furnishings share space with potted greens and knickknacks. Room accents include tile stoves, old-fashioned fixtures, quilts, and Native American blankets. The ample breakfast, which is available to the public on a pay basis, includes home-baked breads and pastries, jellies, and blue-corn waffles, a unique local treat. ✉ *122 Grant Ave., 87501,* ☎ *505/983–6678,* 𝔽𝔸𝕏 *505/983–1526. 7 rooms, 2 share bath, 1 minisuite, 2 rooms in nearby hacienda. MC, V.*

$$ ▣ **Inn of the Animal Tracks.** Three blocks east of the Plaza is this restored Pueblo-style home, with beamed ceilings, hardwood floors, handcrafted furniture, and fireplaces. Each guest room is decorated with an animal theme, such as Soaring Eagle or Gentle Deer. Be prepared for cuteness: The Whimsical Rabbit Room, for instance, is filled with stuffed and terra-cotta rabbits, rabbit books, rabbit drawings, and bunny-rabbit slippers tucked under the bed. Also note that this room opens directly onto the kitchen, where the cook arrives at 6 AM. A full breakfast and afternoon snack are served. In summer the backyard is delightful, and in-room air conditioning—rarely needed in Santa Fe—provides respite on hot days. ✉ *707 Paseo de Peralta, 87504,* ☎ *505/988–1546. 5 rooms. AE, D, MC, V.*

$$ ▣ **Preston House.** This 1886 Queen Anne house, the only one of its kind in the city, is tucked away in a quiet garden setting not far from the Plaza. Its pleasant rooms highlight period furnishings, Edwardian fireplaces, and stained-glass windows. Fruit bowls and fresh-cut flowers add to the appeal. ✉ *106 Faithway St., 87501,* ☎ 𝔽𝔸𝕏 *505/982– 3465. 15 rooms, 13 with bath. AE, MC, V.*

$$ ▣ **Pueblo Bonito B&B Inn.** Rooms in this charming but aging adobe compound, built in 1873, feature handmade and hand-painted furnishings, Navajo weavings, sandpaintings and pottery, locally carved santos, and Western art. All have fireplaces, and many have kitchens. A filling breakfast is served in the main dining room. ✉ *138 W. Man-*

hattan Ave., 87501, ☎ 505/984–8001 or 800/461–4599, FAX 505/984–3155. 11 rooms, 7 suites. Coin laundry. MC, V.

Campgrounds

With its wide open spaces, decent roads, and knock-'em-dead scenery, northern New Mexico draws camping enthusiasts and RV road warriors like hummingbirds to flowers. The Santa Fe National Forest is right in the city's backyard and includes the Dome Wilderness (5,200 acres in the volcanically formed Jemez Mountains) and the Pecos Wilderness (223,333 acres of high mountains, forests, and meadows at the southern end of the Rocky Mountain chain). Public campsites are open from May through October.

For specifics, call the **Santa Fe National Forest Office** (✉ 1220 S. St. Francis Dr., Box 1689, 87504, ☎ 505/988–6940). Some private campground operators provide literature at the **La Bajada Welcome Center** (✉ La Bajada Hill, 13 mi southwest of Santa Fe on I–25, ☎ 505/471–5242).

$ ⛺ **Babbitt's Los Campos RV Resort.** The only full-service RV park within the city limits, Los Campos even has a swimming pool. Tucked behind a car dealership on one side, it offers open vistas on the other: poplars and Russian olive trees, a dry riverbed, and mountains rising in the background. ✉ 3574 Cerrillos Rd., 87505, ☎ 505/473–1949. 94 RV sites. Rest rooms, showers, LP gas, pool, picnic tables.

$ ⛺ **Rancheros de Santa Fe Campground.** This beautiful camping park is on a hill in the midst of a piñon forest. ✉ On I–25N, Old Las Vegas Hwy., 87505 (exit 290 on the Las Vegas Hwy., 10½ mi from the Santa Fe Plaza), ☎ 505/466–3482. 95 RV sites, 37 tent sites. Rest rooms, hot showers, LP gas, grocery, ice, pool, coin laundry.

$ ⛺ **Santa Fe KOA.** In the foothills of the Sangre de Cristo Mountains, 20 minutes southeast of Santa Fe, this large campground is covered with piñons, cedars, and junipers. ✉ Old Las Vegas Hwy. (NM 3), Box 95-A, 87505, ☎ 505/466–1419. 44 RV sites, 26 tent sites, 10 cabins. Rest rooms, hot showers, LP gas, grocery, recreation room, coin laundry.

$ ⛺ **Tesuque Pueblo RV Campground.** This campground, operated by the Tesuque Pueblo, is on an open hill with a few cedar trees dotting the landscape; off to the west is the Tesuque River. ✉ Box 360-H, Tesuque 87501 (10 mi north of Santa Fe; take the St. Francis exit off I–25), ☎ 505/455–2661. 68 RV sites, 26 tent sites. Rest rooms, showers, drinking water, security gate, coin laundry.

NIGHTLIFE AND THE ARTS

Santa Fe is perhaps America's most cultured small city. Year-round, the city offers a wide slate of cultural activities—from gallery openings and poetry readings to plays and dance concerts to live music in a historic bar. Known for its opera and its chamber music festival, its galleries and museums, and its large population of artists, Santa Fe has something artistic at every turn. Check the entertainment listings in Santa Fe's daily newspaper, the *New Mexican,* or the weekly *Santa Fe Reporter* for special performances and events. Activities peak in the summer.

The Arts

Music

One of the world's most renowned chamber music series, the **Santa Fe Chamber Music Festival** (✉ Museum of New Mexico in the Palace of the Governors, 113 Lincoln Ave., 87501, ☎ 505/983–2075, FAX 505/

986–0251) is held in July and August at the beautiful St. Francis Auditorium.

Artistically and visually the city's crowning glory, the famed **Santa Fe Opera** (☎ 505/986–5900, FAX 505/986–5999) is housed in a strikingly modern structure—a spectacular, 1,173-seat, indoor-outdoor amphitheater with excellent acoustics and sight lines. Carved into the natural curves of a hillside 7 mi north of the city on Highway 84-285, the opera overlooks a vast panorama of mountains, mesas, and sky. Add some of the most acclaimed singers, directors, conductors, musicians, designers, and composers from Europe and the United States, and you begin to understand the excitement that builds every June. Founded in 1956 by John Crosby, who remains its general director, the company offers five works in repertory each summer—a blend of seasoned classics, neglected masterpieces, and innovative world premieres. Many shows sell out far in advance, but inexpensive standing-room tickets are often available on short notice.

The **Santa Fe Symphony** (✉ Box 9692, 87504, ☎ 505/983–3530, FAX 505/982–3888) performs seven concerts each season (September through May) to sold-out audiences at Sweeney Center (✉ 201 W. Marcy St.).

Orchestral and chamber concerts are given at varying venues by the **Santa Fe Pro Musica** (✉ Box 2091, 87504, ☎ 505/988–4640) from September through May. Baroque and classical compositions are the normal fare; the annual Christmas and Holy Week performances are highlights.

Santa Fe Summerscene (☎ 505/438–8834) offers a series of free concerts (rhythm and blues, light opera, jazz, Cajun, salsa, folk, and bluegrass), and dance performances (modern, folk) on the Santa Fe Plaza every Tuesday and Thursday from mid-June through August at noon and 6 PM.

Theater

The beautiful **Greer Garson Theater** (✉ College of Santa Fe, St. Michael's Dr., ☎ 505/473–6511), stages at least four productions of comedies, dramas, and musicals from October through May.

The well-regarded **Santa Fe Community Theater** (✉ 142 East de Vargas, ☎ 505/988–4262) has been presenting an adventurous mix of avant-garde pieces, classical drama, melodrama, and musical comedy since it was founded in 1922. The **Children's Theater** (☎ 505/984–3055) also performs here year-round; call for times and dates.

Santa Fe Stages (☎ 505/982–6683), an international theater festival, is held from June through August at the Greer Garson Theater (☞ *above*) and includes dance performances and classical and contemporary theater productions.

On Friday, Saturday, and Sunday nights during July and August, **Shakespeare in Santa Fe** (☎ 505/982–2910) presents free performances of the Bard's finest in the courtyard of the John Gaw Meem Library at St. John's College (✉ 1160 Camino Cruz Blanca). The music begins at 6, the show at 7. Bring a picnic basket or buy food at the concession stand. Seating is limited to 350, so it's best to get tickets in advance.

Nightlife

Most of the leading hotels in Santa Fe provide some type of live entertainment nightly. There are also a handful of bars that offer a modest selection of entertainment, from lively dancing at a frontier saloon to quiet cocktails beside the flickering embers of a piñon fire.

The **Catamount Bar** (⊠ 125 E. Water St., ☎ 505/988–722) is popular with the post-college set; there's live music on weekends and some weeknights. **Club Alegria** (⊠ NM 6, Agua Fria Rd., near Siler, ☎ 505/471–2324) is the venue for touring bands—mostly rock, blues, and alternative—and Friday night salsa dance parties. The **Dragon Room** (⊠ 406 Old Santa Fe Trail, ☎ 505/983–7712) at the Pink Adobe restaurant has been the place to see and be seen in Santa Fe for decades; flamenco and other similar, light musical fare entertains the packed bar.

The **Santa Fe Music Hall** (⊠ 100 N. Guadalupe, ☎ 505/983–3311 or 800/409–3311) is the venue for a variety of concerts—flamenco, jazz, rock, blues—featuring both local and nationally known performers. It also offers occasional dinner-theater performances.

Evangelo's (⊠ 200 W. San Francisco St., ☎ 505/982–9014) has pool tables in a smoky basement, 200 types of imported beer, and live music on many weekends. **El Farol** (⊠ 808 Canyon Rd., ☎ 505/983–9912) is where locals like to hang out and listen to live music nightly; it's packed on weekend nights in summer. **Rodeo Nites** (⊠ 2911 Cerrillos Rd., ☎ 505/473–4138) attracts a country-western crowd.

OUTDOOR ACTIVITIES AND SPORTS

On a shelf between the southernmost range of the Rocky Mountains, the Sangre de Cristos, and the high desert of north-central New Mexico, Santa Fe is a great place for outdoor activities. Head to the mountains for fishing, camping, and skiing, to the nearby Rio Grande for kayaking and rafting, and almost anywhere in the area for bird-watching and biking.

Participant Sports

Bicycling
Santa Fe is an ideal size for biking. A suggested map of bike trips can be picked up at the **Convention and Visitors Bureau** (⊠ 201 W. Marcy St., ☎ 505/984–6760). Rentals are available at **Palace Bike Rentals** (⊠ 409 E. Palace Ave., ☎ 505/986–0455).

Bird-Watching
At the very end of Upper Canyon Road, alongside the Santa Fe River, is the **Randall Davey Audubon Center**—a 135-acre nature sanctuary that harbors a surprisingly diverse number of bird species and other wild animals. The site was once the home and studio of Randall Davey, one of the most prolific early Santa Fe artists. The center offers educational programs and free on-site bird walks on weekends, June–August. The Davey House can also be visited one afternoon a week, June–August (the day varies from year to year; call for information). ⊠ *Upper Canyon Rd.,* ☎ *505/983–4609.* ▣ *Free.* ☉ *Daily 9–5 for self-guided tours.*

Golf
Cochiti Lake Golf Course (⊠ 5200 Cochiti Hwy., Cochiti Lake, ☎ 505/465–2230), set against a stunning backdrop of steep canyons and red-rock mesas, is a 45-minute drive southwest of the city. It has been rated among the top 25 public golf courses in the country.

Pendaries Village Golf (☎ 505/425–6018), near Las Vegas, is almost two hours from Santa Fe, but its setting beneath the Sangre de Cristo peaks is impressive. It features an 18-hole course, a putting green, a snack bar, and a lodge with a restaurant.

Santa Fe Country Club (⊠ Airport Rd., ☎ 505/471–0601), a close-to-town, tree-shaded, semiprivate course, has a driving range, putting range, and pro shop, club and electric-cart rentals, and private lessons by appointment.

Horseback Riding

New Mexico's rugged countryside has been the scene of many Hollywood Westerns, including, in recent years, *Wyatt Earp*. Whether you want to ride the range that Kevin Costner and Gregory Peck rode or just go out and feel tall in the saddle, you can—year-round, depending on weather conditions. Rentals average about $20 an hour.

Bishop's Lodge (⊠ Bishop's Lodge Rd., ☎ 505/983–6377) provides rides and guides April–November.

Galarosa Stable (⊠ Galisteo, ☎ 505/983–6565 or 800/338–6877) provides rentals by the half day or full day south of Santa Fe in the panoramic Galisteo Basin.

Vientos Encantados (⊠ Round Barn Stables, Ojo Caliente, one hour north of Santa Fe on U.S. 84/285, ☎ 505/583–2233) offers trail rides and pack trips near the Ojo Caliente mineral springs. After a long ride, a hot soak may be in order!

Jogging

With the city's 7,000-ft altitude, newcomers to Santa Fe may feel as if they're running in the Chilean Andes. Once they adjust, however, they'll find that it's a great place to run. There's a jogging path along the Santa Fe River, parallel to Alameda, and another at Fort Marcy on Washington Avenue.

Every Wednesday evening, the **Santa Fe Striders** (☎ 505/989–1819) start a run from the Plaza. The **Santa Fe Runaround,** a 10-km race held in early June, begins and ends at the Plaza. The **Women's Five-Kilometer Run** is held in early August. Runners turn out in droves on Labor Day for the most popular run of all, the annual **Old Santa Fe Trail Run.** For information about both races contact the Santa Fe Convention and Visitors Bureau (☞ Santa Fe A to Z, *below*).

River Rafting

White-water rafting is a wet, walloping thrill that suits the rocky, bone-thumping country that gave birth to it. Of course, if you prefer something less invigorating than the heart-stopping, hair-raising Class V rapids near Taos, there are more leisurely sightseeing possibilities on a river trip along the Rio Chama or the Rio Grande's White Rock Canyon. The season generally extends from April through September.

For a list of outfitters who guide trips on the Rio Grande and the Rio Chama, write the **Bureau of Land Management, Taos Resource Area Office** (⊠ 224 Cruz Alta Rd., Taos 87571, ☎ 505/758–8851).

Kokopelli Rafting Adventures (⊠ 541 Cordova Rd., ☎ 505/983–3734 or 800/879–9035) specializes in trips through the relatively mellow White Rock Canyon.

Los Rios River Runners (⊠ Taos, ☎ 505/776–8854 or 800/544–1181, FAX 505/776–1842) provides a variety of white-water adventures, including a run through the famous 17-mi Taos Box of the Rio Grande. In winter, cross-country skiing trips are offered.

New Wave Rafting Company (⊠ 103 E. Water St., Suite F, ☎ 505/984–1444 or 800/984–1444) features full-day, half-day, and overnight river trips, with daily departures from Santa Fe.

Santa Fe Rafting Company and Outfitters (⊠ 1000 Cerrillos Rd., ☎ 505/988–4914 or 800/467–7238) customizes rafting tours. Tell them what you want—they'll do it.

Skiing

The **Santa Fe Ski Area,** usually open from Thanksgiving to Easter, is an excellent, relatively small operation that gets an average of 250 inches of snow a year and is renowned for its sunshine. One of America's highest ski areas—its summit is just over 12,000 ft—it has a variety of terrain and seems bigger than its 1,650 ft of vertical rise and 500 acres. It has some great powder stashes, tough bump runs, and many wide, gentle cruising runs. The 40-some trails are ranked 20% beginner, 40% intermediate, and 40% advanced. The kids' center, Chipmunk Corner, provides day care for infants and supervised skiing for children. Rentals, a surprisingly good cafeteria, a ski shop, and Totemoff's bar are other amenities. For information call the Santa Fe Ski Area (☎ 505/982–4429) or Santa Fe Central Reservations (☎ 505/983–8200 or 800/776–7669 outside New Mexico). For snow-condition information call 505/983–9155.

For cross-country skiing conditions around Santa Fe, contact the **Santa Fe National Forest Office** (☎ 505/988–6940).

Tennis

Santa Fe has 27 public tennis courts available on a first-come, first-served basis, including four asphalt courts at **Alto Park** (⊠ 1035½ Alto St.), four concrete courts at **Herb Martínez/La Resolana Park** (⊠ Camino Carlos Rey), three asphalt courts at **Ortíz Park** (⊠ Camino de las Crucitas), and two asphalt courts at **Fort Marcy Complex** (⊠ Prince and Kearny Aves.). For additional public facilities, call the **City Parks Division** (☎ 505/473–7236). Among the major private tennis facilities, including indoor, outdoor, and lighted courts, are **Club at El Gancho** (⊠ Old Las Vegas Hwy., ☎ 505/988–5000), **Sangre De Cristo Racquet Club** (⊠ 1755 Camino Corrales, ☎ 505/983–7978), **Santa Fe Country Club** (⊠ Airport Rd., ☎ 505/471–3378), and **Shellaberger Tennis Center** (⊠ St. Michaels Dr., ☎ 505/473–6144), which is on the campus of the College of Santa Fe and offers lessons and a pro shop.

Windsurfing

Strong summer breezes and a proximity to numerous lakes have made northern New Mexico a popular windsurfing spot, although the water can be quite chilly and the winds unpredictable. Early morning is the best time to go, as there are often thunderstorms in the afternoon. Devoted regulars head to **Abiquiú Lake,** 40 mi northwest of Santa Fe, via U.S. 84/285 (⊠ Box 290, Abiquiú, ☎ 505/685–4371); **Cochiti Lake** (⊠ Off U.S. 85 between Los Alamos and Santa Fe, Peña Blanca, ☎ 505/242–8302); and **Storrie Lake** (⊠ 1 hr east of Santa Fe, via I–25, Las Vegas, ☎ 505/425–9231). Most of these lakes have no on-site rental facilities, but you can rent equipment from **Santa Fe Windsurfing** (⊠ 1086 Siler Rd., ☎ 505/473–7900).

Spectator Sports

Horse Racing

Horse racing at the **Downs of Santa Fe** (⊠ Off I–25W service road, just 6 minutes southwest of town, ☎ 505/471–3311), a beautiful 1-mi track facing the Sangre de Cristo Mountains, attracts nearly a quarter-million spectators each year. The season usually runs from mid-June through Labor Day. Races are held Thursday–Sunday and on holidays, with post time at 1 PM. The $100,000 Santa Fe Futurity for two-year-olds is New Mexico's richest Thoroughbred purse. There's pari-mutuel betting, of course, and a Jockey Club, a Turf Club, ultramodern grandstands, and plenty of parking.

SHOPPING

Santa Fe has been a trading post for a long, long time. A thousand years ago, the great pueblos of the Anasazi civilizations were strategically located between the buffalo-hunting tribes of the Great Plains and the Native Americans of Mexico. Native Americans in New Mexico traded turquoise, which was thought to have magical properties, and other local valuables with Native Americans from Mexico for metals, shells, parrots, and other exotic items. After the arrival of the Spanish during the early 1600s and the subsequent development of the West in the early 1800s, Santa Fe became the place to exchange silver from Mexico and natural resources from New Mexico—including hides, fur, and foodstuffs—for manufactured goods, whiskey, and greenbacks from the United States. With the building of the railroad in 1880, all kinds of goods came and went through Santa Fe.

The trading legacy remains, but now downtown Santa Fe caters almost exclusively to tourists. Today's major commodity is the Santa Fe style, which is as distinctive as the city's architecture. The style is a mix of simple designs and materials and ethnic influences ranging from Native American to Hispanic to worldwide tribal cultures. Although no longer as popular as it was a few years ago, it will always have its admirers. There was a time, however, when owing to its popularity, it became a bit of a cliché; a locally produced poster, titled "Another Victim of Santa Fe Style," shows a Santa Fean lying faceup on a Native American rug, surrounded by howling-coyote carvings, a kiva fireplace, a beamed ceiling, a sun-bleached cattle skull, and a string of red chile peppers.

Santa Fe may seem like one big shopping mall, but a few shopping areas stand out. Canyon Road is the most famous and most expensive. The downtown district offers a mix of shops, galleries, and restaurants within a five-block radius of the Plaza. The Guadalupe neighborhood, on the southwest perimeter of town, is a great place to window-shop and relax at a sidewalk café.

Art Galleries

Santa Fe's sparkling light, ancient cultures, and evocative landscape of mountains and mesas have long hypnotized artists. "The world is wide here," said Georgia O'Keeffe, in her usual get-right-to-the-point manner. In this century, Santa Fe has emerged as a leading international center of contemporary and traditional Native American art and Western art.

But even before the arrival of such artists as Ernest Blumenschein and John Sloan during the early 20th century, an earlier form of art was popular in northern New Mexico. Bultos and retablos, both commonly known as santos, remain a unique, indigenous, little-heralded art form. These devotional images have been part of everyday life in Mexico and the Southwest since the founding of Christianity in the New World. Today they have captured the attention of serious art collectors and leading museums. No attempt has been made to mass-produce them and no two are exactly alike. Tinwork, straw inlay, furniture-making and weaving are yet other arts refined here by Hispanic artists over the centuries.

Santa Fe has some 150 art galleries (and no one knows how many painters). The following selection represents a good cross section; the Santa Fe Convention and Visitors Bureau (☞ Santa Fe A to Z, *below*) has a more extensive listing. *The Wingspread Collectors Guide to*

Santa Fe Shopping

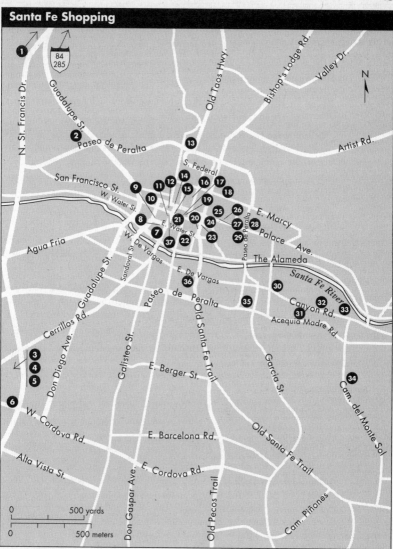

Andrew Smith Gallery, **12**

Arrowsmith's, **36**

Artesanos, **7**

Bellas Artes, **33**

Canyon Road Fine Art, **32**

Charlotte Jackson Fine Art, **18**

Cline LewAllen Gallery, **14**

Collected Works Book Store, **10**

Cristof's, **37**

Dewey Galleries, **23**

Dewey & Sons Trading Co., **20**

Edith Lambert Galleries, **21**

Foreign Traders, **8**

Gerald Peters Gallery, **34**

Jackalope, **3**

Jane Smith, **31**

Joshua Baer & Co., **25**

Kent Galleries, **17**

Montecristi Custom Hat Works, **11**

Montez Gallery, **26**

Morning Star Gallery, **30**

Nedra Matteucci's Fenn Galleries, **35**

New Millenium Fine Art, **9**

Nicholas Potter, **29**

Niman Fine Arts, **16**

Origins, **15**

Packard's Indian Trading Co., **24**

Prairie Edge, **22**

The Rainbow Man, **27**

Santa Fe Boot Company, **6**

Santa Fe Western Mercantile, **4**

Trade Roots Collection, **13**

Trader Jack's Flea Market, **1**

Western Warehouse, **2, 5**

William R. Talbot Fine Art, **19**

Wyeth Hurd Gallery, **28**

Santa Fe and Taos (☞ Books and Videos *in* Chapter 6) is a good bet for those who are seriously interested in buying art in Santa Fe.

Andrew Smith Gallery (☒ 203 W. San Francisco, ☎ 505/984–1234, FAX 505/983–2428) is a significant photo gallery dealing in works by Edward S. Curtis and other 19th-century photographers of the American West; major figures of the 20th century, including Ansel Adams, Eliot Porter, and Alfred Stieglitz; and lesser-known but excellent regional artists including Barbara Van Cleve.

Bellas Artes (☒ 653 Canyon Rd., ☎ 505/983–2745), a landmark gallery and sculpture garden, carries a wide selection of contemporary arts, pre-Columbian and African works, ceramics, and textiles.

Canyon Road Fine Art (☒ 621 Canyon Rd., ☎ 505/988–9511, FAX 505/982–4762) specializes in works by early Santa Fe artists and selected contemporary impressionist painters.

Charlotte Jackson Fine Art (☒ 123 E. Marcy St., ☎ 505/989–8688, FAX 505/989–9898) focuses on contemporary art dealing with light and space, including work by Joe Barnes, Anne Cooper, James Howell, and Roy Thurston.

Cline LewAllen Gallery (☒ 129 W. Palace Ave., ☎ 505/988–8997, FAX 505/989–8702) is a leading center for contemporary arts by internationally known and up-and-coming artists from the Southwest.

Dewey Galleries (☒ 76 E. San Francisco St., ☎ 505/982–8632, FAX 505/983–2625), housed in the historic Spiegelberg Building on the south side of the Plaza, has a great collection of historic Navajo textiles and jewelry, and paintings and sculpture by contemporary Native American artists.

Edith Lambert Galleries (☒ 300 Galisteo, ☎ 505/984–2783 or 800/594–9667, FAX 505/983–4494) represents some of the nation's most promising artists. In addition, groundbreaking special exhibits by renowned metalsmiths, fiber artists, and book artists are held annually.

Gerald Peters Gallery (☒ 439 Camino del Monte Sol, ☎ 505/988–8961, FAX 505/983–2481) is Santa Fe's leading gallery of prominent 19th- and 20th-century classic American and European art. It has works by Charles M. Russell, Albert Bierdstadt, the Taos Society, the New Mexico Modernists, and Georgia O'Keeffe.

Kent Galleries (☒ 130 Lincoln Ave., ☎ 505/988–1001, FAX 505/988–7583) carries a terrific selection of fine crafts—ceramics, glass, furniture, jewelry, and tapestry—as well as fine arts by regionally and nationally acclaimed artisans.

Nedra Matteucci's Fenn Galleries (☒ 1075 Paseo de Peralta, ☎ 505/982–4631, FAX 505/984–0199) has specialized in 19th- and 20th-century American art for more than 25 years. The gallery features works by California regionalists, the early Taos and Santa Fe schools, and masters of American Impressionism and Modernism. Spanish Colonial furniture, Indian antiquities, and a fantastic sculpture garden, complete with a Vietnamese potbellied pig, are other draws of this highly respected institution.

New Millennium Fine Art (☒ 217 W. Water St., ☎ 505/983–2002) is a huge street-level showroom filled with contemporary Native American paintings and antique jewelry, signed posters and prints, and an excellent collection of photographs of Southwestern and Native American subjects.

Niman Fine Arts (✉ 125 Lincoln Ave., ☎ 505/988–5091, ℻ 505/988–1650) focuses on the prolific and outstanding work of two contemporary Native American artists—Hopi painter Dan Namingha and the late Apache sculptor Allan Houser.

William R. Talbot Fine Art (✉ 129 W. San Francisco St., ☎ 505/982–1559) features antique maps of the Americas and natural-history paintings.

Wyeth Hurd Gallery (✉ 301 E. Palace Ave., ☎ 505/989–8380, ℻ 505/820–7122) carries the work of America's most prolific, multigenerational arts family, which includes N. C. Wyeth (who died in 1945), his children Andrew and Henriette Wyeth, Henriette's husband Peter Hurd, Andrew's son Jamie Wyeth, and Henriette and Peter's grandson Peter de la Fuente.

Specialty Stores

Books

Santa Fe is a literary center. To demonstrate, there are more than 20 used bookstores in town, as well as a handful of high-quality new bookshops.

Collected Works Book Store (✉ 208B W. San Francisco St., ☎ 505/988–4226, ℻ 505/988–2208), is a popular stop for art and travel books, Southwestern titles, and paperbacks.

Nicholas Potter (✉ 203 E. Palace, ☎ 505/983–5434) specializes in used hardback books, including some rare titles. The quixotic shop also handles out-of-print LPs and used jazz CDs.

Clothing

Function dictates form in cowboy fashions. A wide-brimmed hat is essential in open country; it protects the wearer from heat, rain, and insects. Cowboy hats made by Resistol, Stetson, Bailey, and other leading firms range in price from $50 to $500, but hats made of exotic materials, such as fur, can go for thousands. Small wonder that when it rains in Santa Fe or Albuquerque, some people are more apt to be concerned about their hats than about getting wet.

The pointed toes of cowboy boots slide easily in and out of the stirrups, and high heels—worn for the same reason by Mongolian tribesmen—help keep feet in the stirrups. Tall tops protect ankles and legs on rides through brush and cactus country and can protect the wearer from a nasty shin bruise from a skittish horse.

Some Western accessories, now mostly worn to be stylish, were once also functional. A colorful bandanna protected an Old West cowboy from sunburn and windburn; it also served as a mask in windstorms, when riding drag behind a herd, or, on occasions far rarer than Hollywood would have us believe, when robbing trains. A cowboy's sleeveless vest offered maneuverability during roping and riding chores and provided pocket space that his skintight pants—snug to prevent wrinkles in the saddle area—didn't. Of all the accessories today, however, belt buckles are probably the most important item—gold ones go for as much as $1,000.

Jane Smith (✉ 550 Canyon Rd., ☎ 505/988–4775) features extraordinary—and pricey—handmade Western wear for women and men, from beaded doeskin gloves to handmade cowboy boots to Plains Native American–style beaded tunics.

Montecristi Custom Hat Works (✉ 322 McKenzie, ☎ 505/983–9598) is where the smart set goes for custom-made straw hats that fit so perfectly they're all but guaranteed to stay on, even when driving in an open convertible.

Origins (✉ 135 W. San Francisco St., ☎ 505/988–2323, FAX 505/989–8288) is the town's oldest apparel and textile store, with a lively assortment of antique and folk costumes, as well as contemporary designs.

Santa Fe Boot Company (✉ 950 W. Cordova Rd., ☎ 505/983–8415) stocks boots by all major manufacturers and more exotic styles designed by owner Marian Trujillo. Hats and Western outerwear are also sold.

Santa Fe Western Mercantile (✉ 6820 Cerrillos Rd., ☎ 505/471–3655) offers a seemingly inexhaustible supply of hats, boots, jeans, English and Western saddles, buckles, belts, and feed and health-care products for horses and livestock.

Western Warehouse (✉ De Vargas Center, ☎ 505/982–3388; ✉ Villa Linda Mall, ☎ 505/471–8775) sells all the top-name hats, boots, belts, and buckles.

Home Furnishings

Artesanos (✉ 222 Galisteo St. and 1414 Maclovia St., ☎ 505/471–8020), is one of the best Mexican-import shops in the nation, with everything from leather chairs to papier-mâché *calaveras* (skeletons used in Day of the Dead celebrations), tinware, and Talavera tiles.

Dewey & Sons Trading Co. (✉ 53 Old Santa Fe Trail, ☎ 505/983–5855 or 800/444–9665) is the place to shop for stunning Western blankets, including the largest selection in the Southwest of Pendleton products, and the Southwest Trail series by Hopi weaver Ramona Sakiestewa.

Foreign Traders (✉ 202 Galisteo St., ☎ 505/983–6441), a Santa Fe landmark—founded as the Old Mexico Shop in 1927 and still run by the same family—offers high-quality handicrafts, antiques, and accessories from Mexico and other parts of the world.

Jackalope (✉ 2820 Cerrillos Rd., ☎ 505/471–8539) sprawls over seven acres, incorporating several pottery barns, a furniture store, endless aisles of knickknacks from Latin America, and a huge greenhouse. It also has a lunch counter, barnyard animals, and a prairie-dog village.

Montez Gallery (✉ Sena Plaza Courtyard, 125 E. Palace Ave., ☎ 505/982–1828) sells Hispanic works of art and decoration, including retablos, bultos, furniture, paintings, pottery, weavings, and jewelry.

Native American Arts and Crafts

Arrowsmith's (✉ 402 Old Santa Fe Trail, ☎ 505/989–7663), offers an eclectic collection of artifacts and early crafts from cowboy-and-Indian days. Prices range from a few dollars for arrowheads to $24,000 for a saddle embellished with 200 pounds of silver.

Cristof's (✉ 106 W. San Francisco St., ☎ 505/988–9881, FAX 505/986–8652) has a large selection of high-quality, contemporary Navajo weavings and Navajo sandpaintings, pottery, and sculpture.

Joshua Baer & Co. (✉ 116½ E. Palace Ave., ☎ 505/988–8944) carries superb historic Navajo textiles and rare antique Pueblo weavings.

Morning Star Gallery (✉ 513 Canyon Rd., ☎ 505/982–8187, FAX 505/984–2368) specializes in antique Native American art and artifacts. In a landmark adobe shaded by a huge cottonwood tree, it's a virtual museum of antique basketry, pre-1940 Navajo silver jewelry, Northwest Coast Native American carvings, classic Navajo weavings, and art of the Plains Buffalo culture.

Packard's Indian Trading Co. (✉ 61 Old Santa Fe Trail, on the east side of the Plaza, ☎ 505/983–9241), is the oldest authentic Native American arts and crafts store on the Santa Fe Plaza. This veritable museum has old pottery, saddles, kachina dolls.

Prairie Edge (✉ 102 E. Water St., El Centro, ☎ 505/984–1336) offers classic Lakota art, artifacts, and jewelry, created by contemporary Sioux artists and craftspeople in the style and tradition of the past.

The Rainbow Man (✉ 107 E. Palace Ave., ☎ 505/982–8706), established in 1945, does business in the rebuilt remains of a building that was damaged during the legendary 1680 Pueblo Revolt. Today, the shop offers an eclectic mix of jewelry, vintage Native American blankets, historic photographs, and railroad memorabilia. The shop's collection of miniature kachina dolls, some standing only an inch tall, is its main attraction.

Trade Roots Collection (✉ 411 Paseo de Peralta, ☎ 505/982–8168) sells Native American ritual objects, such as fetish jewelry and Hopi rattles. It is also a good source of raw materials for craftspeople.

Flea Markets

Trader Jack's Flea Market (✉ 7 mi north of Santa Fe on U.S. 84/285, ☎ 505/455–7874), also known as the Santa Fe Flea Market, is considered the best flea market in America by its habitual legion of bargain hunters. It's open from dawn to dusk every Friday, Saturday, and Sunday, except from December through February—and sometimes even then if the weather's right. You can buy everything here from a half-wolf puppy or African carvings to vintage cowboy boots, fossils, or a wall clock made out of an old hubcap. Sprawled over 12 acres on land belonging to the Tesuque Pueblo, the flea market is right next to the Santa Fe Opera. ("There goes the neighborhood," says Trader Jack, when the opera season starts.)

SIDE TRIPS

One can hardly grasp the profundity of New Mexico's ancient past or its immense landscape without an excursion into the hinterlands. Most of these side trips from Santa Fe should take about a day. But even if you don't have that much time, try, at least, to get to one or two sights outside of town.

Along the Santa Fe Trail

On this daylong outing southeast of Santa Fe along the famed Santa Fe Trail, you can visit Pecos National Historic Park, the site of what was perhaps the greatest Native American Pueblo; Las Vegas, a town that retains a feeling of the old west; and Fort Union, a relic of the American frontier.

Pecos National Historic Park
25 mi southeast of Santa Fe via I–25.

The centerpiece of Pecos National Historic Park is the ruins of Pecos, once a major Pueblo village. Strategically located in a fertile valley between the buffalo hunters of the Great Plains and the farmers of the Rio Grande Valley, Pecos was a trading center centuries before the Spanish conquistadors first visited in 1540. The Spanish later returned to build two missions, in their zeal to convert the Native Americans to Catholicism.

Containing more than 1,100 rooms in a structure as high as five stories, the pueblo once sheltered as many as 2,500 people. It was abandoned in 1838 and its 17 surviving occupants moved to the Jemez Pueblo. The ruins of the missions and of the excavated pueblo may be visited on a self-guided tour, which can be completed in about two hours. The park also has an outlying parcel where the critical Civil War battle at Glorieta took place. At the park's entranceway there is a visitor center. ⊠ *Pecos National Historic Park, Pecos,* ☎ *505/757–6414.* ▧ *$4 per car, $2 per tour-bus passenger.* ⊘ *Memorial Day–Labor Day, weekdays 8–6; Labor Day–Memorial Day, weekdays 8–5.*

Las Vegas
63 mi east of Santa Fe on I–25; 35 mi southeast of Pecos National Park on I–25.

The antithesis of its Nevada namesake, Las Vegas is a town that time seems to have passed by in both appearance and pace. Once an oasis for stagecoach passengers en route to Santa Fe on the Santa Fe Trail, it became, with the arrival of the railroad in the late 19th century, the state's major center of commerce for a brief period. The seat of San Miguel County, Las Vegas lies where the Sangre de Cristo Mountains merge with the high plains of New Mexico, and its name, meaning "The Meadows," reflects its lovely setting. At an altitude of 6,470 ft, its climate is generally delightful both summer and winter, although it can be hit with severe winter storms off the Great Plains.

Las Vegas's 15,000 inhabitants unabashedly live in the past. The town has nine historic districts with old buildings (many of ornate Italianate commercial design—a welcome relief from adobe overload), old hotels, beautiful Victorian houses, and old shops (primarily selling memorabilia and antiques of the period). More than 900 of the buildings are listed on the National Historic Register.

At the Las Vegas Chamber of Commerce building you can go traipsing through the past—back to a time when there were men who were slow on words but fast on the draw. It was once home to Sheriff Pat Garrett, who killed Billy the Kid, and is now home to the **Theodore Roosevelt's Rough Riders Memorial and City Museum.** Teddy Roosevelt gathered many of his famous Rough Riders from this region and, fresh from his triumph at San Juan Hill, announced his candidacy for the vice-presidency in the lobby of the once glorious Castaneda Hotel. The museum houses memorabilia from the Spanish-American War, documents pertaining to the city's history, and Native American artifacts. ⊠ *727 Grand Ave.,* ☎ *505/425–8726.* ▧ *Free.* ⊘ *Mon.–Sat. 9–4.*

LODGING

$$–$$$ 🛏 **Plaza Hotel.** This elegant, historic hotel was built in 1882. Rooms are Victorian in style, with antique furniture and high ceilings. The restaurant, the **Landmark Grill,** serves Mexican food, steaks, and pasta. ⊠ *230 Old Town Plaza, 87701,* ☎ *505/425–3591 or 800/328–1882. 37 rooms. Restaurant, bar, meeting rooms, free parking. AE, D, MC, V.*

Fort Union National Monument
94 mi northeast of Santa Fe on I–25; 28 mi from the north edge of Las Vegas, past Watrous, exit onto NM 161 to get to Fort Union National Monument; you can't miss it—the road dead-ends at the fort.

The ruins of New Mexico's largest American frontier–era fort sit out on the middle of an empty, windswept plain that still echoes with the isolation surely felt by the soldiers stationed here between 1851 and 1890. The fort was established to protect travelers and settlers along the Santa Fe Trail, but with the "taming" of the West, it was abandoned. The visitor center provides interesting historical background about the fort and the Santa Fe Trail. In summer, there are often reenactments of this bygone time. ✉ *Watrous,* ☎ *505/425–8025.* 🎫 *$2 per person, $4 per car.* ☉ *Memorial Day–Labor Day, daily 8–6; Labor Day–Memorial Day, daily 8–5.*

Santa Fe Trail Visitor Information

Ft. Union National Monument (✉ Box 127, Watrous, 87753, ☎ 505/425–8025); **Las Vegas Chamber of Commerce** (✉ 727 Grand Ave., Box 148, Las Vegas 87701, ☎ 505/425–8631); **Pecos National Historic Park** (✉ Drawer 418, Pecos 87552, ☎ 505/757–6414).

Jemez Country

In the Jemez region, the 1,000-year-old Anasazi ruins at the Bandelier National Monument and the vibrant culture of the San Ildefonso Pueblo form a striking contrast to Los Alamos National Laboratory, birthplace of the atomic bomb. A visit to this area is like traveling in time from New Mexico's prehistoric past to its technological present.

This trip, which can be done in a day or extended with an overnight stay en route, offers terrific views of the Rio Grande Valley, the Sangre de Cristos, the Galisteo Basin, and, in the distance, the Sandías. The Anasazi ruins, in the striking canyons of the Pajarito Plateau, are extraordinary, as are the Bradbury Museum and Fuller Lodge in Los Alamos—for different reasons. A beautiful high-forest drive brings you to the awe-inspiring Valle Grande and on to Soda Dam on the Jemez River, Jemez State Park, with its abandoned Spanish mission, and the town of Jemez Springs. There are places to eat and shop for essentials in Los Alamos, a few roadside diners at La Cueva on the highway to Jemez Springs, and accommodations and restaurants in Jemez Springs.

Los Alamos

31 mi west of Santa Fe; drive north out of Santa Fe on U.S. 84/285 to Pojoaque and exit west onto NM 502.

The town of Los Alamos, just 45 minutes from Santa Fe, was founded in absolute secrecy in 1943 as a center of war research, and its existence only became known in 1945 with the detonation of the atomic bombs in Japan. It looks and feels very out of place in northern New Mexico, but it is a fascinating place to visit because of the profound role it played in shaping the modern world.

The **Bradbury Science Museum** is Los Alamos National Laboratory's public showcase. You can experiment with lasers; use advanced computers; witness research in solar, geothermal, fission, and fusion energy; and see World War II's Project Y (the Manhattan Project that built the bomb). ✉ *Los Alamos National Laboratory, 15th St. and Central Ave,* ☎ *505/667–5061.* 🎫 *Free.* ☉ *Tues.–Fri. 9–5, Sat.–Mon. 1–5.*

Fuller Lodge, a short drive up Central Avenue from the science museum, is a massive log building built in 1928 as a dining and recreation hall for the small private boys' school that once occupied this site. In 1942, the school was bought out by the federal government to serve as the base of operations for the Manhattan Project. Today it houses an art center, which features works of northern New Mexican artists and hosts temporary exhibits. ✉ *2132 Central Ave.,* ☎ *505/662–9331.* 🎫 *Free.* ☉ *Winter, Mon.–Sat. 10–4; summer, also Sun. 1–4.*

The **Los Alamos Historical Museum,** in a building adjoining Fuller Lodge, has artifacts of early Native American life on display, as well as photographs and documents of the community's history before and

after World War II. ⊠ *2132 Central Ave.,* ☎ *505/662–4493.* ◩ *Free.*
⊙ *Winter, Mon.–Sat. 10–4; summer, also Sun. 1–4.*

DINING AND LODGING

$–$$ ✕ **Hill Diner.** This large, friendly, reasonably priced diner serves some
of the finest gourmet burgers in town, along with chicken-fried steaks,
homemade soups, and heaps of fresh vegetables. ⊠ *1315 Trinity Dr.,*
☎ *505/662–9745. AE, D, DC, MC, V. Closed Sun.*

$–$$ ✕◩ **Los Alamos Inn.** Rooms in this sprawling ground-level hotel have
modern Southwestern decor and sweeping canyon views. The restau-
rant/bar, **Ashley's,** serves American and Southwestern regional specialties;
the Sunday brunch is a favorite with locals. ⊠ *2201 Trinity Dr., 87544,*
☎ ℻ *505/662–7211. 114 rooms. Restaurant, bar, pool. AE, D, DC,*
MC, V.

$$ ◩ **Hilltop House Hotel.** Minutes from the Los Alamos National Lab-
oratory, this hotel is geared toward traveling scientists and vacation-
ers. Deluxe rooms have kitchenettes; one executive suite offers full kitchen
facilities; all are furnished in modern Southwestern style. A compli-
mentary breakfast is included. The tasteful restaurant, **Trinity Sights,**
offers good American and Southwestern cuisine and fabulous views
of the Sangre de Cristos. ⊠ *400 Trinity Dr. at Central Ave. (Box 250),*
87544, ☎ *505/662–2441,* ℻ *505/662–5913. 87 rooms, 13 suites.*
Restaurant, lounge, indoor pool, exercise room, coin laundry. AE, D,
DC, MC, V.

$–$$ ◩ **Orange Street Inn.** In a rather unremarkable 1948 wood-frame
house in a quiet residential neighborhood, this B&B offers rooms fur-
nished in Southwestern and contemporary style. The public area has
cable TV and a VCR, and you can use the kitchen and the laundry. An
ample continental breakfast is served year-round and, on summer af-
ternoons, wine and hors d'oeuvres are provided. ⊠ *3496 Orange St.,*
87544, ☎ ℻ *505/662–2651. 7 rooms, 3 with bath. D, MC, V.*

Bandelier National Monument

40 mi northwest of Santa Fe. From Los Alamos, take NM 502 (Trin-
ity Dr.) west and then NM 501 (West Jemez Rd.) south until you reach
NM 4 at a "T" intersection. Turn left (east) and drive 6 mi to the en-
trance of Bandelier National Monument.

Seven centuries before the Declaration of Independence was signed, compact city-states existed in the Southwest. Remnants of one of the most
impressive of them can be seen at Frijoles Canyon in Bandelier National Monument. At the canyon's base, beside a gurgling stream, are
the remains of cave dwellings, ancient ceremonial kivas, and other stone
structures that stretch out for more than a mile beneath the sheer walls
of the canyon's tree-fringed rim. For hundreds of years, the Anasazi
people, early relatives of today's Rio Grande Pueblo Native Americans,
thrived on wild game, crops of corn, and beans. Suddenly, for reasons
still undetermined, the settlements were abandoned. Climatic changes?
A great drought? Crop failures? No one knows for sure what caused
the hasty retreat.

You may ponder these and other mysteries while following a paved,
self-guided trail through the site. Using primitive wooden ladders, you
can squeeze through the doorways into some of the cave dwellings and
get a feel for what it was like to live in the cell-like rooms.

Bandelier National Monument, named after author and ethnologist
Adolph Bandelier (his novel, *The Delight Makers,* is set in Frijoles
Canyon), contains 23,000 acres of backcountry wilderness, water-

falls, and wildlife, traversed by 60 mi of trails. A small museum in the visitor center focuses on the area's prehistoric and contemporary Native American cultures, with displays of artifacts from AD 1200 to modern times. ✉ *Bandelier National Monument,* ☎ *505/672–3861.* 🖼 *$5 per car.* ⊙ *Memorial Day–Labor Day, daily 8–6; Labor Day–Memorial Day, daily 8–5.*

Valle Grande

40 mi west of Santa Fe. From Bandelier National Monument, take a left onto NM 4 west and follow the winding, scenic road up through the mountain forest to Valle Grande.

If you're coming from Bandelier National Monument, the drive should take about 45 minutes and is particularly pretty in late September or early October when the aspens turn gold. Valle Grande is one of the world's largest volcanic calderas. You can't imagine its immensity until you spot some cows off on the crater's lush meadow floor, and they look like specks of dirt. The entire 50-mi Jemez range, formed by cataclysmic upheavals, is now filled with gentle streams, hiking trails, campgrounds, and delightful hot springs—reminders of its volcanic origin.

Soda Dam

71 mi northwest of Santa Fe. 15 mi south of Valle Grande on NM 4. 1 mi north of Jemez State Monument on NM 4.

The geological wonder known as Soda Dam was created over thousands of years by travertine deposits—minerals that precipitate out of geothermal springs. With its strange, mushroom-shape exterior and caves split by a roaring waterfall, it's no wonder the spot was considered sacred to Native Americans. Numerous artifacts have been found here. In summer it is a popular swimming spot.

Jemez State Monument

70 mi northwest of Santa Fe. 40 mi southwest of Los Alamos. 1 mi north of Jemez Springs on NM 4.

Jemez State Monument contains both impressive Spanish and Native American ruins. Approximately 600 years ago, ancestors of the people of Jemez Pueblo built several villages in and around the narrow mountain valley. One of the villages was Guisewa, or "Place of the Boiling Waters." The Spanish colonists discovered it and built a mission church beside it, San José de los Jemez, which was abandoned in 1630. Both ruins are protected within this unit of the state park system. The Jemez Pueblo and Reservation are 13 mi south of the monument (☞ *Side Trips in* Chapter 4). ✉ *Box 143, Jemez Springs,* ☎ *505/829–3530.* 🖼 *$2.* ⊙ *Mid-Apr.–mid-Sept., daily 9:30–5:30; mid-Sept.–mid-Apr., daily 8:30–4:30.*

Jemez Springs

69 mi northwest of Santa Fe. 1 mi south of Jemez State Monument on NM4.

The tiny town of Jemez Springs is a year-round vacation destination, with hiking, cross-country skiing, and camping in the nearby U.S. Forest Service areas. There is an old hot-spring retreat, the Jemez Spring Bath House (☎ 505/829–3303), a general store, a wonderful bar-restaurant, and a good B&B.

If you have more time, consider visiting the **Jemez Pueblo** (☞ Side Trips *in* Chapter 4), 10 mi south of Jemez Springs.

$ ✗ **Los Ojos.** Come to this bar-restaurant for tasty burgers, beer, and pool. Take a log stool at the bar or dine in a booth. A huge stone fireplace topped by an elk rack and local cultural doodads tacked to the walls give it a homey feel. ⊠ *"Downtown" Jemez Springs*, ☎ *505/829–3547. D, MC, V.*

$$ ⊡ **Jemez River B&B Inn.** On 5 acres along the Jemez River beneath towering mesa cliffs in a certified hummingbird sanctuary, this inn has lovely rooms with coved ceilings, tile floors, and Native American arts and crafts. All open onto a beautiful plaza with a natural spring and a flower garden that attracts hundreds of hummingbirds. ⊠ *16445 Hwy. 4, 87025,* ☎ FAX *505/829–3262 or 800/809–3262. 6 rooms. Hot tub, massage. AE, D, MC, V.*

Jemez Country Visitor Information

Bandelier National Monument (⊠ Los Alamos 87544, ☎ 505/672–3861); **Jemez State Monument** (⊠ Box 143, Jemez Springs 87025, ☎ 505/829–3530); **Los Alamos County Chamber of Commerce** (⊠ Fuller Lodge, 2132 Central Ave., Box 460 VG, Los Alamos 87544, ☎ 505/662–8105).

Gray Line Tours of Santa Fe (☎ 505/983–9491) runs a four-hour tour of Los Alamos and the nearby Bandelier Cliff Dwellings.

The Southern Loop

This excursion takes you south from Santa Fe through the sublime Galisteo Basin with its immense open spaces to the quiet historic village of Galisteo, then along good country gravel roads to the "Williamsburg of the Southwest"—the living museum of Las Golondrinas. Set aside four or five hours for this jaunt.

Galisteo

23 mi south of Santa Fe: Take I–25 north to U.S. 285 south, then NM 41 south.

Founded as a Spanish outpost in 1614—and built largely out of the rocks from nearby Pueblo ruins—Galisteo is now a charming little village popular with artists and equestrians who keep their horses here (trail rides and rentals are available at local stables). There's a small church, open only on Sunday for services; a graveyard; and an old working brewery that offers tours and occasional tastings.

El Rancho de las Golondrinas

15 mi south of Santa Fe off I–25 in La Cienega. 20 mi northwest of Galisteo.

The "Williamsburg of the Southwest," El Rancho de las Golondrinas (The Ranch of the Swallows) is a reconstruction of a small New Mexican agricultural village. Originally a *paraje,* or stopping place, on El Camino Real, the village has restored buildings from the 17th to 19th centuries.

To get there from Galisteo, pick up graveled and well-maintained County Road 42 in the center of town, next to the church, and head west approximately 10 mi until you hit paved NM 14. Turn north through the scattered dwellings of San Marcos and Lone Butte, where you can grab a bite to eat at a couple of surprisingly good cafés (don't be put off by disheveled appearances). About 3 mi north of where you hit NM 14, exit left onto the graveled NM 586, which zigzags its way west to I–25's service road. Head north on the service road until you reach a bridge over 1–25. Cross to its west side and continue on this two-lane road down into the village of La Cienega, where you will find signs directing you to Rancho de las Golondrinas.

Guided tours at the ranch highlight Spanish Colonial lifestyles in New Mexico from 1660 to 1890: You can view a molasses mill, threshing grounds, and wheelwright and blacksmith shops, as well as a mountain village and a *morada* (meeting place) of the order of Penitentes. Sheep, goats, and other farm animals wander about the sprawling 200-acre complex. During the Spring and Harvest Festivals, on the first weekends of June and October, respectively, the village comes alive with traditional music, Spanish folk dancing, and food and crafts demonstrations. ⊠ *334 Los Pinos Rd., Santa Fe,* ☎ *505/471–2261.* 🖾 *$3.50; $5 during festivals.* ☉ *Apr.–Aug., Wed.–Sun. 10–4.*

The Southern Loop Visitor Information

Rancho de las Golondrinas (⊠ 334 Los Pinos Rd, Santa Fe 87505, ☎ 505/471–2261).

Chaco Culture National Historic Park

Chaco Canyon was the focal point of the amazing Anasazi culture that once dominated the entire Four Corners area of northwestern New Mexico, southwestern Colorado, southeastern Utah, and northeastern Arizona. Seventeen miles long and 1 mi wide, with cliff faces rising 330 ft, the canyon protects the remains of a dozen major pueblo ruins and about 400 smaller settlements. **Pueblo Bonito,** the largest prehistoric Southwest Native American dwelling ever excavated, contains 800 rooms covering more than 3 acres. This dwelling, the magnificent kivas (sunken ceremonial chambers), a 400-mi network of paved roads, and a solstice marker testify that this site was the climax of the Anasazi culture, which peaked about AD 1150. The visitor center has a museum about the canyon, and petroglyphs on display.

This long day trip involves some 380 mi of driving, but it is quite rewarding. To get to Chaco from Santa Fe, take I–25 south to Bernalillo, then NM 44 northwest through Cuba to Nageezi. Turn left onto a dirt road, which runs almost 30 mi south to the park's boundary. The trip takes about 3½ to 4 hours. On your way you might want to stay overnight in Jemez Springs (☞ *above*) or Cuba—or camp in Chaco Canyon, where overnight camping is permitted year-round. ⊠ *Star NM 4 (Box 6500), Bloomfield,* ☎ *505/786–7014.* 🖾 *$4 per car; campsite extra.* ☉ *Visitor Center: Memorial Day–Labor Day, daily 8–6; Labor Day–Memorial Day, daily 8–5. Trails: sunrise–sunset.*

The High Road to Taos

If you are driving from Santa Fe to Taos and you have a few extra hours, skip the main highway (NM 68) and take the far more scenic route, the "High Road to Taos." The drive through the rolling foothills and tiny valleys of the Sangre de Cristos, dotted with orchards, pueblos, and picturesque villages inhabited by weavers and wood carvers, is stunning. A note of caution, however. As pretty as the high-road country is in winter—when the fields are covered with quilts of snow, which trace the lines of homes, fences, and trees like bold pen-and-ink drawings against the sky—the roads can be icy and treacherous. Check on weather conditions before attempting the drive, or stay with the more conventional Santa Fe–Taos route. The scenery is best enjoyed traveling north to south, so you might want to save it for the return trip from Taos.

Nambé Pueblo

Head north from Santa Fe past Tesuque on U.S. 84/285; about 12 mi out of town at Pojoaque turn northeast (right) onto NM 503. Nambé Pueblo is down a side road about 4 mi off NM 503.

At the Nambé Pueblo crafts center, near the Plaza and governor's office, you can purchase notable golden-flecked micaceous pottery, as well as woven belts and jewelry. There's also a lovely picnic area at the base of Nambé Falls and a large fishing lake, open from March through November. The pueblo's main public ceremonial days are July 4 and October 4—the feast day of St. Francis. ⊠ *4 mi off NM503, Box 117-BB, Santa Fe,* ☎ *505/455–2036.*

Chimayó

25 mi north of Santa Fe. From Nambé Pueblo, return to NM 503, then continue on to Chimayó.

Nestled into the rugged hillsides where gnarled piñons seem to grow from bare bedrock, Chimayó—nicknamed "the Lourdes of the Southwest"—is famous for its weavings, its food, and its church.

Once you reach the village, you can't miss the signs for the **Santuario de Chimayó.** This small frontier adobe church has a fantastically carved, painted wood altar and is built on the site where, believers say, a mysterious light came from the ground on Good Friday in 1810. When people from the village investigated the phenomenon, to try to find its source, they pushed away the earth and found a large wooden crucifix. Today the chapel sits above a sacred *pozito* (a small hole), the dirt from which is believed to have miraculous healing properties, as the dozens of abandoned crutches and braces left at the altar—along with many notes, letters, and photos left behind—dramatically testify. The Santuario draws a steady stream of worshipers all year long; during Holy Week as many as 50,000 people visit. The shrine is a National Historic Landmark, but unlike similar holy places, the commercialism is limited to a small adobe shop nearby that sells brochures, books, and religious articles. ☎ *505/351–4889.* ▨ *Free.* ☉ *Daily 9–5:30.*

DINING AND LODGING

$$ ✕ **Rancho de Chimayó.** In a century-old adobe hacienda tucked into the mountains, with whitewashed walls and hand-stripped vigas, cozy dining rooms, and lush, terraced patios, the Rancho de Chimayó is still owned and operated by the family who originally occupied the house. There's a roaring fireplace in winter and, in summer, dining alfresco. ⊠ *NM 520,* ☎ *505/351–0444. Reservations essential. AE, MC, V.*

$ ✕ **Leona's de Chimayó.** This tiny, fast-food-style burrito and chile stand at one of end of the Santuario de Chimayó parking lot has only a few tables, but in summer it's very crowded. The place was so successful that owner Leona Tiede opened a thriving tortilla factory in Chimayó's Manzana Center (☎ 800/453–6627). The specialty is flavored tortillas—everything from butterscotch to jalapeño. ⊠ *Off NM 503,* ☎ *505/351–4569. No credit cards.*

$$–$$$ ▨ **Casa Escondida.** This intimate, serene adobe offers sweeping views of the Sangre de Cristo Mountains. Its rural setting has made it popular with mountain bikers. With Chopin on the CD player and the scent of fresh-baked strudel wafting through the rooms, owner Irenka Taurek, who speaks several languages, provides an international welcome. Rooms are decorated with Native American and regional arts and crafts, and antiques. Ask for the Sun Room, in the main house, which has a private patio, viga ceilings, and a brick floor. The separate one-bedroom Casita Escondida has a kiva-style fireplace, tile floors, and a lovely sitting area. A large hot tub is hidden in a grove behind wild berry bushes. ✉ *Off NM 76 at Rd. Marker 0100 (Box 142), 85722,* ☎ *505/ 351–4805 or 800/643–7201,* FAX *505/351–2575. 5 rooms, 1-bedroom house with full kitchen. Outdoor hot tub. AE, MC, V.*

$$ 🏨 **Hacienda de Chimayó.** Rooms at this hotel are decorated with turn-of-the-century antiques, and each has a private bath and a fireplace. The lovely mountain setting and the charming furnishings make this a delightful accommodation. ✉ *NM 520, 87522,* ☎ *505/351–2222,* FAX *505/351–4038. 6 rooms, 1 suite. AE, MC, V.*

$$ 🏨 **La Posada de Chimayó.** This small, rustic, peaceful B&B offers two guest houses; one was built in the 1890s and has packed earth floors. The cozy rooms have fireplaces, Mexican rugs, handwoven bedspreads, and comfortable regional furniture. Owner Sue Farrington, an expert on Mexico and Mexican cooking, offers a full gourmet breakfast in a variety of south-of-the-border flavors. ✉ *279 Rio Arriba, C.R. 0101 (Box 463), 87522,* ☎ FAX *505/351–4605. 2 rooms, 2 suites. MC, V.*

SHOPPING

Chimayó is known for its colorful weavings. **Ortega's Weaving Shop** (✉ At the junction of NM 520 and NM 76, ☎ 505/351–4215) offers high-quality Rio Grande–style textiles by the family whose Spanish ancestors brought the craft to New Mexico in the 1600s. The **Galeria Ortega,** adjacent to Ortega's Weaving Shop, features traditional New Mexican, Hispanic, and contemporary Native American arts and crafts.

Cordova

28 mi north of Santa Fe. From Chimayó, continue toward Taos, and at the juncture of NM 76, turn right and proceed about 4 mi to the clearly marked turnoff for the town of Cordova.

Hardly more than a mountain village with a small central plaza, a school, a post office, and a church, Cordova is the center of the regional wood-carving industry. The town supports no fewer than 35 full-time and part-time carvers. Most of them are descendants of José Dolores López, who in the 1920s created the unpainted "Cordova Style" of carving that the village is famous for. Most of the *santeros* (makers of religious images) have signs outside their homes indicating that the statues are for sale. The pieces are expensive, ranging from several hundred dollars for small ones to several thousand for larger figures. Collectors snap them up at any price. The **St. Anthony of Padua Chapel,** which is filled with beautiful handcrafted statues and retablos, is worth a visit.

Truchas

35 mi north of Santa Fe; from Cordova, take NM 76 1½ mi north.

Truchas (Spanish for "trout") is where Robert Redford shot the movie *The Milagro Beanfield War* (based on a novel written by Taos author John Nichols). This breathtakingly beautiful village is perched on the rim of a deep canyon with the towering Truchas Peaks, mountains high enough to be almost perpetually capped with snow. The tallest of the Truchas Peaks is 13,102 ft, the second-highest mountain in New Mexico.

SHOPPING

Truchas has a colorful array of shops and galleries. The best known is **Cordova's Weaving Shop** (✉ Box 425, ☎ 505/689–2437). Proprietor Harry Cordova, whose son played a part in the Redford movie, is quick to point out that his shop's back door was also in the film as the front door of the town's newspaper office.

Trampas
42 mi north of Santa Fe; 7 mi north of Truchas on NM 76.

The village of Trampas has a marvelous historic church, **San Tomás,** which dates from 1760 or earlier.

To reach Rancho de Taos, site of the famous San Francisco de Asís Church (☞ The Spanish Colonial Heritage *in* Chapter 3), continue on NM 76 to its intersection with NM 75 and turn right, then left onto NM 518. Turn right on NM 68 for Taos.

The High Road to Taos Visitor Information
Nambé Pueblo (✉ Box 117-BB, Santa Fe 87501, ☎ 505/455–2036).

Pueblos near Santa Fe

This day trip will take you to a handful of the state's 19 pueblos, including San Ildefonso, one of the state's most picturesque, and Santa Clara, whose lands harbor an ancient, spectacular set of cliff dwellings. Plan on about two hours at each pueblo.

Pojoaque Pueblo
12 mi north of Santa Fe on U.S. 84/285.

There is not much to see in the pueblo's plaza area, which hardly has a visible core, but the official state visitor center and adjoining Poeh Center on U.S. 84/285 are worth a visit. The latter is an impressive complex of traditional adobe buildings, including the three-story Sun Tower, which houses a museum, a cultural center, and artist studios. The center frequently hosts demonstrations by artists, exhibitions, and, in warm weather, traditional ceremonial dances. The pueblo's population was decimated and essentially ceased to exist for a number of years, but the survivors eventually began to restore it. Its feast day is celebrated on December 12. ✉ *NM 71 (Box 21), Santa Fe, ☎ 505/455–2278.* ⊙ *Daily 8–5. Sketching and still and video cameras are not allowed.*

San Ildefonso Pueblo
19 mi north of Santa Fe on U.S. 84/285. From the Pojoaque Pueblo, return to U.S. 84/285, but exit almost immediately onto NM 502 toward Los Alamos. Continue for about 7 mi until you reach the turnoff for San Ildefonso Pueblo.

This was the home of the most famous of all pueblo potters, Maria Martinez, whose work is now on permanent display in museums around the world. She first created the exquisite "black on black" pottery in 1919 and in doing so sparked a major revival of all Pueblo arts and crafts. Though she died in 1980, San Ildefonso Pueblo remains a major center for pottery making and other arts and crafts. Many artists sell from their homes, and there are also several trading posts on the pueblo, as well as a visitor center, and a museum where some of Maria Martinez's work can be seen on weekdays. San Ildefonso is also one of the more visually appealing pueblos, with a well-defined plaza core and a spectacular setting beneath the Pajarito Plateau and Black Mesa. Its feast day is celebrated on January 23, when unforgettable Buffalo, Deer, and Comanche dances are performed from daybreak to dusk. ✉ *NM 5 (Box 315-A), Santa Fe, ☎ 505/455–3549 or 505/455–2273.* ▣ *Free.* ⊙ *Daily 8–5. Cameras are not permitted at any of the ceremonial dances but may be used at other times with a permit. Fees are $5 for still cameras, $25 for video recorders, and $15 for sketching.*

Santa Clara Pueblo
27 mi northwest of Santa Fe. From San Ildefonso Pueblo, return to NM 502 and continue west across the nearby Rio Grande to NM 30.

Turn north (right) and continue on 6 mi to the turnoff to the Puyé Cliff Dwellings. Proceed on this gravel road some 9 mi to Santa Clara Pueblo.

Santa Clara Pueblo, southwest of Española, is the home of an historic treasure—the awesome **Puyé Cliff Dwellings**, which are tucked away in a canyon above the village—that also harbors four ponds, miles of stream fishing, picnicking, and camping facilities. In the village, you can find numerous small shops selling the highly sought-after burnished red pottery, as well as engraved blackware, paintings, and other arts and crafts by pueblo artisans. Self-guided and guided tours are offered to the cliff dwellings, which are topped by the ruins of a 740-room pueblo. Puyé is some 9 mi up a gravel road off NM 503 south of the village. The pueblo's feast day of St. Clare is celebrated on August 12. ⊠ *Off NM 30 (Box 580), Española,* ☎ *505/753–7326.* 🎟 *Free.* ☉ *Daily 8–4:30. Permits for the use of trails, camping, and picnic areas, as well as for fishing in trout ponds, are available at the sites. Fees are $5 for photography and video cameras.*

Pueblos near Santa Fe Visitor Information
Pojoaque Pueblo (⊠ NM 71, Box 21, Santa Fe 87501, ☎ 505/455–2278); **San Ildefonso Pueblo** (⊠ NM 5, Box 315-A, Santa Fe 87501, ☎ 505/455–3549 or 505/455–2273); **Santa Clara Pueblo** (⊠ Off NM 30, Box 580, Española 87532, ☎ 505/753–7326).

SANTA FE A TO Z

Arriving and Departing

By Bus
Texas New Mexico & Oklahoma Coaches (⊠ 858 St. Michaels Dr., ☎ 800/231–2222) offers comprehensive daily service to and from Santa Fe's bus station (☎ 505/471–0008).

By Car
Santa Fe is easily accessible by car from several metropolitan areas, north and south, via I–25 or U.S. 84/285.

By Plane
☞ Air Travel *in* the Gold Guide.

By Train
Amtrak's (☎ 800/872–7245) *Southwest Chief* serves Santa Fe via the village of Lamy, 17 mi from town, daily on routes from Chicago and Los Angeles. A connecting Amtrak shuttle-bus service (☎ 505/982–8829; reserve a day in advance) is available to and from town for $14 each way.

Getting Around

The majority of museums, galleries, shops, and restaurants in downtown Santa Fe are in walking distance of the Plaza. You need to take a car or a bus to get to the city's outer reaches, including such attractions as the International Folk Art Museum and the Museum of Indian Arts and Culture. Even a tour of the art galleries along Canyon Road can be a hilly 2-mi stretch.

By Bus
The city's bus system, **Santa Fe Trails** (☎ 505/984–6730 for information) covers six major routes: Agua Fria, Cerrillos, West Alameda, Southside, Eastside, and Galisteo. The fare is 50¢. Buses run approximately every 30 minutes weekdays, every hour weekends. Service begins at 6

AM and continues until 10 PM weekdays and until 8 PM Saturday. There is no bus service on Sunday.

By Car

For car rental companies in Santa Fe, *see* Car Rental *in* the Gold Guide. Parking is difficult, but a number of public and private lots can be found throughout the city.

By Limousine

If you're feeling extravagant or the occasion warrants it, you can call the **Limotion** (☎ 505/471–1265). Fares are $65 per hour, with a two-hour minimum.

By Taxi

Public transportation in town is monopolized by **Capital City Cab Company** (☎ 505/438–0000). The taxis aren't metered; you pay a flat fee determined by the distance you're going. There are no official cab stands in town; you must phone to arrange a ride. Rates for various points within the city range from $4 to $7. You can pick up a 40% taxi discount coupon at the Santa Fe Public Library (☞ Visitor Information, *below*).

Guided Tours

General-Interest

Aboot About (☎ 505/988–2774) leads walking tours on the history, art, and architecture of Santa Fe. Tours leave daily at 9:30 from the Eldorado Hotel; 9:45 from the St. Francis. The fee is $10. **Afoot in Santa Fe Walking Tours** (✉ 211 Old Santa Fe Trail, ☎ 505/983–3701) offers a 2½-hour get-acquainted, close-up look at the city with the help of resident guides. It leaves from the Inn at Loretto Monday–Saturday at 9:30 and 1:30; Sunday at 9:30. The fee is $10.

Discover Santa Fe (✉ 508 W. Cordova, ☎ 505/982–4979) provides specially tailored tours and vacation itineraries for individuals and families, and tour and business groups, including airport transfers, hotel arrangements, and guides. **Gray Line Tours of Santa Fe** (✉ 1330 Hickox St., ☎ 505/983–9491) features a variety of daily tours to Taos, the Bandelier Cliff Dwellings, Los Alamos, and the Santa Clara Pueblo, leaving from and returning to the Santa Fe Bus Depot (hotel and motel pickups by advance arrangement). In winter, tours are subject to road and weather conditions. **Santa Fe Detours** (✉ 107 Washington, outdoor booth Mar.–Oct.; La Fonda Hotel lobby, 100 E. San Francisco St., ☎ 505/983–6565 or 800/338–6877, Nov.–Feb.) includes tours by bus, river, and rail; city walks; trail rides; rafting; and ski packages.

Storytellers and the Southwest (☎ 505/989–4561) is a two-hour literary walking tour of downtown Santa Fe that explores the history, legends, characters, and authors of the region through its landmarks and historic sites. The tours depart from May through September, Monday and Wednesday at 6 PM from the Plaza. Call for reservations.

Learning Experiences

Santa Fe School of Cooking (✉ 116 W. San Francisco St., ☎ 505/983–4511) offers both night and day classes in regional New Mexican fare. The **Travel Photography Workshop** (✉ Box 2847, ☎ 505/982–4979, FAX 505/983–9489) is a weeklong photography blitz headed by Lisl Dennis, a noted photographer whose work appears regularly in *Outdoor Photographer* and who has authored a number of books on photographic techniques.

Special-Interest

Art Tours of Santa Fe (✉ 310 E. Marcy St., ☎ 505/988–3527 or 800/ 888–7679) specializes in five- to seven-day excursions to historic sites, museums, galleries, artists' studios, private homes, and collections; tours are accompanied by authorities on art, archaeology, and New Mexican history.

Behind Adobe Walls and Garden Tours (✉ 54½ E. San Francisco St., ☎ 505/983–6565 or 800/338–6877) generally schedules house and garden tours on the last two Tuesdays of July and the first two Tuesdays of August. The **Santa Fe Botanical Garden** (☎ 505/438–1684) schedules walks and tours of local gardens from May through September.

Recursos (✉ 826 Camino de Monte Rey, ☎ 505/982–9301) runs historical, cultural, and nature tours.

Rojo Tours (✉ 228 Old Santa Fe Trail, ☎ 505/983–8333) designs specialized trips—to view wildflowers, pueblo ruins and cliff dwellings, galleries and studios, Native American arts and crafts, and private homes—as well as adventure tours, such as ballooning, white-water rafting, hiking, and horseback riding.

Southwestern Association for Indian Arts (✉ 552 E. Coronado Rd., ☎ 505/989–5072), which produces the annual famed Santa Fe Indian Market, organizes visits to Native American artists in northern New Mexico.

Contacts and Resources

Emergencies

Fire, ambulance, police (☎ 911); **Medical Emergency Room, St. Vincent Hospital** (✉ 455 St. Michaels Dr., ☎ 505/820–5250); **Lovelace Urgent Care** (✉ 901 W. Alameda, ☎ 505/995–2500; ✉ 440 St. Michaels Dr., ☎ 505/995–2400); **Medical Dental Center** (✉ 465 St. Michaels Dr., Suite 205, ☎ 505/983–8089) will see walk-in patients on an emergency basis.

Late-Night Pharmacy

Walgreens (✉ 1096 S. St. Francis Dr., ☎ 505/982–9811) provides 24-hour service.

Visitor Information

The **Santa Fe Convention and Visitors Bureau** (✉ 201 W. Marcy St., Box 909, 87504, ☎ 505/984–6760 or 800/777–2489, FAX 505/984–6679) has Santa Fe visitor guides, brochures, maps, and calendar listings. The **Santa Fe Chamber of Commerce** (✉ 510 N. Guadalupe St., Suite L, De Vargas Center N, 87504, ☎ 505/983–7317) provides assistance and general information, primarily to traveling business people and individuals relocating to Santa Fe. The **New Mexico Department of Tourism** (✉ Lamy Bldg., 491 Old Santa Fe Trail, 87503, ☎ 505/ 827–7400 or 800/733–6396, FAX 505/827–7402) offers a wealth of booklets and printed material on New Mexico.

Another good source of information is the **Santa Fe Public Library,** whose main branch (✉ 145 Washington Ave., ☎ 505/984–6780), just off the Plaza, carries bus route maps, discount taxi coupons, and a wealth of local literature.

Weather, Time, and Temperature

For information about the weather, time, or temperature, call 505/473–2211.

3 Taos

Taos's essence lies in the commingling of its Native American, Hispanic, and Anglo inhabitants, perhaps most evident in its effusive cultural spirit and eclectic architecture. Its diversity, physical beauty, and Old West feel have lured literary and artistic talents since the early 20th century. Now it also attracts outdoors enthusiasts who come to ski its world-class slopes and raft its rushing rivers.

A SMALL, OLD FRONTIER TOWN steeped in the history of New Mexico, Taos embraces a unique mix of rich cultural heritage and Wild West swagger. Weathered and dusty in summer, Taos seems timeless: stately elms and cottonwood trees, narrow streets, and a profusion of adobe all cast a lingering spell upon the memory.

Updated by
Nancy
Zimmerman

The one- and two-story adobe buildings that line the two-centuries-old Plaza reveal the influence of Native American and Spanish settlers. Overhanging balconies supported by rugged beams were added later by American pioneers who ventured west after the Mexican War of 1846. Hidden courtyards sprinkled through the town recall Spanish haciendas. Some of the roads extending from the Plaza are still unpaved today; when it rains, they're not unlike the rutted streets of yesteryear.

With a population of approximately 5,000, Taos is actually three towns in one. The first is the business district of art galleries, restaurants, and shops likened to Santa Fe before all the glitz and glamour. The second, 3 mi northwest of the commercial center, is the Taos Pueblo where the Taos-Tewa Native Americans still live. The third Taos, 4 mi south of town, is Ranchos de Taos, a farming and ranching community settled by the Spanish centuries ago. A bit scruffy these days, Ranchos de Taos is best known for the San Francisco de Asís Church, its massive buttressed adobe walls a sanctuary for a wealth of important religious artifacts and paintings. Its *camposanto* (graveyard) is one of the most photographed in the country.

Life at the Taos Pueblo predates Marco Polo's 13th-century travels in China and the arrival of the Spanish in America in 1540. The northernmost of the 19 Pueblo Native American settlements in the Rio Grande Valley, Taos Pueblo is now the home of some 200 of the more than 2,000 members, most of whom live in fully modern homes elsewhere on the Pueblo's 95,000 acres. Unlike many nomadic Native American tribes that were forced to relocate to government-designated reservations, the Taos Pueblo Native Americans have resided at the base of the 12,282-ft-high Taos Mountain for centuries, remaining a link between pre-Columbian inhabitants who originally lived in the Taos Valley and their descendants who reside there now.

Scores of renowned painters, photographers, and literary figures were also drawn to Taos's earthy spirit—Georgia O'Keeffe, Ansel Adams, and D. H. Lawrence among them. Add this remarkable artistic heritage to the unique blend of history and culture, and Taos's appeal is evident.

EXPLORING TAOS

Taos packs a punch despite its size. It's hardly a glamorous city, but its multilayered culture makes it an enormously welcoming and comfortable place to visit and explore. On a rolling mesa at the base of the rugged Sangre de Cristo Mountains, where lofty Wheeler Peak rises 13,161 ft, Taos is worth more than a day trip out of Santa Fe. Formidable ski slopes beckon in the winter, and summer brings with it floods of visitors wishing to see this novel town. Galleries and small museums surrounding the historic Plaza continue the city's legacy as an artistic and literary center beginning in the 1920s, attracting collectors and artists today.

One of the pluses of this small, safe community is its walkability. Sites of interest beyond Taos proper, such as the Enchanted Circle, the Rio

Grande Gorge, and the haunts of Taos personalities, require a car. For drivers—a word of caution—traffic can be murderous at peak summer and winter seasons. Be prepared for trying jams and snarls. But there are good sidewalks, well-lighted pedestrian crosswalks, and public parking lots close to the major in-town sights.

Taos Plaza and Bent Street

Walking through the Taos Plaza and the neighboring Bent Street introduces you to that once-upon-a-time-in-the-west feeling that lends the town the rough-and-ready charm of its historical roots. The plaza is the original center of commercial life of both early and modern Taos. Bent Street, where New Mexico's first American governor lived and died, is now the town's upscale shopping area and art gallery enclave.

When exploring Taos keep in mind that a joint ticket to the Kit Carson Historic Museums of Taos can save you money on admission to participating sights. Among the members of this private, nonprofit organization are the Blumenschein Home, the Kit Carson Home and Museum, and the Martínez Hacienda.

Numbers in the text correspond to numbers in the margin and on the Taos map.

A Good Walk

Begin your promenade at the old-fashioned gazebo in the middle of **Taos Plaza** ①. Walk a few hundred yards south behind the plaza along Don Fernando to Manzanares Street to Juanita where the walled residential plaza of protected houses still stands. Make sure you peek into the little *capilla* (chapel) on the corner of this plaza. Look south across the plaza to Hotel La Fonda de Taos, the old hotel where D. H. Lawrence's infamous naughty paintings are tucked away in the manager's office. A small fee gets you in for a peek.

Two blocks off the Plaza is the **Blumenschein Home** ②, a wonderful, small museum. Pick up Ledoux Street from the right-hand corner of La Fonda, and follow it across Ranchitos Road to signs directing you to the home of the famous Taos artist. Pick up the handy, free guidebook at the entrance (oh, and don't miss the kitchen). Just a few feet farther along on Ledoux is the **Harwood Foundation** ③, a collection of paintings of Taos artists in the former home of a member of the original Taos Society of Artists.

Walk back to the Plaza and continue on to the intersection of U.S. 68, which is also the main street of Taos. Cross this thoroughfare and you'll be on Kit Carson Road. Follow it up about 50 ft to the **Kit Carson Home and Museum** ④. When you finish here, go back to Paseo del Pueblo Norte (U.S. 68) and walk north past the Taos Inn to Bent Street, which will be on your left. Spend some time window-shopping at the pretty boutiques and galleries in this area.

Tucked into a tiny plaza of its own, you'll come to the **Governor Bent Museum** ⑤, the modest home of the first Anglo governor of the state. Just across the street is John Dunn House, once the homestead of a notorious Taos gambler and transportation entrepreneur. It's now a small shopping plaza, and you'll find a number of interesting shops (☞ Specialty Shops *in* Shopping, *below*). Farther along Bent you'll come to the corner of Armory and Placitas Road and the Taos Volunteer Fire department building, where you'll find the **Firehouse Collection** ⑥, which doubles as a fire station and an exhibition space for more than 100 Taos artists.

After you've enjoyed the pleasant, upscale Bent Street area, return to Paseo del Pueblo Norte (U.S. 68), turn left, and head north. You'll pass by the **Stables Art Center** ⑦ and **Kit Carson Park** ⑧, where he was buried. Right next to the park, just a few feet farther to the north, is the beau-, tiful **Fechin Institute** ⑨, another Taos artist's home.

TIMING

The entire walk can be done in a half day in any kind of weather, at any time of year. But note that the Fechin Institute is closed from November to Memorial Day, except by appointment; from Memorial Day to October, it is open from Wednesday to Sunday. Some of the museums are closed on the weekend, so you may want to do this walk from Wednesday to Friday. Although mostly interesting, the museums offer little information, and you'll be able to move through each one fairly quickly. You could take a whole day for this walk if you stop for lunch along the way, browse in the galleries, or stay longer at any one of the sights.

Sights to See

★ ② **Blumenschein Home.** Two blocks off the southeast corner of the Plaza is the Ernest L. Blumenschein home, where the Taos Society of Artists headquartered from 1912 to 1927. The charming adobe house full of paintings and antiques blends European sophistication with classic Southwestern architecture. ⊠ *222 Ledoux St.,* ☎ *505/758–0505.* ☞ *$4; combination tickets for 2 sites, $6 (☞ Kit Carson Home and Museum or Martínez Hacienda, below.)* ☉ *Daily 9–5.*

★ ⑨ **Fechin Institute.** The interior of this extraordinary Southwestern adobe house, built between 1927 and 1933 by Russian émigré and artist Nicolai Fechin, is a marvel of beautifully carved Russian-style woodwork and furniture that glistens with an almost golden sheen. Fechin constructed it to showcase his daringly colorful portraits and landscapes. Fechin's daughter Eya oversees her father's architectural masterpiece, and loves talking about Nicolai and life "back then." Listed in the National Register of Historic Places, the Fechin Institute hosts annual exhibits and special workshops devoted to the artist's unique approach to learning, teaching, and creativity. ⊠ *227 Paseo del Pueblo Norte,* ☎ *505/758–1710.* ☞ *$3.* ☉ *Memorial Day weekend–Oct., Wed.–Sun. 1–5:30, or by appointment.*

☙ ⑥ **Firehouse Collection.** More than 100 works of some of the most well-known Taos artists—Joseph Sharp, Ernest Blumenschein, Bert Phillips, and others—are hung, oddly enough, at the Taos Volunteer Fire Department, two blocks north of Bent Street on the corner of Armory Street and Placitas Road. The exhibit space is the meeting hall, adjoining the station house where five fire engines are maintained at the ready. An antique fire engine is housed here as well. ⊠ *323 Placitas Rd. (Box 4591),* ☎ *505/758–3386.* ☞ *Free.* ☉ *Weekdays 9–4.*

☙ ⑤ **Governor Bent Museum.** In 1846, when New Mexico became a United States territory during the Mexican War, Charles Bent, an early trader, trapper, and mountain man, was appointed governor. A year later he was killed in his house by an angry mob protesting New Mexico's annexation by the United States. Governor Bent was married to María Ignacia, older sister of Kit Carson's wife, Josefa Jaramillo. The well-kept adobe building where Bent lived is a bit cluttered and overwhelmed with his family's possessions, furniture, and Western Americana. But the guides are devoted to this museum and are quite knowledgeable. ⊠ *117A Bent St.,* ☎ *505/758–2376.* ☞ *$1.* ☉ *Daily 10–5.*

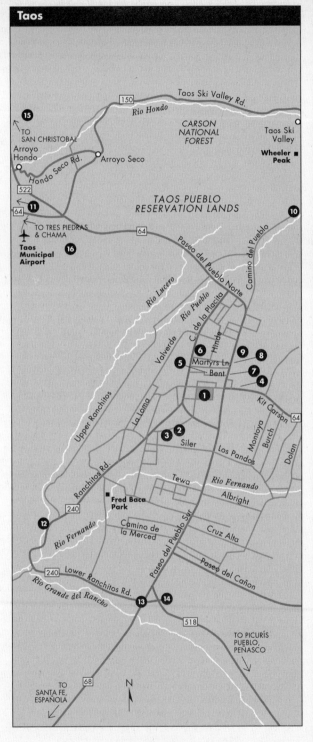

Taos

In case you want to see the world.

At American Express, we're here to make your journey a smooth one. So we have over 1,700 travel service locations in over 120 countries ready to help. What else would you expect from the world's largest travel agency?

do more ®

AMERICAN EXPRESS

Travel

http://www.americanexpress.com/travel

In case you want to be welcomed there.

We're here to see that you're always welcomed at establishments everywhere. That's why millions of people carry the American Express® Card – for peace of mind, confidence, and security, around the world or just around the corner.

do more

In case you're running low.

We're here to help with more than 118,000 Express Cash locations around the world. In order to enroll, just call American Express before you start your vacation.

do more

And just in case.

We're here with American Express® Travelers Cheques and Cheques *for Two*.® They're the safest way to carry money on your vacation and the surest way to get a refund, practically anywhere, anytime.

Another way we help you...

do more ®

AMERICAN
EXPRESS

Travelers Cheques

3 Harwood Foundation. This museum, in the former home of Burt C. Harwood, another member of the original Taos Society of Artists, is a department of the University of New Mexico. If you are a confirmed aficionado of the artwork of the early Taos artists, then this museum is the place for you. Almost all the works come from patron Mabel Dodge Luhan's private collection. At press time the foundation was scheduled to reopen by 1998, after a renovation to increase the exhibition space. ⊠ *238 Ledoux St.,* ☎ *505/758–9826.* 🖾 *$2.* ⊙ *Mon.– Sat. noon–4.*

NEED A
BREAK?

The **Cookie Company** (⊠ 127 Bent St., ☎ 505/758-5867), a snappy bakery tucked into an adobe cottage open daily from 9 to 5, makes scrumptious cookies and delectable veggie empanadas.

☞ 4 Kit Carson Home and Museum. Kit Carson bought this low-slung 12-room adobe home in 1843 as a wedding gift for his young bride, Josefa Jaramillo, the daughter of a powerful, politically influential Mexican family. Josefa was 14 when the twice-married, 32-year-old, dashing mountain man and scout began courting her. Three of the museum's rooms are furnished as they were when the Carson family lived here. The rest of the museum is devoted to basic gun and mountain-man exhibits, early Taos antiques, artifacts, and manuscripts. There's a shop that sells books and gifts. ⊠ *Kit Carson Rd.,* ☎ *505/758–4741.* 🖾 *$4; combination tickets for 2 sites, $6 (☞ Blumenschein Home, above; or Martínez Hacienda, below).* ⊙ *Nov. 2–Mar., daily 9–5; Apr.– Nov. 1, daily 8–6.*

NEED A
BREAK?

Stop at **Caffe Tazza** (⊠ 122 Kit Carson Rd., ☎ 505/758-8706) for great coffee and homemade muffins.

☞ 8 Kit Carson Park. Kit Carson's grave is here marked with a *cerquita* (a spiked wrought-iron rectangular fence), traditionally used to outline and protect grave sites. Mabel Dodge Luhan, the pioneering patron of the early Taos art scene, is also buried here. This 20-acre park has swings and slides for recreational breaks. It's well marked with big stone pillars and a gate. ⊠ *Paseo del Pueblo Norte (U.S. 68), 2 blocks north of Taos Plaza.*

7 Stables Art Center. It was in the stables in back of this house that the Taos Artists' Association first began exhibiting the work of member and of invited nonmember artists from all over northern New Mexico—thus the name. The association purchased the handsome adobe building in 1952, and it is now the visual arts gallery of the Taos Art Association. Exhibits change monthly; all work is for sale. It's next door to the Taos Inn on U.S. 68. ⊠ *133 Paseo del Pueblo Norte, Taos 87571,* ☎ *505/758–2036.* 🖾 *Free.* ⊙ *Daily 10–5.*

1 Taos Plaza. The first European explorers of the Taos Valley came here with Captain Alvarado's 1540 Coronado Expedition. In July 1598, Basque explorer Don Juan de Oñate arrived in Taos and established a mission and trading arrangements with the Taos Pueblos. The settlement actually developed into two plazas: the historic Plaza at the heart of the town became a thriving business district for the early colony; a few hundred yards behind, a walled residential plaza was formed, and it still stands today, going strong with its throng of gift and coffee shops. As authorized by a special act of Congress, the U.S. flag flies in the center of the Plaza day and night in recognition of Kit Carson's heroic stand protecting it from Confederate sympathizers during the Civil War. Next to a covered gazebo, donated by heiress and longtime Taos resident Mabel Dodge Luhan, is the Tiovivo, an antique carousel that thrills children three days a year only during the July Fiestas de Santiago y Santa Ana. Tickets are 50¢ per ride.

Taos Pueblo and Rio Grande Gorge

A drive to the Taos Pueblo is a trip worth making. Pueblo life defined much of the early spirit of Northern New Mexico— and especially Taos— for hundreds of years. The next stop is a spectacular walk across the Rio Grande Gorge Bridge, one of the highest expansion bridges in the world.

A Good Drive

Drive 3 mi north on Paseo del Pueblo Norte (U.S. 68), and keep your eyes peeled for the signs on the right, just beyond the post office, directing you to **Taos Pueblo** ⑩. It is a World Heritage Site and an important view into pueblo ritual and life still upheld today.

After enjoying the wonders of this marvelous pueblo, continue your drive by returning south on U.S. 68 to I–64 west. Drive to the traffic light and continue to follow I–64 west to the **Rio Grande Gorge Bridge** ⑪, a stunning marriage of natural wonder and human engineering. You may want to take along some sturdy hiking shoes and plenty of water and snacks, and take the invigorating walking path down into the gorge. But be warned—what goes down, must come up—and it's quite an arduous path.

TIMING

You'll need two to three hours to enjoy the pueblo. It can get very hot in summer; you may want to go first thing in the morning to try to avoid the heat and crowds. Conversely, in the winter it can get cold and windy; dress warmly. Whatever season you choose, the very best time to visit is during one of the marvelous ceremonial dances—but set aside several hours, because the ceremonies never start on time and they are worth the wait. A half hour should be enough time to see and enjoy the grandeur of the Rio Grande Gorge Bridge.

Sights to See

✋ ⑪ **Rio Grande Gorge Bridge.** It's a breathtaking experience to see the dramatic gorge with the Rio Grande flowing gracefully along 650 ft below. This glorious structure is the second-highest expansion bridge in the country. Hold on to your camera and eyeglasses when looking down, and watch out for low-flying planes. The Taos Municipal Airport is close by, and daredevil private pilots have been known to challenge one another to fly *under* the bridge.

★ ✋ ⑩ **Taos Pueblo.** For nearly 1,000 years, the mud-and-straw adobe walls— several feet thick in places—have sheltered the customs and way of life of the Taos-Tewa Native Americans. Named a United Nations World Heritage Site in 1993, it is the largest existing multistory pueblo structure in the United States. The two main buildings, Hlauuma (north house) and Hlaukwima (south house), separated by a creek, are believed to be of a similar age, probably constructed between AD 1000 and 1450. Once magnificent structures, they now look tired from the passage of time. They have common walls but no connecting doorways. The Tewas gained access to their homes only from the top, via ladders that were retrieved after entering. Small buildings and corrals are scattered about.

The pueblo today appears much as it did when the first Spanish explorers arrived in New Mexico in 1540. The adobe walls glistening with mica caused the conquistadors to believe they had discovered one of the fabled Seven Cities of Gold. The outside surfaces are continuously maintained by replastering with thin layers of mud, and the interior walls are frequently coated with thin washes of white earth to keep them clean and bright. The roofs of each of the five stories are supported by large timbers, or vigas, hauled down from the mountain forests. Rotted vigas are replaced as needed. Pine or aspen *latillas* (smaller pieces of wood) are placed side by side between the vigas; the entire roof is then packed with dirt.

Even after 400 years of Spanish and Anglo presence in Taos, inside the pueblo the traditional Native American way of life has endured. Tribal custom allows no electricity or running water in Hlauuma and Hlaukwima, where approximately 200 Taos Native Americans live full-time. Some 2,000 others live in conventional homes on the pueblo's 95,000 acres, a sea of television antennas. The crystal-clear waters of the Rio Pueblo de Taos, originating high above in the mountains at the sacred Blue Lake, are the primary source of drinking water and irrigation. Bread is still baked in *hornos* (outdoor domed ovens). Artisans of the Taos Pueblo produce and sell traditionally handcrafted wares such as mica-flecked pottery and silver jewelry. Great hunters, the Taos Native Americans are also renowned for their work with animal skins, and their excellent moccasins, boots, and drums.

Although the population is about 90% Catholic, the Tewa, like most of the Pueblo people, observe both Catholic and Native American religious rituals. This derives from the Great Indian Revolt of 1680, when a duly chastised clergy agreed to accept both approaches to religious observation. At Christmas and other sacred holidays, immediately after mass, Native American dancers, dressed in seasonal sacred raiment, proceed down the church aisle, drums beating and rattles moving, to begin their own religious rites.

The pueblo Church of San Geronimo, or St. Jerome, the patron saint of Taos Pueblo, was completed in 1850 to replace the original destroyed by the U.S. Army in 1847 during the Mexican War. With its graceful flowing lines, arched portal, and twin bell towers, the church is a popular subject of photographers and artists (but, please, no photographs inside).

The public is invited to certain ceremonial dances held throughout the year. These include: January 1, Turtle Dance; January 6, Buffalo or Deer Dance; May 3, Feast of Santa Cruz Foot Race and Corn Dance; June 13, Feast of San Antonio Corn Dance; June 24, Feast of San Juan Corn Dance; July 2 weekend, Taos Pueblo Powwow; July 25–26, Feast of Santa Ana and Santiago Corn Dance; September 29–30, Feast of San Geronimo Sunset Dance; Christmas Eve, the Procession; Christmas Day, Deer Dance with *Matachines* (ceremonial dancers). Although there is no charge for general admission (☞ Tourist fees, *below*) certain rules must be observed: Respect the RESTRICTED AREA signs that protect the privacy of pueblo residents and sites of native religious practices; do not enter private homes or open any doors not clearly labeled as curio shops; do not photograph tribal members without asking permission; do not enter the cemetery grounds; and do not wade in the Rio Pueblo de Taos, which is considered sacred and is the community's sole source of drinking water. ⊠ *Taos Pueblo* ☎ *505/758–9593.* ☞ *Tourist fees: $5 per vehicle (for parking), $10 for tour buses (plus $1 per passenger); $5 for a still-camera permit, $10 for a movie-camera permit, $10 for a video-camera permit; artist's sketching fee $15, artist's painting fee $35.* ⊙ *Apr.–Nov., daily 8–5:30; Dec.–Mar., daily 8:30–4:30. Closed for funerals, religious ceremonies, and often for a one-month "quiet time" in late winter or early spring; call ahead before planning to visit at this time.*

NEED A
BREAK?   Look for signs that read FRY BREAD on dwellings in the Pueblo: You can
enter the kitchen and buy a piece of fresh fry bread—bread dough that
is flattened and deep-fried until puffy and golden brown and then
topped with honey or powdered sugar.

The Spanish Colonial Heritage

Driving along the back roads of Taos offers you a glimpse into the Spanish Colonial farm life pervasive in the Taos environs. After the conquistadors permanently colonized this part of Northern New Mexico,
their Spanish culture dominated Taos for centuries. Even today, you'll
hear Spanish spoken in many of the shops and on the street. Foods with
that tasty Spanish tang—staple menu items in the restaurants and area
museums—attest to this heritage.

A Good Drive

Go south on NM 240 (also known as Ranchitos Road) to the **La Hacienda de Don Antonio Severino Martínez** ⑫. You'll be driving through
the no-frills back roads of the town. As you pass by the tiny adobe cottages dotting the landscape, you'll get a sense of an older way of life
that mirrors what you'll see at the hacienda.

When you're ready to continue on, follow Ranchitos Road (NM 240)
farther south 4 mi to **Ranchos de Taos** ⑬ (on U.S. 68), where you'll
come upon the world-famous **San Francisco de Asís** ⑭ church. You can't
miss this minuscule farm village and the church that Georgia O'Keeffe
made famous.

TIMING
This is a great tour for a Sunday after brunch, no matter what the season. Set aside two to three hours.

Sights to See

⑫ **La Hacienda de Don Antonio Severino Martínez.** The spare, fortlike,
18th-century walled farm museum on the banks of the Rio Pueblo served
as a community refuge against Comanche and Apache raids. Built in
progressive additions between 1804 and 1827 by Severino Martínez,
the massive adobe walls without exterior windows protect 21 rooms
around two central courtyards. You will get a glimpse into early Spanish Colonial farm life, when supplies to Taos came by ox cart on the
Camino Real. The restored period rooms display textiles, foods, and
crafts of the time. There's a working blacksmith's shop, and weavers
create beautiful clothes on reconstructed period looms. During the last
weekend in September the hacienda hosts the annual Old Taos Trade
Fair, which reenacts fall trading fairs of the 1820s when Plains Native
Americans and trappers came to trade with Spanish and Pueblo Native Americans in Taos. The two-day event includes traditional crafts
demonstrations, native foods, entertainment, traditional-style cara-
vans, and music. ⊠ *Ranchitos Rd. (NM 240),* ☎ *505/758–1000.* 🖼
$4; combination ticket for 2 sites, $6 (☞ *Blumenschein Home or Kit
Carson Home and Museum, above).* ☉ *Daily 9–5.*

⑬ **Ranchos de Taos.** This Spanish Colonial ranching and farming community was an early home to Taos Native Americans and settled by
Spaniards in 1716. Many of the adobe cottages have seen better days,
but there are various shops, modest galleries, and taco stands, as well
as the famous church painted by innumerable artists over the last century. ⊠ *Paseo del Pueblo Norte (U.S. 68), about 4 mi south of Taos
Plaza.*

OFF THE
BEATEN PATH

PICURÍS PUEBLO – The Picurís (Keresan for "those who paint") Native Americans once lived in large six- and seven-story dwellings similar to those still standing at the Taos Pueblo, but they were abandoned in the wake of 18th-century Pueblo uprisings. Relatively isolated—south from Taos off U.S. 68, between Taos and Española—Picurís is surrounded by the timberland of the Carson National Forest and is one of the smallest pueblos in New Mexico. The 270-member, Tiwa-speaking Picurís tribe governs itself as a separate tribal nation and has no treaties with any foreign country, including the United States. There is a museum with examples of pottery and crafts for sale and a multipurpose building with a restaurant, convenience store, and the Picurís Market. Guided tours explore recent excavations. Fishing, picnicking, and camping are permitted at nearby trout-stocked Pu-Na and Tu-Tah lakes. Fishing and camping permits can be obtained at the Picurís Market. ⊠ *Off U.S. 68, Peñasco,* ☎ *505/587–2957.* ☜ *Fees for guided tours, the ruins, sketching, and video and still cameras.* ☉ *Daily; hrs vary.*

⓮ **San Francisco de Asís Church.** A spectacular example of Spanish Mission architecture, this church was built in the 18th century as a spiritual and physical refuge from raiding Apaches, Utes, and Comanches. In a state of deterioration, it was rebuilt by community volunteers in 1979 using traditional adobe bricks. The earthy, clean lines of the exterior walls and supporting bulwarks—casting shapes and shadows—have inspired generations of painters and photographers. Late-afternoon light offers the best exposure of the heavily buttressed rear of the church; morning light is best for the front. Bells in the twin belfries call faithful Taoseños to services on Sunday and holidays, when worshipers overflow the church. In the parish hall nearby, a 15-minute video presentation every half hour explains the history and restoration of the church, and the mysterious painting *Shadow of the Cross.* In the evening the shadow of a cross appears over Christ's shoulder. Scientific studies made on the canvas and the paint pigments cannot explain the phenomenon. ⊠ *Ranchos de Taos,* ☎ *505/758–2754.* ☜ *$1.* ☉ *Mon.–Sat. 9–4, Sun. and holy days during church services: Mass at 7 (in Spanish), 9, and 11:30* AM.

Artistic and Literary Taos

A drive through the countryside bordering Taos brings you in touch with some of the literary and artistic roots of this historic southwestern town. Once the Taos Society of Artists made known the glories of the New Mexican vistas and Native American lore, this area became a haven for the great and not so great of the New York smart set—from socialite Millicent Rogers to Mabel Dodge Luhan, D. H. and Frieda Lawrence, and painter Georgia O'Keeffe. They bought houses and began either writing about the deserts or capturing them on canvas—while others just collected the works.

A Good Drive

The English writer D. H. Lawrence loved the dry, sunny climate of New Mexico but only lived in Taos for a couple of years in the Kiowa Ranch north of town. Now the property of the University of New Mexico, the **D. H. Lawrence Ranch and Shrine** ⓯ is on the grounds. The shrine, amid gorgeous surroundings, may be visited, but the buildings are closed to the public. Take I–64 west, and at the traffic light, go north on NM 522. Keep an eye out for the clearly marked sign that points to the ranch and shrine. This is about 10 mi from Taos.

Head back south to Taos along NM 522 about 5 or 6 mi to the traffic light again. At that corner watch for the signs directing you to the

Millicent Rogers Museum ⑯. Keep a sharp watch for this turn and those signs. This rural road ultimately connects back onto Upper Ranchitos Road. If you miss the turn, go back into town, pick up NM 240 (Ranchitos Road), and turn left onto Upper Ranchitos. You'll feel as if you're driving off the edge of the earth, but after about 4 mi or so, you'll see the big adobe wall and the sign for the museum.

A pilgrimage to Georgia O'Keeffe country—to complete your exploration of artistic Taos—may leave you with as many questions as do her most mysterious paintings. Ghost Ranch and her property in Abiquiú, a good 60 mi southwest of Taos, are not public monuments, so the trip is what you make of it (☞ Off the Beaten Path, *below*). If you wish to see some of her original works, Santa Fe has museums and a gallery with a solid collection (☞ Exploring Santa Fe *and* Shopping *in* Chapter 2).

TIMING

How much time you spend will depend a lot on how much the Millicent Rogers Museum engages your attention. Two hours will get you through its galleries and exhibits. The D. H. Lawrence shrine should take about a half hour to visit.

Sights to See

⑮ **D. H. Lawrence Ranch and Shrine.** The noted British author lived in Taos for about 22 months over a three-year period between 1922 and 1925. He and his wife, Frieda, arrived in Taos at the behest of Mabel Dodge Luhan, who collected famous writers and artists the way some people collect butterflies. Luhan provided them with a place to live, Kiowa Ranch, on 160 acres in the mountains north of Taos. Rustic and remote, it's now known as the D. H. Lawrence Ranch, although Lawrence never actually owned it. Nearby is the smaller cabin where Dorothy Brett, the traveling companion of the Lawrences, stayed. The houses, now owned by the University of New Mexico, are not open to the public, but you can visit the nearby D. H. Lawrence Shrine on wooded Lobo Mountain. A small white shedlike structure, it is simple and unimposing. The writer fell ill while visiting France and died in a sanatorium there in 1930. Five years later, his wife, subsequently married in Italy to Angelo Ravagli, had Lawrence's body disinterred, cremated, and brought back to Taos. Frieda Lawrence is buried, as was her wish, in front of the shrine. ⊠ *NM 522, San Cristobal,* ☎ *505/ 776–2245.* ⊑ *Free.* ⊙ *Daily.*

⑯ **Millicent Rogers Museum.** Founded in 1953, it contains more than 5,000 pieces of Native American and Hispanic art, the core of Standard Oil heiress Millicent Rogers's impressive private collection. Displayed is an excellent collection of baskets, blankets, rugs, jewelry, kachina dolls, carvings, paintings, and rare pieces of Hispanic religious and secular artifacts. A recent acquisition of major importance is the pottery and ceramics of Maria Martinez and members of the famous San Ildefonso family of potters. There are permanent and changing exhibits, guided tours on request, lectures, films, workshops, demonstrations, and a gift shop. The museum is about 4 mi northwest of the Plaza along NM 522. ⊠ *NM 522 (Box A),* ☎ *505/758–2462,* 🆇 *505/758–2462.* ⊑ *$4.* ⊙ *Daily 9–5; closed Mon. Nov.–Mar.*

OFF THE
BEATEN PATH

GHOST RANCH/ABIQUIÚ – Georgia O'Keeffe wrote, "When I first saw the Abiquiú house it was a ruin...As I climbed and walked about in the ruin I found a patio with a very pretty well house and a bucket to draw up water. It was a good-sized patio with a long wall with a door on one side. That wall with a door in it was something I had to have. It took me 10 years to get it—three more years to fix the house up so I could live in it—and after that the wall with the door was painted many times." The artist first stayed on the hauntingly beautiful Ghost Ranch, owned by a family who let her use the ranch to paint. In 1949 she moved to her permanent ranch in Abiquiú, 20 mi south of Ghost Ranch, and continued to paint her dreamy landscapes and beguiling still lifes.

Upon her death in 1986 at the age of 98, O'Keeffe had special provisions in her will to ensure the houses would never be public monuments or tourist arenas. Therefore, the rocky desert vistas between Ghost Ranch and Abiquiú are all that remain open to public scrutiny. Part of Ghost Ranch is a living museum today (☞ Side Trip, *below*), but it shows no trace of O'Keeffe to the public eye; her Abiquiú home is rarely open. This call for privacy seems appropriate for her persona of grace and paintings of puzzling beauty. To venture to O'Keeffe country, take U.S. 68 south to Española, I–84 west to Abiquiú; look for a dirt road off I–84 marked with a cattle-skull highway sign.

The Enchanted Circle

The 84-mi day trip through the Enchanted Circle, a breathtaking panorama of alpine valleys and the towering mountains of the lush Carson National Forest, in many ways takes you into another century. Its charming name is the brainchild of hard-working marketers, but you won't really argue with the choice. The trip can easily be combined with the drive to Artistic and Literary Taos (☞ A Good Drive, *above*) because both the D. H. Lawrence Ranch and the Millicent Rogers Museum are on the loop.

Numbers in the text correspond to numbers in the margin and on the Taos Environs: The Enchanted Circle map.

A Good Drive

Traveling east from Taos along I–64 you'll soon be winding through Taos Canyon, climbing your way toward 9,000-ft-high Palo Flechado Pass. On the other side of the pass, in about 25 mi you will come to **Angel Fire** ⑰, now primarily a ski resort, named for the glow that covers the mountain in the late autumn and early winter. Continue east on I–64 about 14 mi to tiny **Eagle Nest** ⑱, an old-fashioned ski-resort village. Next you'll get on U.S. 38 going northwest and head over Bobcat Pass, just under 10,000 ft in elevation, about 16 mi to **Red River** ⑲. In winter stop at Red River Ski area to get in some super skiing; in summer see a staged shootout or take advantage of the proximity to the Sangre de Cristo Mountains. From Red River, the Enchanted Circle heads west about 12 mi to **Questa** ⑳, amid some of the most beautiful mountain country in New Mexico and the Carson National Forest. Turning left at downtown Questa's main intersection, you're about 20 mi from Taos on NM 522. About 5 mi south along NM 522, the Red River Fish Hatchery is worth a trip (☞ Off the Beaten Path, *below*). This is also the leg where you would stop at the D. H. Lawrence Ranch and Shrine and the Millicent Rogers Museum (☞ Artistic and Literary Taos, *above*).

TIMING

Leave early in the morning and plan to spend the entire day on this trip, spending as much time as you wish in each town. During ski season you may want to make it an overnight trip and get in a day of skiing (☞ Skiing *in* Outdoor Activities and Sports, *below*). Summer, spring, and fall tours will offer easy, safe, and ice- and snow-free driving. But a good, sunny winter day yields some lovely winter scenery—don't forget your sunglasses!

Taos Environs: The Enchanted Circle

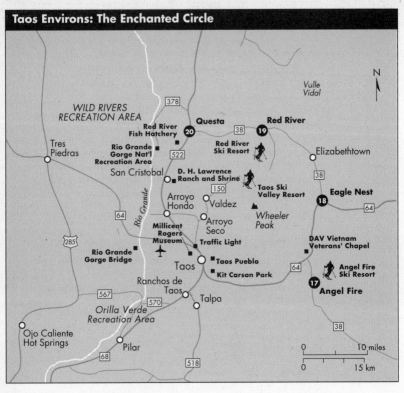

Sights To See

17 **Angel Fire.** Primarily a ski resort, this was for hundreds of years little more than a long, empty valley, and the fall meeting grounds of the Ute Native Americans. Here you'll find the stunning **Vietnam Veterans Memorial,** a 50-ft-high gull wing–shape monument built in 1971 by D. Victor Westphall, whose son David was killed in that war. The memorial's textured surface captures the dazzling, colorful reflections of the New Mexican mountains, changing constantly with the sun's movement. Angel Fire is on the north side of I–64, about 25 mi from Taos.

18 **Eagle Nest.** Surrounded by thousands of acres of national forest, this small, funky village welcomes—even cossets—skiers at the various hotels and B&Bs. Take a walk around to enjoy the old-fashioned shops and to get a feeling for the old New Mexico mining history. It is about 14 mi from Angel Fire.

20 **Questa.** Literally "hill" in the "Heart of the Sangre de Cristo Mountains" it is a small, quiet village nestled between the Red River and Taos amid some of the most beautiful mountain country in New Mexico. Don't miss **St. Anthony's Church,** built of adobe with 5-ft-thick walls and viga ceilings. It is about 12 mi from Red River.

OFF THE BEATEN PATH **RED RIVER FISH HATCHERY –** If you're traveling with children, take them on this fascinating, self-guided visit and see how freshwater trout are hatched, reared, stocked, and controlled. A visitor center has displays and exhibits, a show pond, and a machine that dispenses fish food, so you can feed the trout yourself. The tour can last anywhere from 20 to 90 minutes, depending on how enraptured you become. Guided tours are available for groups upon request. Parking and a picnic area are on the grounds. It is about 5 mi south of Questa along NM 522. ⊠ *NM 522, Questa,* ☎ *505/586-0222.* 🎫 *Free.* ⊙ *Daily 8-5.*

⑲ **Red River.** Another major ski resort, it has 33 trails and a bustling little downtown filled with shops and sportswear boutiques. Red River came into being as a miners' boom town during the last century, taking its name from the river whose mineral content gave it a rich, rosy color. When the gold petered out, Red River died, only to be rediscovered in the 1920s by migrants who were escaping the dust bowl. Rising 8,750 ft above sea level at the base of Wheeler Peak, New Mexico's highest mountain, Red River is the highest, if not the loftiest, town in the state. Much of the Old West flavor remains: Main Street shoot-outs, an authentic melodrama, and plenty of square dancing and two-stepping. In fact, because of its many country dances and festivals, Red River is affectionately called "The New Mexico Home of the Texas Two-Step." ☎ *505/776–5510 for reservations and directions.*

NEED A BREAK?

In Red River stop by the **Sundance** (⊠ High St., ☎ 505/754-2971) for Mexican food or **Texas Red's Steakhouse** (⊠ Main St., ☎ 505/754-2964) for steaks, chops, burgers, or chicken.

DINING

Taos is well on its way to developing a solid restaurant base. Restaurants vary from sophisticated to the less-than-polished basic. Several modest, local eateries serve up basic Southwestern dishes oozing cheese and chiles. Good, upscale places exist, too, and they're a sure bet for fresh ingredients and some flair. For fine dining hit the restaurants with highly trained chefs, first-class service, and delectable food. Tucked in among all these are the usual bacon-and-egg coffee shops and a great Italian deli.

CATEGORY	COST*
$$$	over $15
$$	$10–$15
$	under $10

per person, excluding drinks, service, and sales tax (6.9%)

$$$ ✕ **Apple Tree.** Named for the large tree in the courtyard, this is a great lunch and early dinner spot in a historic adobe Territorial house on Bent Street, a block from the Plaza. It's a bit overpriced but you can rely on fresh ingredients in tasty dishes such as grilled lamb and chicken fajitas. A weekend brunch is served from 11:30 to 3, and weekdays lunch is served from 11:30 to 3. ⊠ *123 Bent St.,* ☎ *505/758–1900. AE, D, DC, MC, V.*

$$$ ✕ **Casa Cordova.** This cozy restaurant, an L-shape adobe building with a wooden portal, serves classic food in a large dining area with two fireplaces. Menu highlights include rosemary crêpes with wild mushrooms and (occasionally) homemade pâté among the appetizers, and fresh trout, steak au poivre, quail, and sweetbreads among the entrées. ⊠ *NM 150 (Ski Valley Rd.) at Arroyo Seco,* ☎ *505/776–2500. AE, MC, V. Closed Sun.*

$$$ ✕ **Casa de Valdez.** A large A-frame building with wood-paneled walls and beamed ceilings, Casa de Valdez has a rustic, mountain-lodge feeling. The tables and chairs are handmade, as are the colorful drapes on the windows. Owner-chef Peter Valdez specializes in hickory-smoked barbecues, charcoal-grilled steaks, and regional New Mexican cuisine. ⊠ *1401 Paseo del Pueblo Sur,* ☎ *505/758–8777. AE, D, MC, V. Closed Wed.*

76

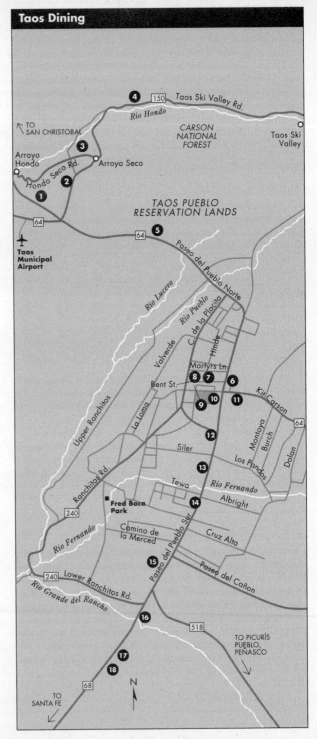

Taos Dining

$$$ ✗ **Doc Martin's.** The restaurant of the **Taos Inn,** Doc Martin's takes its name from the building's original owner, a local physician who performed operations and delivered babies in the rooms that now make up the dining areas. Its Southwestern decor makes a charming setting to enjoy breakfast, lunch, or dinner. Chef Patrick Lambert brings to the table some imaginative dishes such as seared salmon in roasted garlic cream sauce; he also makes a scrumptious Aztec chocolate mousse with roasted-banana sauce. ⊠ *Taos Inn, 125 Paseo del Pueblo Norte,* ☎ *505/758–1977. MC, V.*

$$$ ✗ **Jacquelina's.** A relative newcomer, this is fast becoming a very pop-
★ ular local dining spot. Chef Chuck La Mendole creates food with delicate flair and superb presentation. The grilled salmon with tomatillo salsa is super, as is the barbecued shrimp with *poblano* (a dark green, rich-tasting chile, ranging from mild to fiery) corn salsa. It's the place to go for great upscale Southwestern food, knowledgeable service, and comfortable surroundings. ⊠ *1541 Paseo del Pueblo Sur,* ☎ *505/751–0399. MC, V. Closed Mon. No lunch Sat.*

$$$ ✗ **Joseph's Table.** The former site of a Chinese restaurant has been transformed into a warmly romantic, European-style eatery (but you still enter through the kitchen!). Artfully prepared menu items include roasted duck and steak with garlic "smashed" potatoes. ⊠ *4167 Paseo del Pueblo Sur,* ☎ *505/751–4512. MC, V. Closed Mon. No weekend lunch.*

$$$ ✗ **Lambert's of Taos.** In the historic Randall House, 2½ blocks south of the Plaza, this restaurant serves contemporary American dishes prepared from fresh ingredients. They have a formidable array of fine California vintages and the desserts are tasty. ⊠ *309 Paseo del Pueblo Sur,* ☎ *505/758–1009. AE, DC, MC, V. No lunch weekends.*

$$$ ✗ **Stakeout Grill and Bar.** Tucked into Outlaw Hill, in the foothills of the Sangre de Cristo Mountains 9 mi south of Taos Plaza, this old adobe homestead has 100-mi-long views and sunsets that dazzle. But the main attraction is the food: New York strip steaks, filet mignon, roast prime rib, shrimp scampi, swordfish steak, duck, chicken, and daily pasta specials. Clearly marked by a huge cowboy hat next to the highway turnoff, the restaurant's rustic decor will take you back to the days of the Wild West. ⊠ *Stakeout Dr. (off U.S. 68),* ☎ *505/758–2042. AE, D, DC, MC, V.*

$$$ ✗ **Villa Fontana.** Entering this restaurant is like walking into a so-
★ phisticated Italian country inn: warm coral walls, candlelit dining, gleaming hardwood well-appointed tables, and starched linens. Master chef Carlo Gislimberti prepares classic northern Italian cuisine, including the house special featuring locally picked wild mushrooms, a variety of seasonal game, such as venison and pheasant, and a wonderful grilled whole sole. Siobhan Gislimberti oversees the first-class dining with great charm and the staff is so beautifully trained they seem like ballet dancers going through their paces. Lunch is served in the garden. ⊠ *NM 522, 5 mi north of Taos Plaza,* ☎ *505/758–5800. AE, D, DC, MC, V. Closed Sun. No lunch Nov.–May.*

$$–$$$ ✗ **Trading Post Cafe.** Chic ambience, excellent service, and an imagi-
★ native menu make this relative newcomer the most popular dining spot in town. The simple decor, intelligent wait staff, and plentiful, delicately prepared food are all sure bets. The perfectly marinated salmon gravlax appetizer is exceptional and the paella is a bounty for two. Desserts, such as homemade raspberry sorbet, are delicious. This is an outstanding dining experience. ⊠ *4179 U.S. 68 (at NM 518),* ☎ *505/758–5089. MC, V. Closed Sun.*

$$ ✗ **Bent Street Deli.** This small, unassuming deli offers an extensive selection of great soups, sandwiches, salads, and desserts as well as gourmet coffees, beer, and wine. Among other tempting sandwiches, they do Reubens for East Coasters who can't live without their dose of pastrami. But don't get full—there's cheesecake and other sweet treats in the glass counter at the front. Dinners are a little fancier with fresh salmon, Sumatra primavera pasta with Indonesian peanut sauce, or the ever-popular *camarones* (shrimp) in pesto sauce. Breakfast is served until 11. ⊠ *120 Bent St.,* ☎ *505/758–5787. MC, V. Closed Sun.*

$$ ✕ **Ogelvie's Bar and Grill.** Occupying the second floor of an old two-story adobe building on the east side of the Taos Plaza, Ogelvie's is the perfect spot for people-watching from on high, especially from the outdoor patio in summer. It's clean, comfortable, and reasonably priced. Go there for dependable meat-and-potato dishes and no surprises. Sure bets are Angus beef, grilled Rocky Mountain trout, and meat or cheese enchiladas. A special light-and-healthy menu is available. ⊠ *1031 E. Plaza,* ☎ *505/758–8866. Reservations not accepted. AE, DC, MC, V.*

$$ ✕ **Tim's Chile Connection.** Young skiers flock here for lots of beer—it is also home of the Taos Brewery—western music, and Tim's stick-to-your-ribs Southwestern blue-corn tortillas, homemade salsa, buffalo burgers and steaks, and fajitas. It's a bit pricey for what it serves, but the margaritas are monumental and delicious—even memorable. ⊠ *Ski Valley Rd. (NM 150),* ☎ *505/776–8787. D, DC, MC, V.*

$–$$ ✕ **Fred's Place.** This quirky but congenial spot is so popular with the locals that you might have to wait for a table, but it's worth it. Owner-chef Fred serves northern New Mexico specialties like *carne adovada* (meat, marinated in a spicy sauce) and blue-corn enchiladas prepared with unexpected subtlety and flair. The restaurant is eccentrically decorated (locally carved crucifixes and santos, a ceiling mural of Hell) and peopled with a hip, friendly staff. ⊠ *332 Paseo del Pueblo Sur,* ☎ *505/758–0514. Reservations not accepted. MC, V. Closed Sun. No lunch.*

$ ✕ **Casa Fresen Bakery.** Tucked away in Arroyo Seco, this first-class
★ bakery, espresso bar, and Italian deli is a very popular spot among locals. Enjoy sumptuous imported cheeses—those usually found only in New York City—fresh pâté, and specialty meats as well as homemade breads, muffins, croissants, and pastries. You'll find the most delectable sandwiches you've had in a long time and take-out lunches and picnic baskets that are better than Mom makes. ⊠ *CR 150, Taos Ski Valley Rd.,* ☎ *505/776–2969. MC, V.*

$ ✕ **El Pueblo Café.** This family-owned roadside café on the north side of town serves homemade Southwestern food in a friendly, peaceful atmosphere. It's inexpensive, cheerful, and delicious for a quick no-nonsense meal. ⊠ *625 Paseo del Pueblo Norte,* ☎ *505/758–2053. AE, MC, V.*

$ ✕ **Roberto's.** Bobby and Patsy Garcia serve creative native New Mexican dishes from recipes handed down through the Garcia family for generations. Three intimate Southwestern-style dining rooms are filled with art and cherished family antiques. The chiles rellenos are particularly good. ⊠ *122B E. Kit Carson Rd.,* ☎ *505/758–2434. AE, D, MC, V. Closed Tues.*

$ ✕ **Tapas de Taos Café.** Sugar skulls stare from the counters and paper skeletons dance from the ceiling at this funky café. But beyond the Mexican *Dia de los Muertos* (Day of the Dead) paraphernalia, the food is fresh and well made. The specialty is tapas, which usually means small versions of burritos, empanadas, and tacos. You can mix and match from the menu and have a great time. In summer there are two pleasant patios for people-watching or sipping lemonade in the shade of huge trees. ⊠ *136 Bent St.,* ☎ *505/758–9670. D, MC, V.*

LODGING

Taos's range of hotels and motels along U.S. 68, also known as the Paseo del Pueblo Sur and Norte, suits every need and budget. Big-name chains to smaller establishments offer basic accommodations with no drastic variation in hotel rates from season to season.

Expect higher lodging rates during the two high seasons: ski season (usually late December–early April, depending upon snow conditions) and summer (July–August). Reservations are highly recommended during these times. Skiers now have many deluxe resorts to choose from, both in town and on the slopes.

By far the best deals in town are the bed-and-breakfasts. Family-owned and carefully decorated, they provide personal service, delicious breakfasts, and many extras that hotels charge for. The B&B's are often in comfy old adobes that have been lovingly refurbished with style and flair. Owners love to suggest interesting adventures and great restaurants, or just sit and chat over a glass of wine or a cup of tea.

CATEGORY	COST*
$$$	over $95
$$	$50–$95
$	under $50

All prices are for a standard double room, excluding 3.5% city room tax or 3% county room tax, 6.9% city sales tax or 6.3% county sales tax, and service charges.

Hotels

$$$ ☷ **Fechin Inn.** Taos's first new hotel in 10 years is a graceful Pueblo Revival sprawl on the grounds of the Fechin Institute (to which guests have free admission) and adjacent to Kit Carson Park. Fechin's daughter, Eya, participated in the planning; Fechin reproductions adorn the rooms and hallways, and the woodwork in the large, comfortable lobby is based on the artists designs. A generous Continental breakfast is available every morning in the lobby, as are cocktails in evening. Rooms are comfortable, if somewhat nondescript; most have a private balcony or patio. Pets are welcome. ✉ *227 Paseo del Pueblo Norte, 87571,* ☎ *505/751–1000 or 800/811–2933,* ℻ *505/751–7338. 85 rooms and suites. Massage, exercise room, ski storage, meeting rooms, free parking. AE, D, DC, MC, V.*

$$$ ☷ **Sagebrush Inn.** Built in adobe Pueblo-Mission style in 1929, this beautiful inn is graced with authentic Navajo rugs, rare pottery, Southwestern and Spanish antiques, fine carved pieces, and paintings by Southwestern masters. Georgia O'Keeffe once lived and painted in one of the third-story rooms. Many of the bedrooms have kiva-style fireplaces; some have balconies looking out to the Sangre de Cristo Mountains. The Sagebrush Village offers condominium family lodging, too. ✉ *1508 Paseo del Pueblo Sur (3 mi south of the Plaza), Box 557, 87571,* ☎ *505/758–2254 or 800/428–3626,* ℻ *505/758–5077. 100 rooms and suites. 2 restaurants, lounge, pool, 2 hot tubs. AE, D, DC, MC, V.*

$$–$$$$ ☷ **Taos Inn.** Only steps from the Taos Plaza, this hotel is an historic landmark listed in the National Register of Historic Places. The guest rooms are pleasant and comfortable. In summer there's dining alfresco on the patio. The lobby, which also serves as seating for the **Adobe Bar,** is built around an old town well, from which a fountain now bubbles forth. Most of the town's shops and restaurants are within walking distance of the hotel. ✉ *125 Paseo del Pueblo Norte, 87571,* ☎ *505/*

80

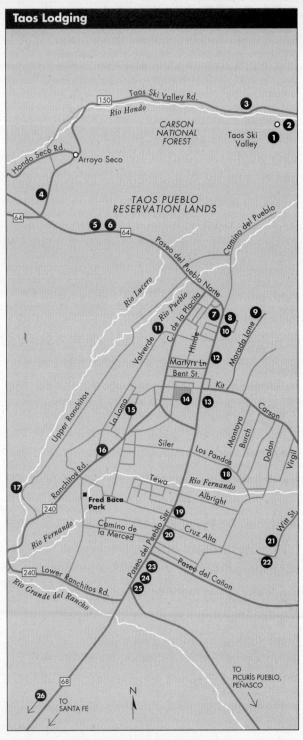

Taos Lodging

758–2233 or 800/TAOS–INN, FAX *505/758–5776. 36 rooms. Restaurant, bar, lounge, library. AE, DC, MC, V.*

$$–$$$ 🏨 **Comfort Suites.** The owners of the Sagebrush Inn next door opened this complex of 60 suites in December 1996. Each unit features a living room with a sofa bed plus a bedroom with a king- and a queen-size bed, television in both rooms, microwave oven, coffeemaker, and refrigerator. Complimentary breakfast is served in the expansive breakfast room in the main lobby. ✉ *1500 Paseo del Pueblo Sur (Box 1268), 87571,* ☎ *505/751–1555 or 888/751–1555. 60 suites. Hot tub, pool. AE, D, DC, MC, V.*

$$ 🏨 **Don Fernando de Taos Holiday Inn.** This seven-year-old hotel is built in a distinct Pueblo-style design, with rooms grouped around central courtyards and connected by meandering walkways. Rooms are tastefully appointed with hand-carved New Mexican furnishings and kiva-style fireplaces. ✉ *1005 Paseo del Pueblo Sur, Drawer V, 87571,* ☎ *505/758–4444 or 800/759–2736,* FAX *505/758–0055. 126 rooms. Restaurant, bar, lounge, pool, hot tub, tennis court. AE, D, DC, MC, V.*

$$ 🏨 **El Pueblo Lodge.** This low-to-the-ground Pueblo-style adobe only blocks north of the Taos Plaza has practical amenities: in-room refrigerators, kitchenettes, and complimentary guest laundry rooms. Traditional Southwestern furnishings and fireplaces give the rooms a homey feel. Free Continental breakfast is served in the lobby. ✉ *412 Paseo del Pueblo Norte (Box 92), 87571,* ☎ *505/758–8700 or 800/ 433–9612,* FAX *505/758–7321. 60 rooms. Pool, hot tub. AE, D, MC, V.*

$$ 🏨 **Hotel La Fonda de Taos.** Here's a hotel that has seen better days but once was a place of pride in town. On the south side of the Plaza, it is worth a visit if only to walk through the foyer full of old newspaper clippings and grandiose paintings. But, even more, $3 will get you into the manager's cluttered office to view erotic paintings by D. H. Lawrence. Banned in London in the 1920s, they'd hardly cause you to bat an eye now. Far more interesting are the innumerable photographs of some of the famous literary figures of the town, lolling around being literate and precious. Also displayed is a hodgepodge of Western paintings, Hopi shields, portraits, busts, Mexican paintings and artifacts, and mounted bullfighters' costumes in full pose, often mistaken by older guests for bellhops. ✉ *Taos Plaza (Box 1447), 87571,* ☎ *505/ 758–2211 or 800/833–2211,* FAX *505/758–8508. 24 rooms. Lounge. AE, MC, V.*

$$ 🏨 **Kachina Lodge de Taos–Best Western.** A large and comfortable lodge, this hotel is built in a two-story Pueblo-style adobe. Every night from Memorial Day through Labor Day, a troupe from the nearby Taos Pueblo performs ritual dances outside by firelight. Not surprisingly, the kachina theme is carried throughout, and guest rooms continue the Southwestern Native American theme with handmade and hand-painted furnishings and colorful bedspreads. It is just down the road from Taos Pueblo and minutes from the Taos Plaza. ✉ *413 Paseo del Pueblo Norte (Box NN), 87571,* ☎ *505/758–2275 or 800/522–4462,* FAX *505/758–9207. 118 rooms. Restaurant, bar, coffee shop, pool, hot tub, shops. AE, D, DC, MC, V.*

$$ 🏨 **Rancho Ramada Inn de Taos.** More Taos than Ramada, the two-story adobe-style hotel welcomes you with a lobby fireplace, desert colors, Western art, and Native American pottery. The rooms have an inviting Southwestern-style flavor. The Fireside Cantina specializes in spicy Southwestern cuisine and American favorites, and you can enjoy hors d'oeuvres here while sitting by a cozy fireplace. There is also live music here during peak summer months. ✉ *615 Paseo del Pueblo Sur, Box 6257, 87571,* ☎ *505/758–2900 or 800/272–6232,* FAX *505/758–*

1662. 124 rooms. Dining room, lounge, pool, meeting rooms. AE, D, DC, MC, V.

$ 🖭 **Sun God Lodge.** Some of the movie *Twins* was filmed here. Though inexpensive, this motel has old adobe charm with basic amenities—a good deal for the price. Right on the main highway, the lodge is convenient to the restaurants and historic sites. ⊠ *909 Paseo del Pueblo Sur, 87571,* ☎ *505/758–3162 or 800/821–2437. 55 rooms. Hot tub. AE, D, MC, V.*

Bed-and-Breakfasts

$$$ 🖭 **Adobe & Pines.** This delightful bed-and-breakfast has expansive views of Taos Mountain. Opened in 1991, the inn's main house is replete with Native American and Mexican artifacts, gorgeous Mexican-tiled baths, cozy kiva fireplaces, fluffy goose-down pillows, and comforters. A separate cottage and two new equally handsome casitas also house guests. The owners serve gourmet breakfasts in a charming, sunny, glass-enclosed patio. If you like the food, they also sell a small cookbook of their favorite recipes. ⊠ *U.S. 68 (Box 837), Ranchos de Taos 87557,* ☎ *505/751–0947 or 800/723–8267,* ℻ *505/758–8423. 4 rooms, 1 cottage, 2 casitas. No smoking. 4 Jacuzzis, sauna. MC, V.*

$$$ 🖭 **Casa de las Chimeneas.** Just 2½ blocks from the Plaza, "the house ★   of chimneys," with regional art, tile hearths, French doors, and traditional viga ceilings, is secluded behind thick adobe walls. The grand interior of this Spanish-style hacienda was originally built in 1912. Each room has its own private entrance, a fireplace, handmade New Mexican furniture, and a tile bar stocked with complimentary juices, sodas, and mineral waters. All rooms overlook the formal gardens and fountains. The two-course breakfasts—maybe featuring an artichoke mushroom omelette with corn muffins—and late-afternoon hors d'oeuvres are delicious and change daily. ⊠ *405 Cordoba Rd. (Box 5303), 87571,* ☎ *505/758–4777,* ℻ *505/758–3976. 3 rooms, 1 suite. No smoking. Outdoor hot tub. AE, MC, V.*

$$$ 🖭 **Inn on La Loma Plaza.** The walls surrounding this Spanish-style inn, formerly the Taos Hacienda Inn and listed on the National Register of Historic Places, were built in the early 1800s to protect a small enclave of settlers from invasions. Now, guests can enjoy the privacy and relax after skiing or sightseeing. This rambling inn is lovely; its rooms have handcrafted Southwestern decor and fireplaces with sitting areas. Breakfast is served in the dining room or the plant-filled sunroom. The eclectic, comfortable living room has an interesting antique camera collection and a formidable library; it's perfect for reading and relaxing. ⊠ *315 Ranchitos Rd. (Box 4159), 87571,* ☎ *505/758–1717 or 800/ 530–3040,* ℻ *505/751–0155. 5 rooms, 2 artist studios with kitchenettes. AE, MC, V.*

$$–$$$ 🖭 **Casa Europa.** This pleasant B&B, its original adobe bricks and wood viga ceiling intact, is a classic estate set on six acres overlooking pastures and the surrounding mountains. The rooms are nicely furnished with an eclectic collection of European antiques and Southwestern pieces, including the oldest door in Taos. The main guest areas are light and airy with comfortable chairs to relax in and listen to the fire crackle. Breakfasts are elaborate, and complimentary homemade afternoon pastries are served daily except during the ski season, when they're replaced by evening hors d'oeuvres. ⊠ *840 Upper Ranchitos Rd., HC 68 (Box 3F), 87571,* ☎ *505/758–9798 or 888/758–9798. 6 double rooms. Hot tub, sauna. MC, V.*

$$–$$$ 🖭 **La Posada de Taos.** Just a couple of blocks from the Taos Plaza is this provincial adobe with beamed ceilings, a portal, kiva-style fireplaces, and the intimacy of a private hacienda. Four of its five guest rooms are in the main house; the fifth is a separate cottage with a queen-size four-poster bed, a sitting room, and a fireplace—all cozy and pretty enough to be dubbed *La Casa de la Luna de Miel* (The Honeymoon House). Adobe fireplaces can be found in four of the five guest rooms, which have either mountain or flowering-courtyard views. Innkeepers Bill Swan and Nancy Brooks-Swan offer a full, hearty breakfast, from traditional ham and country eggs to spicy burritos. ⊠ *309 Juanita La. (Box 1118), 87571,* ☎ *505/758–8164 or 800/645–4803. 5 rooms, 1 cottage. No credit cards.*

$$–$$$ 🖭 **Mabel Dodge Luhan House.** This National Historic Landmark was once the home of this heiress and professional friend to the literati of the area. Past guests, from pre-bed-and-breakfast days, included D. H. and Frieda Lawrence, Georgia O'Keeffe, and Willa Cather. There are nine guest rooms in the main house, and eight more in a separate guest house, as well as a two-bedroom gatehouse cottage. The inn is frequently used for literary, artistic, cultural, and educational meetings and workshops. A full Southwest-style buffet breakfast is served. Don't expect glamour—this is one of the most basic B&Bs in town. The buildings are rumpled and frayed and the stairs creak. Meal service is available for groups, and public tennis courts are nearby. ⊠ *Box 3400, 240 Morada La., 87571,* ☎ *505/758–9456 or 800/846–2235,* ℻ *505/751–0431. 12 rooms with bath, 5 without bath, 1 cottage. Meeting rooms. AE, MC, V.*

$$–$$$ 🖭 **Touchstone Inn.** D. H. Lawrence visited this house when Miriam De-
★ Witt owned it in 1929. The owner, Taos artist Bren Price, has filled the elegant rooms, named after famous Taos literary figures, with a tasteful mix of antique and modern pieces. The grounds overlook part of the Taos Pueblo lands, and this makes for a pleasantly quiet stay. Some suites have fireplaces. Early morning coffee is served in the gracious living room, and gourmet breakfasts with inventive presentations are served in the glassed-in patio. ⊠ *0110 Mabel Dodge La. (Box 2896), 87571,* ☎ *505/758–0192 or 800/758–0192,* ℻ *505/758–3498. 8 rooms. In-room VCRs, hot tub. MC, V.*

$$ 🖭 **Brooks Street Inn.** An elaborately carved corbel arch, the handiwork of Japanese carpenter Yaichikido, spans the entrance to a shaded, walled garden. The guest rooms show great attention to detail with fresh flowers and fluffy pillows. Paintings by local artists adorn the walls. The full breakfast is dreamy: blue-corn pancakes with pineapple salsa, stuffed French toast with apricot glaze, and other home-baked delights, all served with good, fresh coffee, espresso, and cappuccino. In warm weather breakfast is served at umbrella tables on the patio; in winter it's served by the fireplace. ⊠ *119 Brooks St. (Box 4954), 87571,* ☎ *505/758–1489 or 800/758–1489. 6 rooms. No smoking. AE, MC, V.*

$$ 🖭 **Hacienda del Sol.** Art patron Mabel Dodge Luhan bought this
★ house in the 1920s and lived here with her fourth husband, Tony Luhan, while building their main house, Las Palomas de Taos. It was also their private retreat and guest house for visiting notables; author Frank Waters wrote *People of the Valley* here. Most of the rooms feature kiva-style fireplaces, Spanish antiques, Southwestern-style handcrafted furniture, and original artwork. The secluded outdoor hot tub has a crystalline view of Taos Mountain. The jet-black bathroom of Los Amantes Room is a celebration in decadence with its huge black hot tub amid a jungle of potted plants and a skylight for stargazing. A full gourmet breakfast is served. ⊠ *109 Mabel Dodge La. (Box 177), 87571,* ☎ *505/758–0287,* ℻ *505/758–5895. 9 rooms. Outdoor hot tub. MC, V.*

$$ 🖭 **Old Taos Guesthouse.** Once a ramshackle adobe hacienda, this homey bed-and-breakfast has been completely and lovingly outfitted with the owners' handmade furniture, Western artifacts, and antiques.

Some rooms have the smallest bathrooms you'll ever encounter, but they all have private entrances and some have fireplaces. There are 80-mi views from the outdoor hot tub. The owners welcome families and personal checks. ✉ *1028 Witt Rd. (Box 6552), 87571,* ☎ *505/758–5448 or 800/758–5448. 9 rooms. Hot tub. MC, V.*

$$ 🏨 **Orinda.** Built in 1947, this is a dramatic adobe estate with spectacular views and country privacy. The spacious one- and two-bedroom suites have separate entrances, kiva-style fireplaces, traditional viga ceilings, and Mexican-tile baths. Two rooms share a common sitting room. The thick adobe walls ensure peace and quiet. A common area with a fireplace and a picture window faces Taos Mountain. A hearty breakfast is served family-style in the soaring two-story sun atrium amid a gallery of artwork, all for sale. ✉ *461 Valverde (Box 4451), 87571,* ☎ *505/758–8581 or 800/847–1837,* ℻ *505/751–4895. 4 rooms. No smoking. AE, D, MC, V.*

$$ 🏨 **San Geronimo Lodge.** Tucked away along a small street off Kit Carson Road, this lodge sits on 2½ acres that front the majestic Taos Mountain and back up to the Carson National Forest. The owners have a collective eye for retaining its original 1925 charm. There's a balcony library, attractive grounds, and two beautifully appointed rooms designed for people with disabilities. Many rooms have fireplaces. The hotel staff will arrange ski packages. ✉ *1101 Witt Rd., 87571,* ☎ *505/751–3776 or 800/894–4119,* ℻ *505/751–1493. 18 rooms. Hot tub, pool, massage. AE, D, DC, MC, V.*

Resorts and Ski Lodges

$$$ 🏨 **Inn at Snakedance.** This modern, spotlessly clean resort hotel epitomizes the rustic, elegant tradition of European Alpine lodges. Right on the slopes, the inn has a handsome library where guests can enjoy an après-ski coffee or after-dinner drink by a fieldstone fireplace. The dining room has a soaring ceiling with 100-year-old beams originally cut for the copper mines down the road. Chef Harold Orner oversees imaginative food with a Southwestern flair. Rooms have a pleasant Southwestern motif and some have fireplaces. In summer the hotel offers weeklong vacation packages, including a cooking school and several fitness adventure courses. ✉ *Box 89, Taos Ski Valley 87525,* ☎ *505/776–2277 or 800/322–9815,* ℻ *505/776–1410. 60 rooms. Minibars, refrigerators, hot tub, massage, sauna, exercise room. AE, MC, V. Closed mid-Apr.–Memorial Day.*

$$$ 🏨 **Thunderbird Lodge and Chalets.** Only 150 yards from the main lifts, on the sunny side of the Taos Ski Valley, this large, two-story wood-frame inn is nothing fancy, but it's great for families with kids. A large conference room doubles as a game room, with board games and a library. Supervised children's activities include early dinners, movies, and games. Lodge rooms are small and functional; the Chalet rooms are larger, with king-size beds. ✉ *Box 87, Taos Ski Valley 87525,* ☎ *505/776–2280 or 800/776–2279,* ℻ *505/776–2238. 32 rooms. Restaurant, bar, hot tub, massage, sauna, conference room. MC, V.*

$$–$$$$ 🏨 **Austing Haus.** This beautifully decorated hotel is 1½ mi from the
★ Taos Ski Valley. Owner Paul Austing constructed a lot of the building and its furnishings himself. The dining room has picture windows for walls, stained-glass paneling, a fireplace, and a Native American loom with a partially completed blanket mounted on the wall. Guest rooms are pretty and quiet with harmonious, peaceful colors; some have romantic four-poster beds and fireplaces. The restaurant's house specialties are veal Oscar and steak au poivre. During the winter, the inn offers weeklong ski packages. ✉ *Taos Ski Valley Rd., NM 150 (Box 8), Taos Ski Valley 87525,* ☎ *505/776–2649, 505/776–2629, or 800/748–2932,* ℻ *505/776–8751. 44 rooms. Restaurant, hot tub. DC, MC, V.*

$$–$$$$ ☎ **Quail Ridge Inn Resort.** On the way to the Taos Ski Valley, this large resort has one- and two-story modern adobe bungalows that are comfy and efficient. Some suites have kitchens. The resort offers a host of recreational amenities, from organized trail rides to hot-tub soaks. Complete ski, tennis, rafting, mountain-bike, and fly-fishing packages are available for groups or individuals. ⊠ *Ski Valley Rd., NM 150 (Box 707), Taos 87571,* ☎ *505/776–2211 or 800/624–4448,* ℻ *505/776–2949. 110 rooms and suites. Restaurant, lounge, pool, hot tub, 8 tennis courts, exercise room, racquetball, squash, volleyball. AE, D, DC, MC, V.*

Campgrounds

Thousands of miles of unspoiled wilderness await campers in and around the Taos area. A number of commercial campgrounds can be found as well.

$ ⛺ **Carson National Forest.** Within the rugged forest are 30 campgrounds dotted along 400 mi of cool mountain trout streams and lakes. You may also choose your own site, anywhere along a forest road. Contact the forest service for the latest information on camping and exploring the forest (☞ Side Trip, *below*). ⊠ *Forest Service Building, 208 Cruz Alta Rd., Taos 87571,* ☎ *505/758–6200. 30 RV and tent sites. Rest rooms.*

$ ⛺ **Orilla Verde Recreation Area.** Camping, hiking, fishing, and picnicking along the banks of the Rio Grande can be done from this area, 10 mi south of Taos town. It's open year-round. ⊠ *Bureau of Land Management, Cruz Alta Rd., Taos 87571,* ☎ *505/758–8851. About 70 tent sites. Rest rooms.*

$ ⛺ **Questa Lodge.** This campsite is just off the beaten path of the Enchanted Circle, 2 blocks from NM 522. Sites here are on the Red River, and open from May to mid-October. ⊠ *08 Lower Embargo Rd. (Box 155), Questa 87556,* ☎ *505/586–0300 or 800/459–0300. 26 RV sites. Rest rooms, hot showers, basketball, croquet, volleyball, playground, coin laundry.*

$ ⛺ **Taos RV Park.** This park in the foothills of the Sangre de Cristo mountains, 3½ mi from Taos Plaza. The sites are grassy, with a few small trees. It's open year-round. ⊠ *U.S. 68, 1799 Paseo del Pueblo Sur (Box 729F), Ranchos de Taos 87557 (next to the Taos Motel, just off the intersection of NM 518),* ☎ *505/758–1667 or 800/323–6009. 29 RV and tent sites. Rest rooms, hot showers, horseshoes, video games, playground.*

$ ⛺ **Roadrunner Campground.** A river runs through it—the Red River— right through this spectacular woodsy mountain campground. Grounds are closed from mid-December to early spring. ⊠ *NM 578 (Box 588), Red River 87558,* ☎ *505/754–2286 or 800/243–2286. 155 RV sites. Rest rooms, hot showers, grocery, tennis court, video games, playground, laundry, meeting room.*

NIGHTLIFE AND THE ARTS

Evening entertainment is a modest affair in Taos. On weekends the local motels and hotels offer a pleasant variety of music in their bars and lounges. Everything from down-home blues bands to Texas two-step dancing blossoms on Saturday and Sunday nights in the winter. Come summer, things heat up during the week as well. For information about what's going on around town, get a copy of **Taos Magazine** (⊠ Box 1380, Taos 87571, ☎ 505/758–5404), published eight times a year. The weekly paper, *Taos News*, published on Thursday, has detailed information in the "Tempo" entertainment section.

The Arts

The **Taos Community Auditorium** (⊠ 145 Paseo del Pueblo Norte, ☎ 505/758–4677) offers performances of modern dance groups and the local theater group, concerts, movies, and even the sounds of Andean folk music. Contact the Taos Art Association (⊠ 133 N. Pueblo Rd., Taos 87571, ☎ 505/758–2052) for ticket information.

The **Taos Spring Arts Festival,** held throughout Taos May 1 to May 15, highlights the visual, performing, and literary arts of the community and allows you to rub elbows with the many artists who call Taos home. For information contact the Taos County Chamber of Commerce (☞ Visitor Information *in* Taos A to Z). The **Taos Fall Arts Festival,** September 19 to October 5, is the major arts gathering, celebrated throughout Taos when buyers are in town and many other events, such as a Taos Pueblo feast, are going on. Contact the Taos County Chamber of Commerce (☞ Visitor Information *in* Taos A to Z).

The **Wool Festival,** held in Kit Carson Park late September or early October during the same time as the Taos Fall Arts Festival, features everything from sheep to shawl, with demonstrations of shearing, spinning, and weaving, handmade woolen items for sale, and tastings of favorite lamb dishes. For information contact the Taos County Chamber of Commerce (☞ Visitor Information *in* Taos A to Z).

Film

Taos Talking Picture Festival (⊠ 216M N. Pueblo Rd. #216, ☎ 505/751–0637, FAX 505/751–7385), is a multicultural celebration of cinema artists, with a focus on Native American film and video makers. Each year in mid-April the festival presents new independent films, documentaries, animation, and some classic cinema. Each year they recognize a "Maverick" of the cinema.

Music

From mid-June through early August, the Taos School of Music and the International Institute of Music fill the evenings with the sounds of chamber and symphonic orchestras at the **Taos Chamber Music Festival** (⊠ Taos School of Music, Box 1879, ☎ 505/776–2388). This is America's oldest summer music program and possibly the largest enclave of professional musicians in the Southwest. It has been furthering the artistic growth of young string and piano students for more than 30 years. Concerts are presented every Saturday evening from mid-June through August at the Taos Community Auditorium (☞ *above*). Tickets cost $12. The Taos School of Music also gives free weekly summer concerts and recitals, from mid-June to early August, at the **Hotel Saint Bernard** (⊠ Box 88, Taos Ski Valley, ☎ 505/776–2251) at the mountain base (near the lifts) of the Taos Ski Valley.

Music from Angel Fire (⊠ Box 502, Angel Fire, ☎ 505/758–4667 or 505/377–3233) is a series of classical and jazz concerts presented at the Taos Community Auditorium (☞ *above*) and the Angel Fire Community Auditorium (⊠ Town center) from August 21 through September 2. Tickets cost about $12 per concert.

Nightlife

Bars and Lounges

Fernando's Hideaway (⊠ Holiday Inn, Paseo del Pueblo Norte, ☎ 505/758–4444) presents live entertainment nightly, alternating rock, jazz, blues, vocals, and country music. Saturday is reserved for karaoke. Lavish complimentary happy-hour buffets are offered on weekday evenings. **Hacienda** (⊠ 1321 Paseo del Pueblo Sur, ☎ 505/758–8610) features dancing and live rock or country entertainment on weekends. The **Adobe Bar** (⊠ Taos Inn, 125 Paseo del Pueblo Norte, ☎ 505/758–2233), Taos's local meet-and-greet spot, books talented local live acts, from a flute choir to individual guitarists and small jazz, folk, and country bands.

Cabaret

The **Kachina Lodge Cabaret** (⊠ 413 Paseo del Pueblo Norte, ☎ 505/758–2275) brings in headline acts, such as Arlo Guthrie and the Kingston Trio, on a regular basis and has dancing.

Coffeehouses

Caffe Tazza (⊠ 122 Kit Carson Rd., ☎ 505/758–8706) has a variety of free evening performances throughout the week—folk singing, poetry readings, open mike nights, and more.

Country-and-Western Clubs

The **Sagebrush Inn** (⊠ Paseo del Pueblo Sur, ☎ 505/758–2254) offers live music and dancing in its spacious lobby lounge. There's no cover charge, and if you show up on a Thursday, you can learn to two-step.

Jazz Clubs

Thunderbird Lodge (⊠ 3 Thunderbird Rd., ☎ 505/776–2280) in the Taos Ski Valley, has free jazz nights. The Thunderbird Jazz Trio performs every Sunday. On Wednesdays the lodge brings in a more modern group called Groove Junkies.

OUTDOOR ACTIVITIES AND SPORTS

Whether you plan to cycle around town, jog along Paseo del Pueblo Norte, or play a few rounds of golf, remember, the altitude in Taos is over 7,000 ft. With decreased oxygen content and decreased humidity you may experience some or all of the following symptoms: terrible headaches, nausea, insomnia, shortness of breath, diarrhea, sleeplessness, and tension. To deal with this radical altitude change sensibly, try to avoid alcohol and coffee, which aggravate "high-altitude syndrome," drink a lot of water and juice, and keep physical exertion to a minimum until your body acclimates. After a few days you should be your old self again and hit the road running.

Participant Sports

Bicycling

The Taos-area roads are steep and hilly, and none have marked bicycle lanes. Be cautious: drivers, many from out of state, may be as unfamiliar with a passing bicycle as they are with a passing deer.

"Gearing Up" Bicycle Shop (⊠ 129 Paseo del Pueblo Sur, ☎ 505/751–0365), is a full-service bike shop that also has information on tours and guides.

Hot Tracks, (⊠ 214 Paseo del Pueblo Sur, ☎ 505/751–0949), is where the Taos Cycle Club meets. The staff sells all kinds of bikes and is knowledgeable about the best places to go.

Serious bikers may want to participate in the annual autumn **Enchanted Circle Wheeler Peak Bicycle Rally** and the **Aspen-cade,** both held in late September: Hundreds of cyclists challenge the 100-mi route through Red River, Taos, Angel Fire, Eagle Nest, and Questa, past a brilliant blaze of fall color. Contact the Taos County Chamber of Commerce (☞ Visitor Information *in* Taos A to Z, *below*) for more information.

Golf

If golf's your game, take your clubs to Angel Fire's 18-hole PGA mountain course, one of the highest in the nation. Contact the **Angel Fire Pro Shop** (⊠ Angel Fire, ☎ 505/377–3055 or 800/633–7463) for tee times and greens fees.

The **Taos Country Club** (⊠ South of Taos at NM 240, ☎ 505/758–7300), is an 18-hole championship course with a separate practice facility.

Health Clubs

Hotel health facilities are generally reserved only for the use of guests. The **Northside Health & Fitness Center** (⊠ 1307 Paseo del Pueblo Norte, ☎ 505/751–1242) is a spotlessly clean health facility with indoor and outdoor pools, a hot tub, tennis courts, and aerobics classes. The center offers paid child care with a certified Montessori teacher. Available are 7-, 14-, 21-, and 30-day passes. Nonmembers pay $9 per day.

Jogging

The Taos mountain roads are challenging to a runner, to say the least. You might try the running track at the football field at **Taos High School** (⊠ 134 Cervantes St., ☎ 505/758–5230). It isn't officially open to the public, but no one seems to object if nonstudents, within reasonable numbers, jog there. The paths through **Kit Carson Park** are also suitable (☞ Taos Plaza and Bent Street *in* Exploring Taos, *above*).

River Rafting

White-water rafting through the wild and scenic Rio Grande is a growing sport in the region. The **Bureau of Land Management** (☎ 505/758–8851) has a list of registered river guides and further information on running the river on your own.

Far Flung Adventures (⊠ Box 707, El Prado 87529, ☎ 800/359–2627 outside Taos, 505/758–2628 in town) offers half-day, full-day, and overnight rafting trips along the Rio Grande and the Rio Chama.

Kokopelli Rafting (⊠ 541 Cordova Rd., Santa Fe, ☎ 800/879–9035) takes you through either the Taos Box, along the Lower and Upper Gorge, or down the Rio Grande.

Los Rios River Runners, Inc. (⊠ Box 2734, Taos 87571, ☎ 800/544–1181) will take you to your choice of spots—the Rio Chama, the Lower Gorge, or the Taos Box.

Skiing

RESORTS

In winter, within a 90-mi radius, Taos offers five ski resorts with beginning, intermediate, and advanced slopes, as well as snowmobile and cross-country skiing trails. All of these ski resorts offer excellent lodging accommodations and safe, modern child-care programs at reasonable prices.

Angel Fire Resort (⊠ Drawer B, Angel Fire 87710, ☎ 505/377–6401 or 800/633–7463 outside NM) has a hotel and is open from December 15 through the first week in April.

Red River Ski Area (⊠ Box 900, Red River 87558, ☎ 505/754–2382) is open from Thanksgiving to Easter.

Sipapu Lodge and Ski Area (⊠ NM 518, Box 29, Vadito 87579, ☎ 505/587–2240) is open from mid-December to the end of March.

Ski Rio (⊠ Box 159, Costillo 87524, ☎ 505/758–7707) opens for daily business from December 17 to April 7. The resort has 83 runs and makes its own snow.

Taos Ski Valley (⊠ Box 90, Taos Ski Valley 87525, ☎ 505/776–2291, 800/776–1111 or 505/776–2233 for reservations, FAX 505/776–8596) is open from November 22 through the first week in April.

CROSS-COUNTRY

At the **Enchanted Forest Cross-Country Ski Area** (⊠ Box 521, Red River 87558, ☎ 505/754–2374), the season runs from the end of November to Easter.

The **Carson National Forest** (⊠ Forest Service Building, 208 Cruz Alta Rd., Taos 87571, ☎ 505/758–6200) can provide a good self-guided map of cross-country trails throughout the park (☞ Side Trip, *below*).

Swimming

The **Don Fernando Municipal Swimming Pool** (⊠ 124 Civic Plaza Dr., ☎ 505/758–9171) is open for recreational swimming weekdays, 1–4:30 and weekends 1–5. The charge is $2.

Tennis

Kit Carson Park (⊠ Paseo del Pueblo Norte, 2 blocks north of Taos Plaza) and **Fred Baca Park** (⊠ 301 Camino de Medio) both have free public tennis courts, available on a first-come, first-served basis. Contact the Town of Taos Convention and Recreation Services (⊠ 120 Civic Plaza Dr., ☎ 505/758–4160) for information. The **Quail Ridge Inn and Tennis Ranch** (⊠ Taos Ski Valley Rd., ☎ 800/624–4448) has eight Laykold tennis courts (two indoor), which are free to guests and cost $30 per hour (indoor courts) for visitors. Each summer the resort offers a series of tennis programs with Tim Cass, the head coach of the University of New Mexico's Men's Tennis Team. Check with the resort for times and costs.

Spectator Sports

Spectator sports include the annual **Rodeo de Taos,** held at the Taos County Fairgrounds in mid-June, and the **Taos Mountain Balloon Rally,** held in a field south of downtown during the last week in October in conjunction with the "Taste of Taos" food and wine tasting. Contact the Taos County Chamber of Commerce (☞ Visitor Information *in* Taos A to Z, *below*) for more information.

SHOPPING

Shopping in Taos has a personality all its own, and enough originality to pique anyone's interest. Although the predictable Indian braves and bronco-bustin' cowboy statues are inevitable at some shops, you will also find serious talent. Small clothing stores and shops specializing in hand weavings, pottery, clever metalwork, and beautiful turquoise abound. Taos's bookstores offer a good selection of Southwestern history, Hispanic literature, and Native American history.

Shopping Districts

The concentration of shops directly on or just off the historic central Plaza generally focus either on quality Native American artifacts and jewelry or outright tourist kitsch. It is in the Bent Street district that the more upscale galleries and boutiques have a home. Kit Carson Road, also known as I–64, has a mix of the old and the new. There's plenty of metered municipal parking in town, but the downtown traffic bottleneck is at times beyond comprehension. It's a lot of fun poking through these shopping areas because the town is small and the owners want to put their best foot forward—even if it's to sell a ceramic chile ashtray.

The Ranchos de Taos area, 4 mi south of the Plaza, also has some shops. When you visit the church at Ranchos de Taos, these stores are worth taking a look at.

Galleries

Bert Geer Phillips and Ernest Blumenschein, traveling from Denver on a planned painting trip into Mexico in 1898, stopped in Taos to have a broken wagon wheel repaired. Enthralled with the dramatic Taos landscape, earth-hued adobe buildings, thin, piercing light, and clean mountain air, they decided to stay. Word of their discovery soon spread to fellow artists and, in 1912, they formed the Taos Society of Artists. Blumenschein and Phillips, with Joseph Henry Sharp and Eanger Irving Coue Couse, all graduates of the celebrated Parisian art school Académie Julian, made up the heart of the group. Later, others such as Nicolai Fechin moved to town, adding their gifts to the mix, and Taos became a world-famous art colony.

Most of the early Taos artists spent their winters in New York or Chicago teaching painting or illustrating to earn enough money to summer in New Mexico. Living conditions were primitive then: no running water, electricity, or even indoor plumbing. But these painters happily endured such inconveniences to fully indulge their fascination with Native American customs, modes of dress, and ceremonies. Eventually, they co-opted the Native architecture and dress and, rather presumptuously, fancied themselves spiritually akin to the Indian culture. The society was disbanded in the late 1920s, but Taos continued to attract artists. Several galleries opened, and in 1952 local painters joined to form the Taos Artists' Association, forerunner to today's highly active Taos Art Association. At present, more than 80 galleries and shops display art, sculpture, and crafts.

Carol Savid Gallery (⊠ 103B Bent St., ☎ 505/758–1128) displays the artist's luminous sculptural, architectural, and functional glass pieces, all created with dichroic glass.

Clay and Fiber Gallery (⊠ 126 W. Plaza, ☎ 505/758–8093), on the southwest corner of the Plaza, showcases the first-rate ceramics, glass, pottery, and hand-painted silks and weavings of many local artists.

El Taller Taos Gallery (⊠ 237 Ledoux St., ☎ 505/758–4887) exclusively represents Amado Peña, a contemporary Southwest artist working on various media. It also handles sculpture, jewelry, weavings, glass, and clay.

Franzetti Metalworks (⊠ 120G Bent St., ☎ 505/758–7872), displays the owner Pozzi Franzetti's metalwork creations—from sophisticated sculptures to sprightly wall hangings of western motifs.

Mission Gallery (⊠ 138 E. Kit Carson Rd., ☎ 505/758–2861), features early Taos artists, early New Mexico modernists, and important contemporary artists. The gallery is in the former home of early Taos painter Joseph H. Sharp.

Navajo Gallery (⊠ 210 Ledoux St., ☎ 505/758–3250) offers the varied works of owner and Navajo painter R. C. Gorman. This much-admired Native American artist, known for his ethereal interpretations of Indian images, opened his shop in 1968, becoming the first Native American artist to operate his own gallery.

R. B. Ravens Gallery, (✉ St. Francis Plaza, Ranchos de Taos, ☎ 505/758–7322) presents paintings by the founding artists of Taos, pre-1930s weavings and ceramics.

Shriver Gallery (✉ 401 Paseo del Pueblo Norte, ☎ 505/758–4994) handles traditional bronze sculpture and paintings, including oils, watercolors, and pastels, as well as drawings and etchings.

Six Directions (✉ 110 S. Plaza, ☎ 505/758–4376), established in 1985, handles paintings, alabaster and bronze sculpture, Native American artifacts, silver jewelry, and pottery. Bill Rabbit and Robert Redbird are among the artists represented here.

Specialty Stores

Books

Brodsky Bookshop (✉ 218 Paseo del Pueblo Norte, ☎ 505/758–9468) has a casual atmosphere. Books can sometimes be piled every which way but the shop has plenty of contemporary literature, Southwestern classics, and a light, airy children's book corner. It also carries tapes and CDs. The staff is helpful and nice.

Fernandez de Taos Book Store (✉ 109 N. Plaza, ☎ 505/758–4391), on the Plaza, offers a comprehensive selection of a variety of magazines, major out-of-town newspapers such as the *New York Times* and the *Washington Post,* and many Southwestern culture and history books.

G. Robinson Old Prints and Maps (✉ 124D Bent St., ☎ 505/758–2278), in the John Dunn House, has a wide, and good, selection of original 16th- to 19th-century antique maps and prints, Edward Curtis Native American photographs, and rare books.

Merlin's Garden (✉ 127 Bent St., ☎ 505/758–0985) is a funky, pleasant store selling metaphysical books and literature from Ram Dass to Thomas More. They also carry tapes, incense, crystals, and jewelry.

Moby Dickens (✉ No. 6, John Dunn House, 124A Bent St., ☎ 505/758–3050) has lots of windows that let in the bright Taos sun; it's great for browsing. A bookstore for all ages, it has a reliable collection of contemporary best-sellers and an outstanding selection of books on the Southwest.

Mystery Ink (✉ 121 Camino de la Placita, ☎ 505/751–1092) specializes in high-quality used books, especially murder mysteries. They also carry some foreign-language literature.

Taos Book Shop (✉ 122D Kit Carson Rd., ☎ 505/758–3733), the oldest bookshop in New Mexico, founded in 1947, specializes in out-of-print and Southwestern books. The founders, Genevieve Janssen and Claire Morrill, compiled the reminiscences of their Taos years in the interesting *A Taos Mosaic* (University of New Mexico Press). Book signings and author receptions are frequently held.

Clothing

Mariposa Boutique (✉ John Dunn House, 120F Bent St., ☎ 505/758–9028) sells original contemporary Southwestern clothing and accessories by leading Taos designers. They also sell handcrafted jewelry.

Martha of Taos (✉ 121 Paseo del Pueblo Norte, ☎ 505/758–3102) next to the Taos Inn, specializes in Southwestern-style dresses, pleated "broomstick" skirts, Navajo-style blouses, and velvet dresses.

Overland Sheepskin Company (✉ NM 522, ☎ 505/758–8822) has a huge selection of high-quality sheepskin coats, hats, mittens, and slippers, many using Taos beadwork, Navajo rug insets, and buffalo hides for exotic new styles. There are branches in Santa Fe, San Francisco, and the Napa Valley area of California.

Taos Moccasin Co. Factory Outlet (⊠ 216 Paseo del Pueblo Sur, ☎ 505/758–4276) sells a wonderful variety of moccasins made in the building next door for men, women, and children and sold all over the United States. There's everything from booties for babies to men's rugged high and low boots. This shop has great discounts and interesting designs.

Home Furnishings

Casa Cristal Pottery (⊠ On NM 522, El Prado 87529, ☎ 505/758–1530), 2½ mi north of the Taos Plaza, has it all: stoneware, serapes, clay pots, Native American ironwood carvings, ceramic sunbursts, straw and tin ornaments, ristras, fountains, sweaters, ponchos, clay fireplaces, Mexican blankets, clay churches, birdbaths, baskets, tile, piñatas, and blue glassware from Guadalajara. Also featured are antique reproductions of park benches, street lamps, mailboxes, bakers' racks, and other wrought-iron products. Casa Cristal also has an outlet in Colorado Springs, Colorado.

Country Furnishings of Taos (⊠ 534 Paseo del Pueblo Norte, ☎ 505/758–4633) sells marvelous and imaginative folk art from Northern New Mexico. They offer handmade furniture, metalwork lamps and beds, and many other delightful, colorful accessories for the home.

Hacienda de San Francisco (⊠ 4 St. Francis Plaza, Ranchos de Taos, ☎ 505/758–0477) has an exceptional collection of Spanish Colonial antiques.

Lo Fino (⊠ 201 Paseo del Pueblo Sur, ☎ 505/758–0298), in a contemporary adobe, has sophisticated Northern New Mexican–style handcrafted furniture. They carry the works of the 10 top Southwestern furniture and lighting designers. There are hand-carved beds, tables, and chairs, as well as some Native American alabaster sculptures, basketry, and pottery.

Partridge Company (⊠ 131 Bent St., ☎ 505/758–1225) is a charming shop spread through several pretty rooms. It sells top-quality linens for beds and tables, rugs, beautifully woven bedcovers, and elegant accessories with a Southwestern theme.

Taos Blue (⊠ 101A Bent St., ☎ 505/758–3561) specializes in Taos-style interior furnishings. They also have some Pawnee/Sioux magical masks; "storyteller figures" from the Taos Pueblo; ceramic dogs baying at the moon; and Native American shields and rattles, sculptures, leather hassocks, and painted buckskin pillows.

Taos Company (⊠ 124K Bent St., ☎ 800/548–1141) sells magnificent Spanish-style furniture, chandeliers, Mexican *equipal* (wood and leather) chairs, and other accessories with a Southwestern motif. Its spacious showroom also displays beautiful rugs and textiles.

Native American Arts and Crafts

Broken Arrow (⊠ 222 N. Plaza, ☎ 505/758–4304) specializes in collector-quality Native American arts and crafts, including sandpaintings, rugs, prints, jewelry, pottery, artifacts, and Hopi kachina dolls.

Buffalo Dancer (⊠ 103A E. Plaza, ☎ 505/758–8718) buys, sells, and trades Southwestern Native American arts and crafts, including pottery, belts, kachina dolls, hides, and silver-coin jewelry.

Don Fernando Curio and Gift Shop (⊠ 104 W. Plaza, ☎ 505/758–3791) This store opened in 1938 and is the oldest Native American arts shop on the Taos Plaza. Try this shop for good turquoise jewelry, kachinas, straw baskets, and colorful beads.

El Rincón (⌧ 114 E. Kit Carson Rd., ☎ 505/758–9188), is housed in a large, dark, incredibly cluttered turn-of-the-century adobe. The owners consider their store more a trading post than a shop because Native American items of all kinds are bought and sold here. There are drums, feathered headdresses, Navajo rugs, beads, bowls, baskets, shields, beaded moccasins, jewelry, arrows, and spearheads. They have a back room packed with Indian, Hispanic, and Anglo Wild West artifacts. Don't miss a peek at Kit Carson's buckskin pants.

Southwest Moccasin & Drum (⌧ 803 Paseo del Pueblo Norte, ☎ 505/758–9332 or 800/447–3630) has one of the country's largest selections: 716 native moccasin styles and 72 sizes of drums, many painted by local artists.

Taos Drums (⌧ Santa Fe Hwy., U.S. 68, ☎ 505/758–3796 or 800/424–3786) is the factory outlet for the Taos Drum Factory, 5 mi south of the Taos Plaza on U.S. 68 (look for the large tepee). They offer authentic handmade Pueblo log drums, leather lamp shades, and wrought-iron and Southwest furniture.

Taos General Store (⌧ 233 C Paseo del Pueblo Sur, ☎ 505/758–9051) is a large, airy shop specializing in a good selection of Navajo, Zuñi, and Hopi jewelry and pottery at reasonable prices. There's also a small area in the back offering Mexican peasant artifacts and home accessories.

SIDE TRIP

There are many natural wonders—of forest, field, and mountain—surrounding Taos. Take the time to enjoy the wild beauty found in these parts with a side trip to the vast Carson National Forest.

Carson National Forest

Taos is surrounded by the Carson National Forest; the closest boundary is only 4 mi east of Taos.

Carson National Forest spans approximately 200 mi across northern New Mexico, covering some expanses from Bloomfield to Cimarron at points east and west, and from the Colorado and Penasco at points north and south. It encompasses mountains, lakes, streams, villages, and much of the Enchanted Circle. Here, you may explore the great outdoors with numerous activities: hiking, skiing, horseback-riding, mountain biking, backpacking, trout fishing, boating, and even wildflower viewing. The forest is home to big game animals and many species of smaller animals and songbirds; you can see them at the Ghost Ranch Living Museum in Abiquiu. Wheeler Peak is one of the designated wilderness areas, which allow no mechanized equipment and are restricted to travel on foot or horseback; a hike through this undisturbed nature will make for an unforgettable side trip. Exploration of the Carson National Forest should be approached sensibly: contact the Carson National Forest for maps, safety guidelines, and the latest information on restrictions before enjoying its splendor. ⌧ *Forest Service Building, 208 Cruz Alta Rd., Taos 87571,* ☎ *505/758–6200.* ⊙ *Weekdays 8–4:30.*

The 13,000-ft-high **Wheeler Peak,** part of the expansive Sangre de Cristo Mountain Range, is the highest peak in the state. Vigorous hiking for those experienced can be had in this wilderness. Dress warmly, even in summer, take plenty of water and food, and pay attention to *all* warn-ings and instructions distributed by the forest rangers before you start. To reach the 7-mi hike to the peak, start at the Taos Ski Valley 15 mi northeast of Taos (☞ Outdoor Activities and Sports, *above*). ⊠ *Forest Service Building, 208 Cruz Alta Rd., Taos 87571,* ☎ *505/758–6200.* ⊙ *Weekdays 8–4:30.*

Questa's **Cabresto Lake,** in the Carson National Forest about 23 mi north of Taos, has trout fishing and boating, and is open from about June to October. Be careful driving there: 2 mi of deeply rutted, narrow roads are along the drive, so you must have a four-wheel-drive vehicle. For trout fishing far off the beaten path, try **Hopewell Lake,** in the Carson National Forest 30 minutes by car from Tre Piedras (35 mi west of Taos). The lake is open from about May through October. For information on getting fishing licenses from local vendors, call the New Mexico Department of Game and Fish (⊠ Box 25112, Santa Fe 87504, ☎ 800/275–3474).

A highlight of the Carson National Forest is the **Ghost Ranch Living Museum** in Abiquiú, 60 mi southwest of Taos. It has almost every animal calling Northern New Mexico home, including an eagle and a mountain lion. The museum is also a botanical garden and serves as the Carson National Forest's environmental education center. This museum is part of Georgia O'Keeffe's former ranch (☞ Artistic and Literary Taos *in* Exploring Taos, *above*). ⊠ *HCR 77, I–84 (Box 15), Abiquiú,* ☎ *505/685–4312.* 🖼 *Donation $3.* ⊙ *Tues.–Sun. 8–4:30.*

Carson National Forest Visitor Information

Carson National Forest (⊠ Forest Service Building, 208 Cruz Alta Rd., Taos 87571, ☎ 505/758–6200); **New Mexico Department of Game and Fish** (⊠ Box 25112, Santa Fe 87504, ☎ 800/275–3474).

TAOS A TO Z

Arriving and Departing

By Bus

Texas, New Mexico & Oklahoma Coaches, a subsidiary of Greyhound/Trailways, runs buses once a day from Albuquerque to the Taos Bus Station (⊠ 1353 Paseo del Pueblo Sur, ☎ 505/758–1144).

By Car

The main route from Santa Fe to Taos is U.S. 68. From points north, take NM 522; from points east or west, take I–64. Roads can be treacherously icy during the winter months; call New Mexico Road Conditions (☎ 800/432–4269) before heading out. The altitude in Taos will affect your car's performance, causing it to "gasp" because it's getting too much gas and not enough air. If a smooth ride matters, you can have your car tuned up for high-altitude driving.

By Plane

The closest major airport is in Albuquerque, 2½ hours south of Taos. The **Taos Municipal Airport** (⊠ U.S. 64, ☎ 505/758–4995), 12 mi west of the city, services only private planes and air charters. For air-charter information, call ☎ 505/758–4995.

Pride of Taos (☎ 505/758–8340) runs daily shuttle service to the Albuquerque Airport ($35 one-way, $65 round-trip) and between Taos and Santa Fe ($20 each way). Advance reservations are strongly recommended. **Faust's Transportation** (⊠ In nearby El Prado, ☎ 505/758–3410 or 505/758–7359) offers radio-dispatched taxis between the Taos Airport and town ($12), and between the Albuquerque airport and Taos ($35 one-way, $65 round-trip).

By Train

Amtrak (☎ 800/872–7245) provides service into Lamy Station (✉ County Rd. 41, Lamy 87500), a half hour outside Santa Fe, the closest train station to Taos. **Faust's Transportation** (✉ In nearby El Prado, ☎ 505/758–3410 or 505/758–7359) offers radio-dispatched taxis to the train station.

Getting Around

Taos radiates around its famous central Plaza and is easily maneuvered on foot. The Plaza is the starting point for getting oriented to the city: Many restaurants, stores, boutiques, and galleries are on it or within its vicinity. The main street through town is Paseo del Pueblo Norte coming down from Colorado; the route becomes Paseo del Pueblo Sur and heads out toward Santa Fe.

By Car

Major hotels have ample parking. Metered parking areas are all over town; during the peak seasons—summer and winter—traffic and parking can be a headache. To reach many of the sights of interest outside town, transportation is necessary.

By Taxi

Taxi service is sparse. However, **Faust's Transportation** (☎ 505/758–3410 or 505/758–7359), in nearby El Prado, has a fleet of radio-dispatched cabs.

Guided Tours

Orientation

Pride of Taos Tours (✉ Box 1192, Taos, ☎ 505/758–8340) provides 70-minute narrated trolley tours of Taos highlights, including the San Francisco de Asís Church, Taos Pueblo, and a Taos drum shop. Tours run May through October and cost $15 each.

Special-Interest

Native Sons Adventures (✉ 715 Paseo del Pueblo Sur, Taos, ☎ 505/758–9342 or 800/753–7559) organizes biking, backpacking, rafting, snowmobiling, and horseback and wagon expeditions. **Roadrunner Tours** (✉ Box 274, Angel Fire, ☎ 800/377–6416) is run by Nancy and Bill Burch, who offer car, Jeep, ski, and horseback rentals, as well as snowmobile tours and sleigh rides. **Taos Indian Horse Ranch** (✉ 1 Miller Rd., Taos Pueblo, ☎ 800/659–3210) features two-hour trail rides, as well as old-fashioned horse-drawn sleigh rides through the Taos Pueblo backcountry—winter weather permitting—complete with brass bells, a Native American storyteller, toasted marshmallows, and green-chile roasts. Also, escorted horseback tours and hayrides are run through Native American lands during the remainder of the year. Tours are by reservation only; no liquor is permitted. The ranch closes for 42 to 48 days each year to observe the Taos Pueblo Sweats Ceremony. Call the Taos Pueblo Governor's Office (☎ 505/758–9593) for exact dates.

Contacts and Resources

B&B Reservation Agency

Taos Bed and Breakfast Association (✉ Box 2772, Taos 87571, ☎ 800/876–7857).

Emergencies

Ambulance, fire, medical, or **police** (☎ 911); **Taos police** (☎ 505/758–2216); and **state police** (☎ 505/758–8878). **Hospital emergency room:** Holy Cross Hospital (✉ 630 Paseo del Pueblo Sur, ☎ 505/758–8883).

Pharmacies

Taos Pharmacy (✉ Piñon Plaza, 622A Paseo del Pueblo Sur, ☎ 505/758–3342); **Furr's Pharmacy** (✉ 1100 Paseo del Pueblo Sur, ☎ 505/758–1203); **Wal Mart Discount Pharmacy** (✉ 926 Paseo de Pueblo Sur, ☎ 505/758–2743).

Visitor Information

Brochures, maps, a calendar of events, and general information are available from the **Taos County Chamber of Commerce** (✉ 1139 Paseo del Pueblo Sur, Drawer 1, Taos 87571, ☎ 505/758–3873 or 800/732–8267). It's an excellent visitor information center. The center is open 9–6 daily during the summer, 9–5 daily during the rest of the year.

4 Albuquerque

A modest, practical city with a long, fascinating history, Albuquerque is the center of commerce, medicine, and education in New Mexico. Founded in 1706 as an offshoot of the North American Spanish Empire, the city has a rich heritage and a lively culture. Albuquerque and its surroundings also offer dramatic terrain, from the Sandia Mountains to the mesas west of the Rio Grande. And its central location makes it the perfect jumping off point for excursions to other parts of New Mexico.

LARGE, SPRAWLING CITY in the midst of a major growth spurt—its population is nearing the half-million mark—Albuquerque spreads out in all directions, with no apparent ground rules. No cohesive pattern, either architecturally or geographically, seems to hold it together; the city seems as free-spirited as all those hot-air balloons that take part in the Albuquerque International Balloon Fiesta every October.

Updated by
Lois Taylor

It's an unpretentious, practical city, the center of the state's financial, business, education, manufacturing, and medical industries—and its people are friendly. In fact, here, more than anywhere else in New Mexico, the state's three primary cultures rub elbows comfortably. Its citizens are descendants of the Native Americans who first inhabited the land and defended it bravely, of the Spanish who came on horseback to conquer and settle, and of the Anglos who were trappers and hunters and traders and pioneers in a new and often inhospitable land. From its beginning, Albuquerque has been a trade and transportation center. It was an important station on the Old Chihuahua Trail, an extension of the Santa Fe Trail, which wound down into Mexico.

Albuquerque's formidable physical size can be explained in a number of ways. The city was founded in 1706 on the banks of the Rio Grande, near a bend in the river, as a farming settlement. It prospered, thanks to its strategic location on a trade route and its proximity to several Native American pueblos, which offered mutual support: protection from raiding nomadic tribes and commerce. The nearby mountains and river forest yielded ample wood. The settlers built a chapel and then a church, San Felipe de Neri Catholic Church, named after a 16th-century Florentine saint. For protection, homes were built close together around a central plaza, like those in other early Spanish settlements in the hostile new land. The fortresslike community could be entered from the four corners only, making it easier to defend. This original four-block downtown area is now known as Old Town, and it is the city's tourist hub, filled with novel shops, galleries, and restaurants.

It would have made sense for the city to simply continue to grow, progressively expanding from its central hub. But something happened. First the Rio Grande gradually changed its course, moving farther and farther west. The population shifted as a result. Then, in 1880, the railroad came to Albuquerque, its tracks missing Old Town by a good 2 mi and causing another population shift. Old Town wasn't exactly abandoned, but "New Town" sprouted near the depot and grew until it eventually enveloped Old Town.

Then came Route 66, America's first transcontinental highway. Opened in 1926, and nicknamed the "Mother Road" by John Steinbeck, it sparked much of Albuquerque's early economic development. Surging through town during the '30s and '40s, it had as much impact as the railroad and the river combined, and the burgeoning city swelled around the asphalt—motels, gas stations, diners, and truck stops—a sea of neon celebrating America's independent mobility. During World War II Albuquerque flourished with the growth of a major air base, Kirtland, which, with other military-related facilities such as Sandia National Laboratory, are economic linchpins for the city even today.

Albuquerque's economy is still diversifying today. Intel, the world's largest computer-chip maker, has its biggest manufacturing center here, just north of the city in Rio Rancho. The city has a substantial arts scene, apparent from the moment you step off a plane at the attractive Albuquerque International Airport. Exhibits of New Mexican artists ap-

Pick up the phone.
Pick up the miles.

1-800-FLY-FREE

Now when you sign up with MCI you can receive up to 8,000 bonus frequent flyer miles on one of seven major airlines.

Then earn another 5 miles for every dollar you spend on a variety of MCI services, including MCI Card® calls from virtually anywhere in the world.*

You're going to use these services anyway. Why not rack up the miles while you're doing it?

Is this a great time, or what? :-)

Urban planning.

CITYPACKS

The ultimate guide to the city—a complete pocket guide plus a full-size color map.

www.fodors.com

pear throughout the terminal—a part of the Albuquerque Arts Board's 1% For Art Program, which assembles city-funded public art installations. In addition the city has numerous privately owned museums and galleries and is a growing center for artists, writers, poets, filmmakers, and musicians. The city also provides an excellent jumping-off point for trips to nearby towns, parks, and Pueblo reservations, which continue to preserve their customs amid a changing world. Each pueblo has its own personality, history, and specialties in art and design. Visitors are generally welcome.

EXPLORING ALBUQUERQUE

Historic and colorful Route 66 is Albuquerque's Central Avenue, unifying, as nothing else, the diverse areas of the city—Old Town cradled at the bend of the Rio Grande, the downtown business and government centers just east, the University of New Mexico farther east, and Nob Hill, a lively strip of restaurants, boutiques, galleries, and shops still farther east. The railroad tracks and Central Avenue divide the city into quadrants, or quarters—SW, NW, SE, and NE. Once you understand the layout, it's easy to get around. Many attractions are separated by considerable distances. A car is almost a necessity.

Albuquerque's terrain is diverse. Along the river in the north and south valleys, elevations hover at around 4,800 ft. East of the river, the land rises gently to the foothills of the Sandia Mountains; their 10,678-ft summit, Sandia Crest, is a grand spot to view the city spread below and get a feel for its layout. West of the Rio Grande, where much of Albuquerque's growth is taking place, the terrain rises abruptly in a string of mesas topped by seven extinct volcanic cones. The changes in elevation from one part of the city to another result in corresponding changes in temperature, as much as 10°F at any time. It's not uncommon for it to suddenly snow or rain in one part of town and remain dry and sunny in another.

Numbers in the text correspond to numbers in the margin and on the Albuquerque Old Town and Albuquerque maps.

Old Town

Albuquerque doesn't immediately captivate many visitors: strip shopping centers, lots of asphalt, and visual clutter are the first impressions. But tucked away in discreet corners and nooks are a wealth of interesting and diverse attractions, from lovely river walks to world-class museums. The city's old links to Mexico are evident in Old Town, its ties to space-age science are seen at the Atomic Museum, its natural heritage is on view at the Turquoise Museum, and its importance as a locus of Native American history is revealed at the Indian Pueblo Culture Center.

A Good Walk

An exploration of Albuquerque should begin where the city first took root in 1706, in Old Town, whose life was, and still is, centered on **Old Town Plaza** ①. While the modern city grew up all around it, four-square-block Old Town clings fiercely to the past. Today's plaza is much the plaza of the past, except that a graceful white gazebo and lacy wrought-iron benches have been added. Alongside streets, families that have lived here for centuries still go about their business. In many ways, it is far more "real" and charming than the much-touted plazas of Santa Fe and Taos.

After poking around the Plaza itself, cross the street and visit the quiet and lovely **San Felipe de Neri Catholic Church** ②. Cutting diagonally across the Plaza, heading south to the corner of San Felipe Street and Old Town Road, drop in on the **American International Rattlesnake Museum** ③, the largest exhibit of rattlesnakes and rattlesnake memorabilia mounted.

At the corner of Rio Grande Boulevard and Central Avenue, in the run-of-the-mill strip shopping center, you'll find a most unusual and popular attraction—the **Turquoise Museum** ④. The eye-popping displays of this semiprecious gemstone are worth the trip.

Leaving Old Town, take a five-minute stroll over to two of the city's major museums, the solar-heated **Albuquerque Museum of Art and History** ⑤, and the **New Mexico Museum of Natural History and Science** ⑥.

Even though it requires a car, this next stop is not to be missed. The **Indian Pueblo Cultural Center** ⑦ provides excellent insight into the art, culture, and history of New Mexico's 19 pueblos. Retracing your steps back to Old Town, the facility is a 10-minute drive north from Old Town.

TIMING

This walk definitely has a day's worth of sights. The best time to visit Old Town is early in the morning before the stores have opened and the daily rush of activity begins. In the beaming morning light, echoes of the past are almost palpable. Plan to spend an hour and a half at the Old Town sites, an hour in the Albuquerque Museum of Art and History, two hours in the New Mexico Museum of Natural History and Science, and an hour and a half at the Indian Pueblo Cultural Center. If you want to see the Turquoise Museum, don't do this walk on a Sunday, when it is closed. Old Town can be explored in all seasons.

Sights to See

OFF THE BEATEN PATH

ALBUQUERQUE AQUARIUM AND RIO GRANDE BOTANIC GARDEN – Visitors to the Aquarium will follow the story of a drop of water as it enters the upper Rio Grande and eventually reaches the Gulf of Mexico. Among the marine exhibits is a spectacular shark tank with floor-to-ceiling viewing. After refreshments at the San Esteban restaurant (said to be good by the locals), move on to the lovely Spanish-Moorish garden, one of a trio of walled gardens near the entrance of the Botanic Garden. From here it's a short walk to the glass conservatory, which houses two pavilions. The smaller of the two exhibits desert plants and the larger houses the Mediterranean collection. These two facilities, opened adjacent to each other in December 1996, are kid friendly. There is a gift shop. ⊠ *2601 Central Ave. at New York Ave. NW,* ☎ *505/764-6200.* ⊡ *$4.50.* ☉ *Daily 9–5.*

⑤ **Albuquerque Museum of Art and History.** This modern structure houses the largest collection of Spanish Colonial artifacts in the nation, as well as relics of the city's birth and development. The centerpiece of the Colonial exhibit is a pair of life-size models of Spanish conquistadors in original chain mail and armor. Perhaps the one on horseback is Francisco Vásquez de Coronado, who led a small army into New Mexico from Mexico in 1540 in search of gold—the turning point of the region's history. Among the museum's attractions are treasure chests filled with pearls and gold coins, religious artifacts, and early maps, some dating from the 15th century showing California as an island. A multimedia audiovisual presentation chronicles the development of the city since 1875. Changing exhibitions of fine art—both visiting and the best of the city's own sizable art community—go up regularly. A sculpture garden contains some remarkable works as well. ⊠ *2000 Mountain Rd. NW,* ☎ *505/243-7255 or 505/242-4600.* ⊡ *Free.* ☉ *Tues.–Sun. 9–5.*

★ ☞ ❸ **American International Rattlesnake Museum.** Included in this strange collection of living "rattlers" are rare and unusual specimens, such as an albino version. There are also rattlesnake artifacts, videos, and a gift shop. ✉ *202 San Felipe St. NW,* ☎ *505/242–6569.* ✏ *$2.* ☉ *Daily 10–6.*

★ ☞ ❼ **Indian Pueblo Cultural Center.** A rich resource for studies, this museum provides a good overview of the distinguished culture and history of the state's 19 Pueblo Indian tribes. It's one of the largest collections of Native American arts and crafts in the Southwest. The multilevel semi-circular design was inspired by Pueblo Bonito, the famous prehistoric ruin in Chaco Canyon in the northwestern section of New Mexico. Each pueblo has an upper-level alcove devoted to its particular arts and crafts. Lower-level exhibits trace the history of the Pueblo people from prehistoric times to the present. Ceremonial dances are performed during the summer and on special holidays. The Hands-on Corner allows youngsters to touch Native American pottery, jewelry, dried corn, weaving, and tools, and to draw their own petroglyphs or design pots. Original paintings, sculptures, jewelry, leather crafts, rugs, souvenir items, drums, beaded necklaces, painted bowls, and fetishes are for sale. ✉ *2401 12th St. NW,* ☎ *505/843–7270 or 800/766–4405.* ✏ *$3.* ☉ *Daily 9–5:30.*

NEED A BREAK? The **Indian Pueblo Cultural Center** (✉ 2401 12th St. NW, ☎ 505/843–7270) has a restaurant, open for breakfast and lunch, that serves Native American food, including blue-corn enchiladas, *posole* (a thick soup with pork, hominy, chile, garlic, and cilantro), Native American bread pudding, and, of course, fry bread—that addictive popoverlike creation topped with honey, beans, chile, or powdered sugar; or just gobble it up plain!

★ ☞ ❻ **New Mexico Museum of Natural History and Science.** It's just across Mountain Road from **The Albuquerque Museum of Art and History,** and it's an exceptional museum—one of the city's most popular for both locals and visitors. Its simulated active world of wonders includes a simulated active volcano with a river of bubbling hot lava flowing beneath the see-through glass floor; a frigid Ice Age cave; a world-class dinosaur exhibit hall; and an Evolator (short for Evolution Elevator), a six-minute high-tech ride, involving video, sound, and motion, through 35 million years of New Mexico's geological history. A film in the Dynamax Theater makes viewers feel equally involved. If you arrive via the front walkway, you will be greeted by fantastic life-size bronze sculptures of a Pentaceratops, a 21-ft-long horned dinosaur, and a 30-ft-long carnivorous Albertosaur. ✉ *1801 Mountain Rd. NW,* ☎ *505/841–2800.* ✏ *$5.25 for museum; $8 combination ticket for museum and Dynamax Theater.* ☉ *Daily 9–5.*

★ ☞ ❶ **Old Town Plaza.** This small, lovely plaza was laid out in 1706 by Don Francisco Cuervo y Valdes, a New Mexico provincial governor, who was obviously no slouch when it came to political maneuvering; he named the new town after the Duke of Alburquerque, viceroy of New Spain, hoping flattery would excuse the newly formed 15-family community from having the 30 families required to obtain a charter. The Duke of Alburquerque acquiesced, of course, but somewhere along the line the first "r" in his name was dropped. Today the plaza is an oasis of tranquility filled with shade trees, benches, and swatches of grass, surrounded by nearly 200 small shops, restaurants, cafés, galleries, and several cultural sites tucked away in tiny side *placitas* (little plazas) and lanes. Despite its commercial activity, it still has small-town charm. The scents of bubbling vats of green chili, enchiladas, and burritos hang in

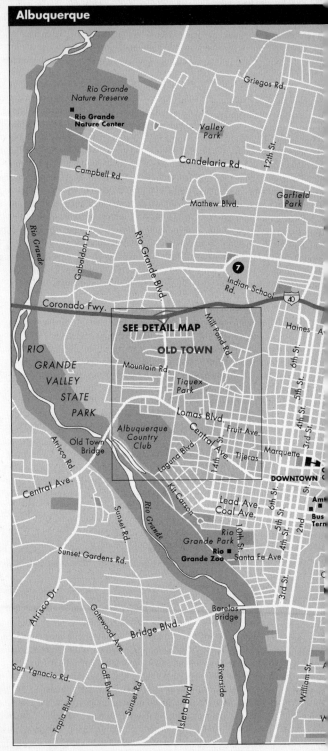

Albuquerque

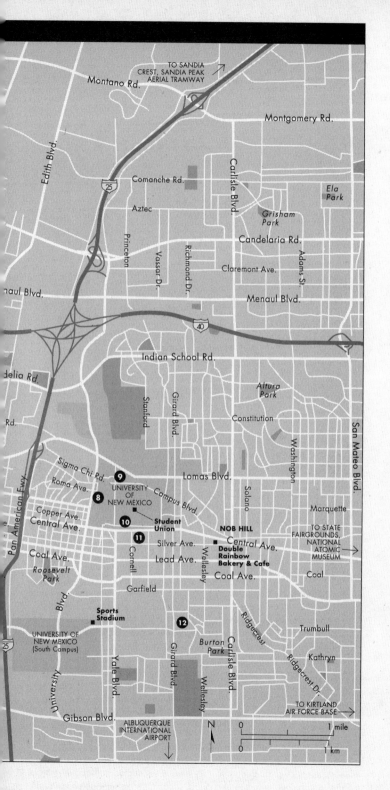

TO SANDIA CREST, SANDIA PEAK AERIAL TRAMWAY

Montano Rd.

Montgomery Rd.

Edith Blvd.

I-25

Comanche Rd.

Ela Park

Aztec

Grisham Park

Princeton

Carlisle Blvd.

Candelaria Rd.

Vassar Dr.

Richmond Dr.

Claremont Ave.

Adams St.

naul Blvd.

Menaul Blvd.

I-40

delia Rd.

Indian School Rd.

Rd.

Altura Park

Stanford

Girard Blvd.

Constitution

Washington

San Mateo Blvd.

Pan American Fwy

Sigma Chi Rd.

Lomas Blvd.

Solano

Roma Ave.

9

UNIVERSITY OF NEW MEXICO

Campus Blvd.

Marquette

Copper Ave.

8

10

Student Union

NOB HILL

TO STATE FAIRGROUNDS, NATIONAL ATOMIC MUSEUM

Central Ave.

Central Ave.

11

Silver Ave.

Cornell

Lead Ave.

Wellesley

Double Rainbow Bakery & Cafe

Coal Ave.

Coal

Coal Ave.

Roosevelt Park

Garfield

Sports Stadium

12

Ridgecrest

Trumbull

UNIVERSITY OF NEW MEXICO (South Campus)

Burton Park

Carlisle Blvd.

Ridgecrest Dr.

Kathryn

I-25

University

Yale Blvd.

Girard Blvd.

Wellesley

TO KIRTLAND AIR FORCE BASE

Gibson Blvd.

ALBUQUERQUE INTERNATIONAL AIRPORT

N

0   1 mile

0   1 km

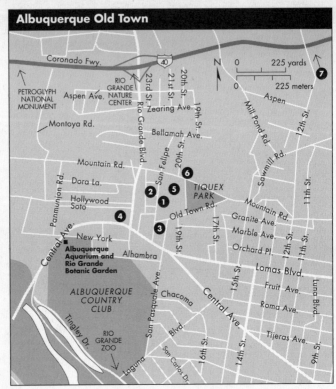

Albuquerque Old Town

the air. Gunfights are staged on Romero Street on Sunday afternoon, and during fiestas, Old Town is alive with mariachi bands and dancing señoritas. You can stroll the Plaza night or day. Event schedules and maps, which contain a list of public rest rooms, are available at the **Old Town Visitors Center** (⊠ 303 Romero St. NW, ☎ 505/243–3215) across the street from the San Felipe de Neri Catholic Church. The center is open daily from 9 to 5, except Sunday, when it opens at 10.

NEED A BREAK?

In Old Town, **Zane Graze Cafe & News** (⊠ 308 San Felipe St. NW, ☎ 505/243–4377) is delightful for lunch or refreshments.

OFF THE BEATEN PATH

PETROGLYPH NATIONAL MONUMENT – Beneath the stumps of five extinct volcanoes, this park protects more than 15,000 ancient Native American rock drawings inscribed on the 17-mi-long West Mesa escarpment overlooking the Rio Grande Valley. Native American hunting parties camped at the base of the cliffs for thousands of years, chipping and scribbling away. Archaeologists believe the petroglyphs were carved on the lava formations between AD 1100 and 1600. Four walking trails provide access to the petroglyphs. Take I-40 west to the NM 448 Coors exit north (just west of the Rio Grande) and take a left off Coors onto Unser Boulevard. ⊠ 4735 Unser Blvd. NW, ☎ 505/839–4429. ☞ $1 weekdays, $2 weekends. ☉ Daily 8–5.

RIO GRANDE NATURE CENTER STATE PARK – This year-round refuge in a portion of The Bosque, the nation's largest cottonwood forest, is home to all manner of birds and migratory fowl. Constructed half above ground and half below the edge of a pond, it has viewing windows to provide a look at what's going on at both levels as birds, frogs, ducks, and turtles do their thing. The park has an active program for both adult and child education and trails for biking, walking, and jogging. ✉ *2901 Candelaria Rd. NW,* ☎ *505/344-7240.* ✆ *$1.* ☉ *Daily 10–5.*

RIO GRANDE ZOO – A lovely oasis of waterfalls, towering canopies of cottonwood trees, and well-designed natural habitats for the animals, this has become one of the nation's best managed and most attractive zoos. Over 200 species of wildlife from around the world live here. The Zoo, in keeping with its mission of wildlife care and conservation, has established captive breeding programs for a number of endangered species. During the summer, concerts are performed on the grounds, and if you are looking for a special place for breakfast, lunch, or dinner, try the very attractive **Cottonwood Cafe,** on the grounds. ✉ *903 Tenth St. SW,* ☎ *505/764-6200.* ✆ *$4.25.* ☉ *Daily 9–5.*

RIO GRANDE ZOOLOGICAL PARK – One of America's best medium-sized zoos—and great if you have kids in tow—is home to more than 1,150 animals, from endangered Mexican wolves and snow leopards to chest-thumping gorillas and ever-playful seals, who frolic in a huge tank with underwater viewing areas. In addition to animal folly, the 60-acre zoo has lush landscaping and a half-dozen waterfalls. ✉ *903 10th St. SW,* ☎ *505/764-6200.* ✆ *$4.25.* ☉ *Daily 9–5.*

② **San Felipe de Neri Catholic Church.** This historic Catholic structure remains active after over two-and-a-half centuries of faithful worship. Though enlarged and expanded several times over the years, its massive adobe walls and other original sections remain intact. Small gardens front and flank it; inside, it's dark, quiet, and still. A small museum with church relics—vestments, paintings, carvings—dating from the 17th century is attached; there is also a gift shop. ✉ *2005 North Plaza NW,* ☎ *505/243–4628.* ☉ *Church always open; museum weekdays 1–4 and Sat. noon–3, but call ahead to confirm hrs.*

④ **Turquoise Museum.** This novel attraction focuses on the beauty, myths, and physical properties of this semiprecious, but widely adored gemstone, which many people rightly associate with the color of New Mexico's skies. After entering through a mine shaft, you'll find one-of-a-kind showpieces and turquoise from more than 60 mines on four continents; displays on how it is formed and its uses by Native Americans in prehistoric times; and an education center where you may learn how to distinguish the real McCoy from plastic. ✉ *2107 Central Ave. NW,* ☎ *505/247–8650 or 800/821–7443.* ✆ *$2.* ☉ *Mon.–Sat. 9–5.*

The University of New Mexico

Established in 1889, the University of New Mexico is the state's leading center for higher education, with internationally recognized programs in anthropology, biology, Latin American studies, and medicine. A mainstay of Albuquerque's cultural life, its many outstanding galleries and museums are open to the public free of charge and should not be missed. It is also noted for its Pueblo Revival–style architecture, including the superb old wing of Zimmerman Library and a campus chapel—both designed by the late, famed architect, John Gaw Meem.

A Good Walk

The impeccably landscaped grounds of the University of New Mexico surround a central area containing knolls, a duck pond, fountains, waterfalls, and benches. Start your walk in this area.

The **Maxwell Museum of Anthropology** ⑧, in the university's Anthropology Building on the western edge of the campus, only a few minutes walk from the duck pond, is a small but outstanding museum with more than 2.5 million artifacts and objects in its vast holdings.

Art lovers shouldn't miss **Jonson Gallery** ⑨, which contains the works of the late, important Transcendentalist painter Raymond Jonson (1891–1982), housed in Jonson's former home and studio. Nor should they overlook the **University Art Museum** ⑩, in the Fine Arts Center (use the Stanford Drive and Central Avenue entrance), which has the state's largest collection of fine art, including a terrific photographic collection.

Yet another stop for art aficionados, at the corner of Central Avenue and Cornell Drive, is the sales and exhibition gallery of the **Tamarind Institute** ⑪, an internationally renowned workshop for lithographers. Tours are available.

A bit of a hike away, 9 blocks south of Central along Girard, you'll find the **Ernie Pyle Branch Library** ⑫, the memorabilia-filled home of the beloved war correspondent.

If you still have any energy left, you might want to take a 15-minute drive off the beaten path to the odd but fascinating **National Atomic Museum** on the grounds of Kirtland Air Force Base.

TIMING

Seeing the University of New Mexico could take a good part of a day. Spend an hour strolling or lolling about the grounds, maybe catching some rays by the duck pond. Allot an hour for each subsequent stop. All facilities are open year-round, but it's best to take this walk Tuesday through Friday because some are closed Monday and weekends.

Sights to See

⑫ **Ernie Pyle Branch Library.** Pyle built this house in 1940 after several visits to New Mexico with his wife, Jerry. Now the smallest branch of the Albuquerque Public Library, it displays photos, handwritten articles by Pyle, and news clippings of his career as a Pulitzer Prize–winning war correspondent and of his death by a sniper's bullet on April 18, 1945, on the tiny Pacific island of Ie Shima. ✉ *900 Girard Blvd. SE,* ☎ *505/256–2065.* ✑ *Free.* ☉ *Tues. and Thurs. 12:30–9; Wed., Fri., and Sat. 9–5:30.*

OFF THE BEATEN PATH

NATIONAL ATOMIC MUSEUM – Odd but fascinating, this museum explores atomic energy and the role New Mexico played in nuclear technology. Exhibits include replicas of Little Boy and Fat Man, the atomic bombs dropped on Japan. In the Missile Park section you can examine a B-52 bomber and an F-105D fighter bomber, touch the rocket that was used to boost Alan Shepard into space, and see an array of historic flying machines with names such as *Hound Dog, Mace,* and *Snark.* David Wolper's film *Ten Seconds That Shook the World* can also be seen here; call ahead for movie times. You'll need a car to get here. ✉ *Kirtland Air Force Base, Wyoming Gate,* ☎ *505/284-3243.* ✑ *Free.* ☉ *Daily 9–5.*

⑨ **Jonson Gallery.** In what was Jonson's home and studio, you'll find the abstract, colorful works on paper of this masterful Transcendentalist American artist who focused on mass and form, as well as works by other contemporary painters. A major retrospective of his work is mounted every summer. ✉ *1909 Las Lomas NE,* ☎ *505/277–4967.* ✑ *Free.* ☉ *Tues.–Fri. 9–4.*

⑧ **Maxwell Museum of Anthropology.** The first public museum in Albuquerque, established in 1932, it shelters over 2.5 million artifacts from diverse ethnic cultures, with real depth in materials from the Southwest. Two permanent exhibitions chronicle 4 million years of human emergence, and the lifeways, art, and cultures of 11,500 years of human occupation in the Southwest. Its photographic archives contain more than 250,000 images, including some of the earliest photo records of Pueblo and Navajo cultures. The museum shop offers a wide selection of traditional and contemporary Southwestern Native American jewelry, rugs, pottery, basketry, beadwork, and folk art from around the world. A children's section has inexpensive books and handmade tribal artifacts for sale. ⊠ *One block north of Grand Ave. on University Blvd. (University of New Mexico campus),* ☎ *505/277–4405.* ▧ *Free.* ◷ *Weekdays 9–4, Sat. 10–4, Sun. noon–4.*

⑪ Tamarind Institute. This world-famous institution played a major role in reviving the fine art of lithographic printing, working with both traditional stone plates and metal plates. Tamarind Master Printer certification is to an artist what a degree from Juilliard is to a musician. A small gallery within the facility exhibits prints and lithographs. Guided tours, conducted on the first Friday of each month at 1:30, are available with reservations. ⊠ *108 Cornell Dr. SE,* ☎ *505/277–3901.* ▧ *Free.* ◷ *Weekdays 9–5.*

⑩ University Art Museum. The state's largest collection of fine art is found in this small, lively, and handsome museum. Works of such Old Masters as Rembrandt and such modern ones as Picasso and (of course) Georgia O'Keeffe grace the walls. The museum also has one of the largest university collections of prints and photographs in the country, with an emphasis on contemporary leaders and early pioneers. It also presents lectures and symposia, gallery talks during the school year, and guided tours. ⊠ *University of New Mexico Center for the Arts (UNM campus),* ☎ *505/277–4001.* ▧ *Free; parking (fee) on campus.* ◷ *Tues. 9–4 and 5–8, Wed.–Fri. 9–4, Sun. 1–4.*

NEED A BREAK?

The university's **Student Union Building** (☎ 505/277–2331), just north of the Stanford entrance off Central Avenue, is a good spot to grab a burger or a snack, or just rest your feet for a while. Here you'll also find changing exhibits and students' artwork in several exhibit spaces, including the Centennial (on the main level), and the ASA (south end, lower level).

Looking for a pick-me-up? Sip a cup of excellent coffee roasted on the premises, and sink your teeth into delectable pastries at the **Double Rainbow Bakery & Cafe** (⊠ Central Ave., ☎ 505/255–6633). Among the offerings are scrumptious soups, quiches, sandwiches, and salads, as well as a complimentary newspaper available for perusing while eating your meal. The café is a block west of Carlisle; its sister café, also called the **Double Rainbow** (⊠ 4501 Juan Tabo, ☎ 505/275–8311), has an even larger selection.

Sandia Peak Aerial Tramway

Rising up like a petrified wave of color about to break on Albuquerque are the majestic Sandia Mountains, which form an ever-changing panoramic backdrop to the city. Hikers, bikers, bird-watchers, climbers, painters, skiers, and sightseers all take advantage of this wild urban refuge. An ideal way to get a lay of the land with spectacular views is the tram ride up to Sandia Peak, which can also include hiking along the rim.

A Good Tour

Approach the Sandia Mountains from the western edge facing the city via the **Sandia Peak Aerial Tramway,** which ascends to the peak. Minimum round-trip time on the tram is 90 minutes; allow more time if you wish to explore the rim and picnic, or have lunch or dinner at the High Finance Restaurant. To reach the tramway base station, take I–25 north to Tramway Road, then head east on Tramway, or take I–40 east to Tramway Road and head north. If you have more time, you may also drive around to the "backside" and ascend to the Sandia Crest. Once descended from the crest, hikers may explore the trails of the Sandias, particularly those facing the foothills on the western face during cold spells; stick to hiking the trails on the summit rim in summer. For information on the hiking trails call the Albuquerque Cultural and Recreational Services Department or the Cibola National Forest (☎ 505/281–3304).

TIMING

The 90-minute tram ride is a perfect activity after a long day of sightseeing, and it's particularly stellar at sunset. This excursion, especially if you will be hiking on the rim, should be done in warm weather. Autumn is an ideal time to view the aspens and scrub oak changing colors, but bring warm clothes for the summit and hiking along the rim.

Sights to See

Sandia Crest. From the western side of this white, limestone upper rim of the Sandia mountains, tremendous views of a huge swath of the state will lie at your feet. Foot trails branch out along the rim from here, offering stunning vistas and an ideal picnic spot in warm weather. You'll be surprised by how much cooler it is here on even the hottest summer day than it is down below in the city. ⊠ *NM 536, Sandia Crest National Scenic Byway.* 🎟 *Free.* ☉ *Year-round.*

😊 **Sandia Peak Aerial Tramway.** Billed as "the longest aerial tramway in the world," both kids and adults are thrilled by the 2.7-mi-long ascent up the steep western face of the Sandias. From the sky-top observation deck at the summit you can see Santa Fe to the northeast and Los Alamos to the northwest—and isn't that Tucson over there? If you're lucky, you may see some of the mountain lions that roam the cliff sides, or some birds of prey. ⊠ *10 Tramway Loop NE,* ☎ *505/856–7325.* 🎟 *$14.* ☉ *Memorial Day–Labor Day, daily 9 AM–10 PM; Labor Day–Memorial Day, Sun.–Thurs. 9–9, Wed. 5 PM–10 PM, Fri.–Sat. 9 AM–10 PM. Closed twice a year for maintenance.*

DINING

Albuquerqueans love to eat out, but exceptional places to dine were a rarity here until the 1980s, when a slew of new, good restaurants opened. This happy trend continues today, though the number of choices still does not match that of Santa Fe. A handful of the city's favorite dining spots specialize in northern New Mexican–style cooking, with flavorful recipes that have been handed down for generations. A waitress sitting down to chat with customers may seem to happen only in TV sitcoms, but in the West—and Albuquerque is the quintessential "Western" city—they really do. This informality rubs off on guests as well: ties come off, boots are pulled on, and the streets outside are littered with briefcases.

CATEGORY	COST*
$$$	over $20
$$	$16–$20
$	under $16

per person, excluding drinks, service, and sales tax (5.8%)

$$$ ✗ **Casa Vieja.** Opened in 1970 in the oldest building in Corrales—a
★ charming 280-year-old adobe that was originally a homestead, then a
church, the territorial governor's home, and a military outpost—it
achieves frontier flavor without straining. The handful of dining rooms
are intimate, with adobe fireplaces, beamed viga ceilings, Native Amer-
ican rugs on the walls, and handsome tinwork on the hand-carved doors.
Owner Rick Gabaldon will offer you French and northern Italian cui-
sine, using quail, duck, and pheasant when in season. There is a patio
for outdoor dining. ⊠ *4541 Corrales Rd., Corrales,* ☎ *505/898–
7489. AE, D, DC, MC, V. Closed Mon. No lunch.*

$$$ ✗ **High Noon Restaurant and Saloon.** In one of Old Town's original
200-year-old adobe buildings, this restaurant was once a woodwork-
ing shop. It now has fine dining in a Territorial setting, with viga ceilings, brick floors, handmade Southwestern furniture, and New Mexican
art. A skylight provides cool, diffused light and glimpses of the stars.
Topping the menu are pepper steak; oven-roasted rack of lamb with
fresh herbs; and panfried trout dusted with blue-corn flour, deglazed
with tequila, and served with pine nuts and leeks and tomatoes. Thursday through Sunday evenings you'll be serenaded by a flamenco gui-
tarist. ⊠ *425 San Felipe St. NW,* ☎ *505/765–1455. AE, D, DC MC, V.*

$$$ ✗ **Monte Vista Fire Station.** This spacious, airy restaurant on Central
Avenue was a working fire station—it even has a brass pole—until 1972.
The adobe-style building, built in 1936, is on the National Register of
Historic Places. Choose from a wide variety of new American seafood,
beef, and pasta dishes, such as green-chile ravioli. A feta quesadilla,
or succulent crab cakes might top the ever-changing list of innovative
appetizers. ⊠ *3201 Central Ave. NE,* ☎ *505/255–2424. AE, D, DC,
MC, V. No lunch weekends.*

$$ ✗ **Artichoke Cafe.** This café is rated highly among locals for its excel-
★ lent service and outstanding French, new American, and Italian dishes
prepared with organically grown ingredients whenever possible. Specialties include grilled duck, pumpkin ravioli with fresh spinach and
butternut squash, and free-range breast of chicken with fresh wild mushrooms. The appetizers are so tasty you may make them a meal. The
building dates to the turn of the century, but the decor is uptown modern. The large dining room on two levels spills onto a small courtyard.
⊠ *424 Central Ave. SE,* ☎ *505/243–0200. AE, D, DC, MC, V. No
lunch Sat.*

$$ ✗ **La Crêpe Michel.** This bistro, offering French country cooking, is a
pleasant alternative to the countless New Mexican restaurants in the
Old Town area. The intimate, rustic Parisian café tucked into the Old
Town Patio del Norte has two lovely patios. The menu emphasizes in-
novative chicken, beef, seafood, vegetarian, and dessert crêpes, as well
as classic French onion soup, escargot, and fresh-baked French bread.
You may notice that the restaurant is missing is a wine list: It's prox-
imity to Old Town's historic San Felipe de Neri Catholic Church pro-
hibits a liquor license. Given the property's popularity, however,
business doesn't seem affected by the absence of alcohol. ⊠ *400 C-2
San Felipe St. NW, Patio del Norte,* ☎ *505/242–1251. MC, V. Closed
Mon. No dinner Sun.*

$$ ✗ **La Placita.** Housed in a historic hacienda on Old Town Plaza, La
Placita offers traditional New Mexican dishes, such as chiles rellenos,
enchiladas, tacos, and sopaipillas, plus a wide selection of American
entrées, including fine steaks. The building dates from 1706, and the
adobe walls are 3 ft thick in places. For years it housed Ambrosio
Armijo's mercantile store, where ladies' lace gloves sold for 10¢ a pair
and gents' linen underdrawers could be purchased for $1. The six din-
ing rooms are art galleries—patrons dine surrounded by outstanding

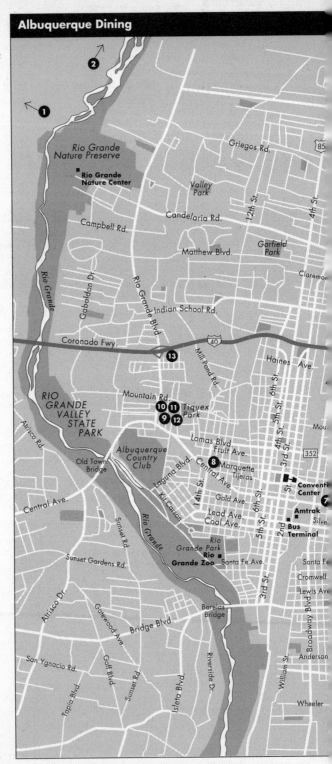

Albuquerque Dining

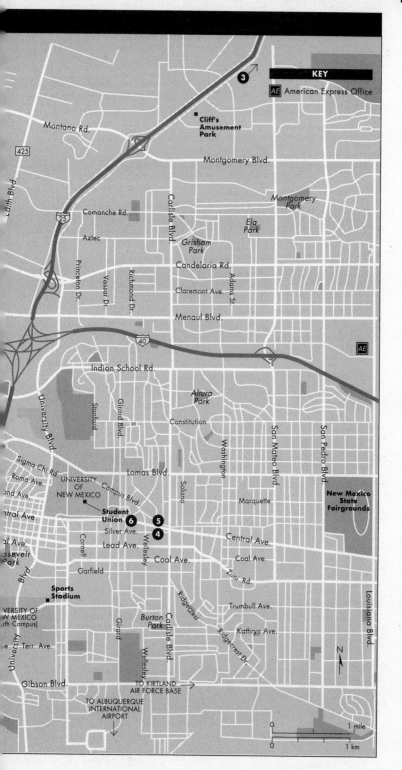

examples of Native American and Southwestern painting. ⊠ *206 San Felipe St. NW,* ☎ *505/247–2204. AE, D, MC, V.*

$$ ✕ **Maria Teresa Restaurant & 1840 Bar.** This nationally preserved landmark in Old Town, next to the Sheraton, is a restored 1840s adobe with 32-inch-thick brick adobe walls plastered with straw and more adobe. The food is standard Continental fare, with beef, seafood, and New Mexican offerings. The interior of Maria Teresa is beautiful; it has early Spanish American furnishings—chests, carvings, and tables—Southwestern paintings, fireplaces, and walled gardens. In summer everyone wants to eat in the courtyard. ⊠ *618 Rio Grande Blvd. NW,* ☎ *505/242–3900. AE, DC, MC, V.*

$$ ✕ **Prairie Star.** The view from the patio of this sprawling but cozy 1940s adobe hacienda in Bernalillo, 15 mi north of Albuquerque, makes it a favorite spot for sipping margaritas at sunset. Inside, you are treated to traditional New Mexican decor in the 6,000-square-ft Pueblo Revival–style building: vigas, *latillas* (ceiling branches set in a crosshatched pattern), kiva-style fireplaces, and *bancos* (small benches that gracefully emerge from the adobe walls). The menu combines New American, Southwestern, and classical cuisine, including *truchas* (trout) with piñon nuts, tender lamb loin, and lightly breaded and fried green-chile appetizers. Homemade bread and desserts are fresh daily. ⊠ *255 Prairie Star Rd.,* ☎ *505/867–3327. AE, D, DC, MC, V.*

$$ ✕ **Scalo Northern Italian Grill.** Nob Hill trendsetters gather at this con-
★ sistently good, informal eatery with a lively bar to experience fine Italian wines and first-rate pasta, seafood, and meat entrées. Most of the multilevel dining area looks onto the bar and an open kitchen, where wonders such as ravioli *al magri con basilico* (filled with spinach and ricotta cheese), *quaglia arrosta con polenta* (quail stuffed with fontina cheese, figs, and prosciutto on creamy polenta with a mushroom reduction), and *calamaretti fritti* (fried baby squid, spicy marinara, and lemon aioli) are created. The homemade desserts are worth splurging for. ⊠ *3500 Central Ave. SE (in Nob Hill Shopping Center),* ☎ *505/ 255–8781. AE, DC, MC, V. No lunch Sun.*

$$ ✕ **Stephen's.** This restaurant has won the Distinguished Restaurants
★ of North America award as well as the Wine Spectator's Award of Excellence. It offers Southwestern and new American food. The three dining areas are pristine: a large Santa Fe–style room with a view of the open kitchen, an enclosed patio enveloped in lush greenery, and a formal dining room with an exposed brick wall that dates from the building's 1915 origins. Choose from pasta and a delectable rack of lamb, to fine grilled fish and piñon tequila chicken. Healthy eaters also enjoy the special spa menu. Service is excellent, as is the selection of more than 300 wines. ⊠ *1311 Tijeras Ave. NW,* ☎ *505/842–1773. Reservations essential. AE, DC, MC, V. No lunch.*

$–$$ ✕ **Andre's.** Since its opening in 1996, owner-chef Andre Diddy's
★ restaurant has been a hot item. Food is imaginative and well prepared, and it's amazingly inexpensive. Check out such blue-plate specials as the sage-roasted duckling with cranberry and port wine sauce or ragout of beef sirloin with olives and peppercorns. Finish your meal off with a Grand Marnier frozen soufflé. There's an extensive wine list and rare beers such as the thirst-quenching New Mexico Desert Pils. ⊠ *9401 Coors Blvd. NW,* ☎ *505/890–2725. AE, D, DC, MC, V. Closed Mon.*

$ ✕ **Il Vicino.** Gourmet pizza—with 25 possible toppings—baked in a European-style wood-fired oven is the drill here. If a snazzy combination escapes you, order pizza rustica, a buttery cornmeal crust topped with roasted garlic, artichokes, calamata olives, and capers, or try one of the other 12 delicious house pizzas. Good salads, pasta, and four to five microbrewed beers round out the menu. ⊠ *3403 Central Ave. NE,* ☎ *505/266–7855. Reservations not accepted. MC, V.*

$ ✕ **Manhattan on the Rio Grande.** This is a new deli but it continues the great sandwich tradition of an old Albuquerque favorite, the now defunct Ned's Restaurant. Said to be the best in the Southwest, here you can get a sandwich big enough to have pleased Henry VIII, and at the same time will console those pining for the Big Apple or Philly. Get a Reuben, a Siciliano or a Stormin Norman (nothing to do with the Gulf War, its named after a famous Lobo basketball coach). Don't plan on making a night of it here, however: The deli is only open until 3:30 PM Monday–Wednesday and 7 PM Thursday–Sunday. ⊠ *910 Rio Grande NW,* ☎ *505/248–1514. AE, MC, V.*

LODGING

As is typical of many large cities in the Southwest today, Albuquerque's hotels offer a comfortable mix of modern conveniences and Old West flavor. The city's accommodations range from budget motels to soaring hotel skyscrapers. A special treat is the large number of bed-and-breakfasts flourishing here, from restored Victorian-era homes downtown to a slew of them just north of town in Los Ranchos and Corrales.

CATEGORY	COST*
$$$	over $100
$$	$65–$100
$	under $65

All prices are for a standard double excluding 5% room tax, 5.8% sales tax, and service charges.

Hotels

Albuquerque

$$$ 🏨 **Albuquerque Hilton.** In this hotel you will find a mix of contemporary sophistication and Southwestern charm—Native American rugs, arched doorways, and Santa Fe–style wooden furniture. Original Native American and Western art is featured throughout. The Ranchers Club restaurant is elegant, with a roaring fireplace. Its authentic grill room—you almost expect to find J.R. Ewing here—features prime meats and fresh seafood prepared over aromatic woods such as piñon or mesquite. The Casa Chaco, the other restaurant, serves coffee-shop breakfast and lunch fare but is transformed at night, when nouvelle Southwestern cuisine is served with candlelight, crisp linen, and sparkling crystal. A business center replete with fax, copy machines, and secretarial services is ideal for business travelers. ⊠ *1901 University Blvd. NE (Box 25525), 87102,* ☎ *505/884–2500 or 800/274–6835,* ℻ *505/889–9118. 264 rooms. 2 restaurants, 2 bars, no-smoking rooms, indoor-outdoor pool, sauna, exercise room, business services. AE, D, DC, MC, V.*

$$$ 🏨 **Albuquerque Marriott.** This 17-story luxury property is tailored to the executive traveler with its special 56-room Concierge Service, complete with smoking and no-smoking choices, faxes, and computer hookups, but it doesn't forget the vacationer either. The region's natural colors and Southwestern touches, such as kachina dolls and Native American pottery and art, are combined elegantly. Rooms are traditional American, with walk-in closets, armoires, and crystal lamps, as well as pay movies. In the hotel is **Allie's American Grill and Bar,** which serves up popular American cuisine. ⊠ *2101 Louisiana Blvd. NE, 87110,* ☎ *505/881–6800 or 800/334–2086,* ℻ *505/888–2982. 410 rooms. Restaurant, bar, indoor-outdoor pool, exercise room, concierge floor, business services. AE, D, DC, MC, V.*

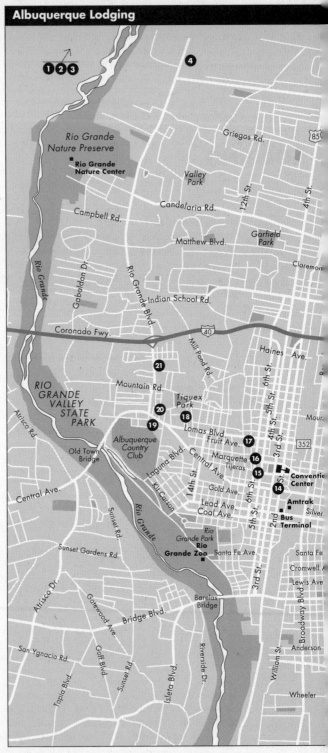

Albuquerque Lodging

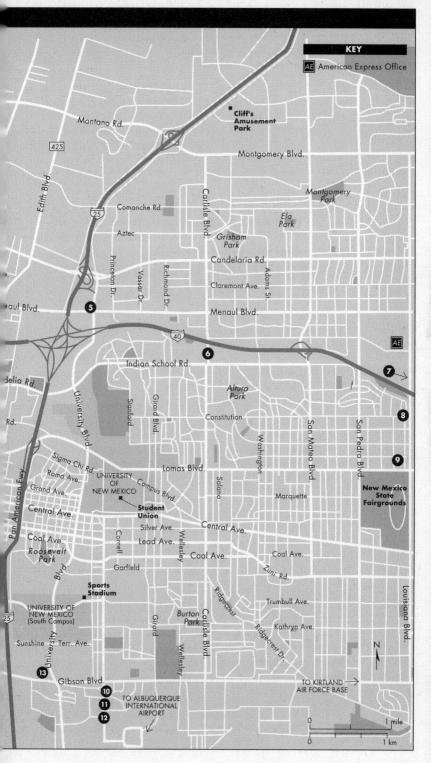

Montano Rd.

Cliff's
Amusement
Park

Montgomery Blvd.

425

Montgomery
Park

Edith Blvd.

Comanche Rd.

Carlisle Blvd.

Ela
Park

25

Aztec

Grisham
Park

Candelaria Rd.

Princeton Dr.

Vassar Dr.

Richmond Dr.

Claremont Ave.

Adams St.

aul Blvd.

5

Menaul Blvd.

40

AE

6

Indian School Rd.

7

delia Rd.

University Blvd.

Stanford

Girard Blvd.

Altura
Park

8

Rd.

Constitution

Washington

San Mateo Blvd.

San Pedro Blvd.

Lomas Blvd.

9

Sigma Chi Rd.

UNIVERSITY
OF
NEW MEXICO

Campus Blvd.

Solano

New Mexico
State
Fairgrounds

Roma Ave.

Marquette

Grand Ave.

Student
Union

Silver Ave.

Central Ave.

Central Ave.

Pan American Fwy.

Coal Ave.

Cornell

Lead Ave.

Wellesley

Coal Ave.

Roosevelt
Park

Coal Ave.

Boulevard

Garfield

Zuni Rd.

Sports
Stadium

UNIVERSITY OF
NEW MEXICO
(South Campus)

25

Girard

Burton
Park

Carlisle Blvd.

Ridgecrest

Trumbull Ave.

Louisiana Blvd.

Sunshine

Terr. Ave.

University

Wellesley

Ridgecrest Dr.

Kathryn Ave.

N

13

Gibson Blvd.

TO KIRTLAND
AIR FORCE BASE

10

11

TO ALBUQUERQUE
INTERNATIONAL
AIRPORT

12

0   1 mile

0   1 km

$$$ 🏨 **Hyatt Regency Albuquerque.** Adjacent to the Albuquerque Convention
★   Center, this occupies one of two soaring desert-colored towers that top
      the city's skyline. The gleaming art deco interior is refined and not over-
      bearing. The spacious, contemporary rooms in mauve, burgundy, and
      tan combine Southwestern style with all the standard Hyatt amenities.
      A private lounge for meetings or social events and special rooms with
      modem hookups are available. Award-winning **McGrath's** serves
      steaks, chops, chicken, and seafood in intimate levels and alcoves. ⊠
      330 Tijeras NW, 87102, ☎ *505/842–1234 or 800/233–1234,* FAX *505/*
      766–6710. 395 rooms, 13 suites, 1 Presidential Suite. Restaurant, 2
      bars, in-room modem lines by request, pool, health club, shops, busi-
      ness services, valet parking. AE, D, DC, MC, V.

$$$ 🏨 **Sheraton Old Town.** This modern, 11-story hotel sits gracefully
      amid Old Town's 400 years of culture and history with no overly jar-
      ring effects. The rooms are large and modern, with tan desert-color
      appointments, hand-wrought furnishings, and large bathrooms with
      vanities. The **Rio Grande Customs House Restaurant,** with a mis-
      placed nautical scheme, serves up well-prepared prime rib, steaks,
      seafood, and poultry; the casual **Café del Sol** has a varied menu with
      lots of Southwestern favorites. This hotel is convenient to Old Town
      sites. ⊠ *800 Rio Grande Blvd. NW, 87104,* ☎ *505/843–6300 or*
      800/237–2133, FAX *505/842–9863. 190 rooms. 2 restaurants, 2 bars,*
      pool, hot tub. AE, D, DC, MC, V.

$$–$$$ 🏨 **Doubletree Hotel.** A two-story waterfall splashes down a marble back-
      drop in the lobby of this 15-story hotel downtown adjoining the Al-
      buquerque Convention Center. The pastel rooms have comfy,
      custom-made Southwestern furniture and regional art. A restaurant at
      the foot of the lobby's waterfall is called, appropriately, **La Cascada**
      (The Cascade). Breakfast, a popular lunch buffet, and dinner, from fresh
      seafood to Southwestern specialties, are served in an airy, open setting.
      ⊠ *201 Marquette NW, 87102,* ☎ *505/247–3344,* FAX *505/247–7025.*
      294 rooms. 2 restaurants, 2 bars, room service, pool, exercise room,
      parking ($5 fee per night). AE, D, DC, MC, V.

$$–$$$ 🏨 **La Posada de Albuquerque.** Opened in 1939 by New Mexico na-
★   tive Conrad Hilton, this highly lauded, 10-story hotel is listed in the
      National Register of Historic Places (and not just because the hotel mogul
      honeymooned there with his bride, Zsa Zsa Gabor). It achieves South-
      western charm naturally with a tiled lobby fountain, an encircling bal-
      cony, massive vigas, and Native American war-dance murals. Ranging
      from small to spacious, rooms have Southwestern and Native Ameri-
      can themes accented with Hopi pottery and R. C. Gorman prints. Din-
      ner at **Conrad's** restaurant focuses on Spanish and Mexican Yucatecan
      cuisine. There's live jazz and blues on weekend nights, and live piano
      on weekday evenings in the popular lobby bar. ⊠ *125 2nd St. NW,*
      87102, ☎ *505/242–9090 or 800/777–5732,* FAX *505/242–8664. 111*
      rooms, 3 suites. Restaurant, 2 bars, beauty salon, health club privileges,
      parking ($5 fee per night), valet parking. AE, D, DC, MC, V.

$$ 🏨 **Barcelona Court All-Suite Hotel.** This colorful, three-story hotel just
      off I–40 has the feel of old Mexico, with tiles and wrought-iron. But
      furnishings are contemporary, with Southwest splashes and regional
      prints. Enjoy complimentary cocktails or breakfast around the large
      atrium fountain. There is no restaurant. Lunch and dinner can be or-
      dered through room service from the nearby **Cooperage Restaurant,**
      specializing in steaks and seafood, but each two-room suite has a gal-
      ley kitchen with a wet bar and a microwave oven. Three rooms have
      hot tubs. ⊠ *900 Louisiana Blvd. NE, 87110,* ☎ *505/255–5566 or 800/*
      878–9258, FAX *505/255–5566. 164 suites. Kitchenettes, minibars, 2*
      pools, sauna, airport shuttle. AE, D, DC, MC, V.

$ ☎ **Budget Inn.** There's nothing really special about this locally owned chain property, but it does offer free local calls, premium cable TV, and coffee. Its rooms are clean, with queen- and king-size beds. ⊠ *2412 Carlise NE (I–40 at Carlise), 87110,* ☎ *505/880–0080,* ℻ *505/880–0053. 38 rooms, 1 suite. AE, D, DC, MC, V.*

At the Airport

$$ ☎ **Courtyard by Marriott.** Take advantage of special corporate rates and amenities—available to everyone—at this haven for business travelers ½ mi north of the Albuquerque International Airport. Rooms, done in blue and pink with Southwest-inspired paintings, have jacks for portable fax machines (and modem lines for some computers), large desks, and long telephone cords that actually reach the work area. The casual **Courtyard Cafe** serves a number of spicy New Mexican dishes as well as pasta, chicken, burgers, and salads. ⊠ *1920 Yale Blvd. SE, 87106,* ☎ *505/843–6600 or 800/321–2211,* ℻ *505/843–8740. 136 rooms, 14 suites. Restaurant, lobby lounge, indoor pool, health club, business services, airport shuttle. AE, D, DC, MC, V.*

$$ ☎ **Radisson Inn Albuquerque Airport.** This hotel is just ¼ mi from the airport. A Southwestern Spanish flavor runs throughout, with arched balconies, tan desert colors, a year-round courtyard pool, and indoor and seasonal outdoor dining. Most of the rooms are standard and comfortable, but there are also VIP executive rooms. No-smoking rooms are available, and pets are welcome in the smoking rooms. **Diamondback's Café** and **Coyote's Cantina** bar look Western and cook northern New Mexican. Guests can use health club facilities 2 mi away, and complimentary car service is available. ⊠ *1901 University Blvd. SE, 87106,* ☎ *505/247–0512 or 800/333–3333,* ℻ *505/843–7148. 148 rooms, 34 VP executive rooms. Restaurant, bar, no-smoking rooms, pool, hot tub, airport shuttle. AE, D, DC, MC, V.*

$$ ☎ **Wyndham Albuquerque Hotel.** Just 350 yards from the airport, **★** this 15-story hotel provides speedy access to your flight, day or night. There is easy access to all major highways and attractions, and you are minutes away from business and government centers. The rooms are decorated in a southwest accent and provide in-room coffee service and large work desks. The hotel's upscale restaurant, the **RoJo Grill,** offers food with a southwestern flare. ⊠ *2910 Yale Blvd. SE, 87106,* ☎ *505/843–7000 or 800/227–1117,* ℻ *505/843–6307. 281 rooms. Restaurant, lobby lounge, pool, sauna, tennis court, exercise room, airport shuttle. AE, D, DC, MC, V.*

$ ☎ **Comfort Inn.** The rooms have uninspired but acceptable decor and furnishings. There's not a restaurant on the premises, but complimentary Continental breakfast is served each morning in the lobby and a full-service restaurant and coffee shop is adjacent to the hotel. The airport is just 1 mi away. ⊠ *2300 Yale Blvd. SE, 87106,* ☎ *505/243–2244 or 800/221–2222,* ℻ *505/247–2925. 114 rooms. Pool, hot tub, airport shuttle. AE, D, DC, MC, V.*

Bed-and-Breakfasts

$$–$$$ ☎ **Casas de Sueños.** Long a historic gathering spot for artists, Casas **★** de Sueños—Houses of Dreams—provides a magical setting amid lush rose gardens, fountains, and quiet patios. The 2-acre compound, adjacent to Old Town, has 19 comfortable casitas with luxurious bedding and Southwestern appointments, and four private hot tubs. Some casitas have kiva fireplaces and kitchens. A breakfast buffet includes decadent French toast or savory eggs, fruit platters, and a selection of fresh breads. Local artists work is displayed in every room. Impeccable service is the hallmark here; a concierge is on the premises to help you plan your stay. ⊠ *310 Rio Grande Blvd. SW, 87104,* ☎ *505/247–*

4560 or 800/242–8987, FAX 505/842–8493. 4 hot tubs, concierge. AE, MC, V.

$$ 🏨 **Bottger Mansion.** The only bed-and-breakfast right in Old Town, this pale blue two-story house is listed on the National Register of Historic Places and dates to 1912, when it was built by a German immigrant, Charles Bottger. Some of the rooms have original pressed-tin ceilings and roomy poster beds. A grassy courtyard fronted by a patio provides a quiet escape from the Old Town crowds. You may have breakfast burritos smothered in green chile, stuffed French toast, and other delectable fare served in your room if you wish. Since Old Town is short on parking space, the management picks up the tab for the parking lot across the street. ⊠ *110 San Felipe St. NW, 87104,* ☏ *505/243–3639. 7 rooms. AE, MC, V.*

$$ 🏨 **Brittania & W. E. Mauger Estate B&B.** Popular with businesspeople because of its downtown location, this fine B&B also has lots to offer travelers. This elegant 1897 residence, the first home in Albuquerque to have electricity, has oval windows with beveled and "feather-pattern" glass, hardwood floors, a bright redbrick exterior, and an "Old West" front veranda. Full breakfasts—home-baked pastries, juice, and coffee—are served in the downstairs sunroom. ⊠ *701 Roma Ave. NW, 87102,* ☏ *505/242–8755. 8 rooms, 1 suite. AE, D, DC, MC, V.*

$$ 🏨 **Casita Chamisa.** In the pastoral cottonwood-shaded North Valley
★   village of Los Ranchos, this B&B has one handsome private room in the main adobe-style house or a separate house for a party of up to six people with two bedrooms, a small sitting room with a fireplace, a kitchenette, and a greenhouse. The furnishings are a comfortable blend of local, Southwestern, and Mexican materials. Opened by Kit and Arnold Sargeant in 1974 as the first B&B in Albuquerque, the property is also an archaeological site, with a prehistoric Native American ruin still visible. Kit, an archaeologist, supervised the dig herself. Kids enjoy the farm animals. Breakfast is country Continental: juices, coffee, breads, and maybe fresh fruit picked from the 14 fruit trees on the grounds. Don't miss Arnold's famous sourdough bread, "with a starter," he says, "that's 115 years old." This B&B is 15 minutes north of Old Town and 12 mi from the airport. ⊠ *850 Chamisal Rd. NW, 87107,* ☏ *505/897–4644. Indoor pool, hot tub. AE, MC, V.*

$$ 🏨 **Corrales Inn.** This Territorial-style adobe, solar-heated home 14 mi north of Albuquerque in picturesque Corrales, was built to serve as a B&B in 1987. Each room has a theme—Asian, Native American, Victorian, Corrales (Southwestern), and Balloon (in honor of the hot-air-balloon festivals held nearby). Rooms have individual temperature controls, as well as a sitting and dressing area. Full gourmet French country breakfasts—quiche, soufflés, omelets, crêpes, croissants—are served in the rooms or in the inn's common room. ⊠ *58 Perea Rd. (behind Plaza San Ysidro), Box 1361, Corrales 87048,* ☏ *505/897–4422,* FAX *505/890–5244. 6 rooms. Hot tub. MC, V.*

$$ 🏨 **Elaine's, A Bed and Breakfast.** This antique-filled three-story log home
★   is set in the evergreen folds of the Sandia Mountain foothills. Four acres of wooded grounds beckon just outside the back door. The top two floors have rooms with balconies, big picture windows that bring the lush mountain views indoors, and massive stone fireplaces. The third-floor room has cathedral ceilings and a brass bed. Breakfast, served in an airy, plant-filled breakfast room or outside on a patio with a fountain, is simple but hearty: fresh fruit, pancakes, or waffles with sausage, but you can have pretty much whatever you request. ⊠ *72 Snowline Rd., Snowline Estate (Box 444), Cedar Crest 87008,* ☏ *505/281–2467 or 800/821–3092. 3 rooms. Jacuzzi. AE, MC, V.*

$$ 🏨 **Inn at Paradise.** On the first tee of the lush Paradise Hills Golf Club, 30 minutes from the airport, this swank B&B resort is a golfer's dream: The 6,895 yards of bluegrass fairways and bent grass greens challenge players of all levels. The 16-room property sits atop the West Mesa. The large, clean rooms show works by local artists and craftspeople. Two suites have fireplaces; a deluxe suite includes a fireplace, full kitchen, and a wet bar. Pastries, fruit, and coffee are served in a breakfast room with a fireplace. Golf packages are available. ✉ *10035 Country Club La. NW, 87114,* ☎ *505/898–6161 or 800/938–6161,* FAX *505/890–1090. 16 rooms, 2 suites, 1 apartment. Spa, golf privileges, airport shuttle. AE, D, MC, V.*

$$ 🏨 **Old Town B&B.** Set on a quiet, tree-lined residential street just a few blocks from Old Town and not far from downtown, the core of this charming place was built by locally renowned architect Leon Watson, a pioneer in the use of adobe in pueblo revival–style home design. The bright, spacious downstairs suite—with a viga and latilla ceiling, kiva fireplace, and *equipal* (Mexican leather) furniture—is very Southwestern without overkill. There is a bathroom with a skylight and hot tub, shared with the owner only, and a sitting room and library. The cozy second-story room offers views of the Sandias and flowering foliage on the property. ✉ *707 17th St. NW, 87104,* ☎ *505/764–9144 or 888/900–9144. 1 double room, 1 suite with shared bath. No credit cards.*

$$ 🏨 **Yours Truly.** This B&B reflects the warm, outgoing personalities of its owners, Pat and James Montgomery; the hot-air-balloon rides James pilots and the roomy outdoor hot tub show their adventurous sides. Perched on a hillside, the inn sports awesome views. Glass blocks set into the walls cast subtle light. The modern adobe rooms are not large, but they're very comfortable and attractive, especially the one with a king-size bed nestled in an adobe banco. Special touches include plush robes, afternoon wine and snacks, and fireplaces in three rooms. Pat pulls out all the stops at breakfast, serving up fresh-baked goods, such as jalapeño toast, and fresh fruit, coffee, and juice. ✉ *160 Paseo de Corrales (Box 2263), Corrales 87048,* ☎ *505/898–7027 or 800/942–7890. 4 rooms. AE, MC, V.*

Campgrounds

$ ⛺ **Albuquerque KOA Central.** At town's edge, off historic Route 66 in the foothills of the Sandia Mountains, this well-equipped campground has expansive views and only a few trees. Most sites are on sand, but a few are on grass. There's even a pet run for Rover. ✉ *12400 Skyline Rd. NE, 87123 (Exit 166 off I–40),* ☎ *505/296–2729. 169 RV sites, 30 tent sites, 16 cabins. Rest rooms, hot showers, LP gas, grocery, pool, hot tub, miniature golf, bicycles for rent, game room, playground, coin laundry, dump facility, meeting room. D, MC, V.*

$ ⛺ **Albuquerque North KOA.** Often called "an oasis in the desert," this park in Bernalillo (12 mi north of Albuquerque) is shaded by some 900 beautiful cottonwoods, pines, evergreens, and willows. Here, you'll get a free pancake breakfast and in summer dinner à la carte and free outdoor movies. ✉ *555 S. Hill Rd., Bernalillo 87004,* ☎ *505/867–5227 or 800/624–9767. 57 RV sites, 36 tent sites, 6 cabins. Rest rooms, hot showers, LP gas, outdoor café, heated pool, badminton, basketball, croquet, horseshoes, video games, coin laundry, meeting room. D, MC, V.*

$ ⛺ **Isleta Lakes and Recreation Area.** Near the pueblo on the Isleta Reservation, this property is replete with cottonwoods and is home to three fishing lakes full of trout, bass, and catfish. ✉ *Box 383, Isleta 87022 (15 min south of Albuquerque); take I–25 south to Exit 215 and pro-*

ceed south on NM 47; ☎ *505/877–0370. 40 RV sites, 100 tent sites. Rest rooms, hot showers, LP gas, grocery, basketball, softball, fishing, coin laundry. MC, V.*

$ ⚘ **Turquoise Trail Campground and RV Park.** This 14-acre park in the Sandias, marked with pine and cedar trees, has hiking trails with access to the Cibola National Forest. Newly opened here is the **Museum of Archaeology and Material Culture,** which chronicles archaeological finds and analyzes artifacts from the Ice Age to the battle at Wounded Knee. The entrance fee to the museum is $2. ⊠ *22 Calvary Rd., Cedar Crest 87008 (15 min east of Albuquerque); go east on I–40 to exit 175, take NM 14 north 5 mi;* ☎ *505/281–2005. 57 RV sites, 30 tent sites, 2 cabins. Rest rooms, hot showers, hot tub, grocery, playground, coin laundry.*

NIGHTLIFE AND THE ARTS

There are many entertainment options in Albuquerque—theater, dance, classical- and rock-music concerts, and films. If you like to two-step to country-and-western tunes, welcome home. Albuquerque's arts community has always performed in the shadow of Santa Fe—although this is still true today, Albuquerque is becoming a serious player. To find out what's on in town, check the Friday and Sunday editions of the *Albuquerque Journal,* the Thursday edition of the *Albuquerque Tribune,* or the *Weekly Alibi.*

The Arts

Music

The conductor of the **New Mexico Symphony Orchestra** (⊠ 3301 Menaul NE, Suite 4, 87107, ☎ 505/881–8999 or 800/251–NMSO), now in its 64th year, swings a wide baton, with presentations of pops, Beethoven, and Handel's *Messiah* at Christmas. Performances are frequently scheduled under the stars at the Rio Grande Zoo Bandshell and at Popejoy Hall on the University of New Mexico campus.

Opera

The **Albuquerque Civic Light Opera Association** (☎ 505/345–6577) is one of the largest community-based producers of musical theater in the country. Its five annual productions are seen by a total of about 66,000 people. Performances are held in the 2,000-seat Popejoy Hall on the University of New Mexico campus.

Popejoy Hall (⊠ University of New Mexico campus, ☎ 505/851–5050 or 800/905–3315), which recently was extensively remodeled and renovated, presents a wide range of musical events, as well as occasional speaking engagements, dance performances, and other touring shows. Concerts range from rock and pop to classical music.

Theater

Albuquerque Little Theater (⊠ 224 San Pasquale Ave. SW, ☎ 505/242–4750), a nonprofit community troupe, combines local volunteer talent with a staff of professionals to present an annual series of comedies, dramas, musicals, and mysteries. The company theater, across the street from historic Old Town, was built in 1936 and designed by famed Southwestern architect John Gaw Meem. It contains an art gallery; a large, comfortable lobby; and a cocktail lounge.

KiMo Theater (⊠ 423 Central Ave. NW, ☎ 505/764–1700 for box office, 505/848–1370 for business office), a 1927 movie palace on Central Avenue restored to its original unique design—Pueblo Deco–style architecture painted in bright colors—offers a varied program: everything from traveling road shows to local song-and-dance acts.

La Compania de Teatro de Albuquerque (✉ KiMo Theater, Box 884, 87103, ☎ 505/242–7929), New Mexico's long-running bilingual theater company, performs classic and contemporary plays in English and Spanish during April, June, October, and December.

Rodey Theater (✉ University of New Mexico Fine Arts Center, ☎ 505/277–4402) stages student and professional plays and dance performances throughout the year, including the acclaimed annual Summerfest Festival of New Plays and the Flamenco Festival.

Nightlife

Bars and Lounges

There is a lively mix of nightclubs, bars, pool halls, late-night dining spots, and live performance spaces now in downtown Albuquerque, all within a 10-minute walk of one another. Other nightlife options are scattered far and wide across the city: more than 62 at last count and growing all the time.

The Dingo Bar (✉ 301 Gold Ave. SE, ☎ 505/243–0663) is a small, funky, downtown nightclub that draws big crowds for its out-of-town road acts. Blues and jazz are its mainstays, though it also books occasional rock, grunge, offbeat country, and world-beat performers.

Fat Chance Bar and Grill (✉ 2216 Central Ave. SE, ☎ 505/265–7531), across the street from the University of New Mexico, is a hangout for rowdy college students. It has booths, a bar, tables, a dance floor, and live entertainment.

Outpost Performance Space (✉ 112 Morningside SE, ☎ 505/268–0044) schedules an eclectic assemblage of live music, from local nuevo-folk to techno, jazz, and traveling East Indian ethnic.

Comedy Clubs

Laff's Comedy Caffé (✉ 3100–D Juan Tabo Blvd. NE, ☎ 505/296–5653) is the place to go for live comedy and dinner Wednesday–Sunday in Albuquerque.

Country-and-Western Clubs

Caravan East (✉ 7605 Central SE, ☎ 505/265–7877) is a granddaddy of country-and-western clubs, having been around for 47 years. Two live bands play nightly, and there's a free buffet and half-price drinks during the 4:30–7 happy hour.

Midnight Rodeo (✉ 4901 McLeod NW, ☎ 505/888–0100) is an enormous country-and-western complex, with a huge racetrack-style dance floor, several bars, and even boutiques. The happy-hour buffet spread, served on Friday and Sunday, is incredible.

OUTDOOR ACTIVITIES AND SPORTS

Albuquerque is blessed with an exceptional setting for outdoor sports, backed by a favorable, yet unpredictable climate. Usually 10°F warmer than Santa Fe, Albuquerque's winter days are often warm enough for playing outdoors. The Sandias tempt you with challenging mountain adventures; the Rio Grande and its thick forest, the Bosque, provide settings for more wild pursuits. There are no major-league sport franchises in the city, but the Triple-A Los Angeles Dodgers' farm team, the Dukes, pitches up some classic baseball, and it's hard to beat the excitement of a University of New Mexico's Lobo home basketball game in the "Pit," with 18,000 rabid fans on hand.

Participant Sports

The **Albuquerque Cultural and Recreation Services Department** (✉ 400 Marquette Ave. NW, Box 1293, Albuquerque 87103, ☎ 505/768–3550) maintains a widely diversified network of parks and recreational programs, encompassing over 20,000 acres of open space, four golf courses, 200 parks, 68 paved tracks for biking and jogging, as well as numerous recreational facilities, such as swimming pools, tennis courts, ball fields, playgrounds, and even a shooting range.

Ballooning

Known for the **Albuquerque International Balloon Fiesta** (☞ Spectator Sports, *below*), Albuquerque also offers myriad opportunities for those who want to take to the skies themselves. If you'd like to give it a try, contact one of the many outfitters that runs ballooning trips: **Braden's Balloons** (✉ 3212 Stanford Ave. NE, ☎ 505/281–2714), **Rainbow Ryders** (✉ 10305 Nita Place NE, ☎ 505/293–0000 or 800/725–2477), or **World Balloon Corporation** (✉ 4800 Eubank Blvd. NE, ☎ 505/293–6800 or 800/351–9588).

Bicycling

Albuquerque is big on biking, both as a recreational sport and as a means of cutting down on automobile traffic and its resulting emissions. In 1973 the city established a network of bikeways, recommending existing streets and roadways as bike routes, lanes, and trails. Few, however, are dedicated just to biking: be careful! Designated Recreational Trails are shared with walkers and joggers and provide the safest off-road area for both (☞ Jogging, *below*). An elaborately detailed **Metropolitan Albuquerque Bicycle Map** can be obtained free of charge by calling 505/768–3550. For information about mountain biking in Albuquerque's adjacent national forest, call the **Sandia Ranger Station** (☎ 505/281–3304).

Bikes can be rented at several locations, including **Rio Mountain Sport** (✉ 1210 Rio Grande Blvd. NW, ☎ 505/766–9970), which is convenient to Old Town, the Rio Grande Nature Center, and the Paseo de Bosque trail.

Bird-Watching

People who love birds love Albuquerque. On one of the continent's major flyways, the Rio Grande Valley, the area attracts many migratory bird species. It also has a great range of microclimates and habitats in a compact area—from alpine to semidesert and riparian—which also favors bird diversity and numbers. For details on bird-watching events and outings, contact the local chapter of the **Sierra Club** (✉ 207 S. Pedro NE, ☎ 505/265–5506, ext. 4).

Good viewing locales include the **Rio Grande Nature Center** (☞ Old Town *in* Exploring Albuquerque, *above*) and the **Ellena Gallegos/Albert Simms Park** (✉ 1700 Tramway NE, ☎ 505/857–8334 or 505/873–6630), a 640-acre reserve at the base of the Sandias adjoining the Sandia Mountain Wilderness Area (☞ Sandia *in* Exploring Albuquerque, *above*).

One of America's favorite bird-watching spots is found just 94 mi south of Albuquerque at the 57,000-acre **Bosque del Apache National Wildlife Refuge** (✉ Box 1246, Socorro 87801, ☎ 505/835–1828).

Golf

The Albuquerque Cultural and Recreation Services Department (☞ *above*) maintains four public golf courses. Greens fees range from $8.90 for nine holes to $14.25 for 18 holes, with special discount rates for sundown play. The courses are open from sunup to sundown. Each has a clubhouse and pro shop, where clubs and equipment can be rented. Weekday play is on a first-come, first-served basis, but reservations are taken for weekend use. The city's **Golf Management Office** (✉ 6401 Osuna Rd. NE, ☎ 505/888–8115) can provide more information.

Arroyo del Oso (✉ 7001 Osuna Rd. NE, ☎ 505/884–7505) has an 18- and a 9-hole regulation course and practice facilities. At one time it was rated by *Golf Digest* as one of the top 50 27-hole public golf courses in the country, with a driving range, rental shop, full-service restaurant, and an up-to-the-hour information line for tee-off status (☎ 505/889–3699).

Ladera (✉ 3401 Ladera Dr. NW, ☎ 505/836–4449) has an 18-hole regulation course, practice facilities, a 9-hole executive course, a large driving range, a restaurant, and a full-service pro shop. It's 10 mi west of downtown.

Los Altos (✉ 9717 Copper Ave. NE, ☎ 505/298–1897) includes an 18-hole regulation course, a short 9-hole course, and practice facilities. One of the Southwest's most popular facilities, Los Altos has a driving range, grass tees, a restaurant serving mainly New Mexican food, instructors for individuals or groups, and a large selection of rental equipment.

Puerto del Sol (✉ 1800 Girard Blvd. SE, ☎ 505/265–5636), near the Albuquerque airport, has a 9-hole regulation course, a lighted driving range, a full-service pro shop, and a snack bar. No reservations are taken for tee times.

The University of New Mexico maintains two public golf courses. **UNM North** (✉ 2201 Tucker Rd. NE, between Stanford Ave. and University Blvd., ☎ 505/277–4146), is a first-class regulation 9-hole course on campus; **UNM South** (✉ Rio Bravo east of I–25, ☎ 505/277–4546), is an 18-hole championship course, including an excellent beginners' 3-hole regulation course. Both are open daily and have full-service pro shops, instruction, and snack bars offering New Mexican favorites.

Health Clubs

Most of the large hotel health clubs are reserved for guests' use only. However, keeping fit in Albuquerque is easy, with numerous health clubs, gyms, and fitness centers from which to choose in virtually every neighborhood. One-day passes can usually be purchased.

Albuquerque Rock Gym (✉ 3300 Princeton Dr. NE, ☎ 505/881–3073) is a complete indoor climbing facility with bouldering ($4) and top-roping ($7). You can rent equipment there. It's one block east of I–25, one block north of Candelaria Road.

4th Street Gym (✉ 1100 4th St. NW, ☎ 505/247–1947), is Albuquerque's newest state-of-the-art gym. Owner Eric Haggard offers a variety of options with your day pass. Just use the gym or get a one-on-one boxing session and then finish your workout with a massage. Call Carla Glaser to make arrangements.

Gold's Gym (✉ 5001 Montgomery Blvd. NE, Suite 147, ☎ 505/881–8500) is a state-of-the-art fitness complex, and part of the national chain. It offers free weights, a cardiovascular deck, aerobics, sportswear, and Pro-line supplements. Nonmembers pay $8 per day.

Liberty Gym (✉ 2401 Jefferson St. NE, ☎ 505/884–8012) is Albuquerque's first coed gym, and it has been in operation for 16 years. Here you will find specialized machines (such as Stairmasters), free weights, and a cardiovascular area, personalized instruction, and nutritional counseling. Nonmembers pay a walk-in fee of $5.

Jogging

The Albuquerque Cultural and Recreation Services Department (☞ *above*) maintains an extensive network of Designated Recreational Trails that joggers share with bicyclists.

Swimming

The City of Albuquerque has at least four year-round pools open for both lap and recreational swimming. Sessions range from two to four hours and schedules change seasonally; the fee is $1.85, which includes one session only. Pools are **Highland** (✉ 400 Jackson St. SE, ☎ 505/256–2096), **Los Altos** (✉ 10100 Lomas Blvd. NE, ☎ 505/291–6290), **Sandia** (✉ 7801 Candelaria Rd. NE, ☎ 505/291–6279), and **Valley** (✉ 1505 Candelaria Rd. NW, ☎ 505/761–4086).

Albuquerque also maintains at least 13 additional outdoor pools all over the city from Memorial Day to mid-August. For information for the specific pools, call the Albuquerque Cultural and Recreation Services Department (☞ *above*).

Tennis

Albuquerque's wide-ranging network of public parks contains nearly 140 courts. Lessons are available at some; others are lighted for night play (until 10 PM). For information call the Albuquerque Cultural and Recreation Services Department (☞ *above*). In addition, the city maintains three tennis complexes.

Albuquerque Tennis Complex (✉ 1903 Av. Caesar Chavez SE, ☎ 505/848–1381) consists of 16 Laykold tennis courts and 4 racquetball/handball courts, which may be reserved by phone or in person; reservations are taken two days in advance at 10 AM. The rate is $2.10 per hour and the complex is open daily from 8 AM to dusk.

Jerry Cline Tennis Complex (✉ Louisiana Blvd. and Constitution Ave., ☎ 505/256–2032 [this is the correct phone number, even though the voice you will hear on the tape does not identify the complex]) has 12 Laykold courts; 3 are lighted. There is no charge, and no reservations are needed to play here.

Sierra Vista Tennis Complex (✉ 5001 Montano Rd. NW, ☎ 505/897–8819) consists of 10 tennis courts (2 Omni courts), 2 platform tennis courts, and an outdoor pool (open summer, daily 12:30–5). Reservations are taken two days in advance at 10 AM; the rate is $2.10 per hour, and the tennis complex is open weekdays 8–8 (on weekends it closes at 5). No racquetball facilities are available.

Along with the numerous tennis courts in the city's various hotels and resorts (☞ Lodging, *above*), a number of private clubs have excellent facilities and generally allow guest privileges at a member's invitation or honor memberships from out-of-town clubs with reciprocal arrangements or equal status. Among these are the **Highpoint Sports & Wellness Club** (✉ 4300 Landau Dr. NE, ☎ 505/293–5820), **Tanoan Country Club** (✉ 10801 Academy Rd. NE, ☎ 505/822–0455), and the **Tennis Club of Albuquerque** (✉ 2901 Indian School Rd. NE, ☎ 505/262–1691).

Spectator Sports

The **Albuquerque Dukes** are the Triple-A farm team of the Los Angeles Dodgers and members of the Pacific Coast League; Orel Hershiser is a Dukes alumnus. Exciting professional baseball can be seen from

April through September at the city-owned Albuquerque Sports Stadium (⊠ 1601 Av. Caesar Chavez SE, 87106, ☎ 505/243–1791), the only stadium anywhere with a drive-in spectator area. Game tickets range from $2 to $5.

Albuquerque National Dragway (⊠ 5700 Bobby Foster Rd., ☎ 505/299–9478) is the state's only sanctioned National Hot Rod Association facility. Races are held year-round, with five major events a year.

The **University of New Mexico**'s (⊠ University and Avenida Chavez, ☎ 505/277–2116 or 800/905–3315) Lobo football and basketball games are also a major draw. The University Arena, affectionately nicknamed "The Pit," has an 18,000-seat capacity to accommodate the city's intensely loyal UNM basketball fans. Across the street is the 30,000-seat Lobo football stadium. Call for schedules and ticket information.

Ballooning

Mention hot-air ballooning to an enthusiast, and Albuquerque automatically comes to mind. The city's high altitude, mild climate, and steady, but manageable winds make it especially suitable. Albuquerque's long history of ballooning dates from 1882, when Professor Park A. Van Tassel, a saloon keeper, made the first balloon ascent at the Territorial Fair. Since those early beginnings, Albuquerque has become the hot-air-balloon capital of the world, partly because of the success of the annual **Albuquerque International Balloon Fiesta** (⊠ 8309 Washington Pl. NE, 87113, ☎ 505/821–1000), the first of which took place in 1972, when 13 balloons participated. Today the nine-day event, held in early October, is the largest hot-air-balloon gathering in the world, with more than 650 registered hot-air balloons and entrants from as far away as Australia and Japan.

A special annual feature is the "balloon glow," when hundreds of tethered balloons are inflated after the sun sets. As propane burners send heat into the colorful envelopes, the balloons light up like giant fanciful light bulbs. Most spectacular are the Saturday- and Sunday-morning ascensions on the opening and closing weekends of the fiesta. At dawn all of the massive balloons are inflated and, although tethered, lift off in a majestic display.

An estimated 1.5 million people attend the nine-day program, and thousands more glimpse the balloons as they float over Albuquerque's backyards, setting off a serenade of barking dogs. It is New Mexico's biggest draw for out-of-state visitors and a delight for those who live here. The entrance fee for the grounds is $4.

SHOPPING

The tourist trail in New Mexico is paved with Native American arts and crafts. Handsome turquoise and silver jewelry, blankets, pottery, Spanish Colonial handmade furniture, leather goods, textiles, colorful items from south of the border, trendy Taos and Santa Fe interior furnishings, and early Western antique mementos abound—everything from Billy the Kid's gun belt (of dubious authenticity) to Kit Carson's hat can be found. Tourist demand has forced prices up, but if you diligently stalk the fairs and powwows, the backstreet shops, flea markets, and secondhand stores, you'll surely come away with a treasure or two.

When purchasing artwork, unless you're really knowledgeable, beware of those high-priced, once-in-a-lifetime purchases. You'll also find some funky, good-natured souvenir art and merchandise that's always worth a few dollars, if only as a keepsake of happy days spent visiting dusty pueblos or flea markets in the sun.

Typical of large Western cities, Albuquerque's main shopping areas and malls are scattered throughout the community. Nob Hill, the city's trendiest district, stretches for seven blocks along Central Avenue from Girard Boulevard to Washington Street. In 1947 it began as one of the nation's first car-oriented shopping centers. Today, neon-lit boutiques, restaurants, galleries, and performing-arts spaces encourage foot traffic day and night. Old Town, at the corner of Central and Rio Grande Boulevard, has the city's largest concentration of one-of-a-kind retail shops, featuring clothing, home accessories, and Mexican imports, as well as a slew of galleries—many featuring fine Native American art. Hours are generally 10–9 weekdays, 10–6 Saturday, and noon–6 Sunday.

Art Galleries

Amapola Gallery (⊠ 2045 S. Plaza St. NW, in Old Town, ☎ 505/242–4311), just west of the Plaza near Rio Grande Blvd., is one of the largest co-op galleries in New Mexico. It has a lovely brick courtyard and an indoor space, both brimming with pottery, paintings, textiles, carvings, baskets, jewelry, and more.

Andrew Nagen (⊠ 4499 Corrales Rd., Corrales, ☎ 505/898–5058, FAX 505/898–5118) has been buying, selling, and appraising antique Navajo, Mexican, Rio Grande, and Pueblo textiles since 1976. His shop is open by appointment only.

Concetta D. Gallery (⊠ 20 1st St. NW, Suite 29, in the First Plaza Galeria, ☎ 505/243–5066) carries a good selection of the early Santa Fe and Taos artists, as well as contemporary regional artists such as Rod Goebel, Walter Chapman, Lincoln Fox, Don Brackett, Clifford Fragua, Ramon Kelley, Joe Horton, Carol McIlroy, Morris Ripple, and Julian Roble working in a wide variety of medias and styles.

DSG (⊠ 3011 Monte Vista Blvd. NE, ☎ 505/266–7751 or 800/474–7751, FAX 505/266–0005), owned by John Cacciatore, handles contemporary and nonobjective New Mexico art by leading regional artists, including Frank McCulloch, Carol Hoy, Leo Neufeld, John Rise, Jane Abrams, Nancy Kozikowski, and Angus MacPherson.

Mariposa Gallery (⊠ 113 Romero St. NW in Old Town, ☎ 505/842–9097), is an excellent venue for contemporary fine crafts, including jewelry, sculptural glass, mixed media, clay works, and fiber arts. The changing gallery exhibits spotlight some of the area's best upcoming artists. The annual October display of *Dia de los Muertos* (Day of the Dead) objects shouldn't be missed.

Richard Levy Gallery (⊠ 514 Central Ave. SW, ☎ 505/766–9888, FAX 505/242–4279) carries works on paper (including photography) and small sculpture by a bevy of major regional artists, including Clinton Adams, Thomas Barrow, Ed Haddaway, Frederick Hammersley, Patrick Nagatani, Ed Ruscha, and Richard Tuttle.

Weems Gallery (⊠ 2801-M Eubank Blvd. NE, ☎ 505/293–6133; ⊠ 303 Romero NW in Old Town, ☎ 505/764–0302) carries a wide selection of unique and affordable pieces by the more than 150 artists it represents. Featured are paintings, pottery, sculpture, jewelry, weaving, stained glass, and original-design clothes.

Specialty Stores

Antiques

Antique Specialty Mall (⊠ 4516 Central Ave. SE, ☎ 505/268–8080) is perhaps Albuquerque's most prestigious center for collectibles and antiques, with special emphasis on memorabilia from the early 1880s to the 1950s. When the set designers for the hit television miniseries *Lonesome Dove* needed special props to establish authenticity, they came here. Objects include Art Deco and Art Nouveau items, Depression-era glass, Native American goods, quilts and linens, vintage clothes, and Western memorabilia.

Cowboys & Indians (⊠ 4000 Central SE, ☎ 505/255–4054) carries the city's largest collection of Native American and cowboy art and artifacts.

Books

Page One (⊠ 11018 Montgomery Blvd. NE, ☎ 505/294–2026), frequently voted the best bookstore in Albuquerque by various polls, is certainly one of the biggest, with the largest selection of books dealing in computer software in New Mexico. It also handles computer software, technical and professional books, maps, globes, racing forms, and 150 out-of-state and foreign newspapers.

Clothing

Wear It! (⊠ 107 Amherst Dr. SE, ☎ 505/266–7764), a Nob Hill highlight, is the place for contemporary clothing and accessories.

Gifts

Beeps (⊠ 3500 Central SE, in the Nob Hill Shopping Center, ☎ 505/262–1900), a card, T-shirt, and novelty store, is a Nob Hill favorite.

Home Furnishings

A (⊠ 3500 Central SE, ☎ 505/266–2222) is a Nob Hill stop for fine housewares, soaps, candles, fine body-care products, and jewelry.

Contemporary lifestyle is the theme at **Moderno** (⊠ 113 Carlisle Ave. SE, ☎ 505/254–0447). Check out the handmade steel beds, chairs, mobiles, and modern locally produced art, rugs, and jewelry.

Mexican Imports

La Piñata (⊠ No. 2 Patio Market in Old Town, ☎ 505/242–2400 or 800/657–6208) specializes in a huge selection of piñatas, perfect for children's birthday parties, as well as papier-mâché products of all kinds.

V. Whipple's Mexico Shop (⊠ 400-E San Felipe St. NW in Old Town's Patio del Norte, ☎ 505/243–6070) is a small, festive shop where you'll delight in the Mexican handblown glassware, tinwork, lead-free dinnerware, Talavera pottery, terra-cotta planters, carved masks, Day of the Dead objects, jewelry, and much more. The owner's vast selection shows her knowledge and appreciation of Mexico's arts and crafts.

Native American Arts and Crafts

Adobe Gallery (⊠ 413 Romero St. NW, ☎ 505/243–8485) specializes in historic and contemporary art of the Southwestern Native Americans: Pueblo pottery; Hopi kachinas; Navajo rugs, blankets, and paintings. Founded in 1978, the shop is housed in a historic *terrones* adobe (cut from the ground rather than formed from mud and dried) homestead that dates from 1878; it is owned and managed by Alexander E. Anthony, Jr. The shop also has an extensive stock of books about Southwestern Native Americans.

Andrews Pueblo Pottery (⊠ Suite 116, 303 Romero NW, ☎ 505/243–0414) handles a terrific selection of Pueblo pottery, fetishes, kachina dolls, and baskets for the beginning and seasoned collector.

Nizhoni Moses, Ltd. (⊠ 326 San Felipe St. NW, ☎ 505/842–1808) features a vast selection of Pueblo pottery, including the black earthenware pottery of San Ildefonso, as well as the work of potters from Acoma, Santa Clara, Isleta, and Zia. Rare Zuni and Navajo jewelry is showcased, as are select Navajo weavings from 1900 to the present.

Skip Maisel Wholesale Indian Jewelry and Crafts (⊠ 510 Central Ave. SW, ☎ 505/242–6526) has been in business since 1905 and has been at its current location since 1929. Even its exterior is a piece of art—check out the excellent murals in the entryway alcove. Inside are quality Native American arts and crafts at truly wholesale prices in a decidedly nonboutique setting. But it's packed with great Zuni, Navajo, and Santo Domingo jewelry; pottery from Santa Clara and Acoma; textiles, paintings, sculpture, and more.

Tanner Chaney Gallery (⊠ 410 Romero St. NW, ☎ 505/247–2242 or 800/444–2242) is housed in a beautiful old pre–Civil War adobe house in Old Town. In several showrooms is an extensive collection of Native American jewelry, sculpture, contemporary and historic pottery, baskets, incredible Navajo weavings, and an extensive selection of books on the Southwest.

Shopping Malls

Among the major shopping malls are: **Coronado Center** (⊠ Louisiana Blvd. NE and Menaul Blvd. NE, ☎ 505/881–4600) and the **Cottonwood Mall** (⊠ Jct. of Coors Blvd. and Coors Bypass, ☎ 505/899–7467), the latter being Albuquerque's largest.

Fashion Square (⊠ 1100 San Mateo Blvd., ☎ 505/265–6931) is anchored by Kistler Collister department store, but it's mostly filled with boutiques selling jewelry, shoes, home furnishings, children's clothes, and beauty products.

First Plaza Galeria (⊠ Downtown at 20 First Plaza, ☎ 505/242–3446) has art galleries, a beauty shop, and retail stores.

Winrock Center (⊠ Louisiana Blvd. exit off I–40, ☎ 505/888–3038) has Dillard's and Montgomery Ward, and 17 restaurants—from fast food to fancy fare.

SIDE TRIPS

Albuquerque is like the hub of an old wagon wheel, with interesting destinations and side trips forming the spokes. Mountain scenery and ghost towns await you; the graves of Billy the Kid and an entire Native American civilization call eerily from their resting places under the sands of time. High, fortresslike plateaus topped by age-old living Native American pueblos and red-rocked canyons dazzle the eye. When visiting pueblos and reservations, there is a certain etiquette you are expected to follow (☞ Pleasures and Pastimes *in* Chapter 1). When scheduling side trips, savvy travelers should check the pueblos and monuments for dates of feast day celebrations and fairs; some pueblos are only open on specific days.

Turquoise Trail and the Sandia Mountains

A scenic drive etched out nearly a quarter century ago and still well traveled is the Turquoise Trail, an old route between Albuquerque and Santa Fe dotted with ghost towns that are being restored by writers, artists, and other urban refugees. Here the pace is slow, the talk is about weather, and Albuquerque seems like another planet. The entire loop of this trip takes a day; the drive up the Sandia crest, a half day.

Tijeras

7 mi east of Albuquerque. From Albuquerque, take I–40 east 7 mi to Tijeras, take NM 337 ½ mi south.

Begin your tour of the Turquoise Trail and the Sandia Mountains with a quick, educational stop in the Tijeras area.

At the **Sandia Ranger Station** you can get pamphlets, maps, and—if there are enough kids in the audience—a fire-prevention program with a *Smokey the Bear* movie. Occasional tours to the nearby **fire lookout tower** and **Tijeras Pueblo ruins** are available. Call to reserve movie and tour times. ⊠ *11776 Hwy. NM 337 (just south of I–40),* ☎ *505/281–3304.* 🖃 *Free.* ⊙ *Weekdays 8–5, weekends 8:30–noon and 12:30–5.*

Kids love **Sierra Goat Farms,** and here you'll meet Carmen Sanchez, the Goat Lady, who owns the farm and delights in teaching children. Ms. Sanchez shows children how to milk the animals and care for them. The farm has plenty of outdoor grills and picnic tables; a variety of goat cheeses, cheesecakes, and chocolates are for sale. ⊠ *NM 337 and Cardinal Rd. (15 mi south of Sandia Ranger Station, 15 mi south of I–40 on NM 337),* ☎ *505/281–5061.* 🖃 *$2.50; free Sun.* ⊙ *Tues.– Fri. 2–4, weekends 1–4.*

Sandia Park

13 mi northeast of Albuquerque. 7 mi north of Tijeras. From Tijeras, take I–40 east and exit north on the Turquoise Trail (NM 14); proceed 6 mi and turn left onto NM 536.

A terrific stop for kids is found in the small community of Sandia Park, bordering the Sandia Mountains.

Both small-fry and grown-ups are enchanted by the **Tinkertown Museum,** which houses a world of miniature carved-wood characters. Owner Ross Ward has spent more than 35 years carving and collecting the 1,200 or so figures that populate this museum, including an animated miniature Western village, a Boot Hill cemetery, and a circus exhibit from the 1940s with wooden merry-go-round horses, a bear act, and tiny vendors selling cotton candy and pink lemonade. Ragtime piano music, a 40-ft sailboat, and a life-size general store are other highlights. ⊠ *121 Sandia Crest Rd. (NM 536),* ☎ *505/281–5233.* 🖃 *$2.50.* ⊙ *Apr.–Oct., daily 9–6.*

Sandia Crest

25 mi northeast of Albuquerque. From Tinkertown Museum, go north on NM 536 12 mi and wind up through the Cibola National Forest to the crest.

For awesome views of Albuquerque and half of New Mexico, take the side road to the Sandia Crest via the "backside" on NM 536, which winds up through the Cibola National Forest. At the summit, explore the foot trails along the rim (particularly in summer) and take in the views, notably a close-up look at the "Steel Forest," the nearby cluster of radio and television towers.

If you are in need of some refreshments or are searching for some inexpensive souvenirs, stop in at the **Sandia Crest House Gift Shop and Restaurant** (☎ 505/243–0605), right on the rim of the crest.

Golden

25 mi northeast of Albuquerque. From the Sandia Crest, take NM 536 south to NM 14 north, the Turquoise Trail; in 20 minutes or so you'll coast into Golden.

Golden, the site of the first gold rush (1825) west of the Mississippi, has a rock shop and a mercantile store. Its rustic adobe church and graveyard send photographers into a state of euphoria. The shop **La Casita** (⊠ North end of village) serves as a kind of unofficial chamber of commerce, in case you've got any questions.

Madrid

37 mi northeast of Albuquerque; 12 mi northeast of Golden on NM 14.

Almost entirely abandoned at one point, Madrid is being rebuilt, but slowly. Weathered old houses and converted company stores have been repaired and turned into shops—and some are definitely worth a visit.

Madrid's **Old Coal Mine Museum** is a remnant of a once-flourishing coal-mining industry. Children love exploring the old coal-mine tunnel with its vein of coal, climbing aboard a 1900 steam train, and nosing through a variety of antique buildings full of marvelous old relics. Tickets for the museum are available at the Mine Shaft Tavern out front. On weekends between Memorial Day and Labor Day, catch the museum's old-fashioned melodrama at the **Engine House Theater,** where you can cheer the hero and hiss the villain in a converted roundhouse machine shop. It's probably the only theater with a full-size steam train that comes chugging onto the stage. In this production, the pretty heroine tied onto the tracks really has something to worry about! ⊠ *Old Coal Mine Museum, Madrid,* ☎ *505/473–0743.* ⊠ *Museum $3, melodrama $9.* ◯ *Daily 9:30–dusk.*

SHOPPING

Madrid has only one street in its town; the shops are easy to find. **Madrid Earthenware Pottery** (☎ 505/471–3450) is a necessary stop for one-of-a-kind handcrafted pottery works. **Maya Jones Imports** (☎ 505/473–3641) has unique Guatemalan imports and other one-of-a-kind creations and an old soda fountain from 1934 that still works. **Primitiva** (☎ 505/471–7904) features handmade Mexican furniture. For hand-loomed knits and rugs, don't miss **Tapestry Gallery** (☎ 505/471–0194).

Cerrillos

40 mi northeast of Albuquerque. 3 mi northeast of Madrid on NM 14.

Cerrillos, yet another echo of bygone days, was a boomtown in the 1880s—its mines brimmed with gold, silver, and turquoise; 8 newspapers, 4 hotels, and 21 taverns flourished. Then the mines went dry, and the town went bust. More recently, Cerrillos has been the site of a number of television and Hollywood Westerns (*Young Guns, Lonesome Dove*). The town has a number of interesting shops along its tree-shaded streets.

Casa Grande (⊠ 17 Waldo, ☎ 505/438–3008), a sprawling 21-room adobe, has a display of early mining exhibits, a gift shop, a petting zoo, and a scenic overlook. Mining exhibit and petting zoo cost $1.

Santo Domingo Pueblo

40 mi northeast of Albuquerque. From Cerrillos, take NM 14 south 9 mi and turn right (west) on NM 301 for about 12 mi to I–25; cross under I–25 onto NM 22 and proceed 4½ mi to the pueblo. To return to Albuquerque from the pueblo, take NM 14 south to I–40 west.

Santo Domingo Pueblo operates a small **Indian Arts and Crafts Center,** where its outstanding *heishi* (shell) jewelry is sold, along with other traditional arts and crafts. Sales are also made from stands along the road, leading into the pueblo. The pueblo's annual three-day Labor Day Arts and Crafts Fair has artists and visitors out in full force. The

August 4th Corn Dance is one of the most colorful and dramatic of all the pueblo ceremonial dances. Held in honor of St. Dominic, the pueblo's patron saint, the dance attracts more than 2,000 dancers, clowns, singers, and drummers. ⊠ *Off NM 22 (4½ mi west of I–25),* ☎ *505/465–2214.* ▣ *Donations encouraged. Still and video cameras, video and tape recorders, and sketching materials prohibited.* ☉ *Daily sunrise–sunset.*

Turquoise Trail and the Sandias Visitor Information

Sandia Ranger Station (⊠ NM 337, Tijeras 87509, ☎ 505/281–3304); **Sierra Goat Farms** (⊠ NM 337 and Cardinal Rd., Tijeras 87509, ☎ 505/281–5061); **Tinkertown Museum** (⊠ 121 Sandia Crest Rd, NM 536, Sandia Park 87047, ☎ 505/281–5233); for Golden, **La Casita** (⊠ North end of Madrid village); for Madrid, call **Johnsons of Madrid** (☎ 505/471–1054); **Old Coal Mine Museum** (⊠ Madrid 87010, ☎ 505/473–0743 for information or 505/438–3780 for theater tickets); **Santo Domingo Pueblo** (⊠ Box 99, Santo Domingo 87052, ☎ 505/465–2214).

Northwest Outing

A pastoral drive from Albuquerque through the tranquil village of Corrales is a tame beginning to this side trip of awe-inspiring natural wonders. You will visit the ruins of an old pueblo near Bernalillo where Coronado is thought to have wintered in 1540—today's Coronado State Monument. Turning northwest you'll skirt the impressive mesas at the southern end of the Jemez Mountains, then slip up a spectacular red-rocked canyon to Jemez Pueblo. This trip will take the better part of a day, depending upon your pace; the round-trip requires about 52 mi of driving.

Corrales

8 mi northwest of Albuquerque. From Albuquerque take I–40 west, take NM 448 to the Coors exit north (just west of the Rio Grande).

Historic, quiet, and beautiful Corrales is dotted with small galleries, shops, places to eat and, during the fall, roadside fruit and vegetable stands.

Coronado State Monument

14 mi northwest of Albuquerque. From Corrales, Continue on NM 448 to NM 528, turn right (north) and go northwest 4.6 mi to the intersection with NM 44, take NM 44 east and in a minute you'll see the entrance on your left.

The area surrounding Coronado State Monument is quite lovely. The Sandia Mountains rise abruptly from 5,280 to 10,678 ft a mere 6 mi away. The community of Bernalillo, settled by Spanish colonists before Albuquerque was founded in 1706, is nearby. In autumn, the views are especially breathtaking, with the trees turning russet and gold.

Coronado State Monument is named in honor of the leader of the first organized Spanish expedition into the Southwest in 1540 to 1542. The prehistoric **Kuaua Pueblo,** on a bluff overlooking the Rio Grande, is believed to have been the headquarters of Francisco Vásquez de Coronado and his army, caught unprepared by severe winter weather during their search for the legendary Seven Cities of Gold. It's worthy of a visit. The museum, in a restored kiva, contains copies of magnificent frescoes done in black, yellow, red, blue, green, and white, depicting fertility rites, rain dances, and hunting rituals; the original frescoes are preserved in a **small visitor center.** Adjacent is **Coronado State Park** (☎ 505/867–5589), which has campsites and picnic grounds, both open year-round. ⊠ *Box 95, Bernalillo 87004,* ☎ *505/867–5351.* 🎫 *May–Sept. $3, Sept.–May $2.* ☉ *Monument grounds and visitor center, daily 8:30–5.*

Jemez Pueblo
26 mi north of Albuquerque. From Coronado State Monument, return to NM 44 and head west (right) 20 minutes or so to San Ysidro, exit onto NM 4 and proceed 5.5 mi to Jemez Pueblo. Return to Albuquerque via NM 44 east and I–25 south.

Jemez Pueblo, in the red sandstone canyon of the Jemez River, is noted for its polychrome pottery. After Pecos Pueblo was abandoned in the 1830s, Jemez was the only Towa-speaking (different from Tiwa and Tewa) pueblo remaining in the state. In addition to the pueblo, the Jemez Reservation encompasses 88,000 acres, with two lakes, **Holy Ghost Springs** and **Dragonfly Lake,** situated just off NM. The lakes are open April through October on weekends and holidays; you must purchase a fishing permit. The only part of the pueblo open to the public is the **Walatowa Visitor Center** (⊠ Along NM 4), which includes a gift shop, photo display, and nature walk. Also, its Jemez **Red Rocks** center hosts arts and crafts fairs the second week in June, the first week in October, and at the end of December. During the weekends (weather permitting), traditional foods are offered and arts and crafts are displayed. There is also a general store where you can get gasoline, which might come in handy since there are no gas stations in the valley. Interesting group educational tours and demonstrations can be arranged in advance; call for information. The ancient ruins of **Jemez State Monument** are some 13 mi north on NM 4 (☞ Side Trips *in* Chapter 2). ⊠ *Trading Post Rd.,* ☎ *505/834–7235.* 🎫 *Free.* ☉ *Walatowa Visitor Center weekdays 10–5, weekends 10–4; Red Rocks weekends 10–6. Photography, sketching, and recording prohibited.*

Northwest Outing Visitor Information
Coronado State Monument (⊠ Box 95, Bernalillo 87004, ☎ 505/867–5351); **Coronado State Park** (⊠ Box 853, Bernalillo 87004, ☎ 505/867–5589); **Jemez Pueblo** (⊠ Box 040, Trading Post Rd., Jemez Pueblo 87024, ☎ 505/834–7235).

Ghosts of the Southeastern Loop

The stops on this daylong tour are linked by legends, mythological figures, and other "ghosts" of the past. First, head out east to an old Western fort and the haunts of Billy the Kid in the town of Fort Sumner, then return west to the lonely ruins of a pueblo driven into extinction by raiding Apache warriors 400 years ago. Finish the loop with a visit to a living pueblo, south of Albuquerque at Isleta, with a historic church where legend has it that the dead rise out of the floor. Note that this outing involves a heavy amount of driving, especially the leg to Fort Sumner.

Fort Sumner
114 mi southeast of Albuquerque. Leaving Albuquerque, head east on I–40 for 62 mi. Just east of Santa Rosa, exit onto U.S. 84 and continue on 45 mi to Fort Sumner. Take U.S. 60/84 east for 3 mi, then turn right (south) onto NM 212 for 4 mi to Fort Sumner.

Established in 1862, Fort Sumner became a state monument in 1968. It is along the east bank of the Pecos River. Artifacts and photographs on display illustrate the history of the site. From 1863 to 1868, it was headquarters for a disastrous attempt to force the Navajo people and some Apache bands—after their defeat on various battlefields in the Southwest—to farm the land, which was far from hospitable. Natural disasters destroyed crops, wood was scarce, and even the water from the Pecos proved unhealthy. Those who survived the harsh treatment and wretched living conditions (3,000 didn't) were allowed to return to reservations elsewhere in 1868. The post was then sold and converted into a large ranch. This is the same ranch where, in 1881, Sheriff Pat Garrett gunned down Billy the Kid, who's buried in a **nearby cemetery.** His headstone was secured inside a barred cage after it was stolen and recovered some years back. ⊠ *Box 356, 88119, on NM 212,* ☎ *505/355–2573.* 🎫 *$1.* ☉ *Year-round.*

Next to the ranch and fort is a small museum, the **Old Fort Museum,** which has some displays about the Kid and ranch life. ⊠ *Billy the Kid Rd.,* ☎ *505/355–2942.* 🎫 *$3.* ☉ *Call ahead.*

While in the area, also be sure to drop in on the **Billy the Kid Museum,** which houses 17,000 square ft of exhibition space on the young scofflaw, as well as antique wagon trains, guns, household goods, and many other novel materials of the frontier era. ⊠ *1601 Sumner Ave.,* ☎ *505/355–2380.* 🎫 *$4.* ☉ *May 15–Sept., daily 8:30–5; Oct.–May 14, Mon.–Sat. 8:30–5, Sun. 11–5. Closed Jan. 1–15.*

Salinas Pueblo Missions National Monument

55 mi southeast of Albuquerque. To reach Salinas Pueblo Missions National Monument from Fort Sumner, head back west on U.S. 60 to the town of Mountainair, you'll notice its Navajo-deco downtown buildings. Turn north (right) onto NM 55 and continue on about 5 mi.

Salinas Pueblo Missions National Monument is made up of three sites, each comprised of ruins of a 17th-century Spanish Colonial Franciscan missionary church and an associated pueblo. The missions have been excavated and the teetering ruins stabilized at each site.

Quarai, one of the sites, was once a flourishing Tiwa pueblo. Located on the fringe of the Great Plains, however, it—like the two other sites—was vulnerable to raids by nomadic Plains Indians, and it was abandoned about 50 years after its mission church, **San Purisima Concepcion de Cuarac,** was built in 1630. Its red sandstone walls still rise up 40 ft out of the earth. Not many people visit the isolated sites, which still seem to echo those troubled times long ago. The monument headquarters is in Mountainair, but each site has a small visitor center. ⊠ *Box 517, Mountainair 87036,* ☎ *505/847–2585.* 🎫 *Free.* ☉ *Labor Day–Memorial Day, daily 9–5; Memorial Day–Labor Day, daily 9–7.*

Isleta Pueblo

13 mi south of Albuquerque. To head to Isleta Pueblo from Salinas Pueblo Missions National Monument, return to U.S. 60 W; 7 mi along, just off the road, is another of the Salinas sites, Abo. Just past Abo you'll top a divide and the broad Rio Grande Valley will suddenly lie before you. Exit onto NM 47 north. At its intersection with NM 304, go north (right), staying on NM 47, and head up the valley through a series of small, historic Hispanic farming villages including Tome; 4 mi or so past Bosque Farms, look for the bridge across the Rio Grande, which will take you directly to Isleta Pueblo.

Of the 15 or so here when the Spanish first arrived, Isleta Pueblo is one of two Tiwa-speaking communities left in the middle Rio Grande Valley. Isleta was one of the few pueblos that didn't participate in the Pueblo Revolt of 1680, during which it was abandoned; some people fled New Mexico with the Spanish to El Paso, where their descendants live to this day on a reservation called Ysleta del Sur; other members went to live with the Hopi of Arizona, but they eventually returned and rebuilt the pueblo.

Facing the quiet plaza is Isleta's historic church, **St. Augustine.** Built in 1629, it is one of the oldest churches in New Mexico, and its massive adobe walls, viga-crossed ceiling, and simple interior decor make it a classic example of Mission-style adobe architecture. Legend has it that the floor has the odd propensity to push church and community figures buried in its floor back up out of the ground; bodies have been reburied several times, only to emerge again.

Polychrome pottery with red-and-black designs on a white background is the specialty here. The pueblo celebrates its feast days on August 28 and September 4, both in honor of St. Augustine. The tribal government maintains picnicking and camping facilities, several fishing ponds, a casino, and it is developing an 18-hole golf course. ⊠ *Box 1270, 87022,* ☎ *505/869–3111 for pueblo, 505/869–2614 for casino.* ⊡ *Free.* ☉ *Year-round. Camera use restricted; only church may be photographed.*

Ghosts of the Southeastern Loop Visitor Information

Fort Sumner State Monument (⊠ Billy the Kid Rd., Box 356, Fort Sumner 88119, ☎ 505/355–2573); **Old Fort Museum** (⊠ Billy the Kid Rd., Fort Sumner 88119, ☎ 505/355–2942.); **Billy the Kid Museum** (⊠ 1601 Sumner Ave., Fort Sumner 88119, ☎ 505/355–2380); **Salinas Pueblo Missions National Monument** headquarters (⊠ Corner of Ripley and U.S. 60, Box 517, Mountainair 87036, ☎ 505/847–2585); **Isleta Pueblo** (⊠ Box 1270, Isleta 87022, ☎ 505/869–3111).

Headin' West

This daylong jaunt heads into the mesa and plateau country west of Albuquerque. Primary stops include Laguna Pueblo, with its lovely church and Native American arts and crafts shops, and Acoma Pueblo's Sky City—one of America's oldest continually inhabited sites atop a 36-story-high rock mesa.

Laguna Pueblo

46 mi west of Albuquerque. Leave Albuquerque by heading west on I–40 and go some 46 mi to Laguna Pueblo.

Scattered about the Laguna Pueblo reservation are six villages, but most visitors are drawn to **Old Laguna,** capped by the eye-catching white facade of **San Jose,** which is visible from I–40. The church, built in 1699, is a National Historic Landmark. Laguna Pueblo is one of the youngest of the New Mexican pueblos, having been established in 1697 by refugees from Zia, Cochiti, and Santo Domingo pueblos. Shops and artist homes identified with signs sell fine pottery decorated with geometric designs. The pueblo's various villages celebrate many feast days and dances, including San José (March 19), Virgin Mary (September 8), and Saints Margaret and Mary (October 17), but all join at Old Laguna on September 19 to honor St. Joseph with Buffalo, Corn, and Eagle dances and a fair. ⊠ *Box 194, Laguna Pueblo 87026,* ☎ *505/ 552–6654.* ⊡ *Free.* ☉ *Daily 8–5. Photography regulations vary in each village; contact the governor's office (*☎ *505/552–6654) for information.*

Acoma Pueblo

66 mi west of Albuquerque. From Laguna Pueblo, return to I–40 and continue west another 6 mi to the Casa Blanca exit and head south on BIA Road 22 for 13 mi to reach Acoma. To return to Albuquerque, head back east on I–40.

Acoma Pueblo's **Sky City** is like nowhere else you've ever been. Atop a 367-ft mesa that rises abruptly from the valley floor, this terraced, multistory, multiunit dwelling is aptly nicknamed. Archaeologists say it is one of the oldest continually inhabited spots in North America, with portions believed to be more than 1,500 years old. Captain Hernando de Alvarado, with Coronado's Expedition of 1540, was the first European to see Acoma. He reported that he had "found a rock with a village on top, the strongest position ever seen in the world." However, the Spanish succeeded, eventually, in conquering the Acomas, and the immense adobe church, **St. Esteban del Rey,** that stands to this day was built with Pueblo labor. The church's ceiling logs were cut more than 20 mi away on Mt. Taylor and carried overland; even the dirt used for the adobe walls—which measure 60 ft tall and 10 ft thick at points—had to be hauled to the mesa top! The mesa-top pueblo is still inhabited by a handful of people full-time. Most Acomans, though, return only during the pueblo's many public and private celebrations, the primary one being St. Esteban's feast day on September 2.

Acoma artisans are known for their fine, thin-walled pottery, hand-painted with intricate geometrical patterns, especially with animals. Sky City may be visited only on guided foot tours; a bus leaves every hour from the center. The visitor center also has a museum, a restaurant, and a crafts shop. There is a casino on the reservation. ⊠ *Acoma Tourist Center, Box 309, 87034,* ☎ *800/747–0181, 800/552–6017 for casino.* ▧ *$6.* ☉ *Spring and summer, daily 8–7, tours daily 8–6; fall and winter, daily 8–4:30, tours daily 8–3:30 (call ahead for dates). Closed Easter weekend, July 10–13, 1st or 2nd weekends of Oct., and occasional other days. Movie and video cameras are prohibited; $5 charge per camera for still photos.*

Headin' West Visitor Information

Laguna Pueblo (⊠ Box 194, Laguna Pueblo 87026, ☎ 505/552–6654); **Acoma Tourist Center** (⊠ Box 309, Acoma 87034, ☎ 800/747–0181).

ALBUQUERQUE A TO Z

Arriving and Departing

By Bus

Greyhound and **Texas New Mexico & Oklahoma Coaches** will get you to Albuquerque, but there are no direct connections from the Greyhound station (⊠ 300 2nd St. SW, ☎ 505/243–4435 or 800/231–2222) to the center of the city. You will have to either phone for a taxi or walk down the road two blocks to get a public bus.

By Car

The main routes into Albuquerque are I–25 from points north and south and I–40 from points east and west.

By Plane

Albuquerque International Airport (☎ 505/842–4366) is the major gateway to New Mexico, just 5 mi south of downtown Albuquerque. Car rentals, air taxis, and bus shuttles are readily available at the airport, which is 65 mi southwest of Santa Fe and 130 mi south of Taos (☞ Air Travel and Airport Transfers *in* the Gold Guide).

The trip into town from the airport takes about 10–15 minutes, and there is a variety of ground transportation from which to choose. Taxis, available at clearly marked stands, charge about $7 plus 50¢ for each additional rider (☞ By Taxi, *below*). Sun Tran buses pick up at the sunburst signs every 30 minutes; the fare is 75¢ (☞ By Bus, *below*). Some major hotels provide shuttle service to and from the airport. If you like to go in high style, limousines (☞ *below*) are the way to go;

car-rental companies (☞ Car Rental *in* the Gold Guide) are another option.

By Train

Amtrak's (☎ 800/872–7245) *Southwest Chief* services **Albuquerque Station** (✉ 214 1st St. SW, ☎ 505/842–9650) daily to and from Los Angeles and Chicago.

Getting Around

Unlike more compact Taos and Santa Fe, Albuquerque sprawls out in all directions, so you'll need transportation to get wherever you're going.

By Bus

The **Sun Tran** buses (✉ 601 Yale SE, 87106, ☎ 505/843–9200) blanket the city with connections about every 30 minutes, less frequently in the more remote areas of the city and on weekends, but the substantial distances one must cover between sites doesn't make bus service a very good option for travelers in Albuquerque. The fare is 75¢. Bus stops are well marked with the line's sunburst signs.

By Car

Getting around Albuquerque by car is easy, and there is plenty of parking. For information about renting a car, *see* Car Rental *in* the Gold Guide.

By Limousine

Albuquerque has several limousine companies. Rates start at $35–$45 per hour for standard limousines and can range up to $95 per hour for stretch limos; there is usually a two-hour minimum. Call for special airport shuttle rates. Companies include: **At Last, The Past, Antique Limousine Service** (☎ 505/298–9944), **Classic Limousine** (☎ 505/247–4000), **Dream Limousine** (☎ 505/884–6464), and **Lucky Limousine Service** (☎ 505/836–4035 or 800/936–4035).

By Taxi

Taxis are metered in Albuquerque, service is around the clock, and rates run about $3.40 for the first mile and $1.60 for each additional mile; each additional passenger is charged $1. Contact **Albuquerque Cab** (☎ 505/883–4888) or **Yellow Cab** (☎ 505/247–8888).

Guided Tours

Orientation

Gray Line of Albuquerque (✉ 800 Rio Grande NW, Suite 22, ☎ 505/242–3880 or 800/256–8991) offers several daily and seasonal tours (May–October). Among them is a three-hour Albuquerque city tour, including the University of New Mexico campus, historic landmarks, and the Indian Pueblo Cultural Center.

Special-Interest

Explora Tours (✉ 3901 68th St. NW, 87120–1631, ☎ 505/831–6135 or 800/639–8735) conducts custom van tours on history, minerals, mining, photography, archaeology, and other subjects.

Gray Line (☞ Orientation, *above*) offers special tours to Acoma Indian Pueblo, the Anasazi cliff dwellings at Bandelier National Monument, and other Native American sites. Departure days and times vary depending on the destination.

Many operators offer early morning **hot-air-balloon tours** of Albuquerque (☞ Ballooning *in* Outdoor Activities and Sports, *above*).

International Universities (✉ 1101 Tijeras Ave. NW, ☎ 505/246–2233 or 800/547–5678) has fascinating educational seminars and excursions that focus on the culture and history of New Mexico, including Indian Pueblos, Santa Fe, and the Turquoise Trail. Customized group tours only.

Mountain Aviation Enterprises (✉ 2505 Clark Carr Loop SE, 87106, ☎ 505/263–3637) tours regional canyons, mesas, ghost towns, and mountains via the skies.

South Mountain Wilderness Tours (✉ Box 638, Edgewood, 87015, ☎ 505/281–9638) leads hikes, camping trips, and outings focusing on bird-watching and geology.

Southwest Explorers (✉ 8904 San Francisco NE, 87109, ☎ 505/821–7096) organizes customized educational, historical, or adventure tours.

Walking

The **Albuquerque Museum** (☎ 505/243–7255) leads hour-long historical walks through **Old Town** at 11 AM Tuesday–Sunday. The tour is free and is available on a first-come, first-served basis; meet in the lobby of the Albuquerque Museum. Tours do not run from December 15–March 15.

Contacts and Resources

Dentists
Dentist referrals (☎ 505/260–7333).

Emergencies
Fire, medical, or police (☎ 911).

Police nonemergency (☎ 505/242–COPS); **fire nonemergency** (☎ 505/243–6601).

Hospital emergency rooms: University Hospital (✉ 2211 Lomas NE, ☎ 505/843–2411), Presbyterian Hospital (✉ 1100 Central Ave. SE, ☎ 505/841–1111). Call either for locations of Urgent Care Centers around the city.

Late-Night Pharmacies
Walgreens offers a 24-hour prescription-refill service at two locations (✉ 6201 Central Ave. NE, ☎ 505/255–5511; ✉ 5001 Montgomery NE, ☎ 505/881–5050).

Road Conditions, Time, and Temperature
Road conditions (☎ 505/827–5213 or 800/432–4269). **Time and temperature** (☎ 505/247–1611).

Visitor Information
The **Albuquerque Convention and Visitors Bureau** (✉ 20 1st Plaza NW, No. 601, Albuquerque 87102, ☎ 505/842–9918 or 800/284–2282) publishes a variety of informative materials, including quarterly calendars of events and brochures describing local and out-of-town driving tours. A tape-recorded bulletin on current local events in Albuquerque can be reached after 5 PM on weekdays and all day Saturday and Sunday by phoning 505/848–1161 or 800/284–2282; the same numbers can be used to request an information packet. The bureau also maintains an information center on the lower level of the airport at the bottom of the escalator; it is open daily from 9:30 to 8.

5 Carlsbad and Southern New Mexico

There is beauty in simplicity—in the graceful curve of a stark white dune or the smooth dome of a cave formation millions of years in the making. In the immense southern New Mexico desert, seemingly barren hills are transformed at sunset into moonscapes of shadow, light, and color. Southern New Mexico was one of the country's last frontiers, and its simple charm can still be found in the lingering patches of unspoiled wilderness.

BURSTING WITH GEOLOGICAL CONTRAST, southern New Mexico is home to the spectacular caves of Carlsbad Caverns, the glittering desert of White Sands National Monument, and the pristine Sacramento Mountains. Cultural diversity, too, is a trademark of the area. Spanish conquistadors first explored here almost five centuries ago, and their travels helped establish the *Camino Real* (King's Highway), the ancient trade route through the Mesilla Valley. Mescalero Apaches and other Native American tribes lived throughout the region, sometimes launching vicious attacks against invaders to protect their homelands.

Updated by
Marilyn
Haddrill

In the late 1800s, Fort Selden, north of Las Cruces, harbored several units of Buffalo Soldiers, a cavalry of African-Americans vital to the protection of pioneers claiming unsettled land. Buffalo Soldiers also were stationed at Ft. Bayard, near Silver City, to shield miners and travelers from Apache Indian attacks. The grasslands were ruled by cattle kings such as the legendary John Chisum, who moved from Texas in 1872 to establish a ranch at a site near present-day Roswell. During the infamous Lincoln County War, which raged during the first half of 1878, baby-faced outlaw Billy the Kid became legend throughout the region (you'll find many "Billy the Kid was here" references at sites). The infamous outlaw also spent part of his childhood in the mountainous Silver City area, famous for its ghost towns and historic buildings preserved as relics from early copper, silver, and gold mining operations. Besides its historic importance, southern New Mexico plays a key role in U.S. space exploration and defense research. Alamogordo's Space Center museum and Hall of Fame illustrate rocketry developments, including experimental programs at nearby White Sands Missile Range and NASA's restricted White Sands Test Facility.

Pleasures and Pastimes

Dining

The Mesilla Valley and Las Cruces rival Santa Fe with impressive numbers of excellent Mexican restaurants, ranging from mom-and-pop operations to elaborately decorated tourist stops. Almost any Mexican-style eatery in the Valley is sure to please, especially if you're a fan of the green chiles grown in abundance in this fertile agricultural region. In southeastern New Mexico you'll find thick steaks and barbecue, characteristic of "cowboy country." The mountain resort town of Ruidoso has especially notable restaurants serving gourmet food. Look for excellent baked goods and specialty sandwiches in several of the delicatessens found in Silver City's historic district.

CATEGORY	COST*
$$$	over $25
$$	$10–25
$	under $10

per person, excluding drinks, service, and 5.6%–7% tax, depending on the county

Lodging

Southern New Mexico has the usual offering of standard chain motels, as well as unique bed-and-breakfasts and luxurious resorts.

CATEGORY	COST*
$$$	$100–$150
$$	$65–$100
$	under $65

All prices are for a standard double room, excluding 5.6%–7%, depending on the county.

Hiking

From desert foothills to dense mountain forests, southern New Mexico offers a variety of terrains for hiking. Trails run throughout Carlsbad Caverns National Park and Lincoln National Forest, where there are dizzying vistas. The town of Carlsbad has a paved walkway along the scenic Pecos River for a gentler hike. In the Mesilla Valley, several footpaths penetrate the base of the Organ Mountains. Visit the Gila National Forest and Gila Wilderness (the nation's second largest) near Silver City to explore hundreds of miles of both desert and alpine trails.

Exploring Southern New Mexico

Three distinct regions are found in the south-central and southeast portions of New Mexico, which span the upper Chihuahuan desert and the Guadalupe and Sacramento mountains. In the east the Pecos River slices through the Pecos Valley, where you'll find the Carlsbad Caverns National Park and the towns of Carlsbad, Artesia, and Roswell. Farming here is devoted mainly to growing cotton and alfalfa hay, used to feed dairy herds. In the west the Rio Grande carves through the fertile Mesilla Valley, famous for its plump green chiles. During the fall harvest, the Valley is scented with the delicious aroma of roasting chiles. The wildly rugged mountain ranges of the Guadalupes and Sacramentos cut through the south-central portion of the state, dividing the Pecos and Mesilla river valleys. In southwestern New Mexico, the vast and scenic Gila National Forest includes the Black Range mountains and surrounds the charming mining town of Silver City.

Great Itineraries

Make a visit to the gargantuan cavern system of Carlsbad Caverns your first priority: It is truly one of the world's greatest natural wonders. New Mexico is an expansive state, and the trip south from Albuquerque covers more than 300 sometimes monotonous miles—allocate more than a half day to cover the trip. You can see most of the region in three days, but you won't be able to spend much time in any one place. More time will allow you to savor the dramatic landscape and explore all the small towns. If you want to head for the mountains, pick Ruidoso, which offers a wide selection of hotels, restaurants, and activities. If you seek a mountain getaway without the crowds, try Cloudcroft. On the west side of the Sacramento mountains, stop at White Sands National Monument for a frolic in bright gypsum dunes, then drive south to Old Mesilla, one of New Mexico's last unspoiled examples of a genuine Mexican-style adobe village.

The Silver City area of southwestern New Mexico requires a special trip, since it's 55 mi northwest of I–10, the nearest interstate. It's lush with points of interest to be found in rugged mountain views, historic buildings, ghost towns, and outdoor adventures such as hiking, fishing, or camping in the Gila National Forest or Gila Wilderness.

IF YOU HAVE 3 DAYS

Spend at least a morning in the main cavern and the visitor center at **Carlsbad Caverns National Park.** That afternoon tour **Living Desert Zoo And Garden State,** then take a late-evening stroll along the paved walkways of the **Lake Carlsbad Recreation Area.** Stay overnight in the town of ⬚ **Carlsbad** or at one of the campgrounds near the park. On day two, drive north on U.S. 285 to **Roswell,** and stop at the **Roswell Museum and Art Center** to see the Goddard rocketry display and paintings by renowned area artists. From Roswell, travel west on U.S. 70–380 to ⬚ **Ruidoso** for a day and a night: Here you can take scenic drives, fish in mountain lakes, hike through tall pines, or browse in the town's galleries and shops. In summer, there is weekend horse racing at Ruidoso Downs, and in winter, fine skiing at Ski Apache Ski Resort. On the third day, drive south from Ruidoso on U.S. 70 to **Alamogordo** and visit the Space Center. Then, keep driving south on U.S. 70 for about 15 mi to **White Sands National Monument** and spend at least a few hours viewing the brilliant white dunes. At the end of the day, continue your drive south on U.S. 70 to ▦ **Las Cruces** and the Mesilla Valley. Visit the shops, galleries, and restaurants in the authentic Mexican-style adobe village of ▦ **Old Mesilla,** southwest of Las Cruces.

IF YOU HAVE 5 DAYS

Spend a whole day exploring the wondrous caves at **Carlsbad Caverns National Park** and stay the night in ▦ **Carlsbad** or in a campground near the park. Set aside several hours the next day to visit the **Living Desert State Park** and take a drive through Walnut Canyon, returning to Carlsbad for the night. Head to **Roswell** on the morning of the third day and to ▦ **Ruidoso** in the afternoon. On the fourth day, stop at the Space Center in **Alamogordo,** then go to **White Sands National Monument** for the afternoon. Drive on to ▦ **Las Cruces** and ▦ **Old Mesilla** and spend the night. Take time on your fifth day to veer off I–10, and head northwest for **Silver City,** the **Gila Wilderness,** and **Gila National Forest.** If you're driving back to Albuquerque via I–25, take a short side trip to **Fort Selden,** home to such military greats as General Douglas MacArthur.

When to Tour Southern New Mexico

Winters tend to be gentle in the desert regions of southern New Mexico, but be advised that May through early September can produce some blistering hot days. Even mountain regions can be uncomfortably warm during a hot spell. In summer try to plan outdoor excursions in the cooler early morning or late-evening hours. Wear sunscreen, sunglasses, and hats in the midday sun and make sure you carry plenty of water. Spring is cooler, but it's often accompanied by nasty, dust-laden winds. Your best bet is late September through early November, when skies are a sharp, clear blue and the weather is balmy.

CARLSBAD CAVERNS NATIONAL PARK AND ENVIRONS

One of New Mexico's most popular attractions, Carlsbad Caverns National Park draws almost three quarters of a million people each year to its huge, subterranean chambers, fantastic rock formations, and delicate mineral sculptures. Nearby, in the town of Carlsbad, you can find numerous restaurants, hotels, and campgrounds and the pretty Pecos River recreational area, which is perfect for picnicking and water sports. Some of the city's most elegant houses occupy quiet residential areas built up along the riverbanks.

Carlsbad Caverns National Park

★ *320 mi south of Albuquerque via I–25, U.S. 380, and U.S. 285 or take I–40 east and U.S. 285 south. 167 mi west of El Paso, Texas, via U.S. 180.*

Although the Carlsbad Caverns National Park is in the Chihuahuan Desert, near the rugged canyons and peaks of the Guadalupe mountain range and the piñon and ponderosa pines of Lincoln National Forest, the most spectacular sights here are all below the earth's surface, with such evocative names as the Green Lake Room, the Kings Palace, the Devils Den, the Klansman, the China Wall, and Iceberg Rock. The park's cave system—hundreds of millions of years in the making—is

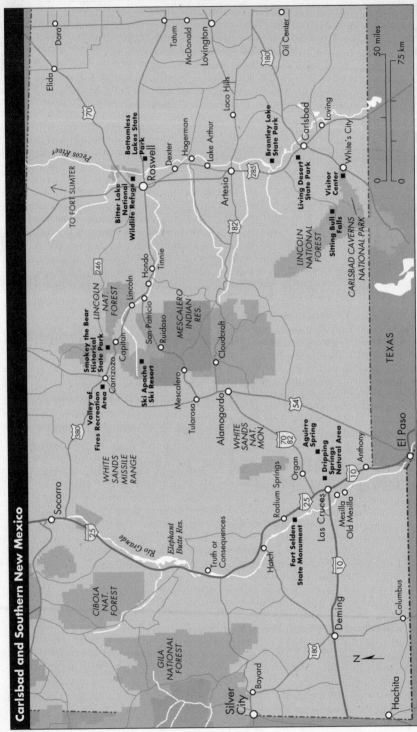

Carlsbad and Southern New Mexico

one of the largest and most impressive in the world. But it was discovered relatively recently. Pictographs near the cave entrance tell us that pre-Columbian Native Americans took shelter in Carlsbad Caverns more than 1,000 years ago, but archaeologists doubt that they ventured very far inside.

It wasn't until the 19th century that nearby settlers rediscovered the caverns, their attention captured by the smokelike appearance of swirling columns of bats leaving each night to feed on insects. Area caves were mined for bat guano (dung), which was used as fertilizer for a number of years. But no one was interested in the caves for any other reason until the early 1920s, when cowboy Jim White began exploring them. White brought a photographer, Ray Davis, to bear witness to his extravagant claims about this amazing underground universe. Davis's photos astounded people and started a rush of interest in the caverns. White turned tour operator, taking people down 170 ft in a bucket left over from the days of mining bat guano. Washington got wind of this natural wonder and, in 1923, inspector Robert Holley was dispatched by the U.S. Department of Interior to investigate. His report was instrumental in getting Carlsbad Caverns declared a national monument by President Calvin Coolidge later that year; in 1930 the area was designated a national park.

The newest discovery in Carlsbad Caverns National Park is Lechuguilla Cave, the deepest limestone cave in the United States. Scientists began mapping the cave network in 1986, and although they've discovered more than 89 mi of caverns extending to a depth of 1,567 ft, there remains more to explore. The cave is not open to the public, but there is an exhibit on it in the visitor center. Of the 83 caves in the park, only a few are open for regular tours. Special permits will be issued to visitors interested in touring the 10 caves; main caverns are available for public viewing.

The origins of Carlsbad Caverns go back some 250 million years, when the 300-mi-long Capitan Reef formed around the edge of the warm, shallow sea that once covered this region. The sea evaporated and the reef was buried until a few million years ago, when a combination of erosion and convulsions brought parts of it back above ground. Rainwater seeping down through the reef's cracks gradually enlarged them into cavities, which eventually collapsed, forming huge rooms. Over eons, the evaporated limestone deposited on the cave ceilings grew into great hanging stalactites, which in turn dripped crystals. Over time the crystals became massive stalagmites and other, more delicate formations, such as cave pearls, draperies, popcorn, and lily pads.

Although you may be tempted to touch the cave's walls and jutting rock formations, heed the ranger's warning against doing so. Oil from the human hand forms a type of waterproofing that inhibits the natural water seepage. You are also not supposed to leave the guided pathways; if you do, you not only risk serious injury, but you can damage the cave as well.

The temperature inside Carlsbad Cavern remains at a constant 56°F, and it's damp, so a sweater or warm clothes are recommended, as are comfortable shoes with rubber soles—because of the moisture, the underground walkways are slippery. But the cavern is well lighted and numerous park rangers are stationed about to offer assistance and information. A new CD-ROM audio guide offers you the opportunity to listen to recorded messages as they take the self-guided Natural Entrance and Big Room routes. The hands-free audio tour is triggered by electronic signals along the trail. As you view the shadowed beauty of this underground domain, you are entertained and educated by recorded commentary from park rangers, geologists, and cavers. Music, interviews, and sound effects help enhance the experience. Food is available both at a restaurant above ground at the visitor center, and at an underground lunchroom. ✉ *Carlsbad Caverns National Park, 3225 National Parks Hwy., Carlsbad 88220,* ☎ *505/785–2232 (for tour reservations, ext. 429, 8:30–4:30).* ✏ *General entrance fee $8 (including audio guide); see individual cave descriptions below for additional fees and hrs of operation.*

There are two self-guided routes into Carlsbad Cavern: **The Natural Entrance Route** and **The Big Room Route.** If you take the former, you'll proceed on foot along the paved walkway that winds down into the caverns' depths for about a mile, passing through a series of underground rooms and descending slowly to a depth of about 750 ft. It takes about one hour to complete; the trail can be slick in parts and the grades are fairly steep, so be prepared for a strenuous hike. The Big Room Route is less difficult. You take a high-speed elevator from the visitor center down 750 ft to an underground lunchroom, and begin your exploration there. This route also takes about an hour to walk and covers a distance of a mile. (The elevator makes a portion of the main cavern accessible to visitors using wheelchairs.) In both cases, you'll visit the Big Room, so called because it's large enough to hold 14 football fields; one corner is as tall as the White House; and the highest ceiling reaches 255 ft. ✏ *Natural Entrance Route and Big Room Route: $8 (including audio guide).* ☉ *Natural Entrance Route: June–mid-Aug., daily 8:30–5; mid-Aug.–May, daily 8:30–2. Big Room Route: June–mid-Aug., daily 8:30–5; mid-Aug.–May, daily 8:30–3:30.*

A third option for exploring the caverns is the ranger-led **Kings Palace Tour** through the Kings Palace, the Queens Chamber, the Papoose Room, and the Green Lake Room. The tour covers about a mile, including an uphill 80-ft climb on a switchback trail and takes about 1½ hours to complete. ✏ *Kings Palace Tour $5, in addition to $8 general entrance fee to caverns.* ☉ *June–mid-Aug., daily and hourly 9–3; mid-Aug.– May, daily at 9, 11, 1, and 3.*

A limited number of other off-trail tours are available within Carlsbad Caverns. **Lefthand Tunnel** is in an undeveloped part of the caverns and contains clear pools and ancient reef fossils. **Lower Cave** is billed as a "moderately strenuous" tour, which involves climbs on 50 ft of vertical ladders. Children younger than 6 are not allowed on this tour. **Hall of the White Giant** is a very strenuous tour that requires squirming long distances on your hands and knees through tight passageways into a very remote chamber with glistening white formations. The tour of "wild" **Spider Cave** takes you through the park's back country and involves tight crawlways; avoid this one if you're squeamish. Call ahead to make reservations and to purchase tickets for special tours. ☎ *505/785–2232, ext. 429.* ✏ *In addition to general entrance fee to cavern: Lefthand Tunnel $4; Lower Cave, Hall of the White Giant, and Spider Cave each $12 (minimum age: 12).* ☉ *Lefthand Tunnel, daily at 9 AM; Lower Cave, daily at 1; Hall of the White Giant, Sat. at 1; Spider Cave (separate from main cavern), Sun. at 1.*

Slaughter Canyon Cave, 25 mi from the main cavern, is much less accessible. Millions of years old, the cave was discovered by Tom Tucker, a local goatherd, in 1937. The cave consists primarily of a single corridor, 1,140 ft long, with numerous side passages. The total extent of the surveyed passage is 1¾ mi, and the lowest point is 250 ft below the surface. Outstanding formations are the Christmas Tree, the Monarch, the Hooded Klansman, the Tear Drop, and the China Wall.

Rangers lead groups of 25 on a two-hour lantern tour of Slaughter Canyon Cave. Children under 6 are not permitted. The cave temperature is a constant 62°F, and the humidity is a clammy 90%. You'll need to bring along your own flashlight, hiking boots or good walking shoes (sneakers aren't recommended), and drinking water. Photographs are permitted, but no tripod setups are allowed since the group moves along at a relatively brisk pace and you *really* wouldn't want to be left behind. Unless you're in great physical shape and have a long attention span, Slaughter Canyon Cave may be more cave viewing than you bargained for. But it's a great adventure for the more daring who want to experience what cave exploration is really like, minus paved pathways and electric lighting.

Reservations are required at least a day in advance; in summer two weeks in advance are recommended. Note that for the last few miles there is a gravel road and that the mouth of the cave is a ½-mi climb up a 500-ft rise. Give yourself plenty of time to complete the drive and the climb to the cave, so you don't arrive late for the tour. ☎ 505/785– 2232, ext. 429. ⌨ $8. ☉ *Tour June–mid-Aug., daily at 10 and 1; mid- Aug.–May, weekends at 10 and 1. Reservations required.*

Apart from the caves themselves, one of the great attractions at Carlsbad Caverns is the **nightly bat flights.** Each evening between late May and mid-October at about sunset, Mexican free-tailed bats exit by the tens of thousands from the natural entrance of the cavern and go flying about scouting for flying insects. Collectively, they consume more than three tons of bugs per night. (No scientist has yet figured out how a bat hanging upside down in a dark cave knows when the sun has set outside.) Because bats are among the most maligned and misunderstood creatures, park rangers give informative talks about them each evening prior to the exodus, at about 7 PM. The time of the bat flights varies over the course of the season, so ranger lectures are flexible as well; the time is usually posted, but if not, check at the visitor center. Lectures are suspended in winter, when the bats leave for the warmer climates of Mexico.

Among the options at Carlsbad is to take the scenic 9½-mi **Walnut Canyon Desert Drive.** This loop begins ½ mi from the visitor center and travels along the top of the ridge to the edge of Rattlesnake Canyon and back down through upper Walnut Canyon to the main entrance road. It's a one-way gravel road, and the backcountry scenery is stunning; go late in the afternoon or early in the morning to enjoy the full spectrum of changing light and dancing colors. You might also spot some of the many inquisitive mule deer that inhabit the park. There's also a self-guided, partially accessible **Desert Nature Walk,** about ½-mi long, which begins near the cavern's entrance.

A very pleasant picnic and recreation area with shade trees, grass, picnic tables, water, grills, and toilets is available at **Rattlesnake Springs** (don't let the name scare you; no one's seen a rattlesnake there in years). It is also a favorite spot for bird-watchers. Near the Black River, Rattlesnake Springs was a source of water for Native Americans hundreds of years ago. Army troops exploring the area used it as well, and today it's the main source of water for all the park facilities. The site is for day use only. No overnight camping or parking is allowed.

Camping

Backcountry camping is by permit only in Carlsbad Caverns National Park; free permits can be obtained at the visitor center, where you can also pick up a map of areas closed to camping. You'll need to hike to campsites, which may not be seen from established roadways. There are no vehicle or RV camping areas in the park.

Nearby Brantley Lake State Park (☞ *below*) and Lincoln National Forest both have camping facilities. In addition a number of commercial sites are available at White's City (☞ *below*), 7 mi northeast of Carlsbad Caverns, and in Carlsbad (☞ *below*), 27 mi northeast.

Outdoor Activities and Sports

BIRD-WATCHING

From turkey vultures to golden eagles, more than 200 species of birds have been identified in Carlsbad Caverns National Park. The best place to go bird-watching in the park, if not the entire state, is **Rattlesnake Springs** (☞ *above*). Ask for a checklist at the visitor center and then start looking for red-tailed hawks, red-winged blackbirds, white-throated swifts, northern flickers, pygmy nuthatches, yellow-billed cuckoos, roadrunners, mallards, American coots, and green-winged and blue-winged teal.

HIKING

Backcountry hiking in **Carlsbad Caverns National Park** can be exhilarating—the desert terrain is stark and awe-inspiring—but few trails are marked. A topographical map, available at the visitor center, is helpful for finding some of the old ranch trails. Permits aren't required, except for overnight backpacking, but all hikers are requested to register at the information desk at the visitor center. Bring plenty of water, as there's none available. No pets or guns are permitted. A less rugged option is to hike in the stunningly beautiful **McKittrick Canyon,** in nearby **Guadalupe Mountains National Park**—a desert oasis with a clear, running stream and cool, green vegetation—accessible only by foot.

Carlsbad

25 mi north of Carlsbad Caverns National Park.

With the world-famous caverns nearby, the town of Carlsbad is among the most popular tourist destinations in New Mexico. On the Pecos River, which affords it 27 mi of beaches and picturesque pathways, Carlsbad is an attractive town of 25,000 that seems pleasantly suspended between the past and the present. Its **Territorial town square,** only a block from the river, encircles a pueblo-style country courthouse designed by the famed New Mexican architect John Gaw Meem, who also designed many of the buildings on the University of New Mexico campus in Albuquerque.

Carlsbad puts on quite a show on the Fourth of July and Christmas holidays, with special events worthy of national attention. A boat parade and spectacular evening fireworks traditionally attract thousands of visitors to the **Lake Carlsbad Recreation Area** for Fourth of July festivities. Right around Thanksgiving, dazzling Christmas displays are put up in backyards and lots along a 2½-mi stretch on the Pecos River for the city's annual **Christmas on the Pecos River** boat tours offered through Christmas and for several days after. Tickets for the event usually sell out early, so make sure to buy them in advance; they are available beginning August 1. The night breeze blowing across the water can be chilly, so dress warmly. Boats leave from the **Pecos River Village** (✉ 710 N. Muscatel), which was once an amusement park and is now a convention center, art gallery, and snack shop. For reservations call the Carlsbad Chamber of Commerce (☎ 505/887–6516). Boat tours are $7.

The **Carlsbad Museum and Arts Center,** on the town square, houses Apache relics, Pueblo pottery, Native American art, early cowboy memorabilia, and remains of meteorites. The prize, however, is the

McAdoo Collection, with works by painters of the Taos Society of Artists. The museum also has changing monthly shows that feature the works of local and nationally recognized artists. ✉ *418 W. Fox St.,* ☎ *505/ 887–0276.* 🎫 *Free.* ◷ *Mon.–Sat. 10–5.*

Atop Ocotillo Hills, about 1½ mi northwest of Carlsbad (off U.S. 285; look for the signs), **Living Desert Zoo And Gardens State Park** contains an impressive collection of plants and animals native to the Chihuahuan Desert (which extends north from Mexico into southwestern Texas and southeastern New Mexico). Like many deserts, it's surprisingly rich in animal and plant life, as the park reveals. The Desert Arboretum has hundreds of exotic cacti and succulents and the Living Desert Zoo—more a reserve than a traditional zoo—is home to mountain lions, deer, elk, wolves, buffalo, rattlesnakes, and other indigenous species. There are numerous shaded rest areas, rest rooms, and water fountains. In hot weather try to visit during cooler early morning or late afternoon hours. But remember that all tours end 1½ hours before closing time. In spring the Living Desert hosts the four-day Annual Mescal Roast and Mountain Spirit Dances demonstrated by members of the Mescalero Apache Indian Tribe. Tribal members once harvested the revered desert plant, mescal, for food from nearby regions. ✉ *1500 Mielhs Dr., Carlsbad,* ☎ *505/887–5516.* 🎫 *$3.* ◷ *Memorial Day–Labor Day, daily 8–8; Labor Day–Memorial Day, daily 9–5. Tours are self-guided and must begin at least 1½ hrs before closing.*

OFF THE BEATEN PATH

SITTING BULL FALLS – From Carlsbad, take U.S. 285 north about 12 mi, then turn west on NM 137. Drive about 27 mi and you'll find a lovely desert riparian area, with fern, watercress, and cottonwoods, created by Sitting Bull Spring. The water cascades off a cliff face and creates clear, sparkling pools below. Swimming is allowed and limited picnic facilities and rest rooms, maintained by Lincoln National Forest, are available. Forest officials warn against climbing the slippery rocks and cliff facings. The area is for day use only. If you would like to camp overnight, keep driving southwest on NM 137 until you reach the New Mexico–Texas state line and **Pine Springs Campground,** a developed site in forested surroundings maintained by Guadalupe Mountains National Park.

Dining and Lodging

$–$$ ✕ **Cortez Café.** This charming Mexican restaurant, with an all-brick interior and photo murals of Old Mexico, has been in business for more than a half century. Ownership changed in late 1996, but tasty, traditional dishes have retained the same quality under supervision of the Gregory and Azzinaro families. Try the combination plate, fajitas, or sour-cream enchiladas. ✉ *506 S. Canal St.,* ☎ *505/885–4747. D, MC, V.*

$–$$ ✕ **Lucy's.** At this family-owned oasis of great Mexican food, the motto is: "the best margaritas and hottest chile in the world." All the New Mexican standards are available in Southwestern surroundings, along with some not-so-standard items, such as chicken fajita burritos smothered with chef Adam's *queso* (cheese), Tucson-style chimichangas, and brisket *carnitas* (meat sautéed with chile and seasonings). The restaurant also offers an unusual line of low-fat and fat-free Mexican cuisine. ✉ *701 S. Canal St.,* ☎ *505/887–7714. AE, D, DC, MC, V.*

$ ✕ **Furr's Cafeteria.** This Carlsbad establishment offers exceptionally good food, particularly for a chain restaurant. The roomy dining area is ideal for tour groups and large families. Usual entrées include fried chicken, roast beef, and special dishes such as lasagna. ✉ *901 S. Canal St.,* ☎ *505–885–0430. AE, D, MC, V.*

$ ✕ **La Fonda.** While en route to or from Carlsbad Caverns, consider
★ stopping over in Artesia (off U.S. 285, about 38 mi north of Carlsbad)
to dine at a regionally popular restaurant known for its milder style
of Mexican cuisine. The interior is tastefully decorated with green
plants and bright Southwest scenes. Many recipes are unique to this
establishment, founded in 1965. Try the house special, the Guadalajara, for a palate-pleasing blend of seasoned beef, cheese, and guacamole
(made from avocado) served on a corn tortilla. ⊠ *210 W. Main St.,
Artesia,* ☎ *505/746–9377. AE, D, MC, V.*

$ ✕ **Red Chimney.** If you hanker for some sweet and tangy barbecue, try
this popular locally owned restaurant with its log-cabin decor and early
American atmosphere. Sauce from an old family recipe is slathered on
chicken, pork, beef, turkey, and ham. Or, you can order up fried cat-
fish or other home-style cooking. Carryout is available. ⊠ *817 N. Canal
St.,* ☎ *505/885–8744. MC, V. Closed weekends.*

$$ 🏨 **Holiday Inn Carlsbad Downtown.** Rugs, paintings, and room decor
★ in this attractive two-story lodge all harmonize with the building's Ter-
ritorial New Mexican theme. The hotel's Phenix [sic] Bar & Grill is a
pub that earned its name and quirky spelling from a rip-roaring Old
West town that once existed a few miles away. Ventanas (Windows),
the gourmet restaurant, offers fine continental cuisine. Kids under 19
stay free if they're in a room with their parents. ⊠ *601 S. Canal St.,*
☎ *505/885–8500 or 800/742–9586,* 𝔽𝔸𝕏 *505/887–5999. 100 rooms.
2 restaurants, bar, pool, hot tub, exercise room, playground, laundry
service. AE, D, DC, MC, V.*

$–$$ 🏨 **Days Inn.** Carlsbad's newest motel is 23 mi (about a 30-minute drive)
north of Carlsbad Caverns and is the first lodging you'll see as you ap-
proach the city. Rooms have Southwestern decor, king-size beds, and
sofa beds. A Continental breakfast is included in the room price. ⊠
3910 National Parks Hwy., 88220, ☎ *505/887–7800,* 𝔽𝔸𝕏 *505/885–
9433. 42 rooms, 8 suites. Indoor pool, airport shuttle. AE, D, DC,
MC, V.*

$–$$ 🏨 **Quality Inn.** One mile from the airport, this two-story, stone-face
property encloses a landscaped patio with a pool and a sundeck about
as large as an aircraft hangar. Rooms are comfortable, with undistin-
guished modern furnishings. The **Cafe in the Park** is open for breakfast, and the more formal **Chaparral Grill Room** is open for dinner. ⊠
3706 National Parks Hwy., 88220, ☎ *505/887–2861 or 800/321–
2861,* 𝔽𝔸𝕏 *505/887–2861. 120 rooms. 2 restaurants, bar, pool, hot tub,
shop, laundry service, airport shuttle. AE, D, DC, MC, V.*

$ 🏨 **Best Western Motel Stevens.** Elegance at bargain prices can be
★ found at this locally owned establishment. Scenes of cavern formations
and Carlsbad's historic courthouse are etched in mirrored glass and
carved into wooden doors. Prints of Western landscapes decorate spacious rooms, some with kitchenettes. Palm trees are scattered throughout the large, landscaped area. Rooms now have voice mail and
computer data ports. Prime rib and steaks are served up in the evenings
at the motel's excellent Flume Room, and Mexican food and sandwiches
are served throughout the day at the Green Tree Room. On Saturday
night, even knowing Carlsbad's ex-mayor, Bob Forrest, who owns the
motel, won't get you a table at the **Silver Spur bar and Lounge** when
popular country-western groups play. ⊠ *1829 S. Canal St. (Box 580),
88220,* ☎ *505/887–2851 or 800/730–2851,* 𝔽𝔸𝕏 *505/887–6338. 202
rooms. 2 restaurants, bar, pool, wading pool, playground, coin laundry. AE, D, DC, MC, V.*

$ 🏨 **Carlsbad Super 8.** This three-story motel, 2 mi from the airport and
1 block from the Convention Center in Carlsbad, has rooms decorated
in Southwestern tones with generic furnishings. A free Continental break-

fast is served in the morning. The closest restaurant is Jerry's, which serves fast-food fare 24 hours a day. ⊠ *3817 National Parks Hwy., 88220,* ☏ *505/887–8888,* ℻ *505/885–0126. 60 rooms. Pool, hot tub. AE, D, DC, MC, V.*

$ ⊡ **Continental Inn.** This place is south of Carlsbad, on National Parks Highway, and about 30 minutes from Carlsbad Caverns. The simple rooms have matching curtains and bedspreads in Southwestern patterns. The small grounds are well kept. Jerry's, which offers fast-food fare 24 hours a day, is within walking distance. ⊠ *3820 National Parks Hwy., 88220,* ☏ *505/887–0341,* ℻ *505/885–1186. 57 rooms, 3 suites. Pool, airport shuttle. AE, D, DC, MC, V.*

$ ⊡ **Stagecoach Inn.** This family-style motor inn is close to many of the major Carlsbad attractions and offers basic rooms at affordable rates— although they go up during peak holiday periods. There's a tree-shaded park with playground and picnic area. ⊠ *1819 S. Canal St., 88220,* ☏ ℻ *505/887–1148. 57 rooms. Restaurant, pool, wading pool, hot tub, laundry service. AE, D, DC, MC, V.*

$ ⬥ **Brantley Lake State Park.** Twelve miles north of Carlsbad via Highway 285, the campground in this state park is filled with Afghanistan pines, Mexican elders, and desert plants. Some camp and picnic sites offer views of the 3,000-acre lake and dam, an inviting oasis in this upper Chihuahuan desert region. ⊠ *Hwy. 285, Box 2288, 88221,* ☏ *505/457–2384. 52 RV sites (water and electric hookups $11); primitive-area camping with no immediate facilities ($6). Rest rooms, showers, picnic areas, grills, playground, boat ramps, fishing, dump station. Reservations not accepted. No credit cards.*

$ ⬥ **Carlsbad Campgrounds.** This tree-filled, full-service campground right inside the city limits has level gravel sites and a seasonal, indoor swimming pool. Reservations are advised in summer and a professional RV service is next door. A grocery and gift shop can be found on the premises. ⊠ *4301 National Parks Hwy., 88220,* ☏ *505/885–6333. 95 RV sites (full hookups $19.75, 41 tent sites $16.50). Rest rooms, hot showers, indoor pool, grills, public phones and phone hookup, sewage disposal, coin laundry. D, MC, V.*

Nightlife

Like many small towns, Carlsbad tends to fold up at night—so you're pretty much limited to special events and the lounge circuit. If you like live country-western music and dancing, try the **Silver Spur Lounge** in the Best Western Motel Stevens (☞ *Lodging, above*).

White's City

20 mi southwest of Carlsbad, off U.S. 62–180 on entrance road to Carlsbad Caverns.

At the turnoff from the highway to Carlsbad Caverns, the tiny resort town of White's City offers a quick fix for essentials—restaurants, saloon, motels, campground, grocery store, post office, gas station, souvenir shops, museum, and even a live melodrama—all along its old-fashioned, western boardwalk.

Million Dollar Museum has 11 big rooms on two levels filled with Early American memorabilia and artifacts—antique dolls and dollhouses, guns and rifles, music boxes, old cars, and a 6,000-year-old mummified Native American. An arcade and shooting gallery are next door. ⊠ *21 Carlsbad Caverns Hwy.,* ☏ *505/785–2291.* ⊡ *$2.50.* ☉ *Mid-May–mid-Sept., daily 7 AM–8 PM; mid-Sept.–mid-Mar., daily 7–6.*

★ **Granny's Opera House** is the place to go if you're ready to shed some inhibitions and whoop it up. In this old-fashioned melodrama, you can boo at the villain, throw popcorn, cheer on the heroes, tune up your vocal cords for a sing-along, and be pulled on stage. ⊠ *12 Carlsbad Caverns Hwy.*, ☎ *505/785–2291.* ⊞ *$5.50, including popcorn to eat and throw.* ☉ *Hour-long shows June–Sept., Fri.–Mon. at about 7:30 PM, depending on when bats fly at Carlsbad Caverns National Park. Call for information regarding special shows.*

Dining and Lodging

$$ ✕ **Velvet Garter Restaurant and Saloon.** Come here for steak, chicken, catfish, shrimp, and Mexican food in an Old West atmosphere. Food prices are old style, too—a 10-ounce rib-eye steak costs $12.95—but a shot of tequila in the saloon will set you back $3.50. ⊠ *26 Carlsbad Caverns Hwy.*, ☎ *505/785–2291. AE, D, DC, MC, V.*

$ ✕ **Fast Jack's.** A good spot to have a hearty breakfast before heading off to the caverns, this fast-food favorite shares an adobe-style building with the **Velvet Garter Restaurant.** Grab a booth and order eggs or a burger, then top it off with a freshly baked piece of pie. An all-you-can-eat breakfast buffet is featured in summer. ⊠ *26 Carlsbad Caverns Hwy.*, ☎ *505/785–2291. No credit cards.*

$$ ⊞ **Best Western Cavern Inn.** This pleasant, New Mexico Territorial–style two-story motor inn, 5 mi from the Carlsbad Caverns main entrance, has rooms decorated in Southwestern decor. It shares a pool with the neighboring Best Western Guadalupe (☞ *below*). Many tour groups and families stay here. ⊠ *17 Carlsbad Caverns Hwy., 88268,* ☎ *505/785–2291 or 800/228–3767,* ⅢX *505/785–2283. 62 rooms. 2 pools, spa, playground. AE, D, DC, MC, V.*

$$ ⊞ **Best Western Guadalupe Inn.** Handmade, Southwestern furniture adds a comfy feel to rooms in this hacienda-style motel next door to Best Western Cavern Inn (☞ *above*). High-desert landscaping with piñon pines, ocotillo cacti, and yucca plants help set the scene. Look nearby for grazing mule deer, which often amble down from their protected haven at the adjacent Carlsbad Caverns National Park. ⊠ *17 Carlsbad Caverns Hwy., 88268,* ☎ *505/785–2291 or 800/228–3767,* ⅢX *505/785–2283. 44 rooms. 2 pools, spa, playground. AE, D, DC, MC, V.*

$ ⚠ **Park Entrance RV Park.** In the heart of White's City, 7 mi from Carlsbad Caverns, this popular RV park offers natural desert sites with canopied shaded tables. ⊠ *17 Carlsbad Caverns Hwy. (Box 128), 88268,* ☎ *505/785–2291 or 800/228–3767. 150 sites. 60 full hookups, 48 pull-throughs ($16 per vehicle for up to 6 people, $3.34 per additional person). Rest rooms, hot showers, grills, LP gas, sewage disposal, 2 pools, tennis court, video games, playground, grocery store, security gates for RV park. AE, D, MC, V.*

ROSWELL AND LINCOLN COUNTY

The area around the town of Roswell is known as Billy the Kid country. Nearby Lincoln County was the site of the infamous Lincoln County War, in the late 1800s. The grassy plains of the Pecos Valley, about 75 mi north of Carlsbad, were once ruled by cattle kings, including the legendary John Chisum. Roswell is also the famous town often mentioned in exposés and movies about UFOs. Between Roswell and Lincoln, on scenic U.S. 70, are the forested Sacramento mountains. Once you get here, you might be tempted to stay for a few days in one of the town's luxurious resorts, rustic cabins, or cozy bed-and-breakfasts.

Roswell

75 mi north of Carlsbad on U.S. 285; 205 mi southeast of Albuquerque.

Roswell (population 50,000) was founded as a farming community in the fertile Pecos Valley almost a century ago. Crops such as alfalfa hay and cotton are irrigated with ample water supplies from underground artesian wells. The town has become known worldwide as the site of "The Roswell Incident," an alleged flying saucer crash that took place near here in 1947. The crash was purportedly covered up in a military conspiracy and only brought to light recently. Skeptics say believers have been breathing too much of the atmosphere typically found on Jupiter or Saturn, but the UFO mania can't be stopped.

The citizens of Roswell are a little chagrined about the town's notoriety, but they have fun with it. There are two UFO museums on Main Street: **Enigma UFO Museum** (✉ 6108 S. Main St. [the museum was scheduled to relocate by 1998, so call first to find out its new address], ☎ 505/347–2275) and the **International UFO Museum and Research Center** (✉ 114 N. Main St., ☎ 505/625–9495, FAX 505/625–1907). The community also sponsors an annual **encounter festival** the first week in July, with guest UFO lecturers and family events such as alien costume competitions. Contact the Roswell Chamber of Commerce (✉ 131 W. 2nd St., ☎ 505/623–5695) for details about the event and information about Roswell.

The **Roswell Museum and Art Center** has works by Peter Hurd, Georgia O'Keeffe, and Luis Jimenez, as well as an extensive assortment of Western artifacts and displays documenting the work of rocketry genius Robert H. Goddard, who conducted some of his early experiments near Roswell. The **Robert H. Goddard Planetarium,** the largest in the state, offers star talks and multimedia programs. ✉ *100 W. 11th St.,* ☎ *505/624–6744,* FAX *505/624–6765.* ⌨ *Free.* ☉ *Mon.–Sat. 9–5, Sun. 1–5. Planetarium shows offered 1 wk each month, Aug.–May, and daily June–July; call for schedule.*

Bottomless Lakes State Park is about 10 mi east of Roswell off U.S. 380. Travel about 2 mi south until you reach a series of small lakes—sinkholes created from dissolved salt and gypsum deposits. Camping facilities are available and swimming is permitted at Lea Lake, where you'll find showers and rest rooms. Paddleboats and paddleboards can be rented during the summer, from Memorial Day through Labor Day. ✉ *HC 12 (Box 1200),* ☎ *505/624–6058,* FAX *505/624–6029.* ⌨ *$3 per vehicle.* ☉ *6 AM–9 PM; overnight camping allowed ($7 plus extra charges for developed sites and hookups).*

Bitter Lake National Wildlife Refuge is just north of Roswell: Turn right on Pine Lodge Road off U.S. 285, and follow the signs 9 mi east to the refuge. Take the 8½-mi self-guided driving tour. Stops along the way offer viewing platforms from where you can watch for snow geese, sandhill cranes, and other exotic birds, among the familiar ducks and various migratory visitors that make this area a popular stopover. ✉ *4065 Bitter Lakes, Roswell, Box 7,* ☎ *505/622–6755.* ⌨ *Free.* ☉ *Daylight hrs.*

OFF THE BEATEN PATH

FORT SUMNER STATE MONUMENT – Take U.S. 285 40 mi north of Roswell, then take the Fort Sumner turnoff and travel northeast on NM 20 for another 45 mi. Fort Sumner was the site where approximately 12,000 Navajo and Mescalero Apache people were interred from 1863 to 1868 and, later, where Sheriff Pat Garrett gunned down outlaw Billy the Kid. *See Side Trips in* Chapter 4 for more information on the Fort Sumner State Monument.

Dining and Lodging

$–$$ ✕ **Cattle Baron.** Grilled meats and spicy sauces distinguish this eatery, which specializes in steaks and seafood served in elegant Southwestern-style surroundings, including a lounge. Salad bar offerings are fresh and varied. ⊠ *1113 N. Main,* ☎ *505/622–2465. AE, D, DC, MC, V.*

$$ ✕🏠 **Sally Port Inn.** The red-tiled roof and white walls of this motel match nearby New Mexico Military Institute, which inspired the name of Sally Port—a passageway in military quarters. J.D.'s Restaurant offers standard fare, breakfast through dinner. ⊠ *2000 N. Main,* ☎ *505/622–6430,* FAX *505/623–7631. 99 rooms, 25 suites. Restaurant, kitchenettes, indoor pool, beauty salon, sauna, exercise room, video games, meeting rooms. AE, D, MC, V.*

San Patricio

45 mi west of Roswell on U.S. 70.

San Patricio, and the nearby tiny villages of Tinnie and Hondo, in the Hondo Valley, are inhabited by ranchers, farmers, artists, and those seeking serenity amidst pastoral scenes of sheep grazing among apple orchards. The Rio Ruidoso flows into the Rio Hondo, helping provide lifeblood for farmers and wildlife alike. During the harvest, fresh cider and locally grown produce are available at roadside stands. The bright white church of San Patricio, with its modest bell tower, will catch your eye as you head to town.

★ Be sure to get to the **Hurd-La Rinconada Gallery,** part of a sprawling art compound on the Sentinel Ranch, which belongs to the Hurd family, one of America's largest art dynasties. Showcased in the unique adobe gallery is the work of the late Peter Hurd, a long-time Hondo Valley resident. Hurd gained world recognition as a regional landscape painter and portraitist—and won perhaps even more fame for a portrait commissioned by President Lyndon B. Johnson who, unhappy with the results, refused to hang it in the White House. Also on display are the works of Hurd's widow, Henriette Wyeth Hurd (Andrew Wyeth's sister), and their son, artist Michael Hurd, who runs the ranch. Michael, who often can be seen on the grounds, is an amiable host who has established his own international reputation with a series of paintings he calls "The Road West." He portrays the stark desert scenery surrounding his home with powerful creations such as "Night Oasis" and "Afternoon at White Sands." Michael's sister, Carole Hurd Rogers, and her husband Peter Rogers, also an artist, live on the ranch as well. Paintings by Andrew Wyeth and his father, N. C. Wyeth, round out the impressive presentation at the gallery. Signed reproductions and some original paintings are for sale. ⊠ *U.S. 70, MM 281,* ☎ *505/653–4331.* ☉ *Mon.–Sat. 9–5, Sun. 10–4. Closed Sun. in winter.*

Dining and Lodging

$–$$ ✕ **Tinnie Silver Dollar.** Once a general store and post office known as
★ Tinnie Mercantile Company, this century-old site has been magically transformed into a sophisticated restaurant. Soak up the Victorian atmosphere while dining on specialty dishes such as prime beef brochette, pasta *diablo* (shrimp sautéed in tomatoes, basil, and crushed red peppers and served on green-chile pasta). ABC newscaster Sam Donaldson, who owns a nearby ranch, can often be spotted here. Watch for the bell tower on the restaurant, and turn fast near mile marker 288 off U.S. 70, or you'll miss this lone establishment. ⊠ *U.S. 70, MM 288 (Box 299), Tinnie,* ☎ *505/653–4425. AE, D, DC, MC, V.*

$$$ ⊞ **Hurd Ranch Guest Homes.** Three adobe casitas on the Sentinel
★   Ranch, adjacent to the Hurd-La Rinconada Gallery, are comfortably
        equipped with modern and Western furnishings and are stylishly dec-
        orated with paintings, sculptures, and Native American artifacts. The
        casitas were once guest houses that the late Peter Hurd made available
        to friends and customers who needed accommodations while he painted
        their portraits. They have washing machines and dryers, fully equipped
        kitchens, and fireplaces. The newest one is named after actress Helen
        Hayes, who was a family friend and frequent visitor. A wing of the Hurd-
        La Rinconada Gallery also has apartments that can be rented. Even
        one night's stay on the ranch offers profound insight into why talented
        Hurd family artists still choose to remain so close to the inspiration of
        contoured hills and the soothing waters of the nearby Rio Ruidoso.
        ⊠ *U.S. 70 (Box 100), 88348,* ☎ *505/653–4331, 800/658–6912,* 𝖥𝖠𝖷
        505/653–4218. 3 casitas and gallery wing. AE, D, MC, V.

Ruidoso

*63 mi west of Roswell on U.S. 70. 50 mi northeast of Alamogordo on
U.S. 70.*

Sprawled at the base of the Sierra Blanca Peak on the eastern slopes
of the pine-covered Sacramento Mountains, Ruidoso is a sophisti-
cated year-round resort town that retains its rustic small-town charm.
In winter the Mescalero Apache–run ski area, Ski Apache, makes Rui-
doso a major ski resort. The summer horse-racing season keeps the town
hopping after the snow melts and the skiers go home. The town's main
street is sprinkled with shops, antiques stores, bars, and restaurants.

★ **Ruidoso Downs,** the self-proclaimed Home of the World's Richest
Quarter Horse Race, offers a fabulous mountain vista as a setting for
cheering the ponies. On Labor Day it is the site of the All-American
Quarter Horse Futurity, with a total purse of as much as $2.5 million.
Purses for other quarter-horse and Thoroughbred events throughout
the season (late May–Labor Day) are almost as spectacular. The **Rui-
doso Downs Sports Complex,** ½ mi east of the track, just off Highway
70 (look for the signs), features year-round pari-mutuel racing plus other
sports events on large-screen TV sets. ⊠ *Hwy. 70 (Box 449), Ruidoso
Downs,* ☎ *505/378–4431.* ⊡ *Racetrack: Open seating free, reserved
seating $2.50 and up, grandstand $2.50–$5.50, Turf Club $8.50
(higher on special weekends). Sports Complex free. Parking $3–$5.*
⊙ *Racing late May–Labor Day, Fri.–Sun.; post time is 1 PM (earlier
on Labor Day). Sports Complex hrs vary depending on the event; call
for schedule.*

☾ The **Museum of the Horse,** about ½ mi east of the racetrack, is home
to a striking, painted bronze sculpture called **Free Spirits at Noisy Water,**
one of the world's largest and most beautiful equine monuments. The
life-sized monument also represents an intricate engineering feat, be-
cause only nine hooves among the eight romping horses actually touch
the ground. The world-class museum also houses the **Anne C. Stradling
Collection,** consisting of over 10,000 pieces related to the horse—
paintings, drawings, and bronzes by master artists; saddles from Mex-
ico, China, and the Pony Express; carriages and wagons, and memorabilia
from Teddy Roosevelt and Frederic Remington. In July 1997, the
Racehorse Hall of Fame opened as a permanent exhibit. Other new
activities include a children's interactive center, featuring pony rides,
live horse demonstrations, puzzles, and access to Old West costumes
that can be tried on. Youngsters also can climb aboard horse mannequins
to have their photos taken in a jockey outfit. ⊠ *Hwy. 70 E (Box 40),*

Ruidoso Downs, ☎ *505/378–4142 or 800/263–5929.* ☞ *$5.* ☉
May–Labor Day, daily 9–5:30; mid-Sept.–Apr., Tues.–Sun. 10–5.

The **Mescalero Apache Indian Reservation,** bordering Ruidoso to the
west, is inhabited by more than 2,500 Mescalero Apaches, most of whom
work in the lumber and fishing industries. The famous **Inn of the
Mountain Gods** (☞ Dining and Lodging, *below*), one of the state's most
elegant resorts, is Apache owned and operated. Other sights on the reservation include a general store, a trading post, and a museum, which
has clothing and crafts displays, a 12-minute video about life on the
reservation, and regular talks about the history and culture of the
Mescalero Apaches. There are also campsites (with hookups at Silver
and Eagle lakes only) and picnic areas. Ritual dances are occasionally
performed for the public, the most colorful of which is on the Fourth
of July. The reservation's **Ski Apache** area offers fine skiing (☞ Outdoor Activities and Sports, *below*). ⊠ *Tribal Office, Hwy. 70 (Box 227),
Mescalero,* ☎ *505/671–4494.* ☞ *Free.* ☉ *Reservation and tribal museum weekdays 8–4:30.*

Spencer Theater for the Performing Arts (☎ 505/336–4800) was
scheduled to open east of Ruidoso by 1998, after construction of the
wedge-shaped structure began early in the year. Designed by architect
Antoine Predock of Albuquerque, the building with its 523 seats is designed for intimate performances by musicians and other guest artists.
Call for information regarding prices and performances.

Dining and Lodging

$$$ ✕ **La Lorraine.** Classic French cuisine, such as chateaubriand, beef
bourguignonne, and sausage-stuffed quail, is served amid elegant colo-
nial French surroundings. ⊠ *2523 Sudderth Dr.,* ☎ *505/257–2954.
AE, MC, V. Closed Sun. No lunch Mon.*

$$–$$$ ✕ **Incredible Restaurant and Saloon.** This rustic Western spot, with a
lounge and atrium for dining under the stars, has been a local favorite
for lobster dinners, prime rib, and filet mignon for more than 30 years.
⊠ *Hwy. 48 N at Alto Village (9 mi north of Ruidoso),* ☎ *505/336–
4312. AE, D, MC, V.*

$–$$ ✕ **Cafe Mescalero.** Chef Tony Carpenter scoured famous restaurants
throughout Mexico for the authentic south-of-the-border recipes fea-
tured in this century-old site. Owned by the Mescalero Apache Indian
Reservation, the building once served as a summer school and retreat
for New Mexico Military Institute cadets from Roswell. Prices are a
bargain for the quality of the cuisine, which includes *bolsa del pobre*
(seafood and vegetables), a specialty from Colima and *pan de cazon*
(grilled shark with black beans and red onions on a tortilla), a dish
originating in Campeche. ⊠ *Carrizo Canyon Rd.,* ☎ *505/257–6693.
AE, D, DC, MC, V.*

$$$ ✕⊡ **Inn of the Mountain Gods.** The Mescalero Apaches own and op-
★ erate this spectacular year-round resort on the banks of Mescalero Lake,
about 3 mi southwest of Ruidoso. Rooms are large and have hand-
some Western and Native American flourishes; each has a balcony. The
inn has its own casinos with poker, lotto machines, and table action.
The 18-hole golf course was designed by Ted Robinson, who also cre-
ated the famous courses at the Acapulco Princess and at California's
Tamarisk. Dine at **Dan-Li-Ka,** which means "good food" in Apache,
while looking out over Mescalero Lake and the Sacramento mountains.
The menu includes Spanish, Native American, and regional New Mex-
ican specialties. If you need a lunch break from casino action, step over
for a burger at the **Apache Tee Cafe** overlooking the golf course. Prices
are reasonable, service is friendly, and you can enjoy the majestic view

of the golf course, Sierra Blanca mountain peak, and lake. ⊠ *Carrizo Canyon Rd. (Box 269), 88340,* ☎ *505/257–5141 or 800/545–6040,* ℻ *505/257–6173. Dan-Li-Ka Restaurant,* ☎ *505/257–5315. 250 rooms. 2 restaurants, bar, pool, hot tub, 18-hole golf course, tennis court, archery, fishing, casinos. AE, MC, V.*

$$ ✕⌷ **Swiss Chalet.** Nestled in the tall pines, this pleasant inn is the closest lodging to the popular Ski Apache slopes only 16 mi away. Owner Hansveli Schlunegger is indeed Swiss, though he now lives in the United States. He has introduced many Swiss and German themes into the lodge's decor, including cow bells, an Alp horn, and cuckoo clocks. Rooms are decorated with hand-painted Swiss-style furniture in light blue or muted red. A German and American menu is featured at the restaurant, named for Schlunegger's granddaughter **Ahna-Michelle.** Hiking trails are available from the lodge. The lounge, **Ol' Barry's Tavern,** has a small, intimate fireplace—perfect surroundings for quiet relaxation after a day of skiing. ⊠ *Hwy. 48, 1451 Mechem Dr., 88345,* ☎ *505/258–3333 or 800/477–9477,* ℻ *505/258–5325. 82 rooms. Restaurant, bar, pool, hot tub, hiking trails. AE, MC, V.*

$$ ⌷ **Shadow Mountain Lodge.** The Ruidoso River is across the street from this small, L-shaped hotel in the historic Upper Canyon. Fieldstone fireplaces in each room add to the lodge's alpine ambience; rooms also come equipped with king-size beds and kitchen facilities. A veranda runs along the front of the hotel, with grills outside for marshmallow and hot-dog toasting. Relax with a good soak in the hot tub, outside in the gazebo. ⊠ *107 Main Rd. (Box 1427), 88345,* ☎ *505/257–4886 or 800/441–4331,* ℻ *505/257–2000. 19 suites. Outdoor hot tub. AE, D, DC, MC, V.*

$$ ⌷ **Sierra Mesa Lodge.** This immaculate, modern bed-and-breakfast near
★ Alto, about 15 mi north of Ruidoso, amidst towering pines, offers a choice of five different rooms delightfully decorated in themes ranging from Oriental to French Country. Quality modern and antique furnishings decorate the premises. There's a toasty fireplace in the living room and a relaxing hot tub. The gourmet breakfast, included in the room rate, is a treat. Owners Larry and Lila Goodman are the perfect hosts, gracious and accommodating in every way. Finding the lodge is a little tricky, so call first for directions. ⊠ *Fort Stanton Rd., Box 463, Alto 88312,* ☎ *505/336–4515. 5 rooms. Hot tub. AE, D, MC, V.*

Outdoor Activities and Sports

Run by the Mescalero Apaches, **Ski Apache Ski Resort,** on Sierra Blanca (11,400 ft) offers fine powder skiing. ⊠ *Hwy. 532 (Box 220), 88345,* ☎ *505/336–4356; 505/257–9001 for snow-report recording* ▤ *Prices change periodically, so call ahead for current fees.* ☉ *Thanksgiving–Easter, daily 8:45–4.*

Capitan

26 mi north of Ruidoso via NM 48. 12 mi west of Lincoln.

If you're headed from Ruidoso toward Lincoln, you'll find that Capitan is right along the way. Capitan is the site of Billy the Kid's famous prison escape, as well as Smokey Bear's birthplace and grave site. Smokey Bear became a symbol of fire prevention in 1950 after he was found as a cub, badly burned in a forest fire in the nearby mountains. He lived in the National Zoo in Washington until his death in 1976 when he was returned home for burial. At the **Smokey Bear Historical State Park** visitor center, displays explain how Smokey became the symbol of forest-fire prevention and how forest fires start; kids can play with computer games and see a puppet show. The 2-acre park has an exhibit at Smokey's grave and information about native plants. The park also includes the village of Capitan's original train depot, which is adjacent to the museum and gift shop operated by the Woman's Club. There's also a picnic area and playground. ⊠ *118 Smokey Bear Blvd. (Box 591),* ☎ *505/354–2748,* ℻ *505/354–3052.* ☜ *25¢.* ⊙ *Daily 9–5.*

Lincoln

12 mi east of Capitan on U.S. 380.

It may not be as well known as Tombstone, Arizona, or Deadwood, South Dakota, but Lincoln ranks right up there with the toughest of the tough old towns of the Old West. The violent Lincoln County Wars took place here more than a century ago, as two opposing factions clashed over winning lucrative government contracts to feed the army and the Native Americans on area reservations. One of the more infamous figures to emerge from the bloodshed was a short, slight, sallow young man with buck teeth, startling blue eyes, and curly reddish-brown hair. His name was Billy the Kid. He is said to have killed 21 men (probably an exaggeration), including Lincoln's sheriff William Brady—for whose murder Billy the Kid was convicted in 1881 and sentenced to hang. But Billy managed to elude the gallows.

On April 28, 1881, though manacled and shackled, Billy made a daring escape from the old Lincoln County Courthouse as he gunned down two men. Three months later, a posse led by Sheriff Pat Garrett tracked Billy down at the home of a friend in Fort Sumner, surprised him in the dark, and finished him off with two clean shots. One of the West's most notorious gunmen, and ultimately one of its best-known folk legends, was dead at 21.

☾ The Lincoln County **Historical Center,** on the eastern end of town, has a 10-minute slide show about Lincoln and exhibits devoted to Billy the Kid, the Lincoln County Wars, cowboys, Apaches, and Buffalo Soldiers, with guides and attendants dressed in period costumes. ⊠ *Hwy. 380, Main St.,* ☎ *505/653–4025.* ☜ *Pass for all sites: May–Sept. $4.50, Oct.–Apr. $4.* ⊙ *May–Sept., daily 9–6; Oct.–Apr., daily 9–5.*

☾ Nothing has changed much at the **Tunstall Store Museum,** just west of the Historical Center. When the state bought the store in 1957, they discovered boxes of unused stock dating from the turn of the century—clothes, hardware, and kerosene lamps, among other items. These are displayed in the store's original cases. ⊠ *Hwy. 380, Main St.,* ☎ *505/653–4049.* ☜ *Pass to all sites: May–Sept. $4.50, Oct.–Apr. $4.* ⊙ *May–Sept., daily 9–6; Oct.–Apr., daily 9–5.*

The **Dr. Woods House** is a fine example of a late-19th-century wealthy person's adobe home. ⊠ *Hwy. 380, Main St.,* ☎ *505/653–4529.* ☜ *Pass to all sites: May–Sept. $4.50, Oct.–Apr. $4.* ⊙ *May–mid-June, daily 9–5; mid-June–Sept., daily 10–6.*

The **Lincoln County Courthouse Museum** is in the building from which Billy the Kid made his daring escape on April 28, 1881. ⊠ *Hwy. 380, Main St.,* ☎ *505/653–4372.* ☜ *Pass to all sites: May–Sept. $4.50, Oct.–Apr. $4.* ⊙ *May–Sept., daily 9–6; Oct.–Apr., daily 9–5.*

OFF THE BEATEN PATH   **VALLEY OF FIRES RECREATION AREA** – About 24 mi west of Capitan, via U.S. 380, and 4 mi west of Carrizo is the most recent lava flow in the continental United States. Covering 44 mi, the dark, jagged landscape resembles a *Star Trek* set. A ¾-mi trail penetrates the site of the volcanic lava, thought to have flowed 1,500 to 2,000 years ago. Caving is allowed with the proper permits. Overnight camping with utility and water hookups is available. ⊠ *U.S. 380, 4 mi west of Carrizozo (Box 871),* ☎ *505/648–2241.* 🖭 *$3 for individual, $5 per carload; $5 for primitive camping, $7 for developed camping, $11 for sites with hookups.* ☉ *Information center daily 8–4.*

Dining and Lodging

$$ ✕ **Hotel Chango.** Despite its name, this is not a hotel, it's a restaurant that serves some of the best food in the area. The owner, Jerrold Flores, is continually experimenting with new dishes, including chicken with lime and tequila sauce, which he complements with a wide variety of wines. Jerrold likes to quote the expression: "bigger isn't better," so expect an intimate dining experience with the owner strictly in charge. Every year Jerrold travels worldwide to buy antiques and artwork, which he uses to decorate the restaurant's warm, brown stucco interior. All of these items are for sale, so you can order some with your meal. ⊠ *103 S. Lincoln St. at junction of Hwys. 380 and 48,* ☎ *505/354–4213. Reservations essential. MC, V. Closed Sun.– Mon.*

$$ ✕🖭 **Ellis Store & Co. Bed-and-Breakfast.** This B&B has a rich history dating back to 1850, when it was a modest, two-room adobe in a territory where the Mescaleros still threatened settlers. During the Lincoln County War, Billy the Kid was known to frequent the place along with many other establishments in the small town of Lincoln. Rooms in the main house are decorated with antiques; those in the Mill House are ideal for families, as there is a large common room. Owner Jinny Vigil cooks gourmet meals in the evening (by reservation only), served in a spacious, wood-paneled dining room. ⊠ *Hwy. 380, MM 98 (Box 15),* ☎ *505/653–4609 or 800/653–6460,* FAX *505/653–4611. 3 double rooms with bath, 4 doubles share 2 baths, extra rooms for kids. Restaurant. D, MC, V.*

$$–$$$ 🖭 **Casa de Patrón Bed-and-Breakfast.** This attractive bed-and-breakfast ★ on Lincoln's main street is in a historic adobe—once the home of Juan Patrón, an early settler and father of three, who was gunned down at age 29 in the violence that swept Lincoln County. Billy the Kid *really* did sleep here, both as a guest of Juan Patrón and while being held by the sheriff under protective custody. The owners have documented evidence that villagers of Lincoln once serenaded Billy here in the evening hours, while he was being held prisoner. The main house has high viga ceilings and Mexican-tile baths; the adjacent Old Trail House has two large rooms—one decorated in Hispanic-cowboy style and the other in a garden motif—with fireplaces. Owners Jeremy and Cleis Jordan also offer two small adobe casitas decorated with traditional New Mexican flavor, cathedral ceilings, vigas, and portals. Casita Bonita, with its circular staircase and loft bedroom is the perfect romantic hideout for couples seeking privacy, while Casita de Paz offers a two-bedroom suite ideal for families. All rooms are furnished with antiques and collectibles and one is wheelchair accessible. Full country breakfasts are served in the main house and Continental breakfasts in the casitas. Jeremy and Cleis are warm hosts, displaying charm and good-natured willingness to share their keen knowledge of this historic area. ⊠ *Hwy. 380 (Box 27), 88338,* ☎ *505/653–4676 or 505/653–4500,* FAX *505/ 653–4671. 5 double rooms, 2 casitas (1 with a 2-bedroom suite). MC, V.*

OTERO COUNTY AND WHITE SANDS NATIONAL MONUMENT

Defense-related activities are vital to the town of Alamogordo and to Otero County, which covers much of the desert Tularosa Basin. Many residents of the area are employed at Holloman Air Force Base and White Sands Missile Range, where the nation's first atomic bomb was exploded at Trinity Site on July 12, 1945. From Alamogordo, take a 20-minute drive due east on U.S. 82 and you'll make an abrupt climb into the small mountain resort town of Cloudcroft. Head south of Alamogordo, about 15 mi on U.S. 70, and you'll find the world-famous desert of White Sands National Monument, which resembles a beautifully stark snowscape.

Alamogordo

55 mi southwest of Ruidoso. 68 mi northeast of Las Cruces off U.S. 70.

Look up as you approach Alamogordo on U.S. 70 and you just might see the dark, bat-shaped outline of a Stealth fighter swooping overhead. Holloman Air Force Base is home to these high-tech fighter planes that played such a crucial role for the United States in the Gulf War. Alamogordo is also known for its space center and space hall of fame.

The **Space Center** and museum, in northeast Alamogordo, is in a striking multistory building on a lofty hill, where it gleams a metallic gold in certain angles of the sun. The center features the **International Space Hall of Fame,** in which astronauts and other space-exploration celebrities are routinely inducted. A simulated, red Mars landscape is among the indoor exhibits. Outside, the **Stapp Air and Space Park** has a rocket sled and other space-related artifacts on display. The scenic **Astronaut Memorial Garden** overlooks White Sands. The **Clyde W. Tombaugh Omnimax Theater and Planetarium** shows Omnimax films and planetarium and laser light shows. ⊠ *At the top of NM 2001,* ☎ *505/437–2840 or 800/545–4021.* 🎟 *Museum $2.50, shows $4.50, combination ticket $6.* ☉ *International Space Hall of Fame: Memorial Day–Labor Day, daily 9–6; Labor Day–Memorial Day, daily 9–5. Tombaugh Omnimax Theater and Planetarium: Memorial Day–Labor Day, shows daily at 10, 11, noon, 2, 3, 4, and 7; Labor Day–Memorial Day, shows weekdays at 10, noon, 2, and 4; weekends at 10, 11, noon, 2, 3, and 4; Fri.–Sun. evening shows at 7. Call for schedules regarding special shows.*

Dining

$ ✕ **Margo's.** Try this family-owned restaurant's specialty Mexican dish, *chalupas* (beans, meat, and cheese served on crisp tortillas). In winter, menudo made of hominy and tripe is served hot and steaming. The family of owner and founder Margo Sandoval has been in the restaurant business in the area for decades. Colorful blankets help provide Southwest decor. ⊠ *504 1st St.,* ☎ *505/434–0689. AE, D, MC, V.*

Cloudcroft

15 mi east of Alamogordo on U.S. 82.

Cloudcroft is a quiet mountain resort town with cabins and church camps tucked into secluded canyons. Longtime weekenders here don't mind telling you that they hope their haven remains a secret. A low-key version of Ruidoso, Cloudcroft has a small strip of specialty shops and a variety of restaurants and lodgings in log cabin–style atmosphere. The Lincoln National Forest Service headquarters has maps showing area hiking trails.

The **National Solar Observatory–Sacramento Peak** in Sunspot, 12 mi south of Cloudcroft on the Sunspot Highway, is designated for observations of the sun at a dizzying elevation of 9,200 ft. A self-guided tour during the day allows you to inspect different telescopes on site. One observation point offers a majestic view of White Sands and the Tularosa Basin. You're even allowed to watch live television views (filtered) of the sun. But this is a working community of scientists—not a tourist attraction—so you're pretty much on your own. ⊠ *National Solar Observatory–Sacramento Peak, Sunspot,* ☎ *505/434–7000.* ▦ *Free.* ☉ *Daily 8–6; guided tour May–Oct., Sat. at 2.*

Dining and Lodging

$$$ ✕▦ **The Lodge.** Originally a retreat for the Alamogordo and Sacra-
★ mento Mountain Railway, this Victorian lodge has entertained hundreds of celebrities, including Pancho Villa, Judy Garland, and Clark Gable. Built in 1899, The Lodge conjures up romantic visions of a Gothic novel with its Bavarian-style interior. Rooms are decorated with chenille bedspreads, period antiques, flocked wallpaper in pastel shades, ceiling fans, and, in many cases, four-poster beds. Elegant dining is offered at Rebecca's, named after a flirtatious and beautiful, redheaded ghost who is said to haunt the hallways in search of a new lover. Executive Chef Timothy Wilkins has won five gold medals in New Mexico culinary competitions for his creations in Southwestern and classic cuisine. The complex also includes the Lodge Pavilion, a rustic 11-room B&B. ⊠ *1 Corona Pl. (Box 497), 88317,* ☎ *505/682–2566 or 800/ 395–6343,* ℻ *505/682–2715. 60 rooms. Restaurant, bar, pool, sauna, spa, 9-hole golf course, volleyball. AE, D, DC, MC, V.*

Outdoor Activities and Sports

Snow Canyon Winter Recreation Area, operated in conjunction with The Lodge (☞ Dining and Lodging, *above*), is 2 mi east of Cloudcroft on U.S. 82. When winter weather cooperates with some hefty snows, slopes are opened for all levels of skiers. Cross-country skis and snowmobile equipment are available. ⊠ *The Lodge, 1 Corona Pl.,* ☎ *505/ 682–2333 or 800/333–7542 for ski conditions,* ℻ *505/682–2715.* ▦ *Call for current prices.* ☉ *Daily 9–4:30, when there is snow.*

White Sands National Monument

★ *15 mi south of Alamogordo off U.S. 70.*

White Sands National Monument, with shifting sand dunes 60 ft high, is a scene out of the *Arabian Nights.* It encompasses 145,344 acres and the largest deposit of gypsum sand in the world (the sand on most beaches is silica; gypsum is used for making plaster of paris), and it's one of the few landforms that is recognizable from space. In the visitor center there is a display about the dunes and how they were formed, an information desk, a bookstore, and a snack bar. From the visitor center, a 16-mi round-trip car ride takes you into the eerie wonderland of gleaming white sand.

It's hard to resist climbing to the top of the dunes for a photograph, then tumbling down, wading knee-deep in the gypsum crystals. But you are cautioned not to tunnel into the sand dunes; in loose sand, tunnels can easily collapse and cause suffocation. When you want to explore on foot, follow the mi-long, self-guided **Big Dune Trail;** the 7½-mi **Alkali Flat Trail;** the 4½-mi **Boardwalk;** and the 6½-mi **Nature Center in the Dunes.** The picnic area has shaded tables and grills. Backcountry campsites are available by permit, obtainable at the visitor center; camping is free, but there aren't any facilities. Once a month from May through October, White Sands celebrates the full moon by remaining open until 11 PM, allowing you to experience the eerie surroundings by lunar light. Call for information and reservations for monthly auto caravans to the source of the gypsum sand deposit, Lake Lucero. During the summer, ranger-led tours are offered daily at sunset. A newly added auditorium features an introductory video about the park. ⊠ *Hwy. 70, Holloman AFB,* ☎ *505/479–6124,* 𝖥𝖠𝖷 *505/479–4333.* ☉ *Daily 7 AM–1 hr past sunset.* ⌹ *$2 per person on foot or on motorcycle, $4 per car.*

THE MESILLA VALLEY

This vast river valley bordered by mesquite-covered sand dunes once was a crossing for Spanish conquistadors, who left behind relics such as armor and helmets during explorations centuries ago. The area later became part of the Camino Real. The Rio Grande cuts through the Mesilla Valley, the area where Cabeza de Vaca is credited with leading the first Spanish explorers to this region in 1593. The Organ Mountains, overlooking the town of Las Cruces, dominate the landscape—the jagged peaks often transformed at sunset into a brilliant magenta color dubbed "Las Cruces purple."

Just west of Las Cruces is the small community of Mesilla, now commonly known as Old Mesilla. This Mexican-style village, which still retains many of its original adobe buildings and plaza, once was the territorial capital of New Mexico and Arizona after the United States acquired the land from Mexico in the Gadsden Purchase of 1853.

Las Cruces

212 mi south of Albuquerque. 68 mi southwest of Alamogordo.

A mixture of old and new, Las Cruces has many diverse neighborhoods, including some near the downtown area that still retain their charming adobe structures dating back more than a century. Other homes are shaded by the many pecan groves in the irrigated farming valley, while newer housing developments are nestled amid lofty sand dunes overlooking the Mesilla Valley. The city and surrounding area represent one of the country's fastest growing metropolitan areas, with an economy closely linked to the border factories of nearby El Paso, Texas, and Juarez, Mexico; defense and commercial activities at White Sands Missile Range; and a major land-grant college at New Mexico State University. If you're in Las Cruces on a Wednesday or a Saturday—and you're up early—drop by the downtown mall (⊠ N. Main St.) for one of the nation's premier outdoor farmers' markets, showcasing locally grown produce, handcrafted items, and baked goods from about 375 vendors.

Old Mesilla

★ *2 mi south of Las Cruces. 220 mi south of Albuquerque: Take NM 28 (Mesilla), exit off I–40 at Las Cruces. 45 mi north of El Paso, Texas.*

Old Mesilla appears much as it did a century ago, with its authentic Mexican-style plaza and charming gazebo where many weddings and fiestas still take place. Shops and restaurants line the cobbled streets. At the plaza's north end, the historic Roman Catholic **San Albino Church** remains an active house of worship.

Stahmann Farms, about 10 mi south of Old Mesilla on NM 28, offers a lovely, shaded drive through rows of pecan trees covering some 4,000 acres—one of the largest pecan orchards in the world. Stop by **Stahmann's Store,** weekdays 9–5:30 and weekends 10–5, to sample some of the farm's pecan products. Call in advance to arrange a tour of the candy plant. ⊠ *NM 28 (Box BB), Las Cruces,* ☎ *505/526–8974 or 800/654–6887.*

Fort Selden State Monument, 13 mi north of Las Cruces at the Radium Springs exit, off I–25, was established in 1865 to protect Mesilla Valley settlers and travelers. Built in typical Southwestern style, the fort has flat-roof adobe brick buildings arranged around a drill field. It housed several units of acclaimed Buffalo Soldiers, African-American cavalry troops. In the early 1880s, Captain Arthur MacArthur was appointed post commander. His young son spent several years on the post and grew up to become World War II hero General Douglas MacArthur. A permanent exhibit called "Fort Selden: An Adobe Post on the Rio Grande" depicts the roles of officers, enlisted men, and women on the American frontier during the Indian Wars. Camping facilities can be found at the adjacent **Leasburg State Park.** ⊠ *I–25 (Box 58), Radium Springs,* ☎ *505/526–8911.* ⊠ *$2.* ⊙ *Daily 8:30–5.*

Aguirre Spring is beneath the towering spires of the Organ Mountains in a juniper-oak woodland zone. Take U.S. 70 northeast from Las Cruces for 12 mi, then turn south at the road marked "Aguirre Springs" for an additional 5 mi. Trails lead into the upper regions of the ponderosa pines, including **Pine Tree Trail** (4-mi loop) and **Baylor Pass National Recreation Trail** (6 mi one-way), two developed paths. Sixty campsites are available. ⊠ *Off Hwy. 70, Bureau of Land Management, 1800 Marquess, Las Cruces,* ☎ *505/525–4300.* ⊠ *$3 per vehicle daily, for camping and day use.* ⊙ *Memorial Day–Labor Day, daily 8–8; Labor Day–Memorial Day, daily 8–6.*

Dripping Springs Natural Area, 10 mi east of Las Cruces on University Avenue, offers day-use access to a now-abandoned mountain resort first built in the 1870s and converted several decades later into a sanatorium for tuberculosis patients. It is also the site of **Hermit's Peak,** a hill where a local legend—Agostini Justiniani, of Italian nobility— lived in solitude during the late 1800s. Agostini was rumored to have miraculous healing powers and received sick people for treatments with his abundance of herbs. He was found murdered at the site in 1869. The area offers a variety of hiking trails to the Organ Mountains. ⊠ *Off University Avenue (Dripping Springs Rd. Ext.) Bureau of Land Management, 1800 Marquess, Las Cruces,* ☎ *505/522–1219.* ⊠ *$3 per vehicle.* ⊙ *Daily 8 AM–sunset.*

☪ **New Mexico Farm and Ranch Heritage Museum,** scheduled to open in the spring of 1998, will feature live demonstrations and massive galleries with farm and ranch artifacts. Occupying a 46-acre site, the $7.5 million museum will include a dairy barn, greenhouse, animal displays, and outdoor pastures. The site is located 1½ mi east of I–25 on University Avenue Extension (Dripping Springs Road) in Las Cruces. ⊠ *4100 Dripping Springs Rd. (Box 1898), Las Cruces,* ☎ *505/522–4100,* ℻ *505/522–3085.* ⊠ *Call for admission prices.* ⊙ *Memorial Day– Labor Day, daily 9–6; Labor Day–Memorial Day, daily 9–5.*

Dining and Lodging

$$–$$$ ✗ **Double Eagle.** Built as a private home in 1848 by the Maes family, this huge mansion on the plaza has chandeliers, turn-of-the-century wall coverings, and gold-leaf ceilings. The site is rumored to have its ghosts, including that of a young man who incurred his mother's wrath by falling in love with a servant girl. The mother is said to have killed both of the young lovers, whose spirits remain here still—happy and in love. Continental cuisine, steaks, and flambé dishes are served in the restaurant, and borderland chile dishes, shark fajitas, and green-chile cheese

wontons are served in Peppers', the adjoining Southwestern-style café-bar. Margaritas are from a secret recipe. ⊠ *308 Calle de Guadalupe,* ☎ *505/523–6700. AE, D, DC, MC, V.*

$$ ✕ **Cattle Baron.** One of the most gracious establishments in the area,
★ this fine restaurant serves prime rib, steak, seafood, and pasta while offering an extensive salad bar. Skylights and greenery brighten the indoor decor, decorated by brass fixtures and wooden tables. An outdoor patio is available for dining in warmer weather, providing a nice view of the city of Las Cruces. This superb regional restaurant chain was founded in Portales, New Mexico, and has been slowing expanding throughout the state as its popularity grows. ⊠ *790 S. Telshor, Las Cruces,* ☎ *505/522–7533,* FAX *505/522–6021. AE, D, MC, V.*

$–$$ ✕ **Giovani's.** Owner and chef Johnny Martin once served a one-year private apprenticeship in Italy, where he learned artful cooking techniques that have earned him a number of blue ribbons. This small and still modest restaurant, founded in late 1996, manifests Martin's dream of owning his own establishment, where secret recipes for pasta and sauces are transformed into mouth-watering gourmet pizzas and other Italian specialties. ⊠ *1706 S. Espina, Las Cruces,* ☎ *505/525–3384. AE, D, MC, V. Closed Sun.*

$–$$ ✕ **La Posta.** This adobe structure once served as a way station for the
★ Butterfield Overland Mail and Wells Fargo stages. A lushly vegetated atrium populated with exotic birds and tropical fish provides a pleasant entrance. Some of the recipes for authentic Mexican food date back a century. The restaurant also serves Southwestern favorites such as chiles rellenos and red or green enchiladas. ⊠ *2410 Calle de San Albino,* ☎ *505/524–3524. AE, D, DC, MC, V. Closed Mon.*

$–$$ ✕ **Lorenzo's.** A hand-painted mural of the Mesilla Valley helps set the scene for this intimate Italian restaurant, with its red tablecloths and bottles of imported oil. Pizzas, pasta, sandwiches, and salads are concocted from secret, Sicilian recipes. Look for this small restaurant in Onate Plaza, near Old Mesilla. ⊠ *2000 Hwy. 292,* ☎ *505/525–3170. AE, D, MC, V.*

$–$$ ✕ **Old Mesilla Pastry Cafe.** Melt-in-your-mouth baked goods and unusual specialty items such as buffalo and ostrich meat make this site an amusing tourist stop for breakfast or lunch. (It's closed evenings.) But if you show up during rush hour, you'll have to elbow your way through the locals who also delight in savory dishes such as green chile chicken pesto pizza. Southwestern-style decor includes tiled flooring, and wooden chairs and tables. ⊠ *2790 Avenida de Mesilla,* ☎ *505/525–2636. MC, V. Closed Tues.*

$$–$$$ 🏠 **Lundeen Inn of the Arts.** A blend of Mexican Colonial and Territorial styles, this century-old home is now an elegant inn and fine-arts
★ gallery. About 300 works of art can be found interspersed throughout the hallways, living room, and guest rooms. Each room is uniquely decorated in honor of various notable artists such as Georgia O'Keeffe; five have balconies. Owners Jerry and Linda Lundeen oversee the inn with warmth and panache. Gourmet breakfasts, included in the room rate, feature such delicacies as Southwestern-style eggs or raisin scones. The entire inn is no-smoking. ⊠ *618 S. Alameda, 88005,* ☎ *505/526–3326,* FAX *505/646–1334. 18 rooms, 2 casitas. AE, D, MC, V.*

$$–$$$ 🏠 **Meson de Mesilla.** This intimate Southwestern resort, decorated in earth tones, occupies one acre of land near Old Mesilla, with striking views of the jagged Organ Mountains and lower mesas. The Southwestern style lodge includes an outdoor courtyard. Most rooms furnished with brass beds and antiques are upstairs, each with access to a large balcony with table and chairs. Breakfasts are available only to guests, but the lodge serves the public for lunches, dinners, and Sunday brunch. Gourmet food such as veal and escargot is offered in charming surroundings decorated with Mexican tile, viga ceilings, and hand-painted murals of the Organ Mountains. ⊠ *1803 Avenida de Mesilla, 88046,* ☎ *505/525–9212 or 800/732–6025,* FAX *505/527– 4196. 13 rooms. Restaurant, pool. D, DC, MC, V.*

Nightlife and the Arts

Check schedules for lectures, concerts, and other special events at **New Mexico State University,** a major land-grant college in Las Cruces. If you want to listen in on local political debates at a traditional adobe watering hole, head for **Chope's Bar & Cafe** (⊠ Hwy. 28 in front of the Post Office, ☎ 505/233–9976), about 15 mi south of Mesilla off NM 28. **Cowboys** (⊠ 2205 S. Main St., ☎ 505/525–9050) is the place to go for good ol' country-western music and dancing.

SILVER CITY AND GILA NATIONAL FOREST

Ghost towns, abandoned cliff dwellings and sprawling ranches interspersed among miles of unspoiled forests are evidence of the rugged adventurers who populated this remote southwestern New Mexico region. Early cliff dwellers mysteriously disappeared sometime after the year 1000, leaving behind the ruins and relics of a culture replaced centuries later by Spanish explorers, roving bands of Apaches, and occasional trappers. Apache leaders including Cochise, Geronimo, and Victorio fought against the onslaught of Mexican and American settlers. For a time, the sheer ruggedness of the mountains helped provide refuge for the Apaches. But the area changed forever when, in the late 1800s, the mineral-laden mountains lured crazed but hardy prospectors determined to make their fortunes in gold, silver, copper, and other minerals found in abundance.

Silver City sprouted as a mining camp in 1870, remaining tough and lawless during its infancy as it struggled to become a more respectable— and permanent—settlement. Henry McCarty spent part of his boyhood here, perhaps learning some of the ruthlessness that led to his later infamy under his better known name—Billy the Kid. While other mining towns in the area sparked briefly and then died, Silver City flourished to become the area's most populated city, now inhabited by about 28,000 citizens.

Even today the Silver City area remains aloof and beautiful, which is part of its charm. Its privacy is buffered by 3.3 million acres of public land that includes the **Gila National Forest** and vast **Gila Wilderness.** This area contains all life zones, including desert and alpine terrain gouged with deeply carved canyons. The jagged scenery ranges from tall timber to the more sparse juniper forests. Scenic drives also lead to several ghost towns, including the old gold mining settlement of **Mogollon.**

Silver City

143 mi northwest of El Paso, Texas, and 233 mi southwest of Albuquerque. Accessible from I–25 (turn west 23 mi north of Hatch onto NM 90) and from I–10 (turn northwest from Deming onto U.S. 180).

Thanks to devoted efforts of historic preservationists, Silver City is one of those delightful communities that has salvaged a number of distinctive houses and storefronts to give visitors a sense of the community's Territorial origins. Silver City is becoming increasingly known as an artists' haven, and a stroll through the historic downtown area will take you by many of the more than 30 art galleries now found in the community.

For more information about Silver City, visit the **Silver City Grant County Chamber of Commerce.** If you're traveling north, NM 90 turns into Hudson Street, where chamber headquarters is located. If you're traveling on Highway 180, this route turns into Silver Heights Boulevard within city limits and intersects Hudson Street, where you'll turn south to reach the chamber office. ⊠ *1103 N. Hudson St.,* ☎ *800/ 548–9378.*

The imposing Ailman House, built in 1881, now serves as headquarters for the **Silver City Museum.** Inside, you can glimpse the area's colorful history in a backlit painting (artist unknown) of the mining and ranching community in 1882. Displays include pottery and other relics from the area's early Mimbres and Mogollon Native American cultures. Climb to the museum's upper level for a view of Silver City's three historic districts. Self-guided walking tours with maps are available in the **Museum Store,** which offers a distinctive selection of Southwest books and gifts. ⊠ *312 W. Broadway St.,* ☎ *505/538–5921.* 🖼 *Free.* ۞ *Tues.– Fri. 9–4:30, weekends 10–4.*

OFF THE
BEATEN PATH

CITY OF ROCKS STATE PARK – About 30 mi southeast of Silver City is this aptly named park, with its wondrous temples and towers of stone. To appreciate this natural marvel, you need to don a pair of good walking shoes and penetrate the interior of this massive collection of stones spewed forth from an ancient volcano. You can't help but imagine yourself in a bizarre city as you peer down "streets" and "alleyways," lined with all shapes and sizes of solid rock structures. The 650-acre park offers 62 campsites, 10 with utility hookups. Fireplaces and picnic tables also are available, snuggled within the shade of the stone monoliths. ⊠ *Off Hwy. 180, Box 54, Faywood,* ☎ *505/536–2800.* 🖼 *$3 per vehicle, day use; $7 per vehicle, overnight camping.*

Dining and Lodging

$ ✕ **Diane's Bakery & Cafe.** In 1997 chef and owner Diane Barrett had big plans to expand her little downtown café, a local gathering place where sandwiches such as roast beef and tuna are served on home-baked bread. Baked goods are light and exceptionally tasty, originating from Diane's background as a Santa Fe pastry chef. Her cinnamon rolls deserve a four-star rating. ⊠ *510 N. Bullard St.,* ☎ *505/538–8722.* ۞ *Tues.–Sat. 10–2:30. No credit cards.*

$ ✕ **Jalisco's.** George and Cecilia Mesa, along with son Michael Mesa, own this family restaurant noted for delicious Mexican dishes such as enchiladas and chile rellenos concocted from old family recipes. Imports from nearby Palomas, Mexico, help brighten the restaurant, which also displays colorful paintings of Mexican marketplaces by local artist Mark Wilson. ⊠ *103 S. Bullard St.,* ☎ *505/388–2060. No credit cards. Closed Sun.*

$ ✕ **Vicki's Downtown Deli.** A touch of Germany can be found in this unique deli, featuring sausages and imported cheeses along with homemade soups and sandwiches. Wash down your meal with a Jamaican Lemonade Spritzer or a Sioux City Sarsaparilla. Baked goods crafted by owner Vicki Sontheim are also sold here. An outdoor patio is open in the summertime. ⊠ *107 W. Yankie,* ☎ *505/388–5430. AE, MC, V. Closed Sun.*

$–$$ 🖼 **Carter House Bed & Breakfast Inn.** This imposing, historic mansion built in 1906 is located right next door to the original site of the "Legal Tender" Silver Mine, which started a frenzy of prospecting in the area in 1870 and led to the mining town's name of Silver City. Four single rooms and one suite, all with private bath, are available for rent, and have sturdy furnishings designed for comfort. No-nonsense breakfasts are served in the mornings, typically an egg dish with sausage along with fruit and baked goods. A hostel is operated—quietly—in the downstairs portion of the building. Managers emphasize privacy for their patrons. The property was for sale in 1997, so it's possible new owners might introduce changes. ⊠ *101 N. Cooper St., 88061,* ☎ *505/ 388–5485. 4 rooms, 1 suite. MC, V.*

$ 🏨 **Palace Hotel.** Owners Nancy and Cal Thompson describe their quaint, restored lodging best: intimate, with the warmth and historic feel of a small European hotel. The Thompsons took over the Palace in 1989 when it was being used for apartments. They succeeded in renovating the grand old building back to its original elegance, when it was opened in 1900 as a first-class hotel. Each of the 22 guest rooms and suites have their own decor, some with Western furnishings and some with a distinctly Victorian flair. An upstairs garden room offers solitude for games or reading. Continental breakfasts are served each morning in the upstairs lobby. Unfortunately, this stately building is next door to a sometimes noisy bar. But the lodging offers convenient access to Silver City's downtown historical district. ⊠ *106 W. Broadway, 88061,* ☎ *505/388–1811. 22 rooms and suites. AE, D, DC, MC, V.*

Shopping

GALLERIES AND SPECIALTY STORES

Yankie Creek Gallery. Traditional and contemporary local artists have formed this cooperative to display a wide range of arts and crafts, including pottery, oils, jewelry and ornaments. ⊠ *217 N. Bullard St.,* ☎ *505/538–5232 or 505/388–4775.* ☉ *Daily 10–5 and by appointment. MC, V.*

Hester House Candy & Gifts. Munch on homemade candy, chocolates, and truffles while admiring this shop's unique gift items: porcelain dolls, Tiffany-style lamps, lotions, and wind chimes. Next door is the **Hester House Annex** (⊠ 106 E. Market St.), a print gallery with fun items such as fantasy hats. Owners Dorothy A. and Carrol A. Porter run both shops. ⊠ *316 N. Bullard St.,* ☎ *505/388–1360.* ☉ *Mon.–Sat. 9:30– 5. D, MC, V.*

Silver Creek Antiques. As much a museum as it is a business, this is a must-see attraction for antique lovers. Owner Robert Burns has assembled memorabilia in nicely arranged displays ranging from Coca Cola bottles to bicycles to relics from the '50s and '60s. A former auto mechanics teacher from Albuquerque, Burns reveals his love of antique machines in displays of a revved up 1966 Chevelle and a 1955 BMW. ⊠ *614 N. Bullard St.,* ☎ *505/538–8705.* ☉ *Tues.–Sat. 11–5. MC, V.*

Gila National Forest

★ This huge area of forest and rangeland covers 3.3 million acres— about 65 mi by 100 mi—which includes the nation's first wilderness so designated by the U.S. Forest Service in 1924. Outdoor opportunities are almost unlimited, with approximately 1,500 mi of hiking trails open for exploration. Developed campgrounds are available, and open camping also is allowed. The forest roads are ideal for mountain biking, although trails tend to be somewhat rough for bicycles. White-water rafting is available, usually in April, if water runoff is ample to support the activity. Fishing is allowed in streams, rivers, and in three lakes.

While almost one fourth of the forest is designated wilderness and closed to vehicular traffic, much of the area remains open for touring. Try the **Inner Loop Scenic Drive,** a gorgeous circling route of about 75 mi. While roads are paved, some of the turns are sharp, narrow, and steep so you're advised against taking large RVs on this route. Starting from Silver City, take NM 15 north to **Gila Cliff Dwellings National Monument.** Here you can view 42 rooms of stone and mud, built by the Mogollon Indians about 700 years ago. From the Gila Cliff Dwellings National Monument, take NM 35—a continuation of the Inner Loop Scenic Drive—to NM 152, leading back to Silver City. ✉ *Rte. 11 (Box 100), Silver City 88061,* ☎ *505/536–9344.* 🎟 *Free.* ☉ *Trail: Memorial Day–Labor Day, daily 8–6; Labor Day–Memorial Day, daily 9–4. Visitor center: Memorial Day–Labor Day, daily 8–6; Labor Day–Memorial Day, daily 8–4:30.*

From Silver City take U.S. 180 west for about 50 mi to Glenwood and the **Whitewater Canyon.** There you'll see the **Catwalk,** a 250-ft metal walkway attached to the sides of boulders. The structure was built in 1935 to grant access to the canyon and a breathtaking view of water cascading over rocks.

From the Catwalk, drive north on U.S. 180 for several miles and turn east onto NM 159 for 9 mi to visit the former ghost town of **Mogollon.** The old gold mining town, built in the 1880's, has been revived by a dozen or so residents who open art galleries and offer tours during summer months. If you want to track down more of the area's ghost towns or view some of the area copper or other mining operations, check at the Gila National Forest Visitor Center (☞ *above*) for maps and information. ✉ *Gila National Forest, 3005 E. Camino del Bosque, Silver City,* ☎ *505/388–8201, 505/388–8485 for hearing and speech impaired,* 𝖥𝖠𝖷 *505/388–8204.* ☉ *Daily 8–4:30 (varies seasonally).*

Dining and Lodging

\$\$ ✕ **Buckhorn Saloon and Opera House.** Mosey up to the wooden bar
★ at this genuine saloon (originally constructed in the 1800s), and slug down a taste of the Old West. You'll be sharing elbow space with some real characters, including dance hall girl "Debbie deCamp"—a life-size doll who strikes a sultry pose while surveying the scene from a balcony overlooking the saloon. After visiting the bar, order up some steak in the adjoining dining room and listen to the mellow crooning of folk singers featured Wednesday through Saturday evenings. This building complex (7 mi northeast of Silver City) in Pinos Altos also includes the recently opened **Opera House,** featuring melodramas and facilities for banquets and private parties. **The Pinos Altos Mercantile,** founded in the 1860s, also is attached to the complex and has been converted to an ice cream parlor and soda shop. ✉ *Hwy. 15, Pinos Altos,* ☎ *505/ 538–9911; 505/388–3848 for opera house.* ☉ *Bar opens at 3, dinner served 6–10; closed Sun. Opera house performances Fri. and Sat. at 8 PM; reservations essential. MC, V.*

Lake Valley National Back Country Byway

This 48-mi scenic drive is accessible via U.S. 180/NM 152 from Silver City or 18 mi west of Hatch off NM 26, where you turn north onto NM 27. Along the route, you'll pass through historic **Hillsboro,** a former boom town that thrived during mining activities of decades past. For a portion of the drive, you'll follow the route taken by the old Kingston Lake Valley Stage Line that ran through a region once terrorized by Apache leaders such as Geronimo and outlaw bands led by notorious figures such as Butch Cassidy. At the **Lake Valley** stop you can view the remnants of an old silver mining town. You'll also see views of the landmark, **Cooke's Peak,** where the first wagon road through the Southwest to California was opened in 1846. This is a remote drive offering an exciting link to the old Wild West. There are no gas stations along the way.

Dining

$ ✕ **Rosie's Restaurant.** Excellent Southwestern cuisine in a relaxed atmosphere can be found in this modest establishment, a great stopover if you've finished or plan to take the Lake Valley scenic drive. The breakfast specialty is *machaca,* shredded beef and onions served with eggs, green chile, and cheese. Try a combination plate (enchilada, taco, and tamale) for lunch or dinner. ✉ *305 Hall St., Hatch,* ☎ *505/267–3700. No credit cards.*

CARLSBAD AND SOUTHERN NEW MEXICO A TO Z

Arriving and Departing

By Bus

Texas, New Mexico & Oklahoma Coaches (☎ 505/887–1108 in Carlsbad) provides transcontinental bus service and connects Carlsbad and White's City, along with all other major cities in listed destinations. **Silver Stage** (☎ 800/522–0162) offers van service to Carlsbad Caverns National Park from any point on the Carlsbad–El Paso route, in addition to shuttle services to Las Cruces from El Paso International Airport. The shuttle also links Silver City to existing routes. The **Las Cruces Shuttle Service** (☎ 505/525–1784) makes regular runs daily between Las Cruces and the El Paso airport and will drop you off at your chosen destination.

By Car

Drive south from Albuquerque on I–25 for about 77 mi, then exit on U.S. 380 East and continue for 165 mi to Roswell. From Roswell, take U.S. 285 to Carlsbad, about 75 mi away (320 mi from Albuquerque). From El Paso, Texas, going east on U.S. 180, the distance to Carlsbad is 167 mi. From Pecos, Carlsbad can be reached via U.S. 285 (off I–10 at Van Horn). Las Cruces is 45 mi east of El Paso off I–10 and 210 mi south of Albuquerque off I–25.

By Plane

The **Albuquerque International Airport,** 380 mi north of Carlsbad, is the gateway to New Mexico and is served by most major airlines. **Mesa Airlines** (☎ 800/637–2247) provides air-shuttle service to Carlsbad and Las Cruces from Albuquerque. The **El Paso International Airport** in Texas also serves as a major hub for air service in the region.

Getting Around

Car rentals and taxi and shuttle services are available at most municipal airports in the region and at most major hotels. Las Cruces operates a citywide public bus system.

Contacts and Resources

Emergencies

Call ☎ 911 for **police, fire,** and **ambulance** services anywhere in southern New Mexico.

Visitor Information

Carlsbad Chamber of Commerce (✉ 302 S. Canal St., Carlsbad 88220, ☎ 505/887–6516, ℻ 505/885-1455); **Carlsbad Caverns National**

Park (✉ 3225 National Parks Hwy., Carlsbad 88220, ☎ 505/785–2232); **Gila National Forest** (✉ 3005 E. Camilno del Bosque, Silver City 88061, ☎ 505/388–8201); **Las Cruces Convention & Visitors Bureau** (✉ 311 N. Downtown Mall, Las Cruces 88001, ☎ 505/524–8521 or 800/343–7827); **Lincoln County Heritage Trust** (✉ Off Hwy. 380, Box 98, Lincoln 88338, ☎ 505/653–4025); **Old Mesilla Association** (✉ c/o Mesilla Book Center, Box 1005, Mesilla Plaza, Mesilla 88046, ☎ 505/526–6220 or 800/343–7827); **Roswell Chamber of Commerce** (✉ 121 W. 2nd St., ☎ 505/623–5695); **Ruidoso Valley Chamber of Commerce–Convention and Visitors Bureau** (✉ 720 Suderth Dr., Box 698, Ruidoso 88345, ☎ 800/253–2255 or 505/257–7395); **Silver City Grant County Chamber of Commerce** (✉ 1103 N. Hudson St., Silver City, NM 88061, ☎ 800/548–9378); **White Sands National Monument** (✉ Box 1086, Holloman AFB 88330, ☎ 505/479–6124); **White's City Visitor Information** (✉ Off Hwy. 70, Box 128, White City 88268, ☎ 505/785–2291).

6 Portraits of New Mexico

"New Mexico," by D.H. Lawrence

Books and Videos

NEW MEXICO

SUPERFICIALLY, the world has become small and known. Poor little globe of earth, the tourists trot round you as easily as they trot round the Bois or round Central Park. There is no mystery left, we've been there, we've seen it, we know all about it. We've done the globe, and the globe is done.

This is quite true, superficially. On the superficies, horizontally, we've been everywhere and done everything, we know all about it. Yet the more we know superficially, the less we penetrate vertically. It's all very well skimming across the surface of the ocean and saying you know all about the sea. There still remain the terrifying underdeeps of which we have utterly no experience.

The same is true of land travel. We skim along, we get there, we see it all, we've done it all. And as a rule, we never once go through the curious film that railroads, ships, motorcars, and hotels stretch over the surface of the whole earth. Peking is just the same as New York, with a few different things to look at; rather more Chinese about, etc. Poor creatures that we are, we crave for experience, yet we are like flies that crawl on the pure and transparent mucous-paper in which the world like a bon-bon is wrapped so carefully that we can never get at it, though we see it there all the time as we move about it, apparently in contact, yet actually as far removed as if it were the moon.

As a matter of fact, our great-grandfathers, who never went anywhere, in actuality had more experience of the world than we have, who have seen everything. When they listened to a lecture with lantern-slides, they really held their breath before the unknown, as they sat in the village schoolroom. We, bowling along in a rickshaw in Ceylon, say to ourselves: "It's very much what you'd expect." We really know it all.

We are mistaken. The know-it-all state of mind is just the result of being outside the mucous-paper wrapping of civilization. Underneath is everything we don't know and are afraid of knowing.

I realized this with shattering force when I went to New Mexico.

New Mexico, one of the United States, part of the U.S.A. New Mexico, the picturesque reservation and playground of the eastern states, very romantic, old Spanish, Red Indian, desert mesas, pueblos, cowboys, penitents, all that film stuff. Very nice, the great Southwest; put on a sombrero and knot a red kerchief round your neck to go out in the great free spaces!

That is New Mexico wrapped in the absolutely hygienic and shiny mucous-paper of our trite civilization. That is the New Mexico known to most of the Americans who know it at all. But break through the shiny sterilized wrapping and actually touch the country, and you will never be the same again.

I think New Mexico was the greatest experience from the outside world that I have ever had. It certainly changed me forever. Curious as it may sound, it was New Mexico that liberated me from the present era of civilization, the great era of material and mechanical development. Months spent in holy Kandy, in Ceylon, the holy of holies of Southern Buddhism, had not touched the great psyche of materialism and idealism that dominated me. And years, even in the exquisite beauty of Sicily, right among the old Greek paganism that still lives there, had not shattered the essential Christianity on which my character was established. Australia was a sort of dream or trance, like being under a spell, the self remaining unchanged, so long as the trance did not last too long. Tahiti, in a mere glimpse, repelled me; and so did California, after a stay of a few weeks. There seemed a strange brutality in the spirit of the western coast, and I felt: O, let me get away!

But the moment I saw the brilliant, proud morning shine high up over the deserts of Santa Fe, something stood still in my soul, and I started to attend. There was a certain magnificence in the high-up day, a certain eaglelike royalty, so different from the equally pure, equally pristine and lovely morning of Australia, which is so soft, so utterly pure in its softness, and betrayed by green parrot flying. But in the lovely morning of Australia one went into a dream. In the magnificent fierce morning of New Mexico one sprang awake, a new part of the soul woke up suddenly, and the old world gave way to a new.

THERE ARE ALL KINDS of beauty in the world, thank God, though ugliness is homogeneous. How lovely is Sicily, with Calabria across the sea like an opal and Etna with her snow in a world above and beyond! How lovely is Tuscany, with little red tulips wild among the corn: or bluebells at dusk in England, or mimosa in clouds of pure yellow among the grey-green dun foliage of Australia, under a soft, blue, unbreathed sky! But for a *greatness* of beauty I have never experienced anything like New Mexico. All those mornings when I went with a hoe along the ditch to the Cañon, at the ranch, and stood in the fierce, proud silence of the Rockies, on their foothills, to look far over the desert to the blue mountains away in Arizona, blue as chalcedony, with the sagebrush desert sweeping grey-blue in between, dotted with tiny cube-crystals of houses, the vast amphitheatre of lofty, indomitable desert, sweeping round to the ponderous Sangre de Cristo mountains on the east, and coming up flush at the pine-dotted foothills of the Rockies! What splendor! Only the tawny eagle could really sail out into the splendor of it all. Leo Stein once wrote to me: It is the most aesthetically satisfying landscape I know. To me it was much more than that. It had a splendid silent terror and a vast far-and-wide magnificence that made it way beyond mere aesthetic appreciation. Never is the light more pure and overweening than there, arching with a royalty almost cruel over the hollow, uptilted world. For it is curious that the land that has produced modern political democracy at its highest pitch should give one the greatest sense of overweening, terrible proudness and mercilessness: but so beautiful, God! so beautiful! Those who have spent morning after morning alone there pitched among the pines above the great proud world of desert will know, almost unbearably how beautiful it is, how clear and unquestioned is the might of the day. Just day itself is tremendous there. It is so easy to understand that the Aztecs gave hearts of men

to the sun. For the sun is not merely hot or scorching, not at all. It is of a brilliant and unchallengeable purity and haughty serenity that would make one sacrifice the heart to it. Ah, yes, in New Mexico the heart is sacrificed to the sun and the human being is left stark, heartless, but undauntedly religious.

And that was the second revelation out there. I had looked over all the world for something that would strike *me* as religious. The simple piety of some English people, the semi-pagan mystery of some Catholics in southern Italy, the intensity of some Bavarian peasants, the semi-ecstasy of Buddhists or Brahmins: all this had seemed religious all right, as far as the parties concerned were involved, but it didn't involve me. I looked on at the religiousness from the outside. For it is still harder to feel religion at will than to love at will.

I had seen what I felt was a hint of wild religion in the so-called devil dances of a group of naked villagers from the far-remote jungle in Ceylon, dancing at midnight under the torches, glittering wet with sweat on their dark bodies as if they had been gilded, at the celebration of the Pera-hera, in Kandy, given to the Prince of Wales. And the utter dark absorption of these naked men, as they danced with their knees wide apart, suddenly affected me with a *sense* of religion. I *felt* religion for a moment. For religion is an experience, an uncontrollable sensual experience, even more so than love: I use sensual to mean an experience deep down in the senses, inexplicable and inscrutable.

But this experience was fleeting, gone in the curious turmoil of the Pera-hera, and I had no permanent feeling of religion till I came to New Mexico and penetrated into the old human race experience there. It is curious that it should be in America, of all places, that a European should really experience religion, after touching the old Mediterranean and the East. . . . A vast old religion that once swayed the earth lingers in unbroken practice there in New Mexico—older, perhaps, than anything in the world save Australian aboriginal taboo and totem, and that is not yet religion.

You can feel it, the atmosphere of it, around the pueblos. Not, of course, when the place is crowded with sightseers and motorcars. But go to Taos pueblo on some brilliant snowy morning and see the white figure on the roof, or come riding through at dusk on some windy evening, when the black skirts of the silent women blow around the white wide boots, and you will feel the old, old root of human consciousness still reaching down to depths we know nothing of: and of which, only too often, we are jealous. It seems it will not be long before the pueblos are uprooted.

But never shall I forget watching the dancers, the men with the fox-skin swaying down from their buttocks, file out at San Geronimo, and the women with seed rattles following. The long, streaming, glistening black hair of the men. Even in ancient Crete long hair was sacred in a man, as it is still in the Indians. Never shall I forget the utter absorption of the dance, so quiet, so steadily, timelessly rhythmic, and silent, with the ceaseless downtread, always to the earth's center, the very reverse of the up flow of Dionysiac or Christian ecstasy. Never shall I forget the deep singing of the men at the drum, swelling and sinking, the deepest sound I have heard in all my life, deeper than thunder, deeper than the sound of the Pacific Ocean, deeper than the roar of a deep waterfall: the wonderful deep sound of men calling to the unspeakable depths.

 NEVER SHALL I FORGET coming into the little pueblo of San Filipi one sunny morning in spring, unexpectedly, when bloom was on the trees in the perfect little pueblo more old, more utterly peaceful and idyllic than anything in Theocritus, and seeing a little casual dance. Not impressive as a spectacle, only, to me, profoundly moving because of the truly terrifying religious absorption of it.

Never shall I forget the Christmas dances at Taos, twilight, snow, the darkness coming over the great wintry mountains and the lonely pueblo, then suddenly, again, like dark calling to dark, the deep Indian cluster-singing around the drum, wild and awful, suddenly arousing on the last dusk as the procession starts. And then the bonfires leaping suddenly in pure spurts of high flame, columns of sudden flame forming an alley for the procession. . . . Never shall I forget the Indian races, when the young men, even the boys, run naked, smeared with white earth and stuck with bits of eagle fluff for the swiftness of the heavens, and the old men brush them with eagle feathers, to give them power. And they run in the strange hurling fashion of the primitive world, hurled forward, not making speed deliberately. And the race is not for victory. It is not a contest. There is no competition. It is a great cumulative effort. The tribe this day is adding up its male energy and exerting it to the utmost—for what? To get power, to get strength: to come, by sheer cumulative, hurling effort of the bodies of men, into contact with the great cosmic source of vitality that gives strength, power, energy to the men who can grasp it, energy for the zeal of attainment.

It was a vast old religion, greater than anything we know: more starkly and nakedly religious. There is no God, no conception of a god. All is god. But it is not the pantheism we are accustomed to, which expresses itself as "God is everywhere, God is in everything." In the oldest religion, everything was alive, not supernaturally but naturally alive. There were only deeper and deeper streams of life, vibrations of life more and more vast. So rocks were alive, but a mountain had a deeper, vaster life than a rock, and it was much harder for a man to bring his spirit, or his energy, into contact with the life of the mountain, and so draw strength from the mountain, as from a great standing well of life, than it was to come into contact with the rock. And he had to put forth a great religious effort. For the whole life-effort of man was to get his life into direct contact with the elemental life of the cosmos, mountain-life, cloud-life, thunder-life, air-life, earth-life, sun-life. To come into immediate *felt* contact, and so derive energy, power, and a dark sort of joy. This effort into sheer naked contact, *without an intermediary or mediator,* is the root meaning of religion, and at the sacred races the runners hurled themselves in a terrible cumulative effort, through the air, to come at last into naked contact with the very life of air, which is the life of the clouds, and so of the rain.

It was a vast and pure religion, without idols or images, even mental ones. It is the oldest religion, a cosmic religion the same for all peoples, not broken up into specific gods or saviors or systems. It is the religion that precedes the god-concept, and is therefore greater and deeper than any god-religion.

And it lingers still, for a little while in New Mexico: but long enough to have been a revelation to me. And the Indian, however objectionable he may be on occasion, has still some of the strange beauty and pathos of the religion that brought him forth and is now shedding him away into oblivion. When Trinidad, the Indian boy, and I planted corn at the ranch, my soul paused to see his brown hands softly moving the earth over the maize in pure ritual. He was back in his old religious self, and the ages stood still. Ten minutes later he was making a fool of himself with the horses. Horses were never part of the Indian's religious life, never would be. He hasn't a tithe of feeling for them that he has for a bear, for example. So horses don't like Indians.

But there it is: the newest democracy ousting the oldest religion! And once the oldest religion is ousted, one feels the democracy and all its paraphernalia will collapse, and the oldest religion, which comes down to us from man's pre-war days, will start again. The skyscraper will scatter on the winds like thistledown, and the genuine America, the America of New Mexico, will start on its course again. This is an interregnum.

—D. H. Lawrence

BOOKS AND VIDEOS

General Interest

Classic books on New Mexico include *Death Comes for the Archbishop,* by Willa Cather, a novel based on the life of Archbishop Jean Baptiste Lamy, who built, among other churches, the St. Francis Cathedral in Santa Fe. *Great River,* by Paul Horgan; *The Wind Leaves No Shadow,* by Ruth Laughlin; *Miracle Hill,* by Barney Mitchell; *Navajos Have Five Fingers,* by T. D. Allen; *Santa Fe,* by Oliver La Farge; *New Mexico,* by Jack Schaefer; and *Moon Over Adobe,* by Dorothy Pillsbury, are all good choices as well. *Lautrec,* by Norman Zollinger, is an entertaining mystery set in Albuquerque. Zollinger also wrote *Riders to Cibola,* which chronicles the conquistadors' search for the legendary Seven Cities of Gold. In 1974 Albuquerque author Tony Hillerman received an Edgar Allan Poe Award from the Mystery Writers of America for his book *Dance Hall of the Dead.* Hillerman also edited *The Spell of New Mexico,* an anthology of New Mexican writers. *A Sense of Place, a Sense of Time,* by pioneering landscape architect and environmentalist John Brinckerhoff Jackson, gives a sense of New Mexico's landscape, past and present. *The Wood Carvers of Cordova, New Mexico,* by Charles L. Briggs, is a prizewinning study of the making and selling of religious images in a northern New Mexico village. *Eliot Porter's Southwest* is the famed photographer's poetic view of the Southwest, much of it focused around his Tesuque, New Mexico, home. *An Illustrated History of New Mexico* is by Thomas E. Chavez, director of the Palace of the Governors in Santa Fe, who uses quotes to underscore his visual chronicle of New Mexican history.

Native American Lore and Pueblo Life

The Man Who Killed the Deer, by Frank Waters, is a classic of Pueblo life. *Masked Gods,* by the same author, has a following that reaches cult proportions. J. J. Brody's profusely illustrated book *Anasazi and Pueblo Painting* is an indispensable volume for art historians and students of Southwestern culture. *Mornings in Mexico,* by D. H. Lawrence, contains a number of essays pertaining to Taos and the Pueblo ritual dances. *Pueblo Style and Regional Architecture,* edited by Nicholas C. Markovich, Wolfgang F. E. Preiser, and Fred G. Strum, covers the evolution of architecture in the Southwest, with particular emphasis on New Mexico. *Nacimientos: Nativity Scenes by Southwest Indian Artists,* by Guy and Doris Monthan, offers photographs and descriptions of ceramic nativity scenes produced by Pueblo Native Americans.

New Mexican Personalities

Billy the Kid: A Short and Violent Life, by Robert M. Utley, a noted historian, is considered the definitive work on the notorious outlaw. *The Life of D. H. Lawrence,* by Keith Sagar, published in 1980, is a good biography of the world-renowned author so strongly associated with (and buried in) New Mexico. Taos is also Georgia O'Keeffe country, and there is a wealth of books about the artist. Among the best is *Georgia O'Keeffe: Arts and Letters,* published by the New York Graphic Society in conjunction with a retrospective of her work at the National Gallery of Art, in Washington, D.C. Also worthy of note is the reissue of the coffee-table book, *Georgia O'Keeffe,* with text by the artist herself. *Portrait of an Artist: A Biography of Georgia O'Keeffe,* by Laurie Lisle, spans the artist's life and career. *Georgia O'Keeffe: Some Memories of Drawings,* edited by Doris Bry, is a collection of the artist's major 1915–1963 drawings, with comments on each.

Albuquerque, Santa Fe, and Taos

Albuquerque—A Narrative History, by Marc Simmons, is a fascinating look at the city's birth and development. *The Wingspread Collectors Guide to Santa Fe and Taos* and *The Wingspread Collectors Guide to Albuquerque and Corrales* (Wingspread, Box 13566-T, Albuquerque 87192) provide high-quality reproductions and useful information about art galleries, art, and crafts of the region; they also include listings of museums, hotels, restaurants, and historic sites. *A Short History of Santa Fe,* by Susan Hazen-Hammond, chronicles Santa Fe's history with text and photos. *Taos: A Pictorial History,* by John Sherman, contains numerous black-and-white historical photographs of the major characters, events, and structures that formed the backbone of Taos, as well as accompanying text.

For information about bed-and-breakfasts in the area, consult *Fodor's The Southwest's Best Bed-and-Breakfasts.*

Videos

Northern New Mexico has provided memorable scenic backdrops for several feature films, particularly Westerns. *Silverado* (1985) and *Wyatt Earp* (1994) are Westerns that were photographed in the Santa Fe vicinity. For television, two miniseries based on popular Larry McMurtry novels with Old West settings, *Lonesome Dove* (1989) and *Buffalo Girls* (1995), were shot near Santa Fe. *The Milagro Beanfield War* (1988), directed by Robert Redford, based on the novel by Taos author John Nichols, was filmed in Truchas, on the High Road to Taos. Other popular movies using Santa Fe area locations include *Late for Dinner* (1991) and *The Cowboy Way* (1994).

The Albuquerque area appears in director Oliver Stone's *Natural Born Killers* (1994). Southern New Mexico provides settings for *Young Guns* (1988), *Gas, Food, Lodging* (1992), *White Sands* (1992), and *Mad Love* (1995). Other movies photographed around New Mexico include *The Cowboys* (1972), starring John Wayne; *Outrageous Fortune* (1987), with Bette Midler and Shelley Long; *Powwow Highway* (1985); and *City Slickers* (1991), starring Billy Crystal.

GLOSSARY

Perhaps more than any other region in the United States, New Mexico has its own distinctive cuisine and unique architectural style, both heavily influenced by Native American, Spanish Colonial, Mexican, and American frontier traditions. The brief glossary that follows explains terms frequently used in this book.

Art and Architecture

Adobe: A brick of sun-dried earth and clay, usually stabilized with straw; a structure made of adobe.

Banco: A small bench that gracefully emerges from the adobe walls. often upholstered with handwoven textiles.

Bulto: Folk-art figures of a santo (saint), usually carved from wood.

Camposanto: A graveyard.

Capilla: A chapel.

Casita: Literally, "small house." The term is generally used to describe a separate guest house.

Cerquita: A spiked, wrought-iron, rectangular fence, often marking grave sites.

Equipal: Pigskin-and-cedar furniture from Jalisco, Mexico. The chairs have rounded backs and bases rather than legs.

Farolito: A small votive candle set in a paper-bag lantern, popular at Christmastime. This term is used in northern New Mexico only. Albuquerque and points south call them *luminarias,* which in the north is the term for the bonfires of Christmas Eve.

Heishi: Shell jewelry.

Hornos: Outdoor domed ovens.

Kiva fireplace: A corner fireplace whose round form resembles that of a kiva; a ceremonial room used by Native Americans of the Southwest.

Latilla: Small pole, often made of aspen, used as a lath in a ceiling.

Placita: A small plaza.

Portal: A porch or large, covered area adjacent to the house.

Pueblo style: Modeled after the traditional dwellings of the Southwest Pueblo Indians. Most homes in this style are cube shaped. Other characteristics are flat roofs, small windows, rounded corners, and viga beams.

Retablo: Holy image painted on wood or tin.

Santero: Maker of religious images.

Territorial style: Modified Pueblo style that evolved in the late 19th century when New Mexico was still a U.S. territory. The territorial home incorporates a broad central hallway and entryway and adds wooden elements, such as window frames, in neoclassical style; some structures have pitched rather than flat roofs, and brick copings.

Terrones adobes: Adobe cut from the ground rather than formed from mud.

Viga: Horizontal roof beam made of logs, usually protruding from the side of the house.

Menu Guide

Aguacate: Spanish for avocado, the key ingredient of guacamole.

Albóndigas: Meatballs, usually cooked with rice in a meat broth.

Bolsa del pobre: A seafood and vegetable dish; a specialty from Colima.

Burrito: A warm flour tortilla wrapped around meat, beans, or vegetables, and smothered in chile and cheese.

Carne adovada: A red chile–marinated pork.

Chalupa: A corn tortilla deep-fried in the shape of a bowl, filled with pinto beans (sometimes meat), and topped with cheese, guacamole, sour cream, lettuce, tomatoes, and salsa.

Chile relleno: A large green chile pepper, peeled, stuffed with cheese or a special mixture of spicy ingredients, dipped in batter, and fried.

Chiles: New Mexico's infamous hot peppers, which come in an endless variety of sizes and in various degrees of hotness, from the thumb-size jalapeño to the smaller and often hotter serrano. They can be canned or fresh, dried, or cut up into salsa.

Chimichanga: The same as a burrito (☞ *above*) only deep-fried and topped with a dash of sour cream or salsa.

Chipotle: A dried smoked jalapeño with a smoky, almost sweet, chocolatey flavor.

Chorizo: Well-spiced Spanish sausage, made with pork and red chiles.

Enchilada: A rolled or flat corn tortilla, filled with meat, chicken, seafood, or cheese; covered with chile; and baked. The ultimate enchilada is made with blue Indian corn tortillas. New Mexicans order them flat, sometimes topped with a fried egg.

Fajitas: Grilled beef, chicken, or fish with peppers and onions and served with tortillas; traditionally known as arracheras.

Flauta: A tortilla filled with cheese or meat and rolled into a flutelike shape (flauta means flute) and lightly fried. When eaten, they're usually dipped in salsa or chile.

Frijoles refritos: Refried beans, often seasoned with lard or cheese.

Guacamole: Mashed avocado, mixed with tomatoes, garlic, onions, lemon juice, and chiles, used as a dip or a side dish.

Huevos rancheros: New Mexico's answer to eggs Benedict—eggs doused with chile and sometimes melted cheese, served on top of a corn tortilla. They're good accompanied by chorizo.

Pan de cazón: Grilled shark with black beans and red onions on a tortilla; a specialty from Campeche.

Posole: Resembling popcorn soup, this is a sublime marriage of lime, hominy, pork, chile, garlic, and spices.

Quesadilla: A folded flour tortilla, filled with cheese and meat or vegetables, and warmed or lightly fried so the cheese melts.

Queso: Cheese; an ingredient in many Mexican and Southwestern recipes.

Ristra: String of dried red chile peppers, often used as decoration.

Sopaipilla: Puffy deep-fried bread, served with honey.

Taco: A corn tortilla, fried and made into a shell that's then stuffed with spicy meat or chicken and garnished with shredded lettuce, chopped tomatoes, onions, and grated cheese.

Tacos al carbón: Shredded pork cooked in a mole sauce and folded into corn tortillas.

Tamale: Ground corn made into a dough and filled with finely ground pork and red chiles, then steamed in a corn husk.

Tortilla: Thin pancake made of corn or wheat flour, used as bread, as an edible "spoon," and as a container for other foods. Locals place butter in the center of a hot tortilla, roll it up, and eat it as a scroll. It is also useful for scooping up the last bit in a bowl of chile.

Trucha en terra-cotta: Fresh trout wrapped in corn husks and baked in clay.

Verde: Spanish for "green." Chile verde is a green chile sauce.

INDEX

X = restaurant, ⊡ = hotel

NOTES

NOTES

NOTES

NOTES

NOTES

NOTES

Fodor's Travel Publications

Available at bookstores everywhere, or call 1–800–533–6478, 24 hours a day.

Gold Guides

U.S.

Alaska	Florida	New Orleans	Seattle & Vancouver
Arizona	Hawai'i	New York City	The South
Boston	Las Vegas, Reno, Tahoe	Pacific North Coast	U.S. & British Virgin Islands
California		Philadelphia & the Pennsylvania Dutch Country	USA
Cape Cod, Martha's Vineyard, Nantucket	Los Angeles		Virginia & Maryland
	Maine, Vermont, New Hampshire	The Rockies	Walt Disney World, Universal Studios and Orlando
The Carolinas & Georgia	Maui & Lāna'i	San Diego	
Chicago	Miami & the Keys	San Francisco	Washington, D.C.
Colorado	New England	Santa Fe, Taos, Albuquerque	

Foreign

Australia	Europe	Montréal & Québec City	Scotland
Austria	Florence, Tuscany & Umbria	Moscow, St. Petersburg, Kiev	Singapore
The Bahamas	France		South Africa
Belize & Guatemala	Germany	The Netherlands, Belgium & Luxembourg	South America
Bermuda	Great Britain		Southeast Asia
Canada	Greece	New Zealand	Spain
Cancún, Cozumel, Yucatán Peninsula	Hong Kong	Norway	Sweden
Caribbean	India	Nova Scotia, New Brunswick, Prince Edward Island	Switzerland
China	Ireland		Thailand
Costa Rica	Israel	Paris	Toronto
Cuba	Italy	Portugal	Turkey
The Czech Republic & Slovakia	Japan	Provence & the Riviera	Vienna & the Danube Valley
Eastern & Central Europe	London	Scandinavia	
	Madrid & Barcelona		
	Mexico		

Special-Interest Guides

Adventures to Imagine	Fodor's Gay Guide to the USA	Halliday's New Orleans Food Explorer	Rock & Roll Traveler USA
Alaska Ports of Call	Fodor's How to Pack	Healthy Escapes	Sunday in San Francisco
Ballpark Vacations	Great American Learning Vacations	Kodak Guide to Shooting Great Travel Pictures	Walt Disney World for Adults
Caribbean Ports of Call			
The Complete Guide to America's National Parks	Great American Sports & Adventure Vacations	National Parks and Seashores of the East	Weekends in New York
	Great American Vacations	National Parks of the West	Wendy Perrin's Secrets Every Smart Traveler Should Know
Disney Like a Pro			
Europe Ports of Call	Great American Vacations for Travelers with Disabilities	Nights to Imagine	
Family Adventures		Rock & Roll Traveler Great Britain and Ireland	Worldwide Cruises and Ports of Call

Fodor's Special Series

Fodor's Best Bed & Breakfasts

America

California

The Mid-Atlantic

New England

The Pacific Northwest

The South

The Southwest

The Upper Great Lakes

Compass American Guides

Alaska

Arizona

Boston

Chicago

Colorado

Hawaii

Idaho

Hollywood

Las Vegas

Maine

Manhattan

Minnesota

Montana

New Mexico

New Orleans

Oregon

Pacific Northwest

San Francisco

Santa Fe

South Carolina

South Dakota

Southwest

Texas

Utah

Virginia

Washington

Wine Country

Wisconsin

Wyoming

Citypacks

Amsterdam

Atlanta

Berlin

Chicago

Florence

Hong Kong

London

Los Angeles

Montréal

New York City

Paris

Prague

Rome

San Francisco

Tokyo

Venice

Washington, D.C.

Exploring Guides

Australia

Boston & New England

Britain

California

Canada

Caribbean

China

Costa Rica

Egypt

Florence & Tuscany

Florida

France

Germany

Greek Islands

Hawaii

Ireland

Israel

Italy

Japan

London

Mexico

Moscow & St. Petersburg

New York City

Paris

Prague

Provence

Rome

San Francisco

Scotland

Singapore & Malaysia

South Africa

Spain

Thailand

Turkey

Venice

Flashmaps

Boston

New York

San Francisco

Washington, D.C.

Fodor's Gay Guides

Los Angeles & Southern California

New York City

Pacific Northwest

San Francisco and the Bay Area

South Florida

USA

Pocket Guides

Acapulco

Aruba

Atlanta

Barbados

Budapest

Jamaica

London

New York City

Paris

Prague

Puerto Rico

Rome

San Francisco

Washington, D.C.

Languages for Travelers (Cassette & Phrasebook)

French

German

Italian

Spanish

Mobil Travel Guides

America's Best Hotels & Restaurants

California and the West

Major Cities

Great Lakes

Mid-Atlantic

Northeast

Northwest and Great Plains

Southeast

Southwest and South Central

Rivages Guides

Bed and Breakfasts of Character and Charm in France

Hotels and Country Inns of Character and Charm in France

Hotels and Country Inns of Character and Charm in Italy

Hotels and Country Inns of Character and Charm in Paris

Hotels and Country Inns of Character and Charm in Portugal

Hotels and Country Inns of Character and Charm in Spain

Short Escapes

Britain

France

New England

Near New York City

Fodor's Sports

Golf Digest's Places to Play

Skiing USA

USA Today The Complete Four Sport Stadium Guide

WHEREVER
YOU TRAVEL,
*H*ELP IS NEVER
FAR AWAY.

From planning your trip to providing travel assistance
along the way, American Express® Travel Service Offices
are always there to help you do more.

Santa Fe

Pajarito Travel (R)
2801 Rodeo Road
Suite B
Santa Fe
505/474-7177

http://www.americanexpress.com/travel

America Express Travel Service Offices are located throughout
New Mexico. For the office nearest you, call 1-800-AXP-3429.